CULTURE OF
MISFORTUNE

CULTURE OF MISFORTUNE

AN INTERPRETIVE HISTORY OF TEXTILE UNIONISM IN THE UNITED STATES

Clete Daniel

ILR Press
an imprint of
CORNELL UNIVERSITY PRESS
ITHACA AND LONDON

Cornell Studies in Industrial and Labor Relations No. 34

First published 2001 by Cornell University Press

Printed in the United States of America

Library of Congress Cataloging-in-Publication Data
Daniel, Cletus E., 1943–
    Culture of misfortune : an interpretive history of textile unionism in the United States / Clete Daniel.
      p. cm.
    Includes bibliographical references and index.
    ISBN 0-8014-3853-5 (cloth : alk. paper)
    1. Textile workers—Labor unions—United States. 2. Labor unions—United States. I. Title.
    HD6515.T4 D36 2001
    331.88'177'00973—dc21   00-011633

Cloth printing   10 9 8 7 6 5 4 3 2 1

This book is dedicated to the generations of men and women who struggled courageously and selflessly in the cause of building and sustaining democratic unionism in the American textile industry, and, in particular, to Sol Stetin and the late Larry Rogin, whose lives of devoted service to their fellow workers embody the best traditions of trade unionism in the United States.

Contents

Acknowledgments

In the course of researching and writing this book I have incurred innumerable debts. I am particularly indebted, however, to the officers and staff of the Rieve-Pollock Foundation, whose unfailing assistance and generosity facilitated my work from beginning to end. That they offered this support unconditionally is a testament both to their collective integrity and to their resolute faith that the most illuminating historical scholarship is that undertaken without fear of learning the full story that honest and rigorous inquiry discloses.

I especially want to thank Keir Jorgensen, whose devotion to this project revealed itself in his tireless efforts both to unearth new documentary sources and to bring other relevant information to my attention. His commitment to the union cause he has served so expertly and faithfully for the whole of his adult life is at once admirable and inspiring. I am also grateful for the help and encouragement I received for Sol Stetin whose enthusiasm and intelligence have been deployed in the service of textile unionism for nearly seventy years, and are still very much in evidence in the work he continues to do on behalf of American workers. Two of those who helped me the most did not live to see the final product of their generosity. Sol Barkin and Larry Rogin rank among the best and brightest people ever to have served the American labor movement, and the knowledge they shared with me informed my understanding of textile unionism in more ways than I can possibly express. Several others also deserve special mention for the valuable assistance they offered, including Scott Hoyman, George Perkel and Peter Goldberger. Peter was especially helpful in the preparation of the last stages of the book and has become a friend as well as a valued collaborator. I would be remiss if I did not also acknowledge the invaluable assistance of my secretary Laura Drysdale. Last, I want to express my deep appreciation to Bruce Raynor, whose friendship I fondly cherish and whose example I greatly admire. With leaders of Bruce's intelligence and devotion to help guide it into the new century, I am encouraged to believe that the labor movement will not waver in its historic commitment to redeem the promise of an authentically democratic life for all American workers.

In the end, the support I received from my wife, Helen, mattered most. Her abiding love and friendship sustained me through every phase of this project, and they remain the gifts I treasure above all others.

CULTURE OF
MISFORTUNE

Introduction

In the history of labor organization in the United States before 1937, a number of periods are notable for the uncommon vitality and resolve evident in workers' efforts to establish an authority equal to that of employers in deciding the terms and conditions of their employment. During these singular periods, when the caution fostered by their chronic vulnerability gave way first to anger and then to action, American workers intruded on the consciousness of the nation. They did so in ways that appeared to contradict the exceptionalist orthodoxy that said that class, as a source of either individual or collective identity, lacked in the United States the compelling force it enjoyed elsewhere in the capitalist world. And even when the demonstrations of uncommon solidarity that defined these infrequent episodes proved unsustainable, they nevertheless suggested that the apparent aversion of American workers to class-conscious behavior was circumstantial rather than intrinsic.

Although ideologues of both the right and the left too readily found in this pattern of episodic insurgency reassuring proof of their otherwise antithetical convictions, the only clear lesson it imparted was that the behavior of American workers did not neatly or inevitably conform to any particular theory or notion of class relations in a capitalist culture. Indeed, the presumably national "environment" of capitalism in the United States was, in truth, a maddeningly complex and bewildering mosaic of contiguous environments which, while uniformly subject to the influences of general forces, were usually most accessible to genuine understanding on the basis of the particular circumstances that obtained in each. Overarching events like war and depression had from time to time created a background against which the common features of these distinctive environments were highlighted in ways that led hopeful class theorists to conclude that a coherent whole was, at last, coming into focus, but discerning the emblematic shapes and forms that confirmed an inexorable momentum toward sharpened class consciousness remained more an act of faith than of dispassionate observation. While one might plausibly discern a legacy of activism when viewing these recurrent periods of heightened labor militancy as a historical continuum, even when that legacy was more patch-work than seamless fabric, deducing the ascending hegemony of class as a source of worker identity was nearly always injudicious.

What this sporadic activism did attest to, despite the endlessly resourceful efforts of American employers to defeat or discourage it, was the enduring allure of the idea of unionism. American workers may well have lagged far behind their British and European counterparts in embracing theoretical expli-cations of class relations under capitalism, but the common expectation of a genuinely democratic life, no matter how vaguely or sporadically conveyed, found expression in their persistent embrace of trade unionism as a goal, if not as a functional reality. Workers might—and usually did—fall short of realizing their trade union ambitions, but even in failure they remained steadfast in the conviction that the country's democratic promise could not be fully redeemed until they collectively secured a measure of equal authority at the point of pro-duction.

What is paradoxical about the history of trade unionism in the United States, however, is that the egalitarian ideal that sustained its promise was rarely evident in the values and attitudes that informed its actual practice before the mid-1930s. The belief that workplace equality was an indis-pensable prerequisite to true democracy was plainly inclusive in its implica-tions, and, the distinctive characteristics that defined workers as individuals notwithstanding, they were a class, inherently whole and indivisible where their fundamental rights were construed theoretically. With surprisingly few exceptions, however, the trade unions forged by American workers prior to the mid-1930s adopted a structure and ethos that announced the practical irrele-vance of class as an organizational premise. Egalitarian idealism might be the theoretical basis upon which labor most plausibly asserted claims of trade unionism's indispensability to real democracy, but its force quickly dissipated in the face of less high-minded contentions that, in practice, for reasons of eco-nomic efficiency and cultural convention, trade unions must be exclusive organizations.

In the end, what tended to matter most in determining the encompassing extent of trade unionism in the United States were not commonalities of class and industry but commonalities of craft, skill, race, ethnicity, and gender. The resultant tradition of worker organization on an exclusive basis was one that strongly discouraged class solidarity and a sense of common identity among American wage earners by institutionalizing their differences. The typical trade unionist might readily concede the unity and mutuality of all wage earn-ers at some level of abstract ratiocination, but, as a practical matter, trade unionism of the exclusive sort most common to the American workplace rarely obliged its adherents to venture beyond the narrow boundaries of group interest. Indeed, at their most uncharitable, craftsmen who had successfully leveraged their skills in the cause of unionism invoked a self-serving Darwinian logic to account for the evident incapacity of less skilled workers to do likewise. When skill and the presumed exigencies of the labor market failed to explain hierarchical tendencies in the working class, unionized craftsmen increasingly drew upon convenient myths of race, ethnicity, and gender to rationalize their "natural" separation from the unorganized.

That unionism in the United States throughout the nineteenth century and well into the twentieth usually occurred on a basis that discouraged solidarity did not mean that the potential advantages of broad-based, inclusive organizations went unrecognized by workers. As early as the 1820s, American workers had demonstrated an understanding that the common disadvantages and discontents attendant to membership in the wage-earning class mitigated the differences among and between them. The character and intent of the various workers' organizations that arose from recurrent realizations of craft unionism's inherent limitations reflected the rapidly changing social, political, and economic circumstances of a nation caught up in a headlong, extemporized rush toward modernity. But whether expressed in efforts to marshal the political power of workers in the interests of democratic reform, movements to incite revolutionary assaults against the wage system and the capitalist values that promulgated it or campaigns to build industrial unions that were unconventional only in their inclusive structure, these periodic challenges to the central premise of insular craft unionism were linked by a transcendent conviction that labor's true and greatest strength lay in unity rather than separation, no matter how alluring exclusivity might be as an expedient.

The most ambitious and extraordinary of these inclusive, class-based organizations, the Knights of Labor and the Industrial Workers of the World, never offered, despite the brief incandescence each achieved as a beacon of far-reaching change, the viable means workers needed to empower themselves on the job or to amplify their collective voice in the democratic arena. More promising in the long run, though their early records did not reveal their full potential, were the few industrial unions that before World War I struggled to carve out jurisdictions for themselves in a craft-dominated labor movement. Determined to organize workers on a basis that rejected craft values in favor of industrial criteria, these new unions, which first gained prominence in the mining and garment industries, attested to unionism's potential accessibility to the millions of semiskilled and unskilled wage earners who constituted the larger portion of the U.S. labor force as the new century began.

From the end of the depression of the 1890s until Americans went to war in 1917, the impressive, if uneven, gains achieved by organized workers redounded mainly to the advantage of craft unionism. But the country's fledgling industrial unions, though few in number and still regarded by hidebound craft loyalists as organizationally untenable, also gained during the prewar era. The United Mine Workers, the International Ladies Garment Workers Union, and the Amalgamated Clothing Workers Union enhanced the credibility of inclusive unionism while advancing and protecting the respective interests of their various constituencies. With the country's entry into the war in 1917, industrial unions, including those of merchant seamen, longshoremen, and meat-packers, were prominent among the worker organizations scrambling to take advantage of the congenial labor policies conceded by the Wilson administration to gain union support for the war effort.

As conducive as wartime conditions were to trade unionism's success, however, the end of hostilities marked a return to labor relations even more bitter and conflict ridden than those of the prewar era. Any expectation harbored by Samuel Gompers and other AFL leaders that labor's conspicuous patriotism during the war entitled trade unions to greater respect and tolerance in its aftermath was quickly dashed by the virulent antiunionism that swept the nation in 1919. The fortunes of industrial unionism, which had improved markedly in the nurturing environment of wartime policies, were subject to especially sharp reversals as employers reasserted control over labor relations. In the steel industry, the focus of a massive organizing campaign launched before the war's end, industrial unionism suffered a particularly debilitating defeat when employers, embolden by a rising tide of both antiradical and antiunion hysteria, ruthlessly crushed a strike involving more than 350,000 workers.

As employers absorbed the evident object lesson of 1919's multiplying labor troubles—that trade unions, despite their impressive wartime gains, were vulnerable—they resolved with increasing frequency and boldness to retake the ground they had earlier conceded to organized workers. Unions everywhere suffered as the open-shop drives of the early 1920s gained momentum, but those organized on an industrial basis were especially vulnerable to coordinated employer assaults. The new industrial unions forged during the war by sailors, longshoremen, and meatpackers quickly faltered in the face of open shop onslaughts, but their older counterparts in mining and the needle trades fared almost as badly. Bolstered by a conservative political climate that favored business and aided by court decisions that limited the ability of unions to fight back, employers had, by the end of the decade, so undercut union power that, where it remained at all, it did so largely at the sufferance of management.

The weakened condition of the labor movement as the economy careened into depression at the end of the 1920s threatened its very survival. In no precinct of the labor movement did the threat of outright extinction loom more menacingly than in the emaciated industrial unions clinging to life on its outskirts. Devout craft unionists had long preached the practical futility of industrial unionism. In the especially acute infirmity of its foremost prototypes they glimpsed the promise of imminent vindication.

Though reduced to the point of institutional impotence by the end of 1932, industrial unionism remained, both in theory and in practice, sufficiently vital to anticipate the coming of the New Deal with cautious expectations of renewal. More because of their political daring and resourcefulness in exploiting the confusion of early New Deal labor policies than due to the Roosevelt administration's always less than ardent commitment to organized labor's revival, the UMW, the ILGWU and the ACW benefited as few other unions did in 1933 and 1934. Seizing upon Sec. 7(a) of the National Industrial Recovery Act as a virtual mandate to organize, rather than accepting it as the empty gesture toward labor that Roosevelt and his advisors intended it to be, John L. Lewis, David Dubinsky, and Sidney Hillman vigorously promoted the revitalization of their unions as an indispensable component of industrial recovery. And because he was unwilling to risk the political backlash that would have resulted from an emphatic assertion that labor had it all wrong in thinking that Sec. 7(a) was an invitation to organize, Roosevelt could do little more than privately lament his unwitting complicity in trade unionism's sudden resurgence.

Beginning in the summer of 1933 and continuing almost without interruption through the fall of 1934, relations between labor and management in nearly every sector of the economy were convulsed by conflicts related to workers' efforts to realize the apparent promise of Sec. 7(a). These battles involved wage earners of nearly every type, from veteran craft unionists in the historic seats of urban labor activism to uninitiated farmworkers in the remote fields and orchards of California's agribusiness baronies. What ultimately distinguished the workplace uprisings of the early New Deal from earlier labor-management conflict was the force and frequency with which they explicitly endorsed and validated the concept of industrial organization. Indeed, what made the greatest labor struggles of the early New Deal truly special was not that they challenged the authority of employers or undermined the corporatist foundations of Roosevelt's new industrial relations policy, but that they decisively rejected craft as the preeminent focus of worker organization in the United States.

Because so many of the hundreds of thousands of workers who joined in the battles of 1933 and 1934 made industrial unionism the common objective of their otherwise separate efforts, the AFL, that once mighty bulwark of craft principles, was as threatened and disconcerted by their activism as employers and the Roosevelt administration were. For most AFL leaders it required no special powers of discernment to see that the industrially structured miners and needle trades unions that they had grudgingly admitted to the "house of labor" were fast becoming, in form and function, a Trojan horse.

Emboldened by the notable successes of their own unions and hopeful that every advance by aroused industrial workers heralded the coming of age of the "new unionism," Lewis, Dubinsky, and Hillman became increasingly insistent in their demands that the craft-dominated executive council of the AFL act decisively to accommodate the burgeoning aspirations of semi-skilled and unskilled wage earners in America's mass-production industries. At the 1934 convention of the AFL, which was held in San Francisco in the still charged atmosphere of the recent general strike in support of Harry Bridges's longshoremen's union, Lewis and his allies demanded that the executive council both initiate an all-out organizing drive in the steel industry and charter new industrial unions in a number of other basic industries, including automobile manufacturing.

At once unwilling to abandon their self-interested craft loyalties and to reject their opponents' demands, members of the conservative majority on the executive council opted for a policy that proved an affront to both logic and good faith. The AFL would sponsor an organizing campaign in steel and issue the industrial union charters insurgents demanded, the council decided, but the rights and interests of all existing craft affiliates would remain intact. That industrial unions in the mass-production industries could be successfully established without infringing on the crafts' claims to exclusive jurisdiction over various skilled occupations was impossible, and the council majority's decision to pursue a clearly untenable policy left its motives open to question.

In the aftermath of the 1934 convention, the AFL's deep ambivalence toward industrial unionism was plain in its ultimate unwillingness to keep the promises made in San Francisco. The AFL made clear that any industrial charter it might issue would have to entrust control over the new unions' affairs to its own hand-picked craft partisans. As for the promised organizing campaign in steel, the undertaking dearest to John L. Lewis's heart, the AFL leadership insisted that it would be launched when the time was right. Of course, the time would never be right.

As the AFL pursued its strategy of purposeful inaction and overt obstruction during the early months of 1935, the prospects for industrial unionism that had appeared so bright the previous summer dimmed alarmingly. Through their bold and often dangerous activism industrial workers in industry after industry had demonstrated with unmistakable clarity during 1933 and 1934 a willingness to take unprecedented risks in the cause of unionism. And yet in 1935 as spring stretched into summer and then summer into fall, the AFL's unwillingness to accept the urgent invitation to mass organization that industrial workers had extended became increasingly evident. Even the enactment in July of the National Labor Relations Act, which not only enabled worker organization but actually embraced collective bargaining as the preferred basis of industrial relations in the United States, failed to rouse the AFL out of its studied lethargy.

Convinced that any reasonable hope of AFL action had long since expired, Lewis and his allies set the stage for a last dramatic confrontation with the federation's craft-union majority at the 1935 convention. Held in the cavernous Atlantic City Convention Hall, the gathering was destined to become the most momentous in the federation's history. Compromise, to which both insurgents and the AFL's old guard had at least pretended earlier, was no longer a viable option. As the delegates arrived in Atlantic City, it was with a rising expectation that the issue of industrial unionism, which had polarized the AFL nearly to the point of paralysis, would finally be resolved once and for all.

In the end, the drama attendant to the debate over industrial unionism at the

1935 convention derived from the volatile relations between its leading participants rather than from any uncertainty over the ultimate outcome. The craft loyalists' decisive majority among convention delegates left little doubt of the results of each of the crucial votes taken on the issue. What Lewis and his allies had at the convention was not so much a chance to win the debate as an opportunity to win the day by exposing to attentive industrial workers the utter futility of trying any longer to advance the cause of the new unionism under AFL auspices.

Although speakers on both sides of the issue unhesitatingly deployed the full arsenal of cogent arguments and personal invective they had stockpiled for the occasion, and while Lewis even contributed a touch of popular theater, and unsubtle symbolism, by abruptly cold-cocking carpenters' union President "Big Bill" Hutcheson during an altercation on the convention floor, the AFL's opposition to industrial unionism was nevertheless endorsed by a comfortable margin. The champions of industrial unionism had never intended to abide by the expressed will of the convention's craft-union majority, however. Rather, they sought to expose the true depth of the federation's commitment to "business as usual." Having accomplished that goal, Lewis, Hillman, and Dubinsky (supported by printers' union President Charles Howard and the heads of the United Textile Workers; Mine, Mill and Smelter Workers; Oil Workers; and the Cap and Millinery Department of the United Hatters Union) defiantly set about building an industrial union movement.

Calling themselves the Committee for Industrial Organization but claiming publicly that they had no desire to defy the AFL by persisting in their open advocacy of industrial unionism, the dissidents acted almost at once to challenge both the authority and the forbearance of the federation's dominant craft faction. Lewis, whose preference for a clean break with the AFL was mitigated by the generally more cautious tendencies of his fellow dissidents, quickly emerged in the public's mind as the personification of what became during the winter of 1935–36 an ever bolder threat to the federation's control over the agenda of organized labor in the United States.

To AFL president William Green, whose personal malleability had commended him to the most forceful members of the federation's executive council as Samuel Gompers' successor ten years earlier, fell the unenviable, and ultimately impossible, task of heading off a complete organizational rupture. At first, Green pleaded with the dissidents to desist from their plan to launch an unauthorized organizing campaign. As anger mounted among the executive council's hardliners, however, Green's earnest entreaties gave way to increasingly pointed threats. Yet whether pleading or threatening, Green was inevitably ignored by Lewis and his compatriots. For all intents and purposes, the breakup that Green labored so earnestly to avoid had already occurred. By the early spring of 1936 the CIO was a functioning entity. And no matter how ardently Green and other would-be peacemakers in the AFL wished it were not so, the mainstream of the American labor movement had abruptly divided along two separate courses, one flowing predictably down a familiar channel methodically dredged by successive generations of craft unionists, the other surging erratically along a widening flume created by it own inexorable advance.

As the chief instigator and strategist of the CIO insurgency, John L. Lewis happily accepted both the congratulations of industrial union enthusiasts and the castigations hurled by defenders of craft orthodoxy. As the force of his personality informed the deliberations of the CIO ever more palpably during the spring of 1936, and the UMW treasury became the readiest source of its financial support, Lewis established a degree of personal authority over the new industrial union movement that verged on proprietorship. Hillman, Dubinsky, and the other trade union leaders who had contributed importantly to the enterprise might speak officially on behalf of the CIO, but it was Lewis's distinctive rumble that resonated most authoritatively among industrial workers and the broader public. More to the point, it was Lewis who charted the CIO's initial course, and that course led the new organization directly into the forbidding maw of antiunionism in the United States, the steel industry.

With the creation in June, 1936, of the Steel Workers' Organizing Committee (SWOC), which was designed to respond to his personal authority, Lewis created the instrument of the CIO's first big push for mass unionism. Simultaneously, his success in wresting jurisdictional rights in the steel industry from the enfeebled clutches of the moribund Amalgamated Association of Iron, Steel and Tin Workers provided the campaign with a cloak of legitimacy that even AFL hardliners were bound to acknowledge, if not to approve.

Because the SWOC drive in the steel industry was the most publicized and generously funded organizing effort of the CIO during the summer and fall of 1936, it necessarily constituted the crucial test of the new organization's ultimate viability. Yet it was hardly the only attempt launched in the latter half of 1936 by industrial union activists intent on planting the CIO's banner in industries previously beyond unionism's reach. Most notably, a group of activist auto workers and their supporters, including a number of able radicals with close ties to the American Communist Party, fashioned a new CIO affiliate from the remnants of several ineffectual AFL federal unions and, without benefit of the impressive resources available to the SWOC, set about the seemingly impossible task of organizing the country's largest automaker. Throughout the fall, organizers from the swelling ranks of the United Auto Workers spread the message of industrial unionism in General Motors plants across the country. And when GM's notoriously pervasive spy system made open advocacy too risky, UAW organizers took their message directly into the workers' homes.

As 1936 came to an end, both the viability and the credibility of the CIO rested on the improbable success of two quite dissimilar organizing drives: one in steel operating systematically and in ultimate obedience to the personal designs of John L. Lewis, the other in autos following an improvised strategy that reflected in equal measures the inexperience and brilliance of its contentious young rank-and-file activists. CIO organizers were, of course, making equally valiant efforts to build new unions in other mass-production industries such as rubber and electrical manufacturing as 1936 came to a close, but the burden of the movement's success in the United States weighed on auto and steel workers as it did on no other groups of would-be unionists. With the steel and automobile industries organized, the industrial union movement could be counted a success, no matter how it fared elsewhere. Conversely, no matter how numerous its organizing successes in other mass industries, the CIO's inability to entrench itself in the dominant companies in autos and steel would inevitably, and not unreasonably, call into question the future of industrial unionism.

Whether the CIO was the real thing or merely the latest in a dishearteningly long series of workers' organizations that had vainly aspired to represent America's industrial masses was a question not long in being answered. By means of successive victories, each of a magnitude unprecedented in the prior history of worker organization in the United States, the SWOC and the UAW, in early 1937, together secured the CIO's standing as both a vehicle for industrial worker empowerment and as a contender for leadership of the larger American labor movement.

The UAW's dramatic confrontation with General Motors, during which the company laid siege to its own factories in Flint, Mich., in an ultimately futile effort to dislodge the sitdown strikers who had seized them, produced after nearly six weeks of tense and bitter struggle a breakthrough for industrial unionism and the CIO whose impact was nothing short of stunning. That General Motors, a company long beyond the reach of worker organization, was now bowing to the pressure of a fledgling union of young militants caused employers across the spectrum of American industry to wonder whether any one of them was safe from the new unionism.

Their unease was exacerbated when, shortly thereafter, United States Steel, long the corporate citadel of the open shop, announced to an astonished nation that it, too, and without having mounted much more than a vigorous skirmish in defense of its antiunion tradition, had reached an accommodation with the SWOC. All of a sudden, it seemed, the CIO had progressed from extravagant ambition to irresistible force. The daunting tests to which the CIO brashly subjected itself in steel and autos had been passed with startling aplomb. And even though Henry Ford and the protolithic heads of the "little" steel companies would shortly demonstrate to overly-confident union enthusiasts in each industry just how much power the open shop retained when it was defended with the ruthless resolve that true devotion compelled, industrial unionism was a force to be reckoned with.

Although the initial victories in autos and steel, because they came against GM and U.S. Steel, probably enhanced the reputation of the CIO in ways that comparable successes in other industries could not have, activist workers and their allies were simultaneously pressing the cause of industrial unionism in diverse centers of mass production across the country. The successive triumphs of auto and steel workers early in 1937 clearly emboldened their counterparts in other industries, but the multiplying affiliates of the CIO were already well on their way to becoming a visible presence in many industrial strongholds. As somewhat less prominent organizing drives by rubber and electrical workers, loggers and longshoremen, packinghouse and oil field workers, metal miners, and glass workers gained measurable momentum, the industrial union idea that had inspired the CIO insurgency only a year earlier assumed increasingly imposing concrete dimensions.

So formidable had the CIO become by the spring of 1937 that the AFL was at last obliged to concede its presence. Confronted by a robust industrial union movement that was largely free of the debilitating ideological burdens that had weighed down earlier challengers to craft's primacy, and increasingly aware that it must follow its rival's example or recede into its burgeoning shadow, the AFL had little choice except to acquiesce in the organization of unskilled and semiskilled workers not long before dismissed as "the rubbish at labor's door." Industrial workers whom AFL traditionalists had long considered unfit for service in labor's cause were, by mid-1937, being ardently courted by federation affiliates, if only to ensure that they did not fall into the clutches of CIO suitors. By year's end, the escalating competition between CIO and AFL unions had swelled their combined memberships to nearly eight million workers, more than double the number counted only five years earlier. More important still, the labor movement, despite its internal disunity, had graduated to a level of participation in the institutional life of the country that would ultimately oblige all other influential institutions—governmental, corporate, religious, educational—to take organized labor into account as they never had previously.

Because the reporting of the CIO's explosive emergence by the country's popular media tended to highlight features common to the exertions of its otherwise distinctive affiliates, the image that was created was that of a monolithic institution. To the extent that the CIO was incarnate in the imposing bulk and overarching authority of John L. Lewis, the public's sense of its unity was confirmed and enhanced. The CIO, with the blustering Lewis at its head, had brusquely intruded on insular power relationships that had endured largely undisturbed since the dawn of the Machine Age, and, as one group of industrial workers after another embraced the activist ethic of the new unionism, those watching from the sidelines were obliged to discard antiquated notions of labor's weakness in favor of fresh impressions commended by multiplying proofs of its growing strength.

Despite the CIO triumphs of 1937, and the broader advances they either prompted or inspired, the record of industrial unionism in the late 1930s and beyond is simply too complex and uneven to support the view that the historic impediments to worker organization in America's mass-production industries had at last been surmounted. It was easy to forget that, at the height of the labor movement's success, most workers remained outside its orbit even as the circumstances of their lives reflected the great benefits its new strength conferred. Within the CIO movement itself, industrial unionism's progress was neither uniform nor symmetrical. And, certainly, the gains that resulted from spectacular successes in industries like steel and autos must be assessed in the light of industrial unionism's much less impressive record of progress in others if its role in the modern history of American labor is to be understood at a level of complexity beyond that accessible through epic interpretations alone. To be understood fully, the CIO must be considered in terms of its defeats as well as its victories, its weaknesses as well as its strengths. To permit the unarguably imposing records of the CIO's most successful unions to define it as a movement is to render too homogeneous and unambiguous a history that, considered in all its aspects, simply will not sustain transcendent interpretations. For all of its suddenly evident utility as a strategy for worker empowerment, industrial unionism was never an irresistible form of labor organization. In manufacturing sectors in which capitalism was slow to adopt a more accommodating perspective and the ancient primacy of employers was abetted by cultural and other forces hostile to the rising ambition of workers to share power, the fallibility of industrial unionism became distressingly obvious.

In no arena of labor-management contention were the limitations of the new unionism more apparent than in the textile industry, and for no labor organization did the challenge to overcome them loom more ominous during the middle decades of the 20th century than for the Textile Workers Union of America. Launched in the immediate wake of the CIO's stunning triumphs over GM and U.S. Steel, the drive to bring industrial unionism to the previously hostile precincts of America's oldest mass-production industry promised, if it succeeded, to match in magnitude and symbolic import the greatest organizational achievements of workers in autos and steel.

The organizing vehicle specially created to accomplish the CIO's grand design in textiles was the Textile Workers Organizing Committee. Intended as the institutional solution to centrifugal tendencies that had long discouraged solidarity among the more than one million employees in the various branches of the textile industry, the TWOC represented a second wave of the CIO offensive against the open shop and craft exclusivity, one presumably rendered all the more formidable because of the momentum bequeathed by earlier victories. The TWOC's prospects for success were further enhanced by the exceptional leadership qualities of the man at its helm. In Sidney Hillman, president of the Amalgamated Clothing Workers and John L. Lewis's chief collaborator in the formation of the CIO, the TWOC had a leader as able and resourceful as any who has served the labor movement in the United States. Aided by veteran militants from the diverse constituencies of the beleaguered United Textile Workers of America and by a cadre of eager activists drawn from an impressive spectrum of labor, religious, and academic backgrounds, Hillman embarked upon the TWOC campaign in an atmosphere laden with expectations of inevitable success.

What follows, however, is not a story of the success that followed Hillman's bold declaration of the CIO's ambitions in the textile industry. Rather, it is an attempt to explain why an undertaking that Hillman and others expected to yield one of industrial unionism's greatest triumphs produced, instead, perhaps its greatest disappointment. More particularly, it is an inquiry into the unique ways in which the prior history of worker organization in the American textile industry confounded the CIO's initial efforts to bring long-suffering millhands into its expanding domain and a study of how inexorable changes in the social, economic, political, and legal context of textile unionism in the years that followed ruinously impeded the Textile Workers Union of America in its exhausting struggle to surmount chronic misfortune. Inevitably, it is also an attempt to understand the singular challenges of leadership in an organization whose internal political culture was increasingly vulnerable to the destructive pressures of apparently irreversible decline and the concomitant ravages of seemingly unavoidable dissention.

Finally, this study discloses that it was the special fate of the TWUA to glimpse the first telltale evidences of America's fall from manufacturing preeminence well before they were discernible to other industrial unions. And in seeking to meet the multiplying challenges to worker organization posed by an industry in the throes of dislocation, relocation and structural transformation, the TWUA unwittingly became the first major union in the United States to confront the specter of postindustrialism in actualized form.

Decades before trade unionists in other mass industries like steel and autos were called upon to cope with the organizational consequences of debilitating change, leaders and members of the TWUA staggered under the weight of new realities that contradicted comforting assumptions of America's manufacturing dominance and industrial unionism's institutional permanence. Though seldom at a loss to appreciate the courage and resolve, if not always the wisdom and efficacy, of the women and men who struggled in the service of textile unionism, other unionists generally were less astute in drawing from the TWUA's undulating fortunes those cautionary inferences that would in time have profound meaning for their own organizations. But whether they knew it or not, the unfolding story of the TWUA was, in a number of significant ways, a daunting forecast of what lay ahead for all American workers who sought to advance the cause of workplace democracy through the agency of trade unionism and the practice of collective bargaining.

CHAPTER 1

A Common Interest

To the extent that the history of textile unionism prior to 1937 provided a basis for forecasting the likely future of the Textile Workers Organizing Committee (TWOC), Sidney Hillman and his colleagues had little reason to be hopeful. The idea of collective endeavor had informed the hopes and fueled the actions of workers from the infancy of the textile industry in the United States, but it had also fallen discouragingly short of redeeming its promise of being the means by which they would democratize workplace decision making.

As America's first mass production industry, textile manufacturing was reliant at a very early stage of its development on a workforce that reflected the profound influences of advancing machine technology. The skilled artisans who comprised the labor force of the weaving trade when it was a mainstay of preindustrial handicraft culture rapidly gave way as the textile industry evolved in the early 19th century to machine tenders, including ever larger numbers of women and children, whose defining characteristics were their lack of skill and their ready availability as a substitute workforce. To be sure, workers possessing various degrees of skill—loomfixers, mulespinners, carders, slashers, and weavers—would remain indispensable members of the labor force throughout the century, but there was no denying that textile manufacturing had become a fixed locus of the machine age and that the machine tender was the ascendant personification of an emerging industrial culture.

The alienation attendant to the industrialization of textile manufacturing in the United States during the early 19th century was not long in manifesting itself in protests by craft and industrial workers alike. The worker organization inevitably inspired by the chronic discontent that ultimately arose among wage earners in America's burgeoning textile industry was sufficiently impressive in its form and frequency to make textile unionism one of the more familiar features of the 19th century industrial landscape. Despite their penchant for collective action, however, textile workers had very limited success in building durable unions. "In no other American industry," one early study concluded, "has unionism had so checkered and uncertain a career as in textiles."[1]

In particular, textile workers found it difficult to agree among themselves on the appropriate compass of solidarity and to muster the will and resources required to sustain unions in an industry whose increasing diversity and chronic volatility discouraged effective activism. The craft-conscious faith to which skilled workers instinctively rallied in the face of roiling industrial change inspired collective action throughout the early 19th century, but the exclusive organizations that gained a tenuous foothold in the leading textile centers—Lowell, Lawrence, Fall River, New Bedford, Mass.; Pawtucket, R.I.; and Manchester, N.H. in New England; and in Philadelphia, Pa., and Paterson N.J., in the Middle Atlantic region—provided only temporary advantages to skilled workers and nothing at all to the growing number of machine operatives whose lack of skills rendered them ineligible for membership.

Even among skilled workers durable solidarity was uncommon. The parochial tendencies fostered by their craft consciousness were reinforced by the strong sense of regional and ethnic identity that often informed their thinking. The early unions among mulespinners, for example, attested to the craft's domination by English and Scottish workers, and often reflected as well the particular tradition of organization associated with one or another of the locales of textile manufacturing in New England and the Middle Atlantic states. Like their counterparts in other crafts during the formative stages of unionism in the United States, skilled textile workers were only rarely disposed to put the concerns of the wider workers' community ahead of their immediate self-interest. On those exceptional occasions when other workers, including the women (first native-born and then immigrant) who supplied the bulk of the industry's semiskilled and unskilled labor, were able to persuade the organized crafts to confront mill owners on a unified basis, any solidarity that resulted dissipated as soon as the immediate crisis that precipitated it had passed.

Indeed, textile unionism in general usually arose from immediate discontents, and, as one commentator noted, too often relied on "the solidarity which can momentarily be achieved by emotion rather than by reason." As a result, the history of collective action among textile workers during the first half of the 19th century was "contained in the accounts of industrial strife rather than in the work of permanent organizations." In the face of repeated wage cuts, which were occasioned by the frequent introduction of new, labor-saving machinery and the substitution of cheaper sources of labor, textile workers became practiced in the conduct of strikes, And although most of these strikes, which "were undertaken only as a result of desperation," proved unsuccessful, textile workers did succeed in fostering a "colorful tradition of guerrilla warfare in defense of what they felt to be their rights."[2]

The latter half of the 19th century witnessed changes in the scope and character of textile unionism, but the fortunes of worker organization in the industry were little improved. Women mill operatives became more prominent activists, but organization among textile workers remained, for the most part, the province of skilled males. The unions formed by textile workers from the 1850s onward offered only very modest rewards to the stalwarts who struggled to sustain them, but the regularity of their appearance, and reappearance, clearly suggested that the idea of collective action had lodged in the hearts and minds of millhands even though they had yet to master its practice.

During the volatile decades of the late 19th century, as the country alternately lurched and careered toward industrial maturity, the sporadic activism of textile millhands was lost in the welter of labor conflict centered in the rapidly growing railroad, mining, and steel industries. Yet if they were cast in what increasingly seemed a less central role in the unfolding class drama of the Gilded Age, textile workers never left the stage entirely. When disaffected radicals departed the International Workingmen's Association in the late 1870s to pursue industrial unionism unencumbered by socialist canons, the organization they founded, the International Labor Union (ILU), gained an especially enthusiastic following among textile workers in New England and the Middle Atlantic region. Indeed, by the time the ILU's brief career came to a close in 1882, it was, despite a well-advertised intention to shelter all industrial workers, almost exclusively an organization of textile millhands.[3]

Textile workers also rallied in even larger numbers to the cause of the meteoric Knights of Labor. Shawl weavers in Philadelphia formed a local assembly of the Knights before the end of 1872, and shortly thereafter the city's carpet weavers followed suit. Like other early recruits to a secret fraternal organization far more concerned in the 1870s with the elaboration of its rituals and the safeguarding of its "mysteries" than with fomenting overt challenges to the wage system of industrial capitalism, textile workers who joined the Knights remained purposely inconspicuous activists. Not until the early 1880s, when the Knights abandoned secrecy in favor of open appeals to the laboring masses, did workers from the broader ranks of the textile industry begin to join the movement. It is likely that more than 25,000 textile workers belonged to the Knights at the height of its success in 1886. And while, as an occupational group, millhands gained no particular prominence in the organization and abandoned the Knights as readily as did other members when its prospects began to plummet toward the end of 1886, they nevertheless confirmed that unionism was an idea that appealed to textile workers in every branch and region of the industry.[4]

Despite its momentary luminescence, the Knights failed both to alter relations between labor and management in the late 19th century and to discourage worker organizations that subordinated class interests to craft desires. For the most skilled textile workers, who seldom let class values intrude on craft concerns, their brief dalliance with the Knights of Labor reflected more a bandwagon mentality than a conscious reconsideration of craft allegiances. "In the course of its brief career in the textile industry," one historian observed,

> the Knights of Labor caught up the existing organization of skilled craftsmen and flung them together with unions of unskilled workers who had never before experienced the urge toward group activity. . . . When the tidal wave subsided the industrial locals were irreparably broken upon the rocks of economic and cultural dissension. The craft assemblies returned to the quieter waters of localism and craft autonomy. When they had recovered from their dizzy but exhilarating whirl, they pointed to the wrecks of their less fortunate brothers as terrible warnings of the fate of wayward industrial youth.[5]

While the resurgence of craft partition at the end of the century was reflected in the efforts of skilled millhands to advance and protect their separate interests through independent organization, the idea of a more inclusive unionism was not completely discredited by the Knights' collapse. The National Union of Textile Workers (NUTW), founded in Lowell, Mass., during the spring of 1890, claimed the middle ground between the Knights and the independent craft unions by seeking to bring all skilled textile workers into a single organization. Chartered by the American Federation of Labor (AFL) in 1891, the NUTW was ultimately more important for the tendency it represented than for any successes it achieved. In its earliest days, the NUTW enjoyed considerable support among the skilled cotton mill workers of Fall River and New Bedford. By the mid-1890s, however, growing political differences, and their still powerful instinct for local craft autonomy, led these workers to abandon the NUTW in favor of independent organizations. The union continued in the late 1890s to claim support from a modest number of textile workers in New England and the Middle Atlantic states—in the woolen mills of Rhode Island and Lawrence, Mass., the silk mills of New Jersey, and the carpet mills and upholstery shops of Philadelphia and New York. As the decade came to a close, however, it was from cotton workers in the Piedmont region of the South, who still felt ardent allegiance to the inclusive values of the Knights of Labor, that the National Union of Textile Workers received its greatest support. Its permanent membership never ranged beyond a few thousand, and, as southern cotton workers extended their domination, it became increasingly isolated, a regional organization whose frequent but unavailing struggles against vehemently antiunion southern mill owners earned it a reputation for courage, if not for stability or effectiveness. Still, the NUTW did reveal that southern millhands were not invariably the docile industrial innocents that boosters of the New South reassuringly described to northern mill owners in their campaigns to hasten the textile industry's southward migration. It also provided additional evidence that textile workers remained cognizant of the potential value of wider, more inclusive organization even though they were still at a loss to know precisely how it might be achieved.[6]

By the end of the century, skilled textile workers almost everywhere were aware of the need for greater solidarity. Yet agreeing on the structure and character of an organization that promoted cooperation across crafts without simultaneously submerging individual craft identities proved difficult. The two leading unions among skilled millhands in New England, representing mulespinners and weavers, regarded the erosion of craft autonomy as an especially dire prospect. Each dominated by workers of English descent who cherished craft principles not least because they embodied the hallowed traditions of their Lancashire forebears, the mulespinners and weavers had fashioned organizations that were models of conservative business unionism. Neither, however, could weather the erosive effects of technological and structural changes in the textile industry as it expanded and diversified.

The mulespinners, whose great skill had afforded them significant leverage where mule spindles were still in use, faced the prospect of virtual extinction as mills adopted new technologies. The introduction of ring-frame spindles, whose relative simplicity of operation permitted the substitution of unskilled workers with only minimal training, posed a threat not just to the elite status of mulespinners, but to their very presence in the American textile industry. By 1900, ring spindles outnumbered mule spindles by nearly three to one, and the few thousand mulespinners still employed were increasingly desperate to devise an effective means of self-preservation, even if it meant compromising their craft autonomy.[7]

Though less immediately threatened by technological change, weavers in New England mill towns also acknowledged the benefits of wider organization as the nineteenth century came to a close. The conservative craft principles that guided weavers in New Bedford, Fall River, and other New England textile centers had largely failed to produce organizations capable of providing the protections they sought. The realization, which was reinforced by increased concern over competition from proliferating southern mills and a surge of European immigrants, prompted them not only to abandon localism in favor of regional organization, but also to take the lead in promoting federation among the textile industry's established craft unions.

Not until the spring of 1900, however, did the National Federation of Textile Operatives, which represented weavers throughout New England, finally succeed in cobbling a loose alliance among most of the region's organized textile crafts. The mulespinners, who had the longest tradition of organization in the industry, were essential recruits to the new federation, but so were a number of other craft unions. Among them was the National Union of Card Room Workers, which in the late 1890s united previously separate carders' unions in Fall River, New Bedford, and Lowell to form the nucleus of what soon became a regional organization. Support also came from the ranks of organized loomfixers in New England. Highly skilled mechanics who repaired and maintained the increasingly complex machinery that dominated production in cotton and woolen mills, members of the National Loomfixers Union, though less vulnerable to employer pressures than other craftsmen, nevertheless endorsed federation out of a gradually dawning realization that greater solidarity would ultimately be advantageous to all skilled textile workers. Finally, federation was also supported by less prominent organizations, including the Fall River Slasher Tenders and Drawing-In Girls Union, whose largely French Canadian membership attested to the special place that immigrants from Quebec had attained in the textile labor force of New England during the late 19th century.[8]

The institutional expression of this emerging consensus was the American Federation of Textile Operatives (AFTO). Founded in Boston during the spring of 1900, the AFTO, though it did nothing to breach the long-standing barrier between skilled and unskilled workers in New England textile mills, did represent a grudging recognition that craft separation no longer made sense in an industry where the boundaries between skilled functions were being redrawn by new means and methods of production. The AFTO also reflected a growing belief among its diverse elements that it was not enough merely to create a new line of defense against relentless employer aggression. The rapid growth of textile manufacturing in the South had generated escalating competitive pressures that made it incumbent upon New England's skilled millhands to create a form of unionism that contemplated the eventual organization of their southern counterparts.[9]

The grand ambition of the AFTO, to establish itself as the preeminent organization of textile craft workers, was immediately challenged by the NUTW, whose straggling remnants maintained a precarious presence in the hostile environs of the southern Piedmont. In possession of an AFL charter that seemed to guarantee its jurisdiction over all textile crafts, the NUTW took the position that it, rather than the upstart AFTO, had the stronger claim to organizational primacy. When the AFTO pressed ahead with its plan to establish formal dominance in the industry, the NUTW, citing federation policy against dual unionism, successfully prevailed upon the AFL to deny the new organization a charter. In the end, however, the shared conviction of skilled textile workers that continued disunity would further their common degradation led both the AFTO and the NUTW to accept an AFL offer to broker a settlement. A series of preliminary meetings between representatives of the AFTO and NUTW quickly followed, and, at an AFL-sponsored convention held in Washington on November 19, 1901, the last structural barriers to craft unity in the textile industry were finally dismantled.[10]

The volatile composite that emerged from the Washington convention, the United Textile Workers of America, was, from the beginning, more unified in theory than in practice. Habits acquired during the era of craft separation were not easily mitigated by the ideal of unity, no matter how compellingly expressed. Those called upon to put aside their separate allegiances in favor of a common affiliation undoubtedly understood and appreciated the new ethic the UTW embodied, but adopting the generic identity that amalgamation imposed was not an easy accommodation. That ambivalence was most evident in the attitudes of the mulespinners, who insisted, at the founding of the UTW, that they be permitted to retain their separate AFL charter until the new organization had demonstrated its viability. Only then, the mulespinners maintained, would they be willing to dissolve their organization and finally join the UTW as local craft affiliates.[11]

As a response to the debilitating tendency among skilled textile workers toward exclusivity, the UTW represented a signal advance, even though its initial membership amounted to less than 2 percent of the total industry labor force. The 10,000 workers who rallied to the UTW did so out of a deepening belief, if not yet a hardened conviction, that industry must replace craft as the ambit of workplace solidarity. Yet, as important as it was as a concession to the reality of industrial culture, the UTW fell far short of being the inclusive organization that less tentative accommodation to industry change might have produced. A minority of UTW members, especially those in the South who still clung to the faded ideal of solidarity championed by the Knights of Labor, clearly preferred a more inclusive organization, but, in general, the UTW was open only to skilled workers who had been eligible for membership in one of the industry's craft unions. Still well outside the newly redrawn boundaries of textile unionism were the semiskilled and unskilled workers, the growing majority of the industry's labor force overall. The UTW failed to reflect the demographics of the textile industry's workforce in other important ways as well. It was, overwhelmingly, a union of northern, native-born male workers of English, Scottish, and Irish descent in an industry whose labor force, particularly its burgeoning semiskilled and unskilled components, was substantially female and recruited, increasing by, from the protean welter of newly arrived southern and eastern European immigrants and the swelling ranks of dispossessed Piedmont farm families.[12]

In the end, defects in the structure and outlook of the UTW proved less daunting impediments to its success than did circumstances beyond the organization's control. The textile industry's early infatuation with machine technology had blossomed by the early 20th century into a devotion that was at once total and irreversible. And as the erosion of status and security that the machine age abetted quickened its relentless progression, skilled millhands were often at a loss to decide whether entrusting their imperiled futures to the UTW, or to any other union, would make things better or worse. This ambivalence was reinforced by chronic labor market conditions. The ready availability of unskilled workers who were eager to claim the opportunities that the machine had already created prompted industry leaders to seek still more labor-saving innovations at the expense of skilled hands. When their anger outweighed their fear, skilled workers might indeed rally to the UTW, but when the emotional imbalance was reversed, they often decided that activism would only hasten the pace of their displacement through further technological change.

The progress of unionism was further impeded by cyclical economic conditions that tended to foster extreme volatility in the major branches of the textile industry. The wildly fluctuating fortunes of most manufacturers ensured that the UTW and other unions that sought to organize the industry's workers rarely enjoyed a stable economic environment. Most American businesses suffered the vagaries of market imbalances during the boom-and-bust decades of the early 20th century, but in the textile industry internal mechanisms to regulate competition were nonexistent, and the trip from prosperity to ruin could be brutally short.

The not-surprising preoccupation with labor costs that this highly competitive environment fostered among employers was heightened further by the chronic wage disparities that emerged between the northern and southern branches of the industry, especially in cotton textiles. Northern employers, whose antiunion credentials were already well-established, felt even more keenly the need to resist unionism and the higher labor costs it threatened as southern textile firms that had proven themselves largely invulnerable to union inroads exploited the competitive advantage that a regional wage disparity afforded them.

Against these and other conditions and circumstances that obstructed the course of textile unionism as the century opened, the newly established UTW could bring little more to bear than a sense that unity was more likely to serve the interests of effective organization than had craft separatism. And as the dominant institutional expression of unionism's promise in the textile industry for the first third of the new century, the UTW was destined to find out, usually the hard way, just how extraordinarily difficult the passage from promise to reality could be.

At its first annual convention in 1902, the UTW claimed a total membership of 10,600 in 185 local unions, or just under 1.5 percent of the more than 700,000 wage earners employed in the various branches of the textile industry in that year. Not until 1913, a dozen years after its founding, was the UTW able to claim a permanent membership that amounted to even 2 percent of the wage labor force in textiles. Except for the period from 1918 to 1920, when the momentum gained from friendly wartime labor policies, favorable labor market conditions, and a rising national tide of union fervor briefly swelled its membership to 100,000 (just over one of every ten textile workers in the country), the UTW was fortunate if its membership represented as much as 3 percent of the industry's workforce.[13]

In many ways, the UTW was an even more marginal presence in the textile industry than its anemic membership totals suggest. From the first, its strength was narrowly concentrated among the minority of skilled workers who had long dominated trade union activities in the leading textile centers of New England and the Middle Atlantic states. In the South, where the industry continued to experience its most significant expansion, the UTW quickly lost the precarious foothold bequeathed to it by the vestigial NUTW. After losing a bitter strike in Augusta, Georgia, in 1902, the UTW largely abandoned further efforts to win the allegiance of southern millhands.[14] This neglect of the South, which had less to do with strategic deliberations than with the new organization's sense of its own limitations, only enhanced the Piedmont's reputation as a region where unionism was an unlikely threat. It also undoubtedly strengthened the resolve of northern textile firms to resist the UTW, lest their ability to compete with their low-cost southern counterparts be further compromised.

Across the expanse of textile manufacturing, which was, in truth, not a single industry but a collection of industries linked in varying degrees by elements of common process, technology, and technique, the UTW's progress tended to be uneven. In the rug- and carpet-weaving industry, which employed a larger proportion of skilled workers than did the other branches and was less vulnerable to destructive competition, the UTW was slightly more successful than in the cotton, silk, hosiery, and knitted goods industries, where workforce composition, competitive structure, and rival unions combined with other factors to severely retard its progress. In the woolen and worsted industry, second only to cotton manufacturing as a source of textile employment, unionism was rare. Centered in Lawrence, Mass., and Passaic, N.J., where the hegemony exercised over largely unskilled, immigrant laborers by the largest mills approximated industrial feudalism, the woolen and worsted industry generally succeeded in limiting the UTW's influence to the dwindling complement of skilled workers it still employed, and even they were often diffident unionists. Finally, in the minor branches of the industry such as cordage and twine, ribbon, linen and lace goods, and among workers in more distant appendages such as dyeing and finishing, the UTW was seldom, if ever, a force of genuine consequence.

The evident tendency among UTW members, especially in the oldest centers of textile manufacturing like Fall River and New Bedford, to indulge local interests and loyalties at the expense of wider solidarity consistently undermined the organization's attempts to achieve the centralization that effective national unionism demanded. The tension between the UTW and its largest local affiliates, in particular, was disturbingly apparent in endless wrangles over the amount of money the former could rightfully collect from the latter by means of a per capita tax. Like other AFL national unions, whose notion of effective centralized authority demanded subordination of the parts to the whole, the UTW relentlessly pressed its local members to agree to a per capita tax large enough to permit the national (or "international," as it would become with the addition of a small Canadian membership) organization to support a benefits program, amass a strike fund, and assist weak locals with the resources collected from strong ones. The amount of the per capita tax, which was always modest except by the standards of a low-wage industry like textiles, quickly became, as one UTW leader later explained, "a kind of barometer indicating the strength of the International at any given time."[15] By that measure, and the frequency with which local unions broke with the national union over the issue, the per capita tax usually attested to the UTW's chronic weakness and incapacity[16].

The vision of effective national unionism that had inspired the creation of the UTW faltered as the daunting barriers to its success rapidly multiplied. Employers were more (rather than less) determined to resist unionism as the industry continued its chaotic development in the early decades of the 20th century, and the union's unfortunate genius for self-destruction revealed itself through an interminable internal debate over money, a crippling aversion to risk, and an inability to jettison the lingering craft values that forestalled its unqualified embrace of the hundreds of thousands of unskilled southerners, French Canadians, Italians, Poles, Greeks, Portuguese and other industrial sojourners—men, women, and children—who tended the machines that were the modern textile mill's commanding feature.

In truth, of course, the vast jurisdiction ceded to the UTW in its AFL charter was undoubtedly more than even the most formidable union could have organized in an era so hostile to labor's ambitions. In the textile industry, as in every other mass-production industry in the United States at the time, the power of employers to resist unions was infinitely greater than the power of workers to build them. And while the UTW was not infrequently an accomplice to its own fecklessness, its weakness was usually best explained as the inevitable obverse of employer strength.

Whatever the causes of the UTW's generally feeble condition, the conspicuous fact of it invited nearly constant competition from rival unions. Within a jurisdiction that covered what one source described as "the most widely diversified group of crafts and jobs assigned to any union in the AFL," dual unionism was hardly unexpected.[17] "The distinguishing characteristic of textile unionism," another observer noted, "has always been its centrifugal tendencies. In no other industry has such a profusion of unions flourished and withered away. Stability and permanence have been a mirage which union leaders have pursued through all manner of policies and philosophies with little reward other than the wisdom of experience or an occasional handful of Judas's silver."[18]

From the beginning, the UTW was confronted by rivals, on both the right and the left, whose intention was to supplant it, either in whole or in part. In Massachusetts, where its membership was concentrated, the UTW was opposed by a number of conservative crafts that had earlier abandoned it because of irreconcilable differences over the per capita tax and assertions of local autonomy. Unions in New Bedford and Fall River, where craft identities were slow to fade, took the lead in forming a loose alliance among those secessionist elements in New England loath to submit a to central authority. The alliance, which in 1916 became the National Amalgamation of Textile Operatives,[19] attested to the residual power of 19th-century craft values among the most skilled textile workers. It also served as a worrisome reminder to the UTW that, should it actually endeavor to practice the form of modified industrial unionism that its more inclusive structure implied, it would probably do so at the cost of further defections by the skilled millhands who were its most valued members.[20]

If the UTW's alleged dilution of craft principles invited opposition from disgruntled rivals on the right, its reluctance to fully embrace the tenets of industrial unionism fostered equally threatening opposition from eager rivals on the left. Just as its failure to mollify unreconstructed craft elements exacted a heavy toll, its inability or unwillingness to address the concerns and aspirations of the semiskilled and unskilled workers also came at a high cost. The radical Industrial Workers of the World (IWW), who promised not merely worker solidarity but worker salvation, found especially attentive audiences among unskilled workers in many northern textile mills precisely because the UTW had so conspicuously and willfully ignored their plight. Unlike the UTW, whose leaders and members often doubted the capacity of what they called the "foreign element," and especially its female component, to discharge the obligations of trade union membership, the IWW assumed that their common exploitation and mutual discontent disposed even the most disparate groups of textile workers to band together.[21] And when Wobblies tested their radical assumption among workers in the woolen and worsted mills of Lawrence in 1912 and among workers in the silk mills of Paterson, N.J., a year later, the results made plain that immigrant millhands, women and children included, were anything but the docile, industrial innocents that the UTW claimed in rationalizing its neglect of them.

The pattern of UTW involvement in these radical-led strikes over the period leading up to America's entry into the war generally conformed to that of other AFL unions confronted by the IWW or some other equally menacing left-wing rival. By denouncing the IWW and other avowedly anticapitalist workers' organizations with a vehemence that rivaled that of the radicals' fiercest critics, AFL unions sought to establish the sort of conservative credentials that might commend them to otherwise hostile employers. By volunteering to interpose themselves between capitalism and its would-be demolitionists on the revolutionary left, the UTW and other AFL unions hoped to establish a reputation among both employers and the public as indispensable collaborators in the system's defense. If employers could be maneuvered into a choice between radicals employing unionism as a means to a revolutionary end and conservatives pursuing unionism as an end in itself, they would almost certainly be willing, according to AFL theorists, to concede the modest cost of the latter in order to spare the unbearable cost of the former.

What seemed likely in theory, however, rarely paid off in practice. The "lesser of two evils" strategy on which conservative business unionists pinned their hopes grossly underestimated the depth of employer opposition to unionism of every type and motive. Of course, anxious employers, including mill owners, did sometimes accommodate small groups of craft unionists when it served to undermine solidarity with the much larger groups of would-be industrial unionists in their employ. But the unwavering preference of nearly all employers was to escape the influence of organized workers of any pedigree.

Yet, even if the UTW and other conservative unions had succeeded in persuading employers that they could be valuable allies in the defense of capitalism, the growing restiveness of industrial workers nevertheless ensured a succession of new claimants to their jurisdictions. During and immediately after World War I, when relentless federal suppression of the IWW effectively eliminated Wobblies from textile manufacturing, the UTW remained vulnerable to challenges from industrial union activists. In most cases, the threat these left-wing upstarts posed was to its reputation rather than to its membership, but they did demonstrate to the hundreds of thousands of semi-skilled and unskilled workers with whom the ultimate future of textile unionism lay that the UTW was unsuited to be the instrument of their collective empowerment.[22] The UTW's conduct during the frequent radical-led strikes of the period left little doubt that its leaders, at least, were willing accomplices to employers' strike-breaking efforts whenever such behavior promised to serve the union's purposes. Practiced in that role, UTW leaders effortlessly matched or exceeded employers in the ardor and vehemence with which they condemned radical-led strikes, even as they blithely conceded the justice of strikers' demands.[23]

While the UTW's membership briefly swelled to an all-time high of 105,000 in 1920, just as the antiradical hysteria that swept the United States was peaking, the increase was due to the residual effects of favorable wartime labor policies and the textile industry's explosive growth rather than to the union's strategy of ingratiation. Mill owners were undoubtedly pleased when the UTW applauded and abetted their efforts to break strikes led by the IWW and other radical unions, but their professed appreciation of "good" unions did not constitute acceptance. Like many other employers during and immediately after the war, mill owners made concessions to unionism when political or economic circumstances dictated a strategic retreat from preferred labor practices, but their historical abhorrence of unions, including conservative ones like the UTW, persisted. Moreover, when deteriorating economic conditions and a resurgence of political conservatism at the beginning of the 1920s afforded mill owners an opportunity to regain the ground earlier ceded to the UTW, they did so unhesitatingly. The vigorous antiunion campaign that resulted quickly restored the open shop as the preeminent feature of industrial relations throughout the textile industry.

The UTW, though it generally resisted employer's within the limits of its always meager resources, saw its membership plummet from 105,000 in 1920 to only 30,000 a year later. Its total membership would have continued to fall had not the American Federation of Full-Fashioned Hosiery Workers, which had seceded from the UTW before the war over the issue of craft autonomy, decided in 1923 to return to the fold. The Hosiery Workers, who would account for well over a third of UTW member, by the end of the 1920s took full advantage of the parent organization's weakened condition by insisting on complete autonomy as a condition of their reaffiliation.[24]

As the economic condition of the textile industry went from bad to worse during the 1920s, wage cuts and the stretch-out became the favored means by which employers sought to reduce labor costs.[25] For the UTW, whose influence on wages, hours, and conditions in the textile industry were usually negligible except where members' skills still afforded a measure of leverage, the inexorable degradation of labor standards during the 1920s was, realistically, more to be endured than opposed. The union perfunctorily donned a brave face on the ever more solemn occasions of its annual conventions, and its leaders ritually predicted that the UTW's resurrection would be accomplished through bold new organizing drives that targeted previously neglected women and southerners and a campaign to convince employers of the mutual advantages of labor-management cooperation.[26] The inescapable truth of the UTW's predicament, however, was that as the "Golden Decade" progressed, its fate was increasingly beyond either its leaders' or its members' control.

Workers in the towns and villages that were home to the various branches of the textile industry, though they had exhibited a remarkably keen devotion to the idea of unionism even as it frequently disappointed them in practice, were generally left to face the multiplying hardships of declining labor standards without the faintest expectation of assistance from the UTW or any other outside organization. Strikes, though fewer in number and smaller in scope as the decade wore on, nevertheless remained a feature of the industry's chronically bitter labor relations. Increasingly confined to single mills and usually undertaken as a last resort and with little or no hope of being won, strikes by textile workers during the 1920s were a better index of the anger and despair fostered by lower wages, longer hours, and greater workloads than of the faith workers retained in the likely benefit of collective struggle.

Its leadership increasingly absorbed in preaching the new gospel of labor-management cooperation to inattentive and uninterested mill owners, the UTW was understandably reluctant to squander scarce resources on unwinnable battles.[27] To salvage what remained of its badly eroded credibility, the UTW was obliged to support a number of strikes, against its leaders' better judgment. When 2,500 workers, three quarters of them women, struck the American Thread Company in Willimantic, Conn., during the early spring of 1925, the UTW reluctantly backed the walkout. Whatever scant assistance the union rendered, however, was undermined by its leaders' undisguised belief that the cause was hopeless from the beginning. In truth, they were right, but their undisguised faintheartedness and openly defeatist attitude did little to boost the UTW's sagging reputation among New England textile workers.[28]

The UTW's reputation suffered another setback in mid-1926 when it was drawn into a particularly bitter and violent struggle by textile workers who had struck months earlier in response to a new round of wage cuts in the worsted mills of Passaic. Initially led by Communists, who found local mill-hands too desperate for help to worry about the politics of those offering it, the Passaic conflict afforded an example of the extraordinary resources and utterly ruthless methods that textile employers, in particular, could bring to bear against striking employees in communities reflexively obedient to their authority. Although at first content to stand on the sidelines, alternately condemning and decrying the strike as an affront to legitimate labor activism, the UTW became a reluctant participant when, after nearly nine months of unavailing struggle, the communist-dominated United Front Committee agreed to surrender control to a new, conservative leadership. In the end, however, the UTW's opportunistic gamble in Passaic did more harm than good. The succession of submissive settlements its representatives negotiated with mill and dye-shop managements in the Passaic area toward the end of 1926 left most strikers feeling betrayed and most employers confirmed in their antiunion convictions.[29]

Curiously, the Communists, whose facile bombast had proven a poor substitute for effective leadership, emerged from the Passaic debacle as militant champions of industrial unionism. Their reputation was further enhanced two years later when more than 25,000 workers in New Bedford, the center of fine cotton goods production in New England, went on strike to protest a 10-percent wage reduction imposed by the New Bedford Textile Manufacturers Association. Although most of the 5,000 or so skilled workers who joined the walkout were members of craft unions affiliated with the American Federation of Textile Operatives, they soon agreed to transfer their membership to the UTW to qualify for strike assistance from the AFL. The more than 20,000 semiskilled and unskilled operatives who also heeded the strike call were entirely unorganized. Largely ignored by their skilled counterparts, these workers, mostly Portuguese immigrants, attracted the immediate attention of Communist organizers, several of whom had taken part in the Passaic conflict.

While the UTW demanded only a rollback or reduction of the wage cut that sparked the strike as the price of labor peace in New Bedford cotton mills, the Communists skillfully played to their followers' anger and militancy by demanding large wage increases, equal pay for equal work, a forty-hour week, and an end to the speed-up. UTW leaders and other conservative elements cited the Communists' unrealistic demands as proof of their ulterior motives, but immigrant strikers without alternative sources of support embraced the Communists as the only allies available to them. Even after strike-breaking activity escalated dramatically in the wake of their blunt rejection of a UTW-sponsored plan to return to work on the basis of a smaller wage reduction than employers had first demanded, the Communists enjoyed the ardent allegiance of their beleaguered following. Not until the conflict was in its sixth month and police had arrested nearly all of their leaders and halted the distribution of all food and other relief did strikers who had loyally followed the

Communists' lead grudgingly drift back to work on terms they had earlier spurned.[30]

Given the punishing defeats they ultimately suffered in both Passaic and New Bedford, the Communists might have reasonably concluded that the textile industry was poor ground for the militant industrial unionism they sought to cultivate. Instead, they were emboldened by the apparent willingness of textile workers, particularly those at the bottom of the industry's occupational hierarchy, to follow their lead. On reflection, Communists no doubt understood that it was their militant style rather than their political message that most fueled the excitement among textile workers in Passaic and New Bedford. And if winning hearts was a necessary prerequisite to winning minds, the Communists' trade union strategy of "boring from within" had prepared them to be patient.

As it happened, however, the end of the New Bedford strike coincided with the inauguration of a new trade union strategy that required U.S. Communists to abandon patient cultivation in favor of the brazenly ideological appeals necessary to the promotion of revolutionary dual unionism. Like the other abrupt policy shifts that punctuated the history of the American party, the Third Period, as the detour into dual unionism between 1928 and 1935 came to be known, was prompted by changing circumstances in the Soviet Union rather than in the United States. Yet, as American Communists dutifully struggled to translate the Communist International's newly promulgated "party line" into a labor policy suited to conditions and circumstances in the United States, they (not surprisingly) focused their initial efforts in the industry that had most recently occupied their attention, textiles. While the ill-fated New Bedford strike was in its final throes, toward the end of 1928, the National Textile Workers Union, the first of what would become an expanding array of Communist-dominated dual unions in the early 1930s, was founded.[31]

In actual practice, the NTWU differed only slightly from the jerrybuilt organizations it superseded. Its name plainly implied an intention to expand beyond the localized efforts that opportunistic party activists had undertaken in Passaic and New Bedford, but the ingrained tendency among Communist organizers in the textile field to exploit spontaneous labor conflicts rather than to build unions through diligent, plodding endeavor gave the NTWU a familiar look. The NTWU also sustained the oddly symbiotic relationship its predecessors had with the equally changeless United Textile Workers. The UTW, conservative, conventional, accommodationist, and still hostage, despite periodic gusts of heartening rhetoric, to attitudes that left unskilled textile workers on the outside looking in, projected an image that made possible the sharp contrast upon which Communists founded the appeals that encouraged otherwise skeptical or wary millhands to overlook the party's largely irrelevant and unpalatable political agenda. In return, Communists in the textile field, like Wobblies before them, afforded the UTW a useful basis upon which to contrast its relatively benign purposes with the extreme motives of unabashed ant-icapitalist revolutionaries. And at their most hopeful, UTW leaders, like many other conservative trade unionists, indulged the belief that a tangible radical menace at capitalism's door increased the likelihood of their success in pro-moting "pure and simple" unionism as an institutional embodiment of true Americanism.

Yet, if these diametrically opposed brands of unionism unwittingly reinforced each other, neither offered much hope to textile workers desperately in need of help as wages and conditions continued to deteriorate at the decade's end. The proof of their mutual impotence was established in an unlikely arena, the upland South. Long neglected by northern unions that gave little serious thought to venturing south as long as problems closer to home continued to consume their meager reserves and energy, textile workers in the multiplying mill towns and villages of Virginia, Georgia, Tennessee, Alabama, and the Car-olinas had generally been left to their own devices in combating the chronic abuses—low wages, long hours, creeping stretch-outs, overbearing paternal-ism—that were particularly egregious features of the industry's regional work culture. The UTW had been lured back to the region during World War I when southern textile workers evinced a renewed enthusiasm for organization, but the industry's mounting economic difficulties ultimately rendered the union incapable of sustaining its early gains. By 1921, when the last of the punishing strikes and lockouts that had convulsed the Piedmont over the preceding three years finally ended, southern textile workers who had struggled so mightily to improve their conditions and establish their rights were again grudgingly sub-mitting to the resurgent authority of mill owners and managers. The UTW, whose reputation among dispirited southern millhands had suffered with each new defeat, drastically scaled back its presence in the region, still as mystified as ever by the Piedmont's singular challenges.[32]

As its membership and resources dwindled in the 1920s, the UTW virtually disappeared from the South. Delegations of union functionaries, usually sup-ported by meager AFL handouts, periodically toured the region during the decade, vainly endeavoring to explain the benefits of labor-management coop-eration to local civic leaders, dutiful churchmen, dubious newspaper editors and curious Rotarians, while southern mill owners, who were not interested, and southern textile workers, who were not consulted, remained oblivious to the UTW's feeble overtures.[33] Not until the end of the 1920s, when steadily deteriorating conditions in southern mills afforded opportunities for new organizing efforts, did either the UTW or the NTWU conclude that the Pied-mont's promise outweighed its dangers.

Even in the midst of the relatively prosperous 1920s, the textile industry still lacked a structure conducive to rational operation and stumbled along on the brink of insolvency. Because most firms were powerless to stave off the ruinous effects of external forces—glutted markets, fluctuating prices for raw mater-ials, changing whims of fashion—they feverishly struggled, as the decade wound down, to cut production costs to the bone. Inevitably, labor costs became the focus of their efforts. As mill owners relentlessly pressured their workers to do more for less they transformed an industrial occupation already notorious for its meager rewards and harsh environment into what was, by 1929, penurious servitude.[34]

The assault on labor standards affected most branches and regions of the textile industry, but nowhere was it more egregious and pitiless than in southern cotton mills. For southern workers, whose long-time habit of moving from mill to mill no longer sufficed as an adequate protest against poor working conditions and the demeaning regimentation of company towns, by the spring of 1929 enough was finally enough.[35] That the first big battle in the widening class war that convulsed the southern textile industry in 1929 was fought by the 5,000 employees of two German-owned rayon spinning plants in the eastern Tennessee mountain town of Elizabethton provided clear evidence that worker discontent in the region was not confined to cotton mills.[36] Yet it was rebellious cotton workers who launched the wider-ranging challenges to employer authority and who attracted the keenest interest among UTW and Communist organizers hoping to secure footholds in the South. It was also cotton workers—especially the women and girls who supplied so much of the cheap labor on which the southern branch of the industry relied—who most forcefully challenged the persistent myth that millhands in the South were too steeped in individualist traditions to match their northern counterparts' appreciation of collective action.

Although organizers from the American Federation of Full-Fashioned Hosiery Workers had been active in the upper Piedmont during the late 1920s, and a diverse group of local union officials in North Carolina had formed the Piedmont Organizing Council in 1927 to encourage a regional campaign under AFL auspices, the strikes that swept across the upland South in 1929, which the *Nation* diagnosed as "symptoms of a fundamental maladjustment," were, for the most part, spontaneous actions by unorganized millhands in the tightening grip of emotions they could no longer suppress.[37]

The Elizabethton strikers, who reportedly acted "without any union impetus," were still battling in early April when angry workers at the Loray mill in Gastonia, N.C., sparked another major conflict. The powerful discontent that led 2,200 long-suffering millhands to shut down the sprawling Loray mill was a variant of the impetuous activism that wage cuts and the stretch-out had fostered across the whole of the textile-manufacturing South by early 1929. What distinguished the Gastonia strike from others arising from the same general causes was the central role that Communists played in leading it. Anxious for an opportunity to showcase their militant brand of unionism in what had become the new center of the U.S. cotton textile industry, the Communists determined, in the fall of 1928, that Gastonia, an area as densely populated with mills and millhands as any in the South, was especially fertile ground for an organizing campaign. When reports of growing restiveness among area millhands confirmed the NTWU's sense of its special possibilities, the union dispatched Fred Beal, a seasoned veteran of the New Bedford strike, to organize Gastonia's disgruntled proletariat.[38]

Given the political innocence and supposed conservatism of southern millhands, even the Communists must have been surprised by how eagerly Gastonia's textile workers accepted their assistance. This curious congeniality was largely a function of sheer desperation. It is also explained, however, by the calming tenor of the Communists' initial overtures, which addressed the workers' most urgent concerns at the expense of the baldly ideological appeals that the party's newly inaugurated Third Period strategy seemed to dictate. "It was a militant campaign," one observer said of the Communists' Gastonia strategy, "which did not differ, on the surface certainly, from that employed by most of the American Federation of Labor unions in their early years."[39]

The remarkable success of the NTWU in Gastonia became fully apparent when nearly every worker in the Loray mill walked out after management fired several of the union's most visible recruits. Within days, as the unrest spread, first to mills in nearby Bessemer City and then to other textile villages in Gaston County, NTWU organizers were besieged by clamorous millhands eager for any help the union could provide. Mill bosses and other critics of the union, including self-interested UTW officials still clinging to the fading hope of ingratiating themselves at the expense of their radical rivals, bombarded strikers with ever more urgent and graphic warnings against forming alliances with the devil. But if millhands who swelled its ranks in the Gastonia area harbored concerns about the NTWU's unsavory auspice, they never let them show.[40] A millhand in Bessemer City, asked why local textile workers were apparently siding with Communists, impatiently answered, "Say you! Listen to me. These people are helping us. They are feeding us." Explaining the woman's succinct exegesis of the sudden affinity between northern Communists and southern hill folk, Tom Tippett, who had traveled south from Brookwood Labor College to chronicle the region's unfolding unrest, later wrote,

> The Bessemer City woman, compelled to work twelve hours a day for a few cents an hour, had not enough time or energy to analyze complicated problems of political economy. She responded to the first avenue which seemed to offer escape and measured the union [NTWU] leaders by what she saw them do in Gastonia. When they denounced the cotton mill and society in general, they were but voicing her own pent-up emotions which she had long wanted to express.[41]

While there is no doubt that the NTWU's communist provenance facilitated the hysterical campaign of Red baiting that characterized strike-breaking efforts in Gastonia, the practiced resort of southern mill owners and their allies to alarmist caveats that all unions were subversive ensured that the tactic would have been used in any case. The antiunionism of the southern textile industry was indiscriminate and adamant, the central canon of an industrial relations theology whose meaning was candid and unambiguous and whose application was swift and certain. The UTW might present a less demonic face than its Communist rival, but, to southern mill owners disposed to detest and oppose unionism in all of its guises the difference between the two was never anything but cosmetic. In times of crisis like those occasioned by the 1929 strikes, more moderate elements convinced of the validity of millhands' complaints and alarmed at the prospect of radicalism's ascendancy might gently counsel mill owners to adopt a less inflexible attitude toward worker organization. Most employers, however, remained convinced of the inerrancy of their antiunion faith, no matter how urgently immediate circumstances dictated doctrinal complacency. The prototypical southern mill owner, this "new master of the South, successor to the plantation owner," was, according to historian Irving Bernstein,

> . . . pathologically opposed to collective bargaining. In his mind there was no distinction between the AFL and the Communists; each represented a fundamental challenge to his conception of southern society. Through the instrumentality of the mill village he could deny the striker a job, evict him from his house, spy on him in private affairs, expel him from church and deny him medical services. As the reward for loyalty, the mill owner could offer the worker the fruits of paternalism.[42]

Certainly, mill owners and their allies in Gastonia betrayed no lack of resolution, either in punishing disloyal workers or in combating the NTWU. The strike-breaking resources of the Loray mill, augmented by local vigilantes and units of the North Carolina National Guard, were ruthlessly deployed to great advantage. Strikers and their Communist backers were subjected to nearly every conceivable form of harassment, intimidation, and assault. The badly overmatched millhands did what they could to sustain the strike, but the tactics used against them, which included mass evictions from company-owned housing and violent disruptions of the meager relief efforts undertaken by the Workers' International Relief and other arms of the Communist Party support apparatus, quickly took their toll.

By the third week of April, the Loray strike, like others in the region, had been effectively smashed. In response, the NTWU, which had earlier been content to make workplace issues the principal focus of its appeal to desperate millhands, dutifully surrendered control of the situation to party propagandists instructed to wring from the Gastonia debacle whatever political recompense it might still yield. Whatever real or imagined propaganda victories the Communists may have realized from their self-indulgent prolongation of a lost cause, they did not nourish the NTWU's resolve to continue its union building among southern textile workers. Indeed, the union's overdue announcement in late September that the strike was over also marked an abrupt end to communist efforts to enlist southern textile workers into the grand army of proletarian revolution. In the wake of their harrowing and costly Gastonia experience, the Communists, it appeared, were willing to cede the textile field to their more conservative but less easily discouraged rival.[43]

As events elsewhere in the Piedmont would make painfully clear, however, the UTW was equally at a loss to seize the apparent opportunity that widespread unrest among southern textile workers presented in 1929. UTW officials had stumbled into the midst of the bitterly contested Elizabethton strike soon after it began. Neither they nor the handful of AFL luminaries, including William Green, who bore personal witness to the innumerable abuses visited upon striking rayon workers by local authorities, state militiamen, and hooded vigilantes could help strikers stave off a calamitous defeat.

It was, however, in Marion, N.C., a small city of 8,000 souls on the leeward slope of the Blue Ridge Mountains, that the UTW's feeble capacity to exploit the southern millhands' revolt was most revealingly confirmed. The three cotton mills in Marion, two owned by a local family and the third controlled by absentee northerners, provided employment for just over 2,100 millhands in the summer of 1929. Low wages, long hours, night work, and the stretch-out, the singularly combustible compound of grievances that had inflamed textile workers throughout the Piedmont, were equally acute sources of unrest and disaffection among Marion's millhands. Indeed, according to some reports, the working and living conditions in Marion were among the worst in the industry. One observer, who claimed a particular knowledge of "the social conditions of southern hill folk," concluded after touring Marion's mill villages that living conditions there were "morally and humanly, almost indescribably degrading."[44]

Prompted by their own relentless degradation and news of the millhands' rebellion spreading across the region, a small group of activists formed a union at the Marion Manufacturing Company in April. In the hope of securing outside help, the Marion activists dispatched an emissary over the mountains to Elizabethton, where UTW representatives were vainly struggling to help striking rayon workers. After receiving a vague promise of assistance, the Marion activists launched an organizing drive, to which millhands from both the East Marion mills and the nearby Clinchfield mills responded enthusiastically.

If tapping the abundant discontent among textile workers in Marion was easy, union leaders soon learned that forging the power that organization promised was not. As soon as the union's activities came to light, the management of the Marion Manufacturing Company summarily fired more than twenty activists. In early July, a delegation of workers presented the union's demands for better conditions and reinstatement of their discharged colleagues to mill president R. W. Baldwin. Described by one detractor as "a man of parts, of which intelligence is not the most outstanding," Baldwin rejected them out of hand.[45] Aware that the UTW was unable to support a strike in Marion because its perennially skimpy treasury had long since been depleted by the Elizabethton conflict, the union representative who finally showed up in the area tried to discourage a walkout. He failed. On July 11, 650 angry employees of the Baldwin mill responded to its management's brusque rejection of their demands by walking off the job.[46]

While the events in Marion attested to the seemingly irreparable state of labor-management relations in the southern textile industry, they also confirmed the congenital impotence of the UTW. Having secured from the AFL the sole legitimate authority to organize the expanse of the American textile industry, the UTW remained conspicuously inadequate to the challenge. With its own diverse and chronically unstable membership either unwilling or unable to contribute support sufficient to its needs, and other unions and the AFL generally inured to the tiresome entreaties of a "poor relation," the UTW seemed forever at a loss to meet the high costs of success. If it could fairly be said of the UTW that its heart was usually in the right place where the well-being of textile workers was concerned, it could be said with equal justice that its ineffectual agency usually rendered it unable to honor its obligations to them.

With little more than advice to offer, UTW representatives observed rather than directed. When they warned 1,500 impatient workers at the nearby Clinchfield mills against joining the strike because available relief was already in desperately short supply, the workers promptly struck anyway. Whatever modest relief suffering millhands did receive during the strike was provided through an informal network of liberal organizations mobilized by graphic accounts of the extraordinary hardship and abuse being inflicted upon them. Socialist Party leader Norman Thomas, who participated in the relief efforts, sharply criticized the mainstream labor movement's failure to reward the "heroism" of Marion strikers as yet another sign of its deepening torpor. The UTW, Thomas insisted, had a chance following the defeat of the NTWU in Gastonia "to show that it could succeed where the Communist philosophy and method could not." Yet the UTW's faintheartedness, in combination with the AFL's indifference, left Thomas convinced that struggling workers like those in Marion were no better served by placing their trust in the conservative labor movement. "I blame the generalship of the American labor movement," Thomas wrote of the inadequate strike relief in Marion, "its lack of plans, vision and machinery adequate to the matter in hand; its ox-cart tactics in an automobile age."[47]

Although a more generous relief effort would have eased the hardship endured by Marion strikers and their families, it is unlikely that it could have altered the outcome. The strikebreaking of southern mill owners, abetted in Marion, as in every other major Piedmont labor dispute in 1929, by state troops who openly sided with employers, overwhelmed even the most courageous and resolute strikers. When impoverished millhands were forced, as they were in Marion, to finance a strike largely from their own scant reserves, a conflict that might have dragged on for months was over in weeks. The willingness of outsiders, and especially the UTW, to champion southern textile workers in their struggles during 1929 attested to their good intentions, but, in the absence of more tangible demonstrations of support, the ultimate outcome of these challenges to employer control was rarely in doubt.

That millhands in Marion appreciated the hopelessness of their situation became evident in early September, when they dejectedly returned to work on the basis of a grudging promise of slightly reduced hours and the reemployment of strikers without prejudice. The conflict soon flared again, however, when mill owners reneged on their pledge that former strikers would not be black-listed. On October 2, after two weeks of vain efforts to reinstate more than a hundred of their fellow workers, millhands working the night shift at the Baldwin mill walked off the job. As they congregated outside the mill in the hope of persuading workers arriving for the day shift to join their protest, the strikers were ordered by the sheriff to disperse. When they hesitated, the sheriff and his eleven deputies, most of whom were on the company's payroll, launched a murderous assault against the unarmed crowd. By the time the gunfire ended, four strikers were dead and more than two dozen, including two who later died, lay seriously wounded. In the aftermath of the carnage, R. W. Baldwin was overheard by several reporters to excitedly exclaim, "Some marksmanship that was. Any time I organize an army the sheriff and his men can join. It took five tons of lead to kill a man in the great war. It took only a few ounces to kill one here in Marion. Some shooting."[48]

The mass funeral for the slain strikers was held in the same vacant lot near the Baldwin mill where millhands had conducted their frequent rallies over the preceding two months. "The only change in the place," Brookwood activist Tom Tippett remembered, "was the addition of wooden frames built by the strikers, on which the caskets rested in front of the speakers' stand."[49] Although a succession of visiting eulogists that included UTW Vice President Francis Gorman confidently assured mourners that the Marion struggle was far from over, shaken millhands at the Baldwin and Clinchfield mills knew better. If righteous anger alone had been enough to sustain their struggle, the Marion strikers, like the thousands of other southern millhands who were in revolt during 1929, would have been assured of victory. Yet because it was the deployment of tangible resources and the exercise of actual power that finally determined the outcome of every strike that rocked the Piedmont, mill owners never had nearly as much to fear as those less familiar with the hard reality of power relationships in the southern textile industry had too readily imagined. Millhands could momentarily disturb the artificial calm that their employers assiduously imposed by means of a stultifying paternalism, but their fundamental powerlessness persisted.

With the defeat of the Marion strike, the fate of the millhands' revolt in the upland South was largely sealed. A long and hard-fought strike by employees of the Riverside and Dan River mills in Danville, Va., during the fall of 1930 offered compelling evidence that not all of the fight had been taken out of southern millhands. But the crushing defeat they ultimately suffered despite the UTW's ardent, if never adequate, support merely reinforced the stark impression of employer invincibility imparted by the successive defeats that southern textile workers had suffered the preceding year.[50]

Beyond fracturing the facile certitude of many northern unionists that the rural backgrounds and agrarian devotions of southern textile workers rendered them unfit for committed service in labor's cause, the Piedmont strikes excited hopes both north and south that the era of the mill owners' absolute hegemony in the region was, despite their momentary triumphs, now destined to fade. "At the moment," the southern writer W. J. Cash readily acknowledged, "the advantage in the struggle is obviously with the [textile] baron and his allied reactionaries, and it will remain there, I suspect, for some while to come. But, as time goes on," he predicted,

> the support of the South will more and more fall away from the baron; his foes at home will become more and more formidable. Indeed, the reactionary South is even now, plainly enough, making its last great stand. The old social-economic system is breaking up. As the rising generation comes to ascendancy among the mill-workers, southern strikes will begin to be won. And the ultimate outcome is as inevitable as the cycle of the sun: *the labor union will conquer.*[51]

Although those AFL officials with first-hand knowledge of the Piedmont strikes were bound to be less sanguine about unionism's future in the region, even they were disposed to agree that the southern millhands' revolt presented the federation with what one historian later described as "its most dramatic challenge of the twenties."[52] But while the strikes excited impassioned comment and resolute pledges of a great southern organizing campaign to come when the AFL began its 1929 convention only three days after strikers in Marion had solemnly buried their dead, the promised shift from talk to action that brought cheering delegates to their feet never materialized.

In place of the massive campaign that UTW delegates fervently urged upon their assembled union brothers and sisters, one that contemplated a war chest large enough to send organizers into every nook and cranny of the southern textile industry, the AFL leadership, still unfailingly obedient to the will of its most conservative craft elements, decided instead that federation president Bill Green should talk the region's mill owners into submission. As the AFL's chief apostle of labor-management cooperation, Green retained the ardent faith of a missionary despite his dismal record in persuading employers of the doctrine's redemptive powers. And when he embarked on his crusade early in 1930, it was with an apparently sincere conviction that the violent anti-unionism of southern mill owners could be overcome by an appropriately soothing and revelatory explication of collective bargaining's therapeutic properties.[53]

In contrast to the violent displeasure with which the Piedmont's ruling elite greeted the arrival of union organizers a year earlier, Green's visit to the heartland of the textile South was bathed in the gracious hospitality for which the region immodestly prided itself. "Mr. Green was well received in the South," Brookwood's Tom Tippett reported,

> There was no attempt of any kind to prevent or oppose his appearances. He spoke in most of the large cities of the industrial section in an atmosphere of friendliness on the part of the ruling power. Bankers and politicians, manufacturers and teachers attended his meetings. The press heralded his coming and devoted news and editorial space to his lectures. Mr. Green addressed himself to the upper classes and the whole setting of his meetings was adapted to this element.

"The president of the American Federation of Labor," Tippett pointedly added, "did not talk at the mill gates."

The calming message that Green imparted to his attentive listeners emphasized, as always, both the benefits and protections that sensible business unionism of the AFL variety was designed to confer. "Mr. Green's speeches," Tippett noted, "were devoted to the class-collaborating-policy of the American Federation of Labor and to long dissertations on the difference between the Communist unions and his own."

"To all of this," Tippett acknowledged,

> the South listened attentively, nodded its head, stood up, out of respect for the labor chief, and applauded him enthusiastically as he walked down the aisle. . . . The bankers, and the business men, even a chamber of commerce here and there, praised the American Federation of Labor and said publicly almost with one voice, "Well if that's what trade-unionism is, we're for it."[54]

"The policies he advocated," the Memphis *Commercial Appeal* approvingly said of Green's ingratiating overture, "might have come with propriety from the president of the American Bankers' Association."[55] Yet, as successful as Green appeared to be in selling trade unionism as an abstraction, its image as a functioning presence in the region's textile mills remained as forbidding as ever to those whose opinions counted most. No matter how attractively Green packaged trade unionism, mill owners were not buying it. "[A]lthough the ruling group listened to and agreed with President Green's sentiments at his meetings," Tippett ruefully concluded,

> this attitude did not carry over into the business offices where the actual mill policy is written. So trade-unions did not automatically appear after Mr. Green's explanation. The opposition to textile unions on the part of the factory owner was just as bitter as though Mr. Green had not come South at all, and when the showdown came, no one else in authority was sufficiently convinced by Mr. Green's visit to make a stand against the cotton mill.[56]

Despite the federation's vain boast that Green's efforts had elicited the "good will and support of leading southern citizens" and had "advanced understanding of trade unionism and . . . made for greater sympathy for our cause," the only genuine interest in trade unionism in the Piedmont resided in the hearts and minds of millhands whom the AFL's strategy bypassed.[57] The drastically scaled-back organizing drive that the UTW did manage with scant AFL support in 1930 demonstrated a still-ardent interest in unionism among southern textile workers despite the chastening memories of their failed revolt the year before.[58] Francis Gorman, who went south to direct the UTW's underfunded and undermanned campaign, claimed at summer's end that nearly 25,000 had been added to the union's rolls. In the end, however, the success that Gorman reported was simply more of the evanescent "progress" that placated UTW functionaries in the North without in any way alleviating the hardship or mitigating the powerlessness of southern millhands. Despite the "reported success" of the UTW's southern organizing campaigns, Tom Tippett observed, "No local union had been recognized and no improvement in wages or work standards had accrued to the operatives. On the contrary," he glumly added, "one wage cut after another had been imposed, flagrant discharge for union membership had occurred, and the bosses were literally daring the union to put up a fight."[59]

If the UTW still had any fight left in it following the unbroken string of setbacks it had already suffered in the South, the total collapse of the Danville strike by the end of 1930 finally depleted its remaining will to carry on in the region. Yet unlike the Communist-led NTWU, which simply wrote off the southern textile industry as a poor investment after the failed Gastonia strike, the UTW was bound to regard its retreat from the region as no more than a strategic maneuver. Organizing the southern textile industry had become, quite simply, the essential challenge the UTW had to meet if it was ever to achieve real institutional viability. Withdrawing from the South, however, did not afford the respite the UTW desperately needed to replenish its resources and restore its resolve. The country's inexorable descent into depression during the early 1930s sent an already "sick" textile industry reeling toward the brink of collapse. And as industry conditions steadily worsened, the long feeble health of textile unionism deteriorated to the point of near attenuation. Every major branch of the American textile industry suffered the debilitating effects of the country's deepening economic crisis. For textile workers, many of whom had struggled at the precipice of abject poverty for the better part of a decade, the depression, when it did not deprive them of employment entirely, plunged already notoriously poor wages and working conditions to new, unimaginable depths.

For the UTW, whose record in the best of times was uninspiring, the still greater challenges that depression bred proved overwhelming. The union's Emergency Committee, the small group of elected officers and other functionaries responsible for the day-to-day operation of the UTW, careened from crisis to crisis during the early 1930s, as embattled local affiliates within its shrinking domain beseeched the national organization for assistance that it was usually powerless to render. Chaired by UTW president Thomas McMahon, an affable Irishman whose trade union career dated from the Knights of Labor, the Emergency Committee increasingly compensated for its inability to deal with deepening problems of real moment to textile workers by immersing itself in bureaucratic squabbles and administrative minutiae. The union's financial resources, which were inadequate even in the best of times, were so depleted by 1933 that the UTW, according to historian Robert R. R. Brooks, "appeared to consist almost entirely of a suite of offices, a complement of officers, and a splendid array of filing cabinets."[60] At the "nadir of its fortunes" in early 1933, Brooks declared, the UTW remained a union more in theory than in practice. "It paid per capita tax to the A.F. of L. on only 15,000 members; it cut its organizing and administrative personnel to the minimum; its officers accepted temporary salary reductions; the *Textile Worker*, having nothing to report, found its covers separated by scanty pages of advertising, desultory organizers' reports, and a few items of flaccid general news."[61]

Beleaguered textile workers who looked to the UTW for help as conditions worsened were usually rewarded with little more than vacuous bromides and stern warnings that strikes, which the national organization was unable to support, would only make bad situations even worse. But while the union's repeated cautions against precipitous strikes made good sense given its indigent condition, millhands at the limits of their endurance were increasingly disposed to interpret the UTW's reluctance to do battle as further evidence of its fecklessness. The NTWU, whose Communist leadership believed that strikes served the party's purposes no matter what the outcome, happily reinforced workers' suspicions and willingly exploited their growing desperation by encouraging struggles which, like those in Lawrence, Mass., and Pawtucket, R.I., in 1931, were doomed to failure from the start. Yet, what tended to stick in the minds of textile workers and their well-wishers alike was not that the Communists had acted irresponsibly but that the UTW was reluctant to act at all.[62]

Although the UTW's leadership had an unwitting talent for exacerbating already difficult problems, not even the most adept stewardship could have spared it the terrible ravages that the Great Depression unleashed. Like the rest of the labor movement, and, indeed, like the rest of the nation, the UTW was adrift in an economic maelstrom that was by 1933 simply too powerful to be navigated by even the most skilled helmsmen. And, like nearly every other storm-tossed institution in the country, the UTW faced an uncertain future certain only in a deepening belief that if and when its equilibrium were finally restored, it would likely be through an auspice infinitely greater than its own.

CHAPTER 2

The Promise of Things to Come

The organized labor movement, though hardly of one mind in the political preferences its diverse components expressed during the 1932 U.S. presidential election, had reason to be heartened by the passing of the Hoover presidency, if only because Herbert Hoover had come to personify the federal government's studied passivity in the face of economic calamity. Yet what, if anything, the labor movement might reasonably expect from the incoming administration of Franklin Roosevelt was unclear. Little was known about the new president's personal views on trade unionism and collective bargaining, and his remarkably infrequent references to labor during the election campaign seemed purposely vague. Despite the absence of specific commitments, however, Roosevelt's credentials, both as a progressive and as an activist, gave organized labor reason to hope that alleviating the desperate plight of the working class would be high on his agenda.[1]

That hope was not long in being realized. The unprecedented legislative activism of Roosevelt's first hundred days was breathtaking in its sweep and magnitude, and boldly announced, as his measured and tepid campaign rhetoric had not, the dawn of a genuinely new era in the domestic political life of the United States. With little hesitation and no more than perfunctory political debates to slow the otherwise dizzying pace of its actions, the Roosevelt administration took full and immediate advantage of the extraordinary latitude that a fearful and despairing people had gladly conceded to it.

Beyond the massive relief programs it inaugurated, which alone revolutionized the relationship between the federal government and individual American citizens by making the former the ultimate guarantor of the latter's survival, the Roosevelt administration's approach to national economic recovery dramatically expanded federal authority and responsibility. The National Industrial Recovery Act (NIRA), passed in the spring of 1933, provided for drastic reorganization of business and commerce by promulgating, under joint public and private authority, codes of fair competition that would govern the conduct of virtually every branch of American industry. As a belated concession to organized labor, whose support for the recovery bill had been only lukewarm as long as it failed to address specific trade-union concerns, the administration grudgingly agreed to the inclusion of language that seemed to guarantee workers' rights to organize and bargain collectively. Embodied in Sec. 7(a) of the NIRA, these new rights were granted out of a smug conviction on the part of New Deal theorists that "organized labor" was too weak and inept to use them effectively. And even if some American Federation of Labor affiliates were able to use 7(a) to prop up the rickety structure of craft unionism, Roosevelt and his advisors had no reason to think that the great majority of unskilled and semiskilled workers employed in America's mass-production industries, workers who had long been scorned and neglected by their skilled brethren, would use the law to empower themselves.[2]

As events were soon to make disturbingly clear to the president and his brain trust, dismissing Sec. 7(a) as an essentially inconsequential appendage of the administration's recovery plan may well have been the most momentous miscalculation of the New Deal. While the administration was probably on solid ground in believing that the craft affiliates of the AFL lacked both the will and the resources to exercise their new rights beyond the boundaries of their immediate and narrow self-interest, it was badly mistaken in its assumption that industrial workers would remain at a loss to organize themselves despite the enabling means that Sec. 7(a) appeared to offer.

Industrial unions like the United Mine Workers, Amalgamated Clothing Workers, and International Ladies Garment Workers, which took particular advantage of Sec. 7(a) because employers in their respective industries were sufficiently demoralized by 1933 to accept unionism as a necessary cost of recovery, were early beneficiaries of the Roosevelt administration's miscalculation. Others, however, including the United Textile Workers, were not long in adopting a similar ambition. After so long a period of spiraling decline, the UTW followed the lead of other traumatized unions in embracing whatever vague hopes the unfolding experiments of the early New Deal sparked. Like their counterparts in the other atrophied branches of a movement that had long since lost its impetus, the leaders of the UTW distilled from a literal rendering of Sec. 7(a) the bracing tonic required to dispel their gloom and revive their ambition. The UTW found special encouragement in the fact that the cotton textile industry, the forbidding arena in which the union's destiny would ultimately be determined, was first in line for a makeover by the newly established National Recovery Administration. If the industrial code that resulted was faithful to the apparent letter and spirit of Sec. 7(a), the union hopefully concluded, textile unionism might emerge from the wreckage of the Great Depression with a brighter future than it had ever known.

Even before Roosevelt formally signed the NIRA into law on June 16, 1933, the UTW's Executive Council had authorized the establishment of a Washington office to ensure that top union representatives would be on hand to see that the rights that Sec. 7(a) conferred would be written into codes affecting "the various divisions of the textile industry."[3] But if UTW leaders believed that placing union representatives in close proximity to the code-drafting process would redound to its advantage, events quickly proved them wrong. When Code of Fair Competition No. 1 was endorsed by the president early in July,[4] it established a new basis for the cotton textile industry's operation that took almost no account of workers' rights or the UTW's desires.[5]

The cotton textile code was nearly exclusively the handiwork of George Sloan, who, as president of the Cotton-Textile Institute and "the guiding spirit of the cotton industry," was careful to produce a document bound to delight employers. Described by one admiring business magazine as a man who "talks, thinks, and wears cotton—underwear, shirt, suit, belt, necktie, and socks," Sloan reportedly "had a cotton code of fair competition ready and in the hands of President Roosevelt a few hours after the National Industrial Recovery Act was signed. . . ."[6]

Sloan, who was promptly appointed chair of the Cotton Textile Code Authority, had willingly incorporated the minimum labor standards the law required. He also readily adopted the language of Sec. 7(a), but only after making certain that the code's administration and enforcement, including the ultimate authority to decide all questions relating to the application of labor standards and the protection of workers' rights, remained solely the province of management.[7] The plaintive objections of the UTW, which had endlessly asserted that it alone was qualified to represent the interests of textile workers, were ignored by industry and NRA officials alike. Even the choice of the labor members of the Cotton Textile National Industrial Relations Board, the tripartite body established to resolve labor disputes under the code, reflected the determination of employers to deny the UTW a voice. Over objections of the UTW and the AFL, Maj. George Berry, president of the Printing Pressmen's Union and a Roosevelt political loyalist largely unacquainted with the unique plight of cotton workers, was appointed to the Cotton Textile Labor Relations Board. And as his detractors feared he would, Berry routinely deferred to his pro-industry colleagues in disposing of millhands' grievances.[8]

Yet despite its inability to influence the content or administration of the cotton textile code, the UTW's enthusiasm for the new approach to industry regulation it the embodied remained remarkably keen during the summer and fall of 1933. Textile workers were among the hundreds of thousands of American wage earners emboldened to join or rejoin unions in the weeks and months following the promulgation of Sec. 7(a), and as its membership rolls expanded dramatically during the late summer, the UTW had reason to be grateful for the organizational stimulus the Roosevelt recovery plan provided, even though it was increasingly disappointed on other grounds. One labor activist wrote of Sec. 7(a),

Though this provision has been reduced to a mockery, and though it exists only on paper and must be enforced on the picket line, it has been of great value in organizing. The initial fear of the worker to defy his boss has been to a certain degree allayed by this very official-looking pronouncement. Added to whatever confidence he has in the strength of the union is the feeling of governmental sanction in his fight, a sort of paternal pat on the back. Though nullified a thousand times later, it helps him over the original Rubicon of doubts and fears.[9]

By mid-September, UTW organizers from New England to the Carolinas were reporting a groundswell of interest in organization among millhands. Total union's membership had grown from some 25,000 workers to approximately 40,000.[10]

Restoring the cotton textile industry to health, however, required more than the positive outlook encouraged by New Deal drumbeaters. The soaring hopes of mill owners prompted large increases in output and employment during the summer of 1933, but in the absence of a commensurate rise in the demand for cotton textiles the industry was returning to old habits by the fall. Labor costs, which were supposed to be removed from competition through the adoption of industrywide standards set forth in the NRA's cotton textile code, came under increasing pressure as despairing mill owners scrambled for advantage. And as worker complaints and protests rapidly mounted in the face of wholesale violations of wage and hour standards and stubborn denials of the organizing and bargaining rights promised in Sec. 7(a), fissures in the Roosevelt administration's recovery plan quickly widened into gaping cracks. The total domination that employers exercised over both the machinery of code administration and enforcement and the adjudication of complaints arising under Sec. 7(a), especially those resulting from discrimination against workers for union activity, ensured that millhands' efforts to protect their interests and secure their rights would be frustrated. It also ensured, however, that the impressive growth that the UTW had realized would be dwarfed by the membership gains that rage fostered when workers realized they had been defrauded. [11]

With the textile labor relations board doing more to promote worker frustration than to relieve it, the likelihood of conflict between millhands and their employers grew exponentially through the winter and following spring. As the tens of thousands of textile workers who had responded to the apparent promise of Sec. 7(a) looked to the UTW for leadership in seizing the bargaining rights that mill owners would not voluntarily concede, the union was forced into a confrontation it had hoped to avoid. The minimum wage specified in the cotton code—$13 a week in the North, $12 a week in the South—had been from the first a source of acute dissatisfaction to textile workers. When employers drove the effective minimums even lower (through a variety of blatant subterfuges that code administrators and NRA officials either willfully ignored or tacitly condoned), discontent transmuted into seething anger. Millhands were further embittered by the similarly unrestrained efforts of southern mill owners in particular to slash labor costs through reduced hours and the stretch-out.[12]

It was, however, the willingness of NRA officials to accede to industry demands to curtail production, which further reduced the meager earnings of increasingly desperate millhands, that finally made serious labor conflicts in cotton textiles unavoidable. Textile workers, including those in silk and hosiery, had seen their wages sharply reduced during the winter of 1933–34, when NRA "czar" Gen. Hugh Johnson granted employers' requests to reduce operating hours temporarily by 25 percent to alleviate mounting problems of overproduction.[13] Based on the same complaint of excess capacity, the Cotton Textile Code Authority beseeched Johnson in May of 1934 to further curtail production. Over the objections of his own staff economists, and with now routine disregard for the interests of textile workers and the UTW, Johnson readily complied.[14]

For the UTW, which had sought to avoid a direct confrontation with the NRA despite the rising anger of its members and the deepening frustrations of its leaders, Johnson's new surrender to industry demands was a provocation too galling to ignore. Even before Johnson reached his decision, UTW members (especially those in the volatile Piedmont) were imploring national union leaders to move beyond flaccid expressions of disappointment and frustration in responding to textile code violations and denials of workers' rights under Sec. 7(a). The *New York Times* reported, as early as May 20, that a strike was likely if industry requests for a production cutback were granted. And once the NRA announced that mill owners would get their way, threats of an industrywide work stoppage quickly escalated.[15] Francis Gorman, whose visibility increased as the crisis deepened, publicly warned both employers and General Johnson that if the approved curtailment of hours was implemented, enraged millhands, more than 200,000 of whom were now said to be union members, would enforce the UTW's threat to shut down every cotton mill in the country.[16]

Employers and their allies were unimpressed. They dismissed the threat as idle bluster by posturing union leaders who had wildly exaggerated worker support for such a plainly dangerous course of action. "To justify his job," *Business Week* patronizingly explained, "the labor leader must appear active in behalf of his membership." Yet in an economically depressed industry like cotton textiles, the magazine concluded, "The general strike threat was worse than futile—it was stupid."[17]

Industry leaders and the Cotton Textile Code Authority were apparently willing to call the union's bluff. Johnson, whose position as NRA chief was growing shakier by the day as labor conflicts erupted in industry after industry in mid-1934, took the threat seriously enough to seek a compromise that would keep the mills operating. After emergency meetings with all parties, including the leadership of the UTW, Johnson announced, on June 2, a settlement that ended the immediate threat of a strike. In return for the union's willingness to call off its threatened strike and acknowledge "the necessity for temporary reductions in machine hours from time to time," Johnson promised to give the UTW an advisory role in shaping future textile code policies, to grant it representation on the Cotton Textiles National Industrial Relations Board, and to instruct NRA experts to study those issues related to wages, hours, and working conditions, including the stretch-out, that had brought despairing millhands to the brink of mass revolt.[18]

Given the UTW's clearly evident inability to carry out its threat of an industry-wide strike during the late spring of 1934, the union's leaders were eager to laud the settlement as a signal triumph.[19] In truth, of course, it was anything but a victory for textile workers. Mill owners remained free to implement the additional production curtailments that had provoked the crisis, while millhands got promises that their grievances would be studied but not that they would be effectively redressed. In light of the UTW's utter lack of preparation and resources, however, its leaders' decision to settle rather than fight made sense. The union plausibly claimed a membership well in excess of 200,000 workers in mid-1934, but relatively few were able or willing to pay dues. Thus, the union was left in the same generally impoverished condition that had long been its institutional hallmark. Moreover, despite the apparent willingness of angry millhands to do battle with their employers, Thomas McMahon, Francis Gorman, and others in the UTW's national leadership, still chastened by past defeats, especially in the South, were convinced that a strike fueled more by emotion than by informed judgment would only create new hardships for both the union and its members.[20]

In the end, however, what UTW leaders thought was irrelevant. The predictable failure of Gen. Johnson's peace plan to alleviate the distress of textile workers created new strike fervor that union leaders were powerless to resist. The passions of American workers were inflamed in the summer of 1934 as they had not been since 1919, and millhands, at the end of their rope, could only have been emboldened by the struggles for workers rights that Toledo autoworkers, Minneapolis truck drivers, and San Francisco longshoremen had already undertaken. The Roosevelt administration's labor policy, an improvised expedient jerrybuilt on the inherently shaky foundation of Sec. 7(a), was destined to come crashing down during the summer of 1934, and disillusioned textile workers were willing accomplices to its piecemeal demolition.[21]

That millhands were determined to strike, with or without the UTW's approval, first became evident in northern Alabama. Some 20,000 workers in the Huntsville area struck two dozen mills in mid-July, after employers summarily rejected their demands for higher wages, better working conditions, and union recognition. Too mad and frustrated to be held back by the financial and institutional calculations that restrained UTW leaders, Alabama millhands struck because, as one explained, there was "no place to go but up."[22]

Had the remarkable solidarity that Alabama millhands achieved in the initial phase of their walkouts crumbled, as many observers predicted, the strike that engulfed the whole of the textile industry only six weeks later might have been forestalled. Doubts about their resolve had led UTW president Thomas McMahon to advise Alabama millhands against the walkouts. Once the conflict was under way, he and other national union leaders expected the worst. Yet, as the days stretched into weeks without a significant break in the strikers' ranks, the strikes reinforced the argument of those urging the UTW to launch an industry-wide walkout. They also contradicted the popular notion that southern millhands were congenitally deficient in the class fortitude required to sustain the battles they too readily joined. As the faith spread among textile workers from New England to the Piedmont that southern millhands were ready and willing to do their part in any struggle that might eventuate, the doubts that had sustained UTW leaders in their opposition to a general strike were effectively refuted. As a reporter for *The New Republic* observed,

> They have been long-suffering and patient, these textile workers; but their day of patience is at an end. . . . Already more than 25,000 are out in Alabama. The others are ready to act—with and through their constituted national officials if they can; without them if they must.[23]

Concerned that events would overtake them if they did not at least attempt to channel the manifest impatience of an increasingly disaffected rank and file, union leaders finally decided, at a contentious meeting of the UTW's Emergency Committee on July 18, to convene "a special convention" in New York City on August 13 to formulate a strategy for "combatting the tactics of employers and to call forcibly to the attention of NRA officials the true conditions in the textile industry."[24] Although they apparently had no clear idea of what the meeting was likely to accomplish, UTW leaders did not originally intend it to be a referendum on the issue of an industry-wide strike. As it became increasingly evident to them in early August that the "studies" undertaken by NRA officials as a condition of the June settlement had gained them nothing, union leaders finally conceded that a general strike might well be their only option. The union's Executive Council, on August 11, unanimously voted to ask delegates to the upcoming special convention to empower UTW leaders "to call a general strike in the cotton industry when, in their judgment, such a strike should be called."[25]

The 500 delegates who attended the convention, a majority of whom represented the union's most militant southern locals, hardly needed to be persuaded that the time for forceful action was now at hand. Almost immediately, UTW leaders lost control of the convention, which at times took on the character of a revival meeting as impassioned southern millhands using their "best pulpit manner" implored fellow delegates to take decisive action. "I have been wounded in the head and shot in the leg," one fiery veteran of the month-old Alabama strikes told his fellow delegates, "but I am ready to die for the union, and I call upon you to do likewise if necessary." In response, a journalist on the scene reported, "Millhands from New England and the South, many of whom had hitchhiked to attend this United Textile Workers convention, . . . roared their approval."[26]

Union president Thomas McMahon, who came to the convention still hoping to sell delegates on some action short of a general strike, quickly saw that they were in no mood to countenance halfway measures. Advocates of an industry-wide strike made it plain to McMahon and other still cautious union officials that their continued faintheartedness would leave delegates no choice except to depose them in favor of more militant leaders like hosiery workers' president Emil Rieve. McMahon got the message. As the convention progressed, one reporter observed, the once "conservative" UTW president had suddenly become "violently pro-strike."[27] The rank and file had "demanded that the union call a strike," UTW Vice President Francis Gorman later recalled, and "there wasn't a thing the leadership could do."[28]

The case for caution having been discredited, and with only ten of the 500 delegates dissenting, the convention thundered its approval for a general strike in cotton textiles to begin on or about September 1. The convention also authorized the special emergency strike committee it created to call additional walkouts in the silk, rayon, and woolen and worsted branches of the industry as soon after September 1 as circumstances permitted.[29]

To chair the strike committee convention delegates turned to the UTW's leading personality and most experienced trouble-shooter, Vice President Francis J. Gorman. Always a union in which conspicuously talented leaders were in short supply, Frank Gorman was easily the best the UTW had to offer. Born in Bradford, England, in 1890, the son of a struggling Yorkshire publican who catered to union activists from the local woolen mills, Gorman spent his early childhood in an atmosphere rife with "legends of British trade unionism, its martyrs and heroes and victories."[30] Only thirteen when he and his family arrived in America, Gorman was quickly initiated into the fetid sanctum of the textile industry, working first as a sweeper and, later, after a three-year apprenticeship, as a journeyman woolsorter in a Providence, R.I., mill, where his keen intelligence and expanding ambition propelled him to prominence in the affairs of the local woolsorters' union. As the president of his local, and then as an organizer for the UTW after it absorbed the Providence woolsorters' union in 1912, Gorman gained the experience and exposure that finally commended his elevation to the vice presidency of the national organization in 1928. Already a skilled navigator through the UTW's labyrinthine political culture, a preternatural realm in which personal élan often trumped formal authority, Gorman further enhanced his stature and influence by assuming a leadership role in the Marion and Danville strikes.[31]

Yet it was the New Deal recovery program, particularly the attention to labor issues that resulted from unending squabbles over the purpose and meaning of Sec. 7(a), that catapulted Gorman and similarly ambitious and resourceful trade union personalities to national prominence, and even celebrity. By the summer of 1934, Gorman was, the nominally superior rank of Thomas McMahon notwithstanding, the UTW's leading figure. When the time came to decide who among a largely bland and uninspiring group of top UTW functionaries was up to the task of leading the union into the biggest fight in its history, Gorman was without serious rivals.

Because mill owners, who continued to doubt that the UTW could make good on its threat, refused even to consider the union's demands, the power to head off an industry-wide strike likely to idle half a million textile workers in more than a dozen states rested solely with the federal government. "President Roosevelt is the only man on God's green earth," McMahon solemnly warned, "who can stop this strike."[32] While the president, whose recovery program was already suffering from an increasingly acute case of terminal disaffection, claimed to be greatly distressed by the prospect of a general strike in one of the country's biggest industries, he was nevertheless unwilling to head it off by weighing in on the side of the UTW's demands. The Roosevelt administration was prepared after the battle was joined to seek a cessation of hostilities based on new, but still pointless, promises to once again "study" the issues that divided millhands and mill owners. Preventing a conflict so long in the making, however, was a goal to which no one, including the president, could reasonably aspire.[33]

The textile strike, which would become the largest in American history, began just after midnight on September 1, the start of the three-day Labor Day weekend. It was led by a union that lacked the resources to sustain it, and was directed against an industry that did not fear a loss of production because it was chronically unable to sell what it had already produced. Notwithstanding these and other factors that combined to make the strike a decidedly bad idea from a bloodlessly rational perspective, nothing short of the visceral gratification that direct action afforded could assuage the anger of millhands who were no longer disposed to "listen to reason."

From his "headquarters" in the Carpenters' Building in Washington, D.C., which *Business Week* mockingly described as "a single easy chair" in a "diminutive office," Gorman endeavored with the help of his indefatigable publicist, Chester Wright, to foster an impression that the UTW was prepared to prosecute the textile strike on hundreds of fronts with a military precision and tactical genius that a German field marshal might have admired.[34]

In truth, the union, which was never fully in control, was starved of resources and largely dependent on the initiative of local millhands, who, more often than not, were oblivious to the "sealed and numbered strike orders" that Gorman regularly dispatched to the roiling conflict's distant fronts. "Whatever slight element of hokum there is in these sealed orders," one of Gorman's admirers nevertheless insisted, "they have given tangible evidence that the Washington headquarters knew what it was about and was proceeding according to plan . . ."[35]

The millhands' overwhelming response to the strike call—the *New York*

Times estimated, on September 14, that as many as 400,000 workers were taking part—and the initial success of the strikers' "flying squadrons" in shutting down mills, especially in the Carolinas and Georgia, gave the public ample reasons to be impressed by the UTW's apparent formidability.[36] Even before the strike began, however, UTW leaders were acutely aware of how little assistance the union would be able to provide once the fight had been joined. The UTW's own resources were as anemic as ever, and the AFL, despite William Green's endorsement of the strike, was not eager to support a cause that had failed to reward past investments.

Notwithstanding the enthusiasm and courage that strikers demonstrated along an intermittent battle line that snaked from Maine to Alabama, and despite the UTW's seeming capacity to do what millowners and others had smugly insisted that it could never do, the vastly superior power of employers was not long in expressing itself through every imaginable channel of legal, political, economic, social, civic, and religious authority. Especially in the scattered mill towns and villages of the southern Piedmont, where their oppressive authority had long since reduced the idea of civil liberties to an irrelevant abstraction, mill owners unleashed a counterattack too overwhelming and ferocious for even the most determined strikers to resist. Local authorities, backed (at the employers' discretion) by National Guardsmen, private detectives, professional strikebreakers, and vigilantes, made the mill owners' fight their own, citing grossly exaggerated reports of violent acts by strikers to justify their own extreme countermeasures. And certainly, southern mill owners and their allies never lacked for firepower. *News-Week* reported that, when employers in the Piedmont set about the task of reopening mills that strikers had earlier closed, they did so with the active backing of 25,000 armed men.[37]

Despite the awful hardships they faced and the demoralizing news that employers were succeeding in reopening struck mills, most of the textile workers on strike in the South took their suffering and their disappointments in stride, heartened by a hope that something might yet be gained and by the knowledge that their fellow strikers in the north were holding out in the face of equally intense pressure. For the most part, northern textile workers had joined the walkout more in solidarity with southern millhands than to protest their own immediate plight. "This strike was forced by the South," one observer noted, and despite the grievances that northern textile workers reasonably harbored, their decision to join the fight was "to a great extent a sympathetic movement . . ."[38] Still, if northern workers, who were more likely to be UTW members, followed rather than led in the fall of 1934, they were not acting out of sympathy alone. The South's newly established dominance in cotton textiles, and its growing importance in nearly every other branch of the industry, left northern millhands little choice except to support their southern counterparts.[39]

Northern workers had much to gain—and very little to lose—by lending themselves to the militant protest that southern millhands had sparked, and they generally refused to let regional prejudices dilute their solidarity. Most of those northern textile centers affected by the strike did not witness the mayhem that engulfed scattered mill towns throughout the Piedmont. Some areas, however, most notably Rhode Island, provided stark evidence that geography conferred no immunity to deadly violence when strikers went all out to resist efforts to reopen struck mills.[40]

As strikers fell back and mill owners gained the upper hand, Gorman and other UTW leaders could only watch with mounting dismay. The union's scant resources had long since been depleted, and with most other unions ignoring its urgent pleas for help, the UTW was confronted with a dilemma: let the strike die a slow death or seize the first opportunity, short of abject surrender, to end it. At the end of the third week of the strike, the Roosevelt administration provided an avenue of escape that Gorman and his colleagues were eager to follow.

Appointed by the president after his earlier efforts to head off the strike had failed, the Board of Inquiry for the Cotton Textile Industry was authorized to either arbitrate the dispute, if the parties were willing, or study the strike's causes for the purpose of proposing a settlement. Chaired by New Hampshire Governor John G. Winant, a progressive Republican who enjoyed Roosevelt's personal confidence, the three-man board soon abandoned any thoughts of arbitration. The mill owners made it plain that nothing less than the UTW's total defeat would satisfy them. As a consequence, the Winant Board pursued its alternative strategy: studying the issues in dispute with the intention of crafting a "peace plan" that Roosevelt might recommend to the parties.

The report that the Winant Board hastily fashioned and forwarded to the president on September 20 was one that, while generally acknowledging the legitimacy of the strikers' complaints, proposed further study rather than immediate improvements in the intolerable terms and conditions of employment against which millhands had rebelled. Still, despite the report's glaring drawbacks, which included a pointed rejection of the UTW's demand for recognized as the workers' bargaining agent, Gorman and the emergency strike committee unanimously endorsed Roosevelt's proposal to end the strike on the basis of the Winant Board's findings. Given that striking millhands, no matter how mightily they endeavored to sustain their struggle, were facing almost certain defeat, Gorman and his fellow strike leaders cannot be faulted for wanting to forestall further suffering and to salvage what remained of the UTW's tattered credibility. The professed desire of the most ardent strikers to fight to the finish, though courageous, failed to take into account the even more terrible hardships that a senselessly prolonged strike was bound to inflict.

Yet Gorman, whose leading role in the strike brought a national prominence that proved more intoxicating than sobering, had his own ego too completely and publicly invested in the conflict to permit its outcome to be viewed as the setback that it plainly was. In recommending to the union's Executive Council on September 22 that strikers be directed to return to work on the basis of the

Winant Board's proposal, Gorman grandly insisted that they could do so with the clear and certain knowledge that they had achieved a "magnificent victory." "It is our unanimous view," Gorman reported on behalf of the strike committee,

> that the union has won an overwhelming victory, that we ought to terminate the strike as no longer necessary and that we now go forth in a triumphant campaign of organization . . . We have been called upon by the President of the United States to join with him in effecting stability in our industry, under a program designed to remedy the abuses against which we struck and we believe it is our clear duty to join with the President in this great effort. We have now gained every substantial thing that we can gain in this strike. Our strike has torn apart the whole unjust structure of NRA, lifting a load from all labor as well as from ourselves.

Gorman was undoubtedly justified in his assertion that the textile strike had further exposed the bankruptcy of NRA labor policies. He can also be forgiven for wanting to put the best possible face on the strike's outcome. His extravagant claims for its "definite" achievements, however, not only undermined his personal credibility but also badly harmed the cause of textile unionism in the South in ways that would become fully evident only in time.

On the basis of utterly unrealistic assumptions that the Winant Board's vague proposals would be accepted and implemented to the UTW's maximum advantage and that mill owners would have to go along, Gorman boldly predicted gains "on a scale so sweeping that we must confess ourselves surprised at the sweeping character of the victory we have won." Not only did the proposed settlement ensure that "[w]e have at last killed the stretch-out," he announced, but it also "definitely" guaranteed new methods of determining wages and hours "on a basis of fact" and secured the "[p]ractical recognition of our union" even if "the cotton mill owners are not required formally to recognize our union at once."

Indeed, as Gorman chose to see things, it was the employers who were the big losers. "The textile employers," he assured the Executive Council, "are now on the defensive, and stand condemned both by the language of the report of the Winant Board, and by the President's approval thereof." Given that "the victory was complete throughout the industry" and that "freedom and justice are available to all of our workers, if we now do our part," Gorman told his colleagues, there was no reason to fight on. "To call off the strike," he insisted,

> will be to gain immediate approval of the public opinion of the land, and the sympathy of the entire Administrative organization. The latter will then be committed to the defense of the worker in any and all of the controversies which are bound to arise in the further working out of the details of the constructive program.
>
> The only possible immediate objective of the strike has been gained: The strike has established the representative character of the United Textile Workers of America for the industry.

"The workers have felt the enthusiasm of a splendid battle," Gorman concluded. "They have been welded together by the great struggle. They will never forget it. It will go down in the history of labor as one of the greatest ever fought."[41]

Gorman's fanciful attempt to couch the UTW's defeat in a proclamation of victory—"a triumph for labor, a complete vindication of its position"—accentuated the positive to a point well beyond the limits of plausibility. Yet with the daunting prospect of almost certain defeat looming before them, with Amalgamated Clothing Workers' president Sidney Hillman strongly endorsing the president's overture and, with little more than a nagging sense of incongruity to deter them, the union's Executive Council unanimously approved Gorman's recommendation.[42] While the discussion was still in progress, however, a few in attendance did wonder aloud whether the union's "victory" was truly of the magnitude Gorman alleged. One skeptic wondered what, if any, real guarantee the strike committee had that southern mill owners, in particular, would honor the President's request that strikers be permitted to return to their jobs without prejudice. Since mill owners had not pledged themselves to accept the Winant Board's settlement plan, either in whole or in part, Gorman and his fellow strike leaders were, in fact, proposing that millhands give up their struggle as an act of faith. Another dubious listener, an organizer from Georgia, beseeched the Executive Council for guidance in explaining the decision to his members, since it "was not what southern people are looking for and it is [a] really big job to go back and convince them."[43]

In the end, the Executive Council's relief at having found a way out of its dilemma apparently overrode any doubts its individual members may have had regarding Gorman's dissembling transmutation of impending defeat into transcendent victory. Those outside the UTW's inner circle, however, were less confused about the difference between winning and losing. The reactions of the press to the union's victory claim ranged from genuine befuddlement to undisguised scorn. "As is always the case after a battle which ends with both antagonists on their feet," the editor of the *Christian Century* observed, "each claims victory." Still, he added, it was "difficult to see" that the UTW had achieved the "triumph" that Gorman claimed. "The basis on which the strike ended is, in fact," he noted, "so vague that it has yet to be proved that individual mill operators will not interpret it as leaving them in a more dictatorial position than they held before the strike was called."[44] Others agreed. "For all the oratory and enthusiasm," *Newsweek* said of the UTW's claims,

> it appeared that the countrys' textile workers had gone back to work with little more than a pious hope. They returned to exactly the same working conditions which they had quit as "intolerable" three weeks earlier.[45]

The *New Republic*, which earlier had been lavish in its praise of Gorman's strike leadership,[46] glumly noted that the UTW was now urging that "strikers return to the mills under a settlement that grants them not one of the demands for which they struck." "For Mr. Gorman and the other UTW officials to hail this 'settlement' as an overwhelming victory is, of course, incomprehensible," its liberal editor insisted, "unless one interprets their elation merely as face-saving."[47] The more left-leaning *Nation* acidly denounced Gorman's "exuberant claims of victory in the textile strike" as a transparent gloss on "one of the worst sell-outs in the history of American labor leadership." In truth, the *Nation* declared, "The workers gain not one of the specific immediate concessions for which they went out on strike." And because it was already abundantly clear that mill owners would not accept even the mildest recommendations of the Winant Board, the editorialist concluded, "The textile worker, who has gone through three payless weeks of dangerous picket duty, martial law, and even concentration camps, has every reason for losing faith in his alphabetical heroes, the NRA and the UTW."[48] Mary Hillyer, also writing in the *Nation,* predicted that, in the aftermath of having "suddenly, inexplicably, sold out" its own followers, the UTW had forfeited its future. "The United Textile Workers declares it will now organize the entire industry," she wrote. "It is an idle boast . . . a dreary camouflage to cover a disastrous defeat." "It would seem less awful," she tartly observed, "if Francis Gorman had been more moderate in his statements during the strike and less eloquent in his claims of victory when finally he offered cooperation to the employers for the 'stabilization and prosperity of the industry.' "[49]

That the liberal and left-wing press, which was ever ready to regret and condemn the "accommodationist" tendencies of most American unions, heartily disapproved the basis on which UTW leaders chose to end the textile strike smarted more than it mattered. What proved far more devastating to the reputation and subsequent credibility of the UTW were the reactions of textile workers to the union's dishonest declaration that the settlement generously compensated for the terrible sacrifice, suffering, and abuse they had endured during the strike. Simply put, the workers knew better. And as the full magnitude of their defeat was highlighted by multiplying reports of widespread discrimination against former strikers throughout the Piedmont, southern millhands who already had reason to doubt the UTW's vitality and competence now had compelling new reasons to doubt its honor and fidelity. Being defeated by employers of vastly superior strength was hardly a new experience for aspiring trade unionists in southern mills. Yet being told by their union leadership that defeat was actually victory, even as thousands of their number faced the prospect of permanent exclusion from the only industrial work accessible to them, was an inexcusable insult to their intelligence.[50]

Many northern millhands, though less vulnerable to employer retribution when the strike ended, had an equally strong reaction to the union's unconditional acceptance of the Winant Board's recommendations. Describing the response of bewildered millhands in New Bedford, Mass., where support for the strike remained strong to the end, Mary Hillyer wrote in the *Nation,*

Stuck to the door of the United Textile Workers' headquarters on the day the strikers were ordered back to work was a roughly drawn cartoon. A hand symbolizing the Winant board was offering strikers the Gorman egg of victory, cracked open and empty. The caption consisted of the cries of the strikers: "Where are your promises Gorman? The thirty-hour week? The end of the stretch-out? The increase in pay? Union recognition?

"We don't know why we've gone back," one puzzled New Bedford weaver complained. "We haven't won anything. We are waiting for [our leader] to come and explain. He's left us holding the bag. Our [local] executive board wired Gorman that we unanimously turned down the Winant report. Then Gorman calls us up and says we are to accept it—it's a wonderful victory. That's a hot one." Gorman had impressed New Bedford millhands in the early days of the strike as "a real fighter," he told Hillyer. "The things he said were great. But he double-crossed us. He sold us out."[51]

While many of the union's critics were willing to concede that winning the textile strike was never a realistic possibility, they remained convinced that the UTW's decision to end the strike without securing the employers' agreement to any of the Winant report's recommendations, including the rehiring of former strikers, constituted an unforgivable breach of trust. Almost at once, the Nation observed, mill owners "made it clear by their actions if not by their public statements that they had very little intention of living up to the ideals of the Winant report."[52]

Reports of discrimination against former strikers flooded union headquarters in the ensuing days and weeks.[53] Gorman admitted to the UTW Emergency Board, on October 26, that at least 363 mills were discriminating against former strikers and that as many as 15,000 millhands had already been blacklisted. He also reported that a new "policy committee" representing mill owners in the Carolinas, Georgia, Alabama, and Virginia had decided following a meeting convened by the southern Manufacturers Association in Greenville, S.C., that it would proceed to "bust the U.T.W. of A."[54] Yet even in the face of this and other evidence of the employers' bad faith, the union's top leaders clung to the frayed hope that the new Textile Labor Relations Board (TLRB) the Winant report gave rise to would, in due course, make things right. Their optimism became untenable, however, as the weeks stretched into months and little or nothing was done to redress workers' grievances. The new labor board, though an improvement over the industry-dominated NRA panel it supplanted, was, from the workers' point of view, equally ineffectual. The TLRB made slight progress in its well-meaning attempts to restore former strikers, but when mill owners persisted in their discriminatory policies the board was powerless to do anything about it. Southern textile employers, in particular, were determined to exploit their strike victory in the service of a broader campaign to purge the last vestiges of trade unionism from their industry. And the TLRB, which hopeful union leaders had lavishly touted as a new and improved bulwark of workers' rights, never became more than a minor impediment to the employers' success.[55]

The ever more obvious failure of the strike settlement to benefit millhands left UTW leaders scrambling to concoct some new interpretation of its value and meaning that would spare them the public embarrassment of recanting their earlier claims of victory. Frank Gorman, who remained the union's most visible spokesperson, alternated between his old assertion that the strike was "one of the most amazing victories ever recorded in the annals" of American labor and a new claim that its real significance was in preparing the ground for the imminent organization of the whole textile industry.

Despite the union's periodic intimations of great things to come, it had no place to go but down in the dreary aftermath of the 1934 strike. The once bracing hope that textile millhands might join Toledo autoworkers, Minneapolis teamsters, and San Francisco longshoremen at the head of a triumphant procession of industrial unionists no longer hostage to the constraints of craft precepts gave way to a more cautious and familiar expectation: that the union could, by not overreaching, maintain a fairly secure presence in the industry's relatively hospitable northern districts. The union was able to retain the allegiance of a dwindling congregation of millhands here and there across the Piedmont, but for most southern millhands, despite the inducements to activism that pitifully low wages and miserable working conditions continued to provide, faith in the UTW was an investment they could no longer justify. Southern millhands did not lose their appreciation of collective action as a result of the failure of the great textile strike. What the experience did foster in many of them, however, was a more evident skepticism, one that led them to hold unions, especially those based in the North, to a much higher standard of proof in deciding whether the benefits that unionism promised were sufficiently within reach to justify the singular risks that worker activism in the South entailed. This new, more exacting calculation of risks and benefits did not constitute a rejection of unionism by southern millhands. It did suggest, however, that among the enduring legacies of the 1934 strike was a greater reluctance among textile workers in the South to give the UTW or its successors the benefit of the doubt when they sought to rehabilitate the union cause.

If the leaders of the UTW understood that southern millhands would be considerably more resistant to organization in the aftermath of the 1934 strike, they did not acknowledge the union's diminished prospects in the Piedmont. On the contrary, UTW leaders who traveled in the region during 1935 and 1936 seized upon even the flimsiest evidence of continuing worker support to claim that the union's subjugation of the textile South was just a matter of time.[56] Behind the bluster and fanciful prophesy, however, was an organization struggling to pay its bills and contain its internal disharmony. Unable to promulgate their own plan for revitalization, union leaders remained wedded, by habit more than by choice, to the vain belief that the Roosevelt Administration, either by refurbishing the NRA's tattered textile code or by hatching some new scheme for the industry's rationalization, might still become the agent of the UTW's salvation. Long after most other union leaders had written off the NIRA as an obstacle to labor's progress, UTW officials continued to look beseechingly toward Washington even as they fervently denounced existing New Deal labor relations policies in the textile industry. Indeed, in March of 1935, only two months before the Supreme Court struck down the section of the NIRA that created it, the National Recovery Administration was unanimously endorsed by the union's Executive Council, which urged UTW locals to do everything in their power to keep it alive. At the same meeting, the Executive Council expressed only perfunctory interest in Senator Robert Wagner's pending National Labor Relations Bill.[57]

The union's fear of being left to its own devices was well-founded. The impression of formidability imparted during the early days of the great textile strike, when 400,000 or so millhands rallied to the union's support, soon gave way to a truer, less sanguine image, one of weakness rather than strength. The powerful sense briefly shared by UTW leaders and members alike that opportunities for labor's advance had never been better collided headlong with the hard truth that theirs was a union still woefully unable to contend against the forces that opposed it. At a time when union leaders were convinced that resources devoted to organizing activities were likely to return unprecedented dividends, they were compelled by the deepening fiscal crisis that membership losses and dues defaults created to reduce the UTW's already inadequate staff of organizers still further. As one discouraged official observed in the fall of 1935, the UTW's financial situation had become so desperate "that at this time this International Union can't afford to spend any more money for organizing—North, East, South or West."[58]

Perhaps inevitably, the malaise into which the UTW descended in 1935 and 1936 created fertile ground for internal dissension and recrimination. The national officers most immediately responsible for directing the union's troubled passage, President Thomas McMahon and First Vice President Frank Gorman, increasingly aired their differences openly, even as they frantically scrambled to deflect a growing barrage of criticism from the ranks. In addition, the already strained relations between the parts that comprised the whole were exacerbated by the new stresses that fresh failures brought. The semi-autonomous federations representing hosiery workers and dyers and finishers, which were relatively prosperous in comparison to the UTW's other main constituencies (cotton, woolen and worsted, carpets and rugs, and silk and rayon), openly questioned the value of continuing their affiliation with a national organization that took ever more from them without giving anything back.[59]

Yet if the UTW's weak and demoralized condition invited gratuitous fault finding and internecine squabbles, it also compelled the union's leaders to take a hard, realistic look at their profoundly troubled organization. The UTW had long claimed exclusive authority to organize America's textile workers, but, by the mid-1930s, the union's blighted record ever more insistently called into question its potential to become, on its own, more than a marginal presence in the industry.

Perhaps, more than anything else, it was the collective resignation that honest introspection fostered among UTW leaders that caused them to conclude, by 1936, that something more than the underpowered vehicle they had relied upon was required to propel textile unionism beyond its historic limitations. Yet it was also the timely discovery of a new propulsive force for industrial labor's advance that kept their resignation from becoming despair, that kept the weight of so many disappointments from crushing their hopes. This new repository of their depleted but still resilient faith was, of course, John L. Lewis's Committee for Industrial Organization. And while it had yet to prove itself as a viable agency of industrial unionism's progress, the CIO quickly commended itself to the UTW as textile unionism's last best hope.[60]

CHAPTER 3

In Praise of the New Unionism

When John L. Lewis acted, in the wake of the 1935 AFL convention, to establish the Committee for Industrial Organization as a thinly disguised opposition movement within the federation, only two other industrial unions, the Amalgamated Clothing Workers and the International Ladies Garment Workers, were in a position to join his United Mine Workers union in contributing significant membership and resources to the enterprise. Among the handful of other discontented but less robust organizations that comprised the rest of the CIO's founding membership, organizations whose weakness consigned them to the shadows of their more forceful collaborators, was the United Textile Workers of America. To a considerable degree, the UTW's relationship with the new CIO was not unlike the one it had always had with the AFL. The UTW was a poor relation whose value lay in its potential rather than its existing assets or organizational prowess. Lewis and his chief allies were also undoubtedly keen to impart an image of the greatest possible breadth of support for their insurgency, and the UTW, along with even less substantial unions representing mine, mill, and smelter workers, oil workers, and cap and hat workers, helped to give the CIO an appearance of mass and strength greater than their own organizations alone could project.[1]

For the UTW, which had come so far to accomplish so little, the risk incurred by openly siding with industrial union dissidents against the AFL's craft majority was minimal. The craft leaders who dominated the federation had been, at best, only grudgingly tolerant of the UTW. And, with the collapse of the 1934 general strike, those among the AFL's top leadership who clung most tenaciously to craft principles found corroboration for their disdain of industrial unionism in the UTW's failures. Of course, any AFL affiliate that chose to follow Lewis's lead invited their scorn, and censure, but the UTW was already held in such low esteem by the federation's craft hierarchy that its declaration of allegiance to the CIO inspired more sneers than concern. Finally, because the AFL had never been other than niggardly in its support of the

UTW, McMahon and his colleagues had no reason to fear that defying the federation would hurt their union financially. On the contrary, the professed willingness of the CIO's prime movers to deploy their respective treasuries in the cause of industrial unionism's broad advance was reason enough for the perennially impoverished UTW to risk estrangement from the AFL. As the feeling grew stronger among UTW leaders after the 1934 strike that a historic opportunity was slipping from their grasp, they increasingly adopted the view that only an abrupt change of course was likely to keep the union from foundering. Until the fall of 1935, however, those at the UTW's helm were at a loss to keep the union afloat much less to steer it toward a brighter future.

Beyond persuading demoralized UTW leaders that they need not acquiesce in the union's evident destiny of drift and decline, the CIO was not disposed, either financially or tactically, to regard the resurrection of textile unionism as an urgent concern. Convinced that the steel and auto industries offered the greatest and most immediate potential for organizational gains, Lewis and other CIO leaders were understandably disinclined to venture into a historic quagmire like textiles when the prospects for industrial unionism were brighter elsewhere.

As a result, the UTW stayed largely on the sidelines during the first year of the CIO's operation, its leaders left with no role other than to support Lewis in his escalating war of words with AFL hardliners during the first half of 1936 and, then, to cheer on steel and auto workers in the latter half of the year as their organizing efforts brought seminal confrontations in both industries ever nearer. Almost anything more was too much for the UTW. When the union appealed to its locals, in the fall of 1936, for donations to support the CIO's organizing efforts, only three responded—with total pledges amounting to $300.00.[2] Even in the best of times, money had been a problem for the UTW. But with its dues-paying membership still in decline more than two years after the end of the 1934 general strike and the need for new operating economies always at the top of its agenda, moral support was all the UTW could contribute to the CIO. In the face of mounting AFL threats, UTW leaders stoutly proclaimed that there was "no turning back from the position we have taken on our affiliation with the . . . CIO," but they also recognized that the immediate fate of industrial unionism would have to rest on shoulders brawnier than their own.[3]

In the end, the UTW's inability to help the CIO hardly jeopardized its success. More troubling, in many ways, was its increasingly evident inability to help itself. The devastation in the wake of the 1934 general strike, which even the most sanguine analysts ultimately agreed was a full-fledged calamity for the cause of textile unionism, continued to be felt at every level of the UTW. In the South, in particular, the decline in membership was so dramatic, by 1936, that the UTW's presence in the region was, except for a few isolated enclaves of continuing support, little more than a fond memory.[4]

As in earlier periods of demoralization, the union's most practiced cheerleaders, Tom McMahon and Frank Gorman, endeavored to find a silver lining in even the darkest clouds. Convincing others that things were not as bad as they seemed, however, proved increasingly difficult. When Emil Rieve, whose largely autonomous hosiery workers' federation continued to be the UTW's most robust constituent, charged that the UTW's troubles were principally a result of mismanagement and poor leadership at the top, Gorman, who was ever at the ready to point out that the union's situation could be even worse, lamely countered that "considering what we have to contend with we have done very well." When pressed by their increasingly contentious colleagues to formulate a strategy for reversing the union's decline, neither Gorman nor McMahon was able to offer much more than a fervent hope of eventual rescue by the CIO.[5]

The UTW did make an effort, in the early fall of 1936, to convince CIO leaders that it was doing its best to solve internal problems that were a particular source of concern to them. The national union's chronic financial difficulties, its critics agreed, was the inevitable consequence of a per capita tax structure hopelessly inadequate for effective operation. Authorized to collect a per capita tax of only twenty cents per month, 25 percent of which it was obliged to return to affiliated departments or federations representing members in nearly every branch of the industry except cotton textiles, the UTW was impoverished by design. Workers in the various branches of the larger industry had long tended to identify more closely with their respective organizations than with an extraneous national body that presumed to represent a largely fictitious whole. And their practiced reluctance to support the UTW more generously derived, in large measure, from the conviction that, in an industry whose branches were all equally prone to instability and hardship, charity had to begin at home. In the mid-1930s this attitude was reinforced by a growing feeling within both the hosiery and the dyers federations, whose relative prosperity obliged them to support the UTW disproportionately, that the national union's ineffectual record in the industry's other major branches— cotton textiles, silk and rayon, woolens and worsteds, carpets and rugs, synthetic yarns—left them throwing good money after bad.

Yet despite the wrangles that had always arisen when the subject of a higher per capita tax was broached, in 1936 the UTW was finally ready to confront the issue. Pressed by the CIO leadership to adopt a dues policy that would permit the UTW to subvent its own revivification, members of the union's Executive Council agreed to recommend doubling the per capita tax to 40 cents per month.[6] As President McMahon warned delegates to the UTW's September convention, the necessity for higher dues could no longer be sidestepped or ignored. "There is only one reason that the United Textile Workers is a backward organization," McMahon told the delegates,

and that is that at these Conventions of ours, delegates think more in terms of their local unions than they do in terms of International organization. We see it today quite plainly . . . Because of the niggardliness of delegates attending the convention, or fear of taking the stand to build up the International Union, we have had no money to give assistance where it was needed.[7]

While UTW leaders ultimately persuaded convention delegates to double the per capita tax, the difficulty the union had always faced in actually collecting it from a preponderantly low-wage membership remained to be overcome. Still, by convincing delegates that the time had finally come to cast off a long-standing restraint on the national union's effectiveness, UTW leaders felt they had made the gesture of good faith necessary to allay CIO concerns about their union's willingness to help itself.

Delegates to the UTW's 1936 convention were far less, successful, however, when it came to dispelling doubts among CIO leaders that the internal dissension that had long plagued their union could be overcome. The fault finding and finger pointing in the wake of the 1934 strike was merely further evidence of the internal fractiousness that had long been one of the UTW's defining characteristics. As it became clear that McMahon and Gorman, the national officials accountable for the organization's deepening torpor, could not agree on how the UTW might arrest its decline, dissidents such as Emil Rieve of the hosiery workers and George Baldanzi of the dyers and finishers were emboldened to press for changes designed to reapportion authority within the union.[8]

In the end, however, the structural reforms adopted by the convention, though they afforded the union's strongest constituencies the greater influence they sought, did nothing to solve the UTW's fundamental problems. Nor did they help to counter the abiding impression of many outsiders that the union's often crippling internecine squabbles were an inevitable consequence of its decentralized structure. Leaders from the union's various branches could, as they did at the close of the 1936 convention, ritually declare their staunch solidarity with the national union, but the structural barriers to true cooperation and fraternity remained in place.

Had John L. Lewis, Sidney Hillman, and other CIO leaders insisted, in the fall of 1936, that the UTW demonstrate its readiness to take advantage of the assistance they seemed disposed to offer, it is doubtful that the union could have done so. In truth, of course, the CIO was so overwhelmed by its existing commitments in the steel and automobile industries that an organizing drive in textiles was still no more than a remote intention.[9] When Hillman addressed the UTW's 1936 convention, he spoke of "the close kinship of the garment and textile workers," but only hinted at the prospect of a CIO campaign in the textile industry. According to Hillman, the most urgent business facing the industrial union movement in the fall of 1936 was not organization but rather the reelection of Franklin Roosevelt, whose continuation in office, he insisted, would help to sustain a national political environment conducive to the CIO's success.[10] Lewis, was equally vague. He instructed his proxy to the convention, CIO Organizing Director John Brophy, to assure delegates that "all of the officers of the Committee for Industrial Organization are tremendously interested in the well-being of the United Textile Workers and its membership," but he was apparently unwilling—or unable—to say when that interest might transmute into action.[11]

Unable to agree on a course of action and lacking the resources to act even if a serviceable consensus had been achieved, UTW leaders could only hope, toward the end of 1936, that when, or if, the CIO's work in steel and autos bore fruit, the million-plus workers in the textile industry would become the next objects of the new unionism's encompassing ambition. The UTW had remained unwavering in its commitment to the CIO, despite escalating AFL threats first to suspend rebel affiliates, then to expel them, but its resolute defiance of the federation had yet to produce tangible benefits.

Certainly, CIO victories over General Motors and U.S. Steel were anything but assured as the separate organizing drives launched against corporate America's most imposing redoubts each reached a stage of final confrontation at year's end. And just as certainly, neither Lewis nor Hillman, or any of the other members of the CIO hierarchy who anxiously awaited the final showdowns in autos and steel, had given more than cursory consideration to the order of battle to be followed once the organization's initial objectives had been secured. So, while the UTW had no choice but to stand by its decision "to go down the line with the CIO," neither its leaders nor its members could say with confidence where the path they had chosen to follow would lead.[12]

What seemed less uncertain to UTW leaders was that, when the CIO finally turned its attention to the textile industry, it would be Sidney Hillman who guided the effort. Hillman's interest in textile unionism was of long standing, and was inspired by institutional expediency as much as by fraternalism. "Our special interest in textile unionism is . . . self-protective," Hillman and his colleagues later acknowledged. "It is in many ways similar, in the underlying motives of self-protection, to the interest of the United Mine Workers in steel unionism." The Amalgamated Clothing Workers union had assumed a direct role in promoting textile unionism as early as 1919, when, under Hillman's leadership, it supported the rise of the Amalgamated Textile Workers of America, which briefly flourished as a left-wing alternative to the still craft-bound UTW.[13] In the years that followed, Hillman divined a natural affinity between the textile and clothing industries. And when the ACWA began to resurrect itself in 1933 as a result of the special impetus it gained from the NIRA and Sec. 7(a), Hillman often alluded to a day not far distant when the renewed strength of his organization might bolster textile unionism's revitalization.

The leaders and members of the UTW were equally disposed to look first to Hillman and the ACWA when they sought the help or advice of outsiders. Hillman had advised the union's top leadership during the most critical phases of the 1934 general strike and had also been the person to whom beleaguered UTW officials most readily turned for guidance as they struggled to navigate the shifting currents of early New Deal labor policies. Moreover, when hopeful

UTW functionaries began to consider the possibilities for renewed activism that the CIO's emergence promised, they rarely did so without considering the special help Hillman and the Amalgamated might be persuaded to give.[14]

Yet, despite the close relations existing between the two unions, and the expectations UTW leaders harbored about the role Hillman was likely to play in textile unionism's resurgence, 1936 ended without a specific promise of future collaboration. After Roosevelt's overwhelming reelection victory in November, Francis Gorman did report to the union's Executive Council that "the first definite move" had been taken to ensure that the UTW's "organizational program" would be "taken up by the CIO." His reference, however, was not to the broad campaign that he and other UTW officials hoped for, but rather to John L. Lewis's vague promise of future help in organizing workers in the only branch of the textile industry with an oligopolistic structure: synthetic yarns.[15]

With no hope of assistance until the CIO's prior commitments in autos and steel were met, the UTW's goal, at the beginning of 1937, was simply to hang on until salvation was finally at hand. Thomas McMahon, who had gone hat in hand, to other unions so frequently that he was known, according to one fellow unionist, as "the pauper President" of the UTW, told his colleagues in late 1936 that defaults on dues payments had forced him to solicit a $10,000 loan from John L. Lewis just "to keep the organization going."[16] It proved to be the last of the many humiliations that McMahon's long service to the UTW exacted. With his appointment as director of Rhode Island's Department of Labor in January of 1937, McMahon resigned the presidency of the union that had held first claim on his loyalty and devotion since the day more than thirty years earlier when he joined Cloth Folders Local 505 of the new UTWA. After fifteen years at the helm of an underpowered vessel perpetually unable to gain the momentum required to propel itself to a safe harbor, McMahon had become the hapless personification of the UTW's inertia and inefficacy. "It was easy," one of his kinder critics later wrote, "to bring an indictment against the old man with the watch-chain over the portly paunch, the erectness and bishop-like dignity that seemed excessive in one below average height. Tom McMahon must have been haunted by the knowledge that he was the president of a union that wasn't there, the step-child, the tin-cup mendicant among the building-trades aristocracy, the union that spoke or mumbled for all but represented less than 3% of textile labor."[17]

Of course, those among his colleagues disposed to be fair to McMahon knew that he was more a reflection of the UTW's weakness than its agent. Certainly, none of his co-functionaries in the UTW, including Francis Gorman, McMahon's constitutionally mandated successor, was any better equipped to accomplish, through personal will or individual genius alone, a reversal of the union's disordered and dysfunctional condition. The two men regarded by outsiders as the UTW's most able leaders, Emil Rieve of the American Federation of Hosiery Workers and George Baldanzi of the Dyers and Finishers Federation, were well-known for their acerbic criticism of the national union's stewardship, but neither had ventured far enough beyond his own insular constituency to attract the broad support required to contest Gorman's ascendancy. Moreover, as leaders of the only two branches of the larger union that were viable at the beginning of 1937, neither Rieve nor Baldanzi had reason to covet Gorman's office. Together, the hosiery workers and dyers accounted for nearly half of the UTW's total membership of 70,000 in early 1937.[18] That fact alone conferred on Rieve and Baldanzi a measure of credibility that the presidency of the UTW (a union that Gorman himself ruefully labeled "a beggar organization") fell conspicuously short of matching.[19]

Although Frank Gorman's name would not have been prominent on any knowledgeable compiler's list of the America's ablest trade union leaders at the beginning of 1937, the pitiable condition of the organization he now presumed to pilot was not amenable to repair through better leadership alone. When Gorman and the other members of the newly expanded Executive Council met on the eve of McMahon's departure to assess the union's immediate prospects, they identified a dispiriting array of apparently intractable difficulties. Notwithstanding the hard-fought decision to ease its chronic destitution by doubling the per capita tax, the UTW remained so impoverished that Secretary-Treasurer James Starr reported that, even after repeatedly raiding the union's unemployment and mortuary funds, he had to further reduce its already woefully inadequate organizing staff. The ensuing discussion, which afforded Gorman's internal critics yet another opportunity to complain about his stewardship of the union's meager finances, also highlighted its untenable organizational structure. Gorman, a frequent target of Rieve's caustic strictures, complained in turn of the grating irony of the hosiery workers' recent decision to donate $50,000 to the CIO while "we [the UTW] are going to the CIO for money." Yet Rieve, whose highly skilled members were easily the best-paid in the UTW orbit, made it plain that his organization was loath to support the national union as long as "lip service" seemed to be its weapon of choice against the severe problems that beset textile unionism. If the textile industry was going to be organized, Rieve contended, it would be the CIO, rather than the UTW, that would get the job done. As a result, he concluded, it made better sense, for those who had money, to spend to support the CIO in its crucial, ongoing struggles in autos and steel than to entrust their funds to the UTW's demonstrably unavailing stewardship.

While most members of the Executive Council were unwilling to adopt Rieve's view that the UTW was a lost cause, they did share his sense that the union's fate rested with the CIO. Only John Peel, the chief UTW functionary in the South, disputed the assertion that the CIO was textile unionism's lone hope of salvation. In relying on the CIO to rescue the UTW, Peel warned his colleagues, the union was simply repeating the error of its earlier futile reliance on the AFL. "We are going to ask the CIO like we asked the AFL," Peel complained. Yet in the end, he maintained: "If the textile workers are organized, it will be because of us."[20]

Notwithstanding Peel's prideful rhetoric, which had a hollow ring given the union's anemic presence in the southern region he headed at the beginning of 1937, the CIO was, in fact, textile unionism's last best hope even if its eagerly awaited intercession was no guarantee of success. In truth, however, the CIO was still an unproven force. Unless and until the United Automobile Workers and the Steel Workers Organizing Committee actually demonstrated the power of the new industrial unionism, the CIO would remain, more than a year after its founding, only a remote menace to managerial authority in America's basic industries. And as the tense, month-long standoff in Flint, Mich., between sitdown strikers and General Motors ominously ground toward an uncertain outcome, and as resolute steelworkers stood toe to toe with U.S. Steel, still anxiously wondering whether the company would fight or talk, even the most astute observers of the labor scene were at a loss to know whether the CIO had a future.

When, finally, the proofs of the CIO's viability came, first in Flint and then in Pittsburgh, they could hardly have been more compelling. The announcement of General Motors's grudging surrender to Flint sitdown strikers on February 11, in addition to leaving a gaping hole in the mighty corporation's once impenetrable anti-unionism, authenticated the CIO as, perhaps, no other victory over big business could have. Less than three weeks later, the CIO's reputation was sent soaring toward the stratosphere when U.S. Steel, whose legendary efficiency in combatting unions had inspired imitators across the industrial spectrum, meekly announced that it was giving in to the Steel Workers Organizing Committee without the bruising fight that, for months, had seemed unavoidable.

For the UTW, whose leaders and members alike had longed for the moment when they would become the focus of the CIO's attention, the victories in autos and steel were essential prerequisites to action in the textile industry. Had either campaign failed, it is unlikely that Lewis and Hillman, knowing well the exceptionally daunting challenges that such an effort was bound to pose, would have been willing to contemplate a major organizing campaign in textiles. Yet in the heady aftermath of triumphs in autos and steel, no challenge seemed beyond the CIO's compass. And as Lewis, Hillman, and their fellow CIO strategists surveyed the new possibilities arrayed before them, even the textile industry, that crowded, forbidding graveyard of so many earlier organizing campaigns, now took on the alluring appearance of fertile ground. Textile workers, too, seemed to sense that they were next on the CIO's organizing agenda. In a letter to Lewis congratulating him on his "generalship in the General Motors strike," L. M. Johnston, a heartened UTW member in Columbus, Georgia, hopefully inquired: "If the question isn't too far fetched, can we look for a campaign to start in Columbus during 1937?"[21]

The first authoritative word that the country's 1,250,000 textile workers were indeed next on the CIO's list of prospective inductees came only two days after the formal signing in Pittsburgh of the new collective bargaining agreement between the Steel Workers Organizing Committee and U.S. Steel. According to the *New York Times,* the decision to launch "the third major offensive of the CIO in the nation's basic industries" was reached during a meeting between Lewis and Hillman on March 4. Assured by Frank Gorman that the UTW would defer to the CIO's authority, Hillman, the *Times* reported, was poised to take charge of a newly-formed Textile Workers Organizing Committee (TWOC) "modeled after the steel committee." Earlier efforts to organize textiles, the *Times* noted, had been "handicapped by lack of funds and small numbers." Now, the CIO intended to undertake a "national campaign to reach every textile operation in the country."

"Under the plan now being discussed," the *Times* reported,

> the textile territory would be divided into several areas, each in charge of a regional director who would be the field marshal for the general committee. Field men would act as organizers in the regions, volunteer organizers would be enrolled from sympathetic employees.[22]

In reporting details of the strategy and tactics that the TWOC intended to employ, the *Times* revealed information that Hillman had made little or no effort to share with UTW officials. Even Frank Gorman, though he had met with Hillman to give his tentative approval to a CIO-led organizing drive in textiles, was probably not privy to the details of its implementation. The UTW's badly tarnished reputation had plainly preceded it, and Hillman, intimately acquainted with the union's chronic debility, apparently believed that its leaders ought participate as little as possible in the planning and execution of the TWOC campaign. The "official" account of the TWOC's creation would later assert that it was the product of lengthy "negotiations" between Hillman and Gorman,[23] but, in fact, the CIO's offer to the UTW was emphatically a "take-it-or-leave-it" proposition.[24] In his admiring biography of Hillman, *New Republic* editor George Soule described the "negotiations" that preceded the TWOC's formation as an occasion when Hillman talked while Gorman dutifully listened. Reconstructing the encounter, Soule's account paraphrased Hillman's stern admonition to Gorman.

> Let's have no misunderstanding about this. In an important project of this kind, there must be no divided responsibility. If the TWOC runs the campaign, it must have full charge. It will utilize the UTW machinery and officers to the full extent of their ability, but it has to be in command. If you don't like this arrangement, the TWOC will step out of the picture and leave the job to the UTW. We will give you financial help as we would to any friendly union. But in that case, you must run your own show and be responsible.[25]

It is clear, of course, that Hillman knew that Gorman and his colleagues had no bargaining leverage, and therefore, no choice except to agree to whatever conditions he might impose. More than simply reflecting his sense of mastery, however, Hillman's brusqueness betrayed his personal disdain for Gorman. Solomon Barkin, who became the TWOC's self-designated director of research, reported that Hillman disdained Gorman because of his inept handling of the 1934 general strike, because of his careless personal habits, and, curiously, because his wife's radical politics situated her beyond the pale of Hillman's ideological tolerance.[26]

That Hillman was generally unwilling to accept Gorman and other long-time UTW leaders as useful collaborators reflected the widespread belief within the CIO that their demonstrated ineptitude disqualified them for anything more than minor roles in the TWOC campaign. More relevant to Hillman's exclusion of UTW leaders, however, was the simple fact that the SWOC organizational model he had adapted for the textile drive made no provision for collaborative leadership. The organizing campaign in steel had been John L. Lewis's show. The CIO's drive in textiles was to be Hillman's. To the extent that UTW leaders would be permitted to participate in the TWOC campaign, it was to be at Hillman's sufferance rather than as an entitlement conferred by their prior service in the cause of textile unionism.[27] From the outset, Gorman later complained, Hillman let UTW officials know that the TWOC campaign would be "conducted by dictum, with no voice either encouraged or permitted from below."[28]

Certainly, the tone and substance of the formal offer of assistance that the CIO presented to the UTW Executive Council at a hastily convened meeting in Washington on Sunday, March 7, left little doubt as to who would be in charge if Hillman's TWOC plan was accepted. Most council members knew almost nothing about the offer, which was brutally curt and simple. In return for the CIO's pledge to undertake a comprehensive organizing campaign in the textile industry, the UTW was obliged, under the proposed agreement, virtually to disappear. As Lewis and Hillman made clear to Gorman, Secretary-Treasurer James Starr, Emil Rieve, and John Peel, the special committee designated by the Executive Council to serve as intermediary between its members and the CIO, the UTW could accept or reject the proposal, but it could not seek to alter its strict and unsparing terms.

The full price the UTW would have to pay for the CIO's help was revealed to the rest of the union leadership when the Executive Council reconvened shortly after two o'clock in the afternoon. The terms of the proposal, which Gorman somberly described as "rather drastic," extinguished whatever hopes UTW leaders had for a partnership with the CIO. Without even an amiable nod in the UTW's direction, the CIO's offer provided (1) that Lewis would appoint a Textile Workers Organizing Committee, only two of whose members would come from the UTW; (2) that the TWOC would have "full authority and power" to administer all existing UTW contracts and to decide all future matters relating to organizing, finances and collective bargaining; (3) that all "officers and agents" of the UTW would "place themselves under the jurisdiction and orders" of the TWOC; and, (4) that the CIO would have "complete power and authority to determine the details incident to the termination of the organizing campaign, the disbanding of the Textile Workers Organizing Committee, and the re-organization of the United Textile Workers of America for the benefit of its present members and new members who join during the organizing campaign."[29]

Although, in the end, Executive Council members voted unanimously to accept the proposal, they were of two minds about its provisions. One faction claimed that the UTW's desperate condition required them to accept the CIO offer without delay, no matter how vague or humiliating its terms. The other acknowledged the union's ruinous state but wanted a fuller explanation of what the agreement entailed. In response to the latter group's concern, however, Gorman could only repeat that Hillman and Lewis, who were awaiting the council's immediate response, would provide details of the CIO offer only *after* it was accepted. Since, as one council member impatiently observed, the only choice before them was to "take it or leave it," they were bound to accept the offer, regardless of the consequences of their decision. Gorman undoubtedly spoke for many of his colleagues when he argued that, despite the misgivings of some about having to decide so momentous an issue on such short notice, "It is up to everyone to forget ourselves personally, our ideas for the moment, and decide now what is the best thing to do for the UTWA."[30]

Although UTW leaders understood that the decision to accept the CIO's offer was perhaps the most fateful one they would ever make, it is unlikely that even the most prescient among them fully understood how little of the organizational structure and culture they had struggled so arduously to sustain was destined to survive the TWOC's unfettered ascendancy. In ceding control over the immediate future of textile unionism to the TWOC, leaders of the UTW were subordinating themselves to what, they quickly discovered, was an organizational apparatus designed to function, as Frank Gorman later groused, "solely according to the dictates of Sidney Hillman."[31] Moreover, by submitting to an agreement that the *New York Times* described as "worded rather more strongly" than even that to which the tottering leadership of the decrepit Amalgamated Association of Iron, Steel and Tin Workers had meekly assented a year earlier, Gorman and his fellow UTW leaders were consigning their individual futures to Hillman's detached, unsparing appraisal.[32] And given that Hillman had done little to conceal his view that the UTW's failure was, in large part, due to ineffective leadership, many of the union's established leaders, including its top officers, had as much reason to regard the coming regime with apprehension as with exultation.

The official announcement of Hillman's appointment as chairman of the TWOC came on March 9, after the CIO's formal ratification of its agreement with the UTW. Thomas Kennedy, one of Lewis's closest colleagues in the

United Mine Workers, was named secretary-treasurer of the committee. In addition, Lewis appointed Thomas Burns of the United Rubber Workers, Charles Weinstein of the Amalgamated Clothing Workers, and Charles Zimmerman of the Ladies Garment Workers Union. (Only Weinstein assumed a direct role in the TWOC's subsequent activities.) The UTW's two representatives on the TWOC were Gorman and Emil Rieve. Gorman's selection was largely a courtesy; Rieve was picked because, as president of the bustling American Federation of Hosiery Workers, he was one of the few leaders associated with the old regime who still commanded Hillman's personal confidence.

Second only to Lewis in the stature he enjoyed within the rapidly expanding orbit of the CIO, Hillman brought to his service in behalf of textile unionism a well-deserved reputation as one of the country's most astute and resourceful labor leaders. Not even Lewis, however, could match the status that Hillman had attained by 1937 in both the administrative and political precincts of the New Deal. His deft navigation of the sprawling bureaucracy spawned by the Roosevelt administration's initial relief and recovery programs had marked Hillman, early on, as a labor leader of uncommon aptitude, and his later prominence in helping to secure the president's reelection marked him as a political figure whose influence extended well beyond the scope of what trade-union leadership had previously conferred.

As a trade unionist, Hillman brought to the particular challenge of organizing textile workers both a generally sound understanding of the industry and a resolute conviction that "responsible unionism" of the type that the Amalgamated Clothing Workers practiced under his leadership could, once the more enlightened and rational mill owners were convinced of its therapeutic powers, help to revive and stabilize a historically blighted sector of manufacturing in the United States. Not unlike men's clothing—the realm in which the utility of Hillman's trade-union philosophy had been tested and, seemingly, validated— most branches, of the textile industry exhibited none of the oligopolistic tendencies that had reshaped other mass-production industries. Characterized by intense competition among a large number of producers, none sufficiently influential in product or labor markets to constitute an industry-wide force for rational operation, textiles exhibited the tell-tale signs of chronic incoherence: low profit margins, excess capacity, irregular production, inadequate capitalization, and a widening technological divide that fostered wildly uneven productivity rates.[33]

Yet if Hillman saw in the textile industry some features that reminded him of men's clothing before the Amalgamated (and the NIRA) moved it in the direction of a more rational dynamic, he could hardly overlook the idiosyncracies of culture and tradition that established the several branches of the textile industry as worlds unto themselves. Nor could he ignore the pronounced North-South bifurcation in cotton textiles that gave what was one branch of industry in theory the appearance of two quite separate and distinct branches in practice. Indeed, Hillman clearly recognized that in the South lay the TWOC's greatest challenge, and that its success elsewhere would mean little if the millhands of the Piedmont, who worked mainly in cotton textiles but also, increasingly, in other southbound branches of the industry like hosiery, knit goods and synthetic yarns, remained beyond unionism's reach.[34] As history was to make abundantly clear, however, understanding the South's crucial importance to the future of textile unionism and overcoming the region's historic aversion to collective bargaining were hardly challenges of a comparable magnitude.

Still, in the spring of 1937, as the TWOC prepared for the difficult work that lay ahead, the prospects for textile unionism's success seemed brighter than ever before. The momentum created by its triumphs in steel and autos and by the lesser but still important victories it had won in rubber, electrical manufacturing, and other mass-production industries over the preceding six months, invested the CIO, during the late winter and early spring of 1937, with a mythic power and presence it would never again enjoy. The sitdown strike, a tactic that, by virtue of its audacity and frequency, came to symbolize the bold and unruly character of the new industrial unionism, was, by the time the TWOC appeared on the scene, so common a feature of the cross-country conflict raging between CIO unions and their corporate adversaries that even the prim young women of Asheville [N.C.] Normal and Teachers College sat down for three days until faculty and administrators agreed to several of their demands for greater social freedom, including "a rule that students may have two dates each week with male friends."[35] On the legislative front, the Wagner Act, though it was not upheld by the Supreme Court until a few weeks after the TWOC campaign began, also abetted the soaring hope of labor activists by endorsing collective bargaining as the only industrial relations policy consistent with the nation's transcendent democratic ideals.

What invested the TWOC campaign with greater promise than any previous organizing drive in textiles had held, however, was money, the essential resource that every earlier effort had conspicuously lacked. Indeed, the willingness of UTW leaders to endure the stinging humiliation that the TWOC agreement inflicted derived from a common conviction that gaining access to the CIO's resources was worth whatever price their prospective benefactors might see fit to exact.[36] As the TWOC apparatus took shape during the middle of March, those anticipating its imminent deployment had good reason to believe that if the effort ultimately faltered it would not be because of the financial constraints that had undermined earlier organizing campaigns. In announcing the TWOC's formation, CIO officials had emphasized that the $500,000 set aside to support its operation was only an "initial" appropriation.[37] Money, they seemed to be telling friends and foes alike, would be no object, and, as an accounting of all expenditures during the two years of the TWOC's operation would ultimately confirm, they were, generally, true to their word. In all, more than $2 million would be spent over the life of the campaign. Hillman's Amalgamated Clothing Workers alone contributed more than $800,000 and other

CIO sources (most notably the United Mine Workers and the International Ladies Garment Workers Union) contributed at least a half million dollars more.[38]

Few of those who eagerly clambered aboard the TWOC bandwagon believed that textile unionism could "buy its way into" an industry so devoutly opposed to collective bargaining, but they could at least be confident that, finally, the money available to them was commensurate with the task at hand. Perhaps the most compelling evidence of the TWOC's singular vitality was the sheer number of organizers that Hillman and his assistants hastily recruited. The staffers came from many sources—but mainly from the Amalgamated, branches of the UTW (in particular the hosiery workers and dyers federations), and a handful of other CIO unions. The organizing staff at Hillman's disposal would number well over 600 at the height of the campaign, nearly 500 of them employed directly by the TWOC. While the quality of service they rendered would—almost inevitably—be uneven, the activists who rallied to the TWOC's service faced the challenges before them with optimism and enthusiasm far greater than any previous organizers in textiles had been able to muster.[39]

At long last, it seemed, the immense institutional possibilities inherent in a textile workers' union of truly encompassing vision and scope were about to be realized.

CHAPTER 4

Trusting in the Strength of Others

In deciding how his swelling army of TWOC organizers would assault the bastions of employer power in textiles, Sidney Hillman pointedly neglected the advice of Frank Gorman and other UTW veterans in favor of that provided by his closest lieutenants from the Amalgamated. Convinced that the UTW's reputation among workers and employers alike was a liability rather than an asset, Hillman ensured that few vestiges of the organization survived in the TWOC. From the balkanized UTW, only the hosiery workers' and dyers' federations, the two constituencies that could pay their own way, were permitted to retain their separate status—and even they were divested of the virtual autonomy each had previously enjoyed.

The UTW had, Hillman and his aides believed, left the idea of unionism in ill repute among textile workers, especially as a result of its incompetent and disingenuous handling of the 1934 general strike. Consequently, they decided that both the UTW and those who personified its failures had to be kept from besmirching the TWOC's reputation. According to TWOC research director Solomon Barkin, this concern led the committee to conclude that, "Persons formerly associated with strike efforts of the UTW, particularly in southern areas, should be shifted to regions where they were less well known." There was, Barkin reported to the first meeting of the TWOC on March 19, a "general feeling that the name CIO was a special advantage and should be capitalized" among textile workers. In short, the committee seemed to believe, the less said about the UTW the better.[1]

Hillman and his ACWU colleagues were equally intent upon making certain that employers in the various branches of the textile industry understood that the UTW, a union that had earned only their enmity and contempt, would have no part in the TWOC campaign. Having advanced the recent fortunes of the Amalgamated as much through conciliatory overtures to employers as through more conventional adversarial methods, Hillman was determined that the UTW's notorious reputation among mill owners not blind them to the possibility that "responsible unionism" could be a rationalizing force in what one observer described as "one of the most confused and unscrupulously competitive industries in the country."[2]

From the moment of the TWOC's birth, Hillman, whom *Newsweek* said had "come to personify efficient, responsible unionism," emphasized to the press the stark differences between what he had in mind and what had occurred under the discredited aegis of the UTW.[3] Describing him as "the Moses who [led] a notorious sweatshop industry out of the industrial jungles into the open clearing of fair trade and wage practices," the labor-friendly *Daily News Record* reported that Hillman's selection as head of the TWOC had "somewhat eased tension . . . in those portions of the industry that are still hostile to Francis Gorman . . . because of the latter's technique in the strike of 1934." Noting that his approach "has been one of conciliation and roundtable discussion rather than to precipitate violent action," the writer confidently guessed, "Under the guidance of Mr. Hillman it may be expected that the development of organization plans will proceed on a quiet and businesslike basis."[4] *Business Week,* which also noted the employers' "extreme distaste" for the UTW because of the 1934 strike, insisted that "mill managers and businesses in all industry could gain some assurance" from Hillman's stated preference for "a calmer, more businesslike line" when it came to worker organization. Claiming that the TWOC, under such reasonable stewardship, would be reluctant to press demands that might do serious injury to a long fragile industry finally on its way to recovery, the *Business Week* writer appreciatively quoted Hillman,

> I never have been much of a believer in the idea of setting up demands at a high peak to use in bargaining for one's real objective, which may be lower. We are trying to make our honest appraisal of what the employer can pay, and from that expect to reach a fair estimate of what labor should receive.[5]

Hillman's expressed devotion to a less adversarial strategy, however, was not merely for public consumption. Keenly aware that strikes had done little to advance the cause of worker organization in the textile industry, Hillman believed that such head-on confrontations were more likely to stiffen employer resistance and to scare off already wary millhands than to achieve the TWOC's ends. Winning decent wages and working conditions and establishing workers' bargaining rights had to be the essential aims of the TWOC campaign, but Hillman plainly hoped that those goals could be achieved by persuading mill owners of "the special advantages of stabilization and fair competition" that industrywide organization would confer.[6] Strikes and other direct actions might be necessary when nothing less drastic would bring the most obdurate employers to terms, but, in general, Hillman believed that the welfare of textile workers and the interests of the TWOC would be best served by relying, first, on the power of persuasion and, then, on the enforcement powers that a sympathetic National Labor Relations Board was prepared to wield on behalf of labor's rights under the Wagner Act.[7]

Given the diversity and geographical sprawl of the textile industry, ensuring that his trade-union philosophy informed the actions of the several hundred organizers to whom the TWOC's initial fortunes were entrusted could easily have been a problem for Hillman. For that reason, he proceeded to place his own Amalgamated subordinates in charge of five of the eight regions (and ninety-six subregions) into which the TWOC's organizing efforts were ultimately divided. Indeed, except for New Jersey, which was assigned to Carl Holderman, a veteran hosiery workers' leader with exceptional knowledge of both the labor and political scenes in the state, every other state outside the South where the TWOC was active was placed under the control of an Amalgamated official.[8] "Fundamentally," one insider later confided, "this was the Amalgamated taking over the organization work lock, stock, and barrel."[9]

Only in the South, a region Hillman tended to regard as inaccessible to genuine understanding except by those born into its singular folkways and steeped in its primordial mysteries, was the Amalgamated's influence, so prevalent elsewhere, kept to a minimum. Hillman and his circle strongly believed that southern-born organizers could best rebut the inevitable charges of practiced union haters in the region that the TWOC was a vehicle for Communist-inspired Yankees and Jews intent on breaching the industrial order and cultural sovereignty of the Christian South through seductive appeals to guileless millhands. Moreover, Hillman was persuaded that if the TWOC was to have any success in convincing the most enlightened southern mill owners that collective bargaining might actually benefit their industry by helping to stabilize it, the message of responsible unionism's salutary promise had to be delivered by a southerner whose personal stature and respectability enhanced its credibility.[10]

To head the region designated as the Lower South, a vast area that encompassed the Carolinas, Georgia, Alabama, Mississippi, Louisiana, Texas, and all but the northeast tip of Tennessee—in short, the whole of the critically important southern cotton textile industry—Hillman found a southerner of requisite reputation and regard in the person of A. Steve Nance. Perhaps, the best-known and most respected labor leader in Georgia, Nance seemed to possess just the right combination of southern breeding, personal esteem, and political acumen necessary to project the image of responsible and constructive purpose that Hillman and others thought would be most conducive to the TWOC's success in the South. He was president of the Georgia State Federation of Labor and a luminary in Atlanta's civic firmament. He had recently declined appointment as the city's postmaster and had had a public school named in his honor in 1936. A longtime craft unionist, he had sided with the CIO in challenging the AFL. And, if Hillman was correct in his assessment of the special leadership that a union breakthrough in the South required, Nance and Franz Daniel, the young southern-born, college-educated Amalgamated organizer assigned to be his second in command, admirably personified the TWOC's emergent promise.[11] "With surprising unanimity," one commentator on the southern labor scene claimed, "employers in many fields agree that *if* unions are inevitable they prefer A. Steve Nance to lead them."[12]

To manage the TWOC's affairs in the Upper South, an area that took in Virginia, West Virginia, Kentucky, northeastern Tennessee, and the Asheville region of North Carolina, and was home to much of the U.S. synthetic fiber industry, Hillman chose John Peel. Unlike Steve Nance, he was a tested, if not unusually accomplished, veteran of Piedmont textile struggles and the only high-ranking UTW functionary to be awarded a leadership position in the new regime. Once a carpenter whose prominence in the central labor council of Durham, N.C., brought him to the UTW's attention, Peel's accomplishments as the union's chief southern representative had been anything but impressive.[13] At the time of the TWOC takeover, the UTW reported a larger dues-paying membership in Oregon, a state in which textile manufacturing was a barely detectable presence, than it could claim in either North or South Carolina, two states that, together, accounted for a majority of the 450,000 mill-hands the southern cotton textile industry was employing in the spring of 1937, according to the *Textile Bulletin*.[14] Yet, given Hillman's conviction that a southern pedigree was essential to effectively representing the TWOC in the South, Peel commended himself for a leadership position despite his lackluster record. By naming him director of the Upper South, however, Hillman did ensure that Peel would not be active in cotton textiles, the branch on which he had earlier concentrated.

Hillman's faith in the presumably unique capacity of native southerners both to persuade and reassure their kinsmen also led the TWOC to enlist the participation of regional activists and luminaries with little or no trade union experience. Lucy Randolph Mason, an otherwise proper southern lady who counted Eleanor Roosevelt among her personal friends and the scions of Virginia's most illustrious families among her direct ancestors, signed on as the TWOC's chief publicist in the South early in the organizing drive. Personally recommended to Hillman by John L. Lewis, who believed that she could help to soften the CIO's image in the South and explain textile unionism's benefits in an accent familiar and soothing to southern ears, the ubiquitous "Miss Lucy" would become one of the TWOC's most visible and indefatigable champions.[15]

An equally unlikely recruit to the cause was the Reverend D. Witherspoon Dodge, another southern-bred activist who could count at least one signer of the Declaration of Independence among his forebears. Expelled from the Presbyterian ministry by the Piedmont Presbytery for believing too ardently in "a God of love, mercy and justice" and not ardently enough in the "monstrous, outmoded doctrines" of predestination to Hell and everlasting punishment to which his outraged accusers subscribed, Dodge was ultimately invited by the more liberal-minded members of the Central Congregational Church of Atlanta to resume his pastoral career as their spiritual guide. A self-styled "rebel" who believed that his own Christian convictions found a truer embodiment in the temporal preachings of Socialist missionaries like Scott Nearing than in the timeless orthodoxies of mainstream southern Protestantism, Dodge was only too happy, one of his detractors scornfully observed, "to stick his snout in the trough of the CIO" when the TWOC came to Dixie.[16] Other southern activists, such as Myles Horton, co-founder of the Highlander Folk School in the mountains of East Tennessee, traveled a shorter, more direct route to the TWOC. Already committed "to educate industrial and agricultural laborers to exert greater control over their jobs and to build a new society embodying the ideals of democracy, brotherhood, and justice," Horton thought that by accepting Nance's invitation to assist the TWOC campaign he was merely pursuing his chosen mission in life along a slightly different path. And while his brief career with the TWOC left him doubting that unions were, in the end, any more eager to accommodate militant southern workers than employers had been, Horton nevertheless proved himself to be an organizer of truly exceptional skills.[17]

Although Hillman had suggested early on that southern cotton mills would be the primary focus of the TWOC's organizing efforts,[18] by the time the drive actually got under way, in late March, other regions and other branches of the industry received as much attention, or more.[19] As events would soon demonstrate, whatever plans the TWOC had were subject to expedient alteration. From the outset, the vitality of the drive in any particular region or industry branch was less a function of strategic dictates than of the effectiveness of the opposition it met. In part, the campaign's uneven progress was also a consequence of its decentralized leadership. However much Hillman had hoped to use the earlier organizing drive in the steel industry as a model for his enterprise in textiles, he soon concluded that the industry's product and geographical diversity rendered his preference for centralized direction and leadership largely irrelevant. The textile campaign was, in fact, several campaigns, which, while linked by common allegiance to centralized policy guidelines and the same broad institutional goals, proceeded at their own pace under the leadership of regional directors whose perceptions and approaches tended to vary greatly. In addition, Hillman's sense of the South as a region too unique to be approached as others would be, gave the TWOC campaign a somewhat schizoid character. At the first meeting of the TWOC, on March 19, Hillman had decreed, "considerable autonomy was to be granted to the South to permit it to develop a program adaptable to southern needs." Lower South regional director Steve Nance assured the committee that "the possibilities for organization were very good" in his region but were likely to be realized only if the campaign was conducted in a patient and conciliatory manner and if "cooperation with industry to stabilize it was . . . the prevailing motif."[20]

Moreover, because it had relatively few strategic targets—mills whose policies and practices exerted industrywide influence in labor matters—cotton textiles left TWOC strategists to guess where, initially, organizing pressures might be most profitably applied. "The cotton textile industry, instead of being a compact cartel in the hands of a comparatively few great companies," the *Daily News Record* noted, "is sprawled out, in 1,200 units, all over the country." And because the TWOC was "well aware of this situation with respect to cotton textiles, . . . it may . . . proceed on a much less spectacular basis than was done in automobile and steel."[21]

An industry of baffling diversity, cotton textiles exhibited few characteristics that were common to all its constituents. Although by 1937 predominantly a southern industry, its surviving northern outposts, especially in New England, retained sufficient vitality and market force in fine goods and other specialty production to defy attempts to explain cotton textiles in the context of a representative manufacturing culture. Few significant commonalities existed—in patterns of ownership, scale of operation, degree of technological sophistication, or modernity of management practices. In cotton textiles, large, modern, technologically advanced mills employing thousands of workers and reflecting a managerial sophistication that compared favorably with the leading manufacturers in America's other mass industries existed alongside small, independently owned and operated mills whose creaking mechanical obsolescence, fetid Dickensian ambience and feudatory paternalism were affronts to modern manufacturing.[22]

The challenges presented by the daunting diversity and geographic vastness of the southern cotton textile industry were compounded by mill owners' vehement and unyielding resistance to what one called "that unholy, foreign-born, Socialistic, despotic thing known as labor unionism." The "apparently irresistible force" that the TWOC had promised to unleash was on a collision course with what seemed an equally imposing "immovable object." "The average outsider," J. H. Marion wrote in the *Christian Century,*

> can scarcely realize with what suspicion, fear, and resentment the ruling classes in the South have regarded the whole labor union movement. Unions to many good people are nothing but rackets, and their leaders an unscrupulous crowd of gangsters. On all sides one can hear men speaking as if John L. Lewis had horns and a forked tail . . . The CIO may yet discover that, compared with southern textiles, steel was a playful kitten![23]

Despite the success of the textile industry in general and its southern branches in particular in defending the sovereignty of management against union encroachments, the threat posed by the CIO-sponsored TWOC was one that mill owners nearly everywhere regarded with special apprehension. Unlike the old UTW, which had so often been unwitting accomplice in its own inefficacy, the TWOC had money, manpower, competent leadership, and the uncommonly potent momentum conferred by recent CIO triumphs. It also expected to benefit from increasing public sympathy with labor's cause and a robust business climate that threatened to make opposition to unionism more costly for employers than it had been when a depressed economy made strikes a less fearsome prospect. The threat the TWOC posed was familiar, but the unprecedented force behind it gave even the most imperious mill owners reason to fear that their mastery over labor was jeopardized as never before.

That employers in all branches of the industry regarded the TWOC as a credible menace was immediately evident. Almost before the ink was dry on the agreement that brought the TWOC into being, mill owners across the industry suddenly expressed enthusiasm for voluntary wage increases. Two of the carpet industry's largest companies, Mohawk and Bigelow-Sanford, acted on March 6 to blunt the TWOC's imminent appeals by announcing a 5-percent wage increase affecting 8,000 workers in upstate New York.[24] On the following day, the *New York Times* reported that southern cotton mill owners were verging on an equally surprising realization that a general wage increase now made a good deal of sense. It was, the *Times* added, "an admission which would not have been forthcoming" before the CIO turned its attention to textile workers.[25] On March 19, the date that Hillman said would mark the official start of the TWOC's organizing campaign, millhands up and down the Atlantic seaboard awoke to the glad tidings that their employers were suddenly volunteering to pay them more. New England cotton mill owners announced a 10-percent wage increase for more than a third of their 90,000 workers.[26] A day later, many more New England millhands, including the 25,000 employees of the American Woolen Company, the industry's dominant producer, benefited from the spirit of generosity sweeping through employers' ranks.[27]

Southern mill owners also found themselves in the grip of this fervent magnanimity. Employers in the Carolinas declared on the day before the TWOC drive officially began that they were boosting the wages of approximately 44,500 millhands by as much as 10 percent. Moreover, the *Charlotte Observer* claimed to have it on good authority from an official of the American Cotton Manufacturers Association that similar wage increases for all other southern millhands were a "definite prospect."[28] That prophesy gained credence nearly at once, when thousands of additional southern millhands, including the more than 18,000 workers employed by the giant Cannon Mills in Kannapolis, N.C., and the 5,200 employees of the Erwin Cotton Mills at Durham, learned they, too, were getting a wage increase.[29]

This enthusiasm for voluntary wage increases spread over most of the textile industry. Yet employers, asked whether this had had any connection to the imminent appearance of TWOC organizers at their mill gates, claimed to be at a loss to understand why either workers or the public should indulge such suspicions. Dr. Claudius Munchison, president of the Cotton Textile Institute, explained the wage increases as only the most recent reflection of his industry's abiding devotion to its workers' welfare. "We will not organize against the CIO threat," Munchison explained, "but we will concentrate action with respect to improved wages, shorter working hours, elimination of child labor, and establishment of fair trade practices."[30] Those closest to the scene, knew better. "Like a boy coming down with measles," one Piedmont correspondent observed,

> the southern textile industry has suddenly broken out with a rash of wage increases. The good grace with which many employers have succumbed to the ailment is awe-inspiring. Only a child, however, will believe that this widespread eruption is, by and large, the result of either prosperity or magnanimity. These southern cotton mill men don't have humanitarian fever; they have the jitters![31]

Although TWOC representatives insisted that millhands would not be fooled by such a transparent antiunion stratagem, the wage increases in nearly every branch of textiles were bound to make an already intimidating venture even more daunting. Organizers nearly everywhere soon discovered, however that the enthusiasm millhands harbored for the militant unionism the CIO symbolized was not much diminished by employers' efforts to buy them off. Their resolve confirmed that anger had come to outweigh fear in mill towns and villages from Maine to Alabama, but it was also helped along by a TWOC policy that allowed organizers to assure prospective union members that they would not begin paying dues until the new organization had won bargaining rights and negotiated a contract for them. Such a policy, which recognized the historic reluctance of underpaid textile workers to pay union dues, undoubtedly encouraged otherwise wary or skeptical millhands to support the TWOC. It also ensured, however, that gauging the TWOC's actual progress and true strength throughout its two-year campaign would be exceedingly difficult because of the disparity between the organization's impressive membership claims and its relatively paltry dues revenue.[32]

Still, considered in the light of textile unionism's history, the TWOC's initial results were nothing short of spectacular. Convinced that organizing the largest companies in each branch of textiles would help to establish patterns for the smaller firms to follow, the TWOC confronted the industry's heavyweights first, whenever possible.[33] In the rug and carpet industry, which employed approximately 25,000 workers, this meant going after Bigelow-Sanford, Mohawk, and Alexander Smith. In woolens and worsteds it meant launching an all-out effort in Lawrence, Mass., where the mills of the American Woolen and Pacific Woolen companies, were located. In the synthetic yarn industry, which employed more than 50,000 workers and where only Celanese employees in Cumberland, Md., were covered by a union contract, the TWOC targeted American Viscose, E. I. Du Pont, and Industrial Rayon.[34]

In cotton, both North and South, and in silk throwing and weaving, two crucially important branches of the textile industry that were less vulnerable to Hillman's follow-the-leader strategy, TWOC organizers took on large and small mills alike. In the northern cotton textile industry, where a generally receptive political climate, the CIO's expanding presence, and a lengthy, if not unbroken, tradition of union activity tended to facilitate organization, organizers found millhands eager to join the TWOC and mill owners sometimes less than adamant in their to opposition. To the extent that mill owners were amenable to Hillman's soothing contention that unionism and collective bargaining could bring order and equipoise to an industry notoriously deficient in both, they were, not surprisingly, in the North rather than in the South, in Massachusetts or Rhode Island rather than in Georgia or the Carolinas.[35]

As TWOC organizers took up their posts throughout the Piedmont during early April, they found that most southern millhands were as eager as their northern counterparts to hear the CIO's message. The bitter memory of the UTW's ignoble performance during the 1934 general strike, and a still evident residuum of fear from the widespread blacklisting that followed, may have disposed southern workers to think twice about the risking that renewed activism posed, but the relentless degradation attendant to mill work nourished a countervailing discontent that led TWOC organizers to conclude that past failures in the region did not preclude future successes. Indeed, in some cases, TWOC organizers reported, they found it harder to restrain southern millhands than to incite them. Both Myles Horton and Paul Christopher, a young college-educated southerner who had seen earlier service with the UTW, claimed that they spent nearly as much time in the early days of the campaign talking millhands out of impetuous strike actions as they did talking them into joining the TWOC.

Piedmont mill owners who had smugly contended that they knew the minds of southern workers as well as they knew their own, still insisted in public that TWOC "agitators" would be met with the same resistance and hostility from millhands that their UTW predecessors had. In private, however, a less sanguine mood prevailed. "Most of the manufacturers came originally from the same red hills as those from which their workers came," southern journalist Jonathan Daniels observed. "They know a secret which they have steadily and loudly denied: they know there is no dependable docility in their cousins at the looms.[36]

For the most part, however, the pace of the TWOC campaign in southern cotton textiles was slow. Nance's strong conviction that enduring success was best achieved by educating southern mill owners and the local power elite that reinforced them to the TWOC's ultimately benign purposes meant that the blustering and confrontational approach organizers used elsewhere was less common in the South. Moreover, with Nance headquartered in Atlanta, remote from the geographical center of the cotton textile industry, TWOC efforts in the Lower South generally lacked the dynamism that appeared to exist where regional directors were in the thick of the fray. Finally, of course, the pace of the TWOC campaign in the South was influenced by the extraordinary opposition it encountered. In standing against unionism, an idea that many southerners were taught from birth to regard as among the most noxious and ungodly ever spawned by miscreant Yankee culture, Piedmont mill owners were entitled by tradition and mutual enmity to assistance from nearly every institutional force in the region, commercial, political, legal, religious, educational, fraternal and civic. Members of the South's social elite might, under normal circumstances, have found it distasteful to stand shoulder to shoulder with hooded Klansman or ill-bred evangelists, but, when unionism threatened to intrude upon the insular "neofeudal" order that sustained cotton textiles in the region, these otherwise diverse and estranged elements of southern society were capable of a solidarity that bridged the widest divides. TWOC activists caught up in the enthusiasm of the moment might fervently believe, as one of their well-wishers prophesied in the spring of 1937, that "even in the insulated South the tide of unionism is coming in," but most soon discovered that union opposition in the Piedmont was built to withstand the mightiest surges.[37]

Given the astonishing successes the TWOC claimed almost at once, however, optimists had reasons to believe that even the South would be hard pressed to resist unionism's advance. Before the drive was a week old TWOC officials were not only reporting impressive gains in membership but also claiming to have wrenched both recognition and contracts from overmatched employers. Sidney Hillman triumphantly informed the press, on March 29, that the 800 employees of the Schlegel Manufacturing Company in Rochester, N.Y., a maker of trim fabrics used in automobiles, had signed a TWOC contract that included provisions for a 15 percent wage increase and a closed shop. He claimed that equally "remarkable results" were being reported by TWOC officials from New England to Georgia.[38] Other TWOC spokesmen reported at the same time that concentrated organizing drives among workers in both major and minor branches of the textile industry were winning converts by the thousands.[39] Before the drive was a month old, Hillman was claiming that, "with a minimum of strikes," the TWOC had won collective bargaining agreements covering more than 60,000 textile workers.[40]

Of course, not every gain to which Hillman laid claim in the early weeks of the drive was, strictly speaking, the result of TWOC efforts. In some branches of the industry, most notably full-fashioned hosiery and dyeing and finishing, independent organizing campaigns were already well under way when his forces took the field. Yet because both the American Federation of Hosiery Workers and the Federation of Dyers, Finishers, Printers, and Bleachers of America were nominal participants in the broader campaign, the TWOC was able to count their triumphs as its own. The impressive membership and bargaining gains won through a series of highly effective strikes by hosiery workers in nearly two dozen mills in and around Reading, Pa., and by the dyers and finishers in several dye shops and cleaning plants in northern New Jersey owed little or nothing to TWOC actions, but they nevertheless helped to inflate its reputation.[41]

For the most part, however, the stunning advances made by workers in various branches of the textile industry from early April onward were directly attributable to the TWOC's exertions. TWOC organizers were a highly visible presence in every important textile center in New England almost as soon as the campaign began. And, while the industry's southward migration had long since dimmed their once commanding preeminence as centers of textile manufacturing in the United States, the legendary milltowns of New England—Fall River, New Bedford, Lawrence, Providence, Pawtucket—were again pulsating with promise as fervent TWOC organizers fanned the dying embers of textile unionism back to full candescence. Likewise, in upstate New York, TWOC organizers quickly succeeded both in breathing new life into moribund remnants of the UTW and in winning new converts to unionism. Within only a few weeks of the campaign's beginning, nearly every carpet mill in the state was under siege by insistent TWOC forces.[42] In New Jersey and Pennsylvania, where vigorous organizing campaigns by the dyers' and hosiery workers' federations had already fostered a climate of labor activism, the TWOC courted every other type of wage earner employed in the region's diverse conglomeration of knitting, silk, rayon, woolen, worsted, and carpet mills.[43]

In the Upper South, home to much of the synthetic yarn industry and to the Riverside and Dan River cotton mills in southern Virginia, the TWOC campaign benefited from the success of Hillman's attempts to bring his personal stature to bear in persuading dubious employers of collective bargaining's hidden virtues. The synthetic yarn industry, the newest, fastest-growing, and most oligopolistic branch of textiles, had long been regarded as the likeliest candidate for organization from above (that is, union recognition resulting from a prior accommodation reached through top-level negotiations between Hillman and a corporate counterpart). The promise of his widely touted personal diplomacy in textile unionism's behalf was handsomely redeemed in mid-April, when Hillman announced that he had concluded a collective bargaining agreement with the American Viscose Company, the nation's leading producer of rayon yarn and employer of over a third of the synthetic industry's more than 50,000 workers. With the American Viscose victory to inspire them, Hillman added, TWOC organizers could reasonably expect that achieving their next objective, bringing the Du Pont Company's 9,000 rayon workers under union contract, "would not be difficult."[44]

Even in the deep South, where a late start and Steve Nance's innate caution combined to slow the TWOC's progress, union enthusiasts had little difficulty finding signs of the campaign's imminent success. Early reports filtering into Nance's Atlanta headquarters from organizers taking up their posts in the Carolinas during April suggested that millhands seemed eager to embrace the TWOC. Union supporters were also cheered by the evident apprehension of southern cotton mill owners, whose scramble to institute across-the-board wage increases fueled speculation that the TWOC already had them on the run.[45] Finally, with the announcement, on April 12, of the Supreme Court decision upholding the Wagner Act, TWOC activists were emboldened to conclude that not even southern mill owners could afford to be so bold as to ignore the now indisputable mandates of federal law. It was increasingly apparent, one sympathetic southern observer declared, that "the tide of union-ism is coming in, and most employers know it. The wiser ones already are preparing to make their peace with the inevitable. Those who oppose the trend will look like children naively trying to sweep back the ocean with a broom."[46]

While the TWOC's ultimate capacity to achieve its announced purposes remained to be proven in the late spring and early summer of 1937, it could nevertheless claim to have propelled the cause of unionism, both qualitatively and quantitatively, well beyond the farthest advance of any earlier organizing effort in the textile industry. What Sidney Hillman had promised to accom-plish when UTW leaders meekly ceded him control over textile unionism's future a few weeks earlier was still a very long way from being fully realized, but certainly enough had been gained to sustain the hope that an industry-wide victory was within the TWOC's grasp. Yet, in transforming the culture of textile unionism, Hillman could claim major accomplishments well before the ultimate magnitude of the TWOC's success was known. Both the antiquated structure and the irresolute ethos of the old order had been unceremoniously swept aside by the TWOC's relentless assumption of jurisdictional primacy. It was his intention, Hillman confided to disaffected union activists in New Bed-ford and Fall River as the TWOC campaign got under way, that the UTW would be "practically dissolved" as the new regime took charge. As one organizing success followed another throughout the spring, the old order had, indeed, faded into a state of musty superannuation. Moreover, as Hillman sent the UTW shuffling toward the sidelines, he also discarded most of its former leaders by decreeing that "merit rather than former affiliation" would dictate who assumed leadership roles within the TWOC.[47] And while UTW president Frank Gorman was permitted to hang around long enough to create the impression of a seamless transition from the old order to the new, by the time the TWOC campaign went into high gear Hillman had safely packed him off to Europe to represent the interests of American textile workers at an interna-tional conference.

The desire of Hillman and his inner circle to create the impression that the UTW had been scrapped, rather than merely supplanted, reflected their under-standable concern that the TWOC would have a hard enough time organizing textile workers without having to lug its predecessor's weighty baggage. The CIO's agreement with the UTW gave the TWOC exclusive authority to issue new union charters, and clearly anticipated that, over time, those locals char-tered under the old regime's now defunct auspices would eagerly trade in an affiliation forever redolent of failure for one that emitted the bracing aroma of success. Sometimes, in their zeal to assert the TWOC's preeminence or to mag-nify its accomplishments, Hillman and his lieutenants verged on proclaiming that textile unionism had hardly existed before their own selfless exertions in its service. When James Starr, the UTW's veteran Secretary-Treasurer, politely asked Hillman to retract a claim published in *The Advance* that the TWOC had "practically nothing" to build on when it entered the textile arena, his appeal was casually dismissed.[48] Plainly, those among the TWOC's leadership whose opinions really mattered were united in the conviction that their cause was better served by burying the UTW than by praising it.

There is little doubt that most of the credit for the TWOC's success during the spring and summer of 1937 properly belongs to leaders who had no previous affiliation with the UTW. Almost without exception, Hillman had entrusted both strategic and day-to-day control of the organizing campaign either to trusted assistants drawn from the ranks of the Amalgamated or to proven leaders recruited from the independently led hosiery and dyers' federations. Even in the Upper South, an area under the nominal authority of UTW veteran John Peel, Hillman's people dominated at critical junctures. For example, when Hillman decided that American Viscose would be the TWOC's first organizing target in the synthetic yarn industry, it was not Peel, but Philadelphia-area director Charles Weinstein, an Amalgamated leader, who took charge of the campaign.[49]

Hillman and his followers were bound to acknowledge that the TWOC's progress among millhands in the North was due, at least in some part, to the tradition of worker activism that the UTW had fitfully endeavored to sustain in the region over the preceding 35 years. Their preferred explanation, however, stressed the commanding example of the CIO and the compelling force of the "new unionism." Certainly, the advantages that derived from the CIO's sponsorship of the TWOC, both in terms of the broad range of support it afforded and the uncommon fervor it excited among millhands across the textile industry, enhanced the likelihood of its success as no other affiliation could have in the late 1930s. The willingness of big companies such as American Viscose in synthetic yarns, J.& P. Coats in the thread industry, and Bigelow-Sanford in carpets and rugs to recognize and bargain with the TWOC well before it had actually proven its mettle attested to the CIO's formidable reputation. Hillman had also used his own special talent for conciliatory bargaining to good advantage, and, whenever it served the TWOC's purpose, he invited the personal intercession of the CIO's ultimate force, John L. Lewis. In 1937, more than any other labor leader in America, Lewis instilled hope and inspired courage in industrial workers and fear and loathing in industrialists.[50]

Encouraged by the mounting evidence of industrial unionism's surging might and mollified by assurances that they would not begin to pay dues to the TWOC until its efforts on their behalf had begun to pay off, millhands continued to respond enthusiastically to the entreaties of organizers during the early summer of 1937. To be sure, the disparity between total union membership and the number of millhands actually covered by collective bargaining agreements continued to cast doubt on the campaign's true progress, but the TWOC seemed well on its way to matching or surpassing CIO gains in both the auto and steel industries. Whether blaring their message from sound trucks that cruised workers' neighborhoods or taking it to one millhand at a time through house-to-house canvassing, the hundreds of organizers to whom the work of building a textile union fell found that their promises of higher wages, shorter hours, and an end to the hated stretch-out were ever more eagerly seized upon as the faith spread that the TWOC could actually redeem them. As the *New York Times* observed, when employers, particularly those in the North, saw the enthusiasm with which their employees welcomed the TWOC's overtures, some concluded that continued resistance to collective bargaining was no longer a viable option. Such resignation was especially common among those mill owners who had also concluded that the legal mandates of the Wagner Act could no longer be ignored.[51]

Where the TWOC found employers still resistant to their employees' expressed desire for union representation, it promptly petitioned the National Labor Relations Board to bring its newly validated authority to bear. In keeping with Hillman's dictum that strikes should be employed only as a tactic of last resort, the TWOC campaign generally proceeded without the diverting pyrotechnics that accompanied other CIO drives. Aroused millhands proved willing, and often eager, to strike when circumstances left them no other option. Hillman's determination to convince employers that collective bargaining could be achieved in the textile industry without a return to the bad old days of unbridled hostilities, however, made him reluctant to sanction extreme measures. Congratulating employers and workers alike on their success in negotiating contracts at two Pennsylvania silk-throwing mills without resort to strikes or strike threats, Hillman declared, "These agreements clearly show that there is an orderly way out of an intolerable condition in the industry, and that the chaos and demoralization with which the industry is beset can be solved only by common sense." Such examples of peaceful dealings, Hillman insisted, offered proof "that enlightened managements are increasingly realizing that stabilization of the silk industry cannot be achieved without the cooperation of labor."[52]

Yet when strike action proved unavoidable, Hillman did not hesitate to deploy the full resources of the TWOC in the cause of victory. Strikes occurred sporadically throughout the initial stages of the campaign, and in early August Hillman authorized what quickly developed into a very bitter but highly effective industrywide strike to bring vehemently antiunion silk and rayon manufacturers to heel. Conducted mainly in New Jersey and Pennsylvania, the silk and rayon throwing and weaving centers, the two-week-long strike involving more than 30,000 workers in approximately 600 mills served, as the TWOC's official history later observed, "to dissipate much of the resistance to textile organization" in a branch of the industry "which previously had stopped all union efforts."[53]

The silk strike, which helped make it possible to bring most of the industry's 60,000 workers under union contracts, was easily the most impressive of the sixty or so the TWOC conducted against obdurate employers during its organizing campaign. Where employers resolved to resist the TWOC at all costs, however, strikes, even when vigorously prosecuted, proved decidedly less effective. The long and costly strikes that the TWOC fought against the Industrial Rayon Company's plants in Covington, Va., and Cleveland, Oh., failed to gain the organization's objectives. They also made it disturbingly clear that Hillman was mistaken in predicting that the union's earlier agreement with American Viscose virtually guaranteed similar successes in its dealings with the synthetic yarn industry's other major producers.[54]

Yet, in the end, strikes, whether won or lost, were never particularly revealing measures of the TWOC's vitality or progress. Hillman's announced aim from the beginning was "to avoid industrial strife," and, where circumstances permitted, the TWOC sought to go over and around barriers rather than to smash through them. That tendency was reinforced by the happy coincidence of the TWOC beginning its drive in textiles almost at the precise moment that the Supreme Court validated the NLRB's authority to enforce the Wagner Act. As a result, whenever TWOC organizers confronted mill owners who refused to abide by the dictates of federal law, they were far more likely to call upon the authority of the NLRB than to take matters into their own hands. The number of board-ordered representation elections the TWOC instigated mounted steadily as the campaign progressed and so did the frequency with which union officials sought NLRB sanctions against recalcitrant employers.

Beyond emphasizing the general point that the law was now on labor's side, the TWOC stressed its commitment to newly established NLRB procedures for the more specific purpose of reassuring employers and millhands alike that the legal machinery now in place to resolve industrial disputes meant that the destructive conflicts of the past were no longer either necessary or reasonable. By the end of September, when its drive was six months old, the TWOC proudly reported that it had decisively won 47 of the 53 representation elections the board had conducted in textiles. These elections, which covered more than 42,000 millhands in various branches of the industry, were eagerly touted by Hillman and others as hallmarks of a new era of American labor relations founded upon orderly, democratic procedures that promised to render recognition strikes increasingly obsolete.[55]

The impressive headway that the TWOC made in the previously impenetrable woolen and worsted industry was heralded by Hillman and other union functionaries as an especially instructive example of how otherwise overmatched millhands could profitably enlist the NLRB in their cause. The chronic inability of the UTW to gain even a modest foothold in Lawrence, the woolen industry's center, had nourished an impression that there were some bastions of antiunion resolve unlikely ever to be breached. That Hillman and his staff well understood both the actual and symbolic importance of Lawrence to the TWOC's future was made plain by their extraordinary efforts to succeed there. Throughout the summer, TWOC organizers, assisted at critical junctures not only by John L. Lewis but also by such sympathetic and influential political luminaries as New York City mayor Fiorello La Guardia, undertook what one described as "an unhurried, intensive, methodical drive" to transform Lawrence's once docile millhands into a militant legion. The union's ultimate goal, however, was to prepare its new recruits, not for an all-out battle against the American Woolen Company, the industry's dominant firm, but for an orderly march into NLRB-supervised polling places.[56] And when Hillman's strategy to overcome the fierce antiunionism of "the U.S. Steel of the woolen industry" was finally put to the test, it could hardly have achieved a more resounding affirmation. On September 15 and 16, millhands in the Wood and Ayer mills, the company's two largest operating units, voted 6,814 to 3,248 to designate the TWOC as exclusive bargaining agent for 11,000 of American Woolen's 28,000 workers. Such emphatic endorsements of unionism, a triumphant Hillman told reporters on September 17, would "unquestionably serve as a tremendous impetus to the organization of workers in other centers, and . . . lead to the establishment of collective bargaining machinery in the entire industry." In a mill town notorious for "industrial strife," Hillman observed, the former combatants had at last "chosen the road of orderly progress."[57]

Added to the impressive victories that it had already won in the carpet and rug, silk and rayon, synthetic yarn, knit goods, and northern cotton industries and in minor branches of textiles (plush and velvet, rope and cordage, jacquard silk, bag and jute, thread and bias binding), its success against a company of American Woolen's commanding stature in woolens and worsteds appeared to confirm the lavish claims of union publicists that the TWOC was not merely a new and improved UTW but a genuinely unprecedented organizational departure that ranked among the CIO's preeminent achievements. Moreover, its champions added, the TWOC had established itself in the textile industry without resort, except on a few occasions, to the extreme measures that CIO unions in other mass industries felt obliged to adopt. "Never," declared one sympathetic journalist, "was a great organizational drive prepared with more care than that of the TWOC. Never have so large a number of workers in an open-shop industry been organized with less fuss and less publicity."[58]

Just how much the TWOC had achieved during its first six months of effort was "officially" disclosed in early October, when Hillman reported on the textile campaign's progress at the national conference of the CIO in Atlantic City. For delegates eager to hear authoritative assurances that the CIO's campaign in textiles had compiled a record of success comparable to what had earlier been achieved in autos and steel and that further justified their perilous decision to rend the labor movement, Hillman did not disappoint. The textile industry, long one of America's darkest, most forbidding realms and a graveyard for so many of labor's noblest endeavors, was, he assured his audience, "organized today as it never has been in its history." More than a quarter of a million millhands, many employed by companies "never under union contract before," were now enjoying the blessings of organization. When the number of workers "who have expressed their desire to become members of the TWOC, who have expressed their loyalty to the CIO," was added to the number already working under union contracts, the organization's total membership exceeded 450,000. In some branches of the industry, he claimed, the TWOC's success was nearly complete. In the synthetic yarn industry, he reported, "more than 70 percent of the workers are covered by TWOC contracts. And in the rug and carpet field, a highly concentrated industry, about 80 percent of the workers are now under contract with the TWOC." In the silk-throwing and weaving industry, the only branch of textiles where the campaign relied on strikes to gain its ends, the TWOC shattered barriers that had blocked every previous union drive. In woolens and worsteds, where NLRB elections had been the strategy of choice, Hillman announced that progress in preliminary negotiations left him "confident that in a short time we shall be able to announce a sole collective bargaining agreement with the American Woolen Company."

In short, Hillman insisted, the TWOC was well on its way to becoming a cornerstone of industrial unionism and a resounding testament to the wisdom of the CIO's decision to follow its own course. "Now, without going into too great detail, which would take too much of your time, I can say, as Chairman of the TWOC, that our record is one of the most encouraging of the drives undertaken by the CIO." Furthermore, he confidently declared, "there is no reason in my mind that if the CIO will carry on, and I am sure it will, . . . we will bring about a complete organization of this great field."

Although his purpose was to emphasize just how much the CIO had already realized from its heavy investments in textile unionism, Hillman could not ignore the whispered doubts of some CIO leaders and members about the TWOC's ultimate prospects. He was acutely aware that the cost of the campaign—close to a million dollars in its first six months—was bound to trouble some, even though his own union had borne more than half the total expense to date. Moreover, the not unreasonable tendency of outsiders to view the TWOC's record in the all-important southern cotton industry as the truest measure of its progress and best indicator of its future prospects left Hillman no choice except to comment on at least a few of the campaign's less heartening aspects.

He acknowledged that the organizing drive in textiles had been costly, but was quick to point out that the expense was not disproportionate to the extraordinary magnitude of the task at hand. It was well to remember, he told the delegates, that what the TWOC achieved conferred benefits "for the millions of workers in all industries, and not alone for the 1,300,000 workers in the textile industry." The TWOC, he added, had adopted a financial plan that guaranteed that it could "carry this program through without embarrassment" for another six months, and that John L. Lewis and the United Mine Workers had demonstrated their continuing faith by pledging $200,000 in additional support.

Whenever possible, Hillman preferred to document the textile campaign's progress by citing the quantifiable gains that his trade union brethren most readily appreciated. In making a case for the TWOC's advances in the South, however, he was forced to substitute articles of faith for hard evidence. Reciting the obligatory litany of special horrors attendant to union activity in the "Bourbon" South, Hillman nevertheless claimed that the TWOC's expanding presence in the region meant that it was now a matter of "when, not if, the 400,000 workers in the South will be organized." There was no doubt, he conceded, that the South would be the definitive test of the TWOC's viability. Nor was there any question, he added, that breaching the political, economic, legal, religious, and social power structure that reinforced employer control in the Piedmont and allaying the fear and suspicion that so often discouraged worker activism were absolute prerequisites to securing collective bargaining. Even so, Hillman insisted, the future was bright. Despite the beatings and shootings, the illegal jailings, the terroristic depredations of Klansmen, the hysterical slanders of overheated editorialists, the fevered harangues of rabid preachers, the TWOC had endured and become a force that the textile South could not long resist. "We have contracts signed in the South, and we have, in addition, over 130,000 pledge cards," he declared. "Our drive will shatter the opposition in the South."[59]

Given the keen desire created by its escalating competition with the AFL to trumpet the "good news" of industrial unionism's relentless advance, the CIO had no more interest in hearing a candid assessment of the TWOC's progress than Hillman had in offering one. The nation's four-year-old economic recovery was rapidly running out of steam. CIO drives in autos and steel were backtracking in the face of fanatical opposition from Ford and the "little steel" companies. With a widening circle of its constituents anxious for fresh assurances that they had committed the sin of dual unionism in a righteous cause, the CIO was disposed to accept Hillman's rosy appraisal at face value.

In truth, the TWOC's progress during its first six months of operation was not nearly as encouraging as Hillman's report suggested and fell far short of validating his bold claim that the CIO's representative in the textile industry would soon join its mainstays in autos and steel as a foundation stone of the new industrial union movement in the United States. Hillman was plainly justified in asserting that the TWOC's accomplishments had propelled textile unionism to new heights, but the generally low standards of performance set by labor's previous efforts in the industry left the true significance of his claim open to interpretation. What the TWOC had achieved, or was on the verge of achieving, in synthetic yarns, silk, carpets and rugs, woolens and worsteds, and several minor industry branches constituted unprecedented advances, but even by its own reckoning the organization's record after six months disclosed at least as many reasons for concern as for optimism.

Of the more than 250,000 millhands reported by Hillman to be working under union contracts, nearly 60,000 were covered by agreements that had been in place before the TWOC appeared on the textile scene. Approximately 200,000 workers had been brought under contract by the TWOC over the preceding six months, but more than 50,000 actually owed their new bargaining rights to the mainly independent exertions of the semiautonomous American Federation of Hosiery Workers and the Dyers Federation. In the end, after credit was apportioned where it was actually due, the TWOC had alone won bargaining rights for fewer than 150,000 millhands. Moreover, the millhands continued to resist paying union dues, despite the more responsible outlook that the TWOC ardently sought to inculcate among its members. Only half of the millhands working under union contracts as of early October were actually paying dues, a fact that helped to explain why the TWOC continued to rely so heavily on the financial support of outsiders, despite its claims of success. Apparently in anticipation of the problem, TWOC negotiators made the check-off, the deduction of union dues by employers, a bargaining priority, but only slightly more than 11 percent of the contracts they negotiated included such a provision.

Also revealing of the TWOC's fragile health was the unevenness of its progress. As impressive as the organization's gains had been in some branches of the industry, in cotton goods, the sector employing by far the largest number of workers, its record was conspicuously unimpressive. In six months, the TWOC had won bargaining rights for fewer than 10,000 cotton mill workers. It was true, as Hillman claimed, that tens of thousands of cotton millhands had signed union pledge cards, but the promise of future gains could not erase the sobering fact that, in the branch of the industry most important to its future, textile unionism's viability remained very much in doubt.[60]

What was most troubling was that the overall weakness of the TWOC in the cotton goods industry attested to the dismal state of affairs in the South. That region had to be organized if textile unionism was ever to be more than a marginal enterprise. In his report to the CIO conference, Hillman, conceded that the South presented exceptional challenges but expressed confidence that the TWOC's deliberate, methodical approach to organizers the region, one as sensitive to the chronic apprehensions of mill owners as to the historic grievances of millhands, would ultimately produce results comparable to those achieved elsewhere.

Even those who agreed that the organizing drive was bound to proceed more slowly in the South had reason to wonder, after six months, just when the extraordinary effort the TWOC had undertaken in the region would finally begin to pay off. The more than one hundred organization assigned to the Lower South were as committed and resourceful as any who had served the cause of textile unionism in the Piedmont.[61] Nearly all born and raised in the South, many had first-hand knowledge of the dispiriting facts of mill village work and life. Despite Steve Nance's tendency to temporize sometimes, his organizers very successfully communicated the TWOC's promise to a skeptical audience. The number of Piedmont millhands willing to sign union pledge cards, though nowhere near the 100,000 that Nance exuberantly claimed before the southern drive was even a month old,[62] did grow fast enough to allay some TWOC officials' fear that the legacy of bitterness and despair resulting from the UTW's fumbling efforts in the region might prove insurmountable. By the TWOC's own calculations (which tended to understate the campaign's progress because of the lag in reporting from remote areas), 65,032 millhands in the Lower South had signed pledge cards by early August.[63] Clearly, the willingness of so many millhands to cast their lot with the TWOC, and in doing so to risk mill owners' retribution, was compelling evidence of their genuine enthusiasm for union organization. It was also the case, however, that millhands were often willing to pledge allegiance to the union because no dues would be collected until binding agreements had been won. As one TWOC recruit explained, "They ain't askin' no dues—not a dime—and they say they won't ask for nothing until they git us something, so I guess it's oke with me and I'll join the CIO."[64]

From the beginning, however, the attitude prevailed that the South was a region unto itself where organizing tactics must be less direct and forceful than those employed elsewhere. Gauging the drive's progress in the Piedmont would also be more difficult. While, in other regions, organizing efforts were measured "by the numbers," its actual progress in the Lower South could only be guessed at, even after six months.

As a consequence, TWOC leaders, Hillman and Nance among them, could fudge. They made ungrounded but sanguine assumptions though they lacked hard evidence. If conventional indices such as dues-paying membership or signed contracts with southern mill owners failed to confirm their upbeat assessments, TWOC spokesmen resorted to the platitude that their plodding educational work among workers and employers in the region would return real dividends soon enough. As Lucy Randolph Mason, the southern patrician who spoke for the TWOC there, naively reminded John L. Lewis in one of her earliest reports, unionism was an idea so fraught with emotion and ignorance in the South that "the approach to the whole subject has to be constructive and conciliatory."[65]

Finding solace in the blithe promise of certain victory, however, became increasingly difficult in the absence of concrete evidence that the TWOC's preparatory efforts in the region were finally paying off. Organizing the South, union officials were forced to conclude, was not going to get any easier, no matter how soothingly they portrayed unionism to mill owners, how artfully they described its mission to millhands, or how doggedly they worked to secure its institutional legitimacy through NLRB remedies.

Where Piedmont millhands welcomed TWOC organizers as their saviors, their devotion to the union cause tended to remain strong, even in the face of fierce employer opposition. It was also the case, however, that where cotton workers reacted to union organizers with hostility or indifference, they were not easily won over, regardless of the blandishments arrayed before them. "TWOC activities present a particular paradox," one friendly commentator said of the southern campaign. "In some mills progress is slow; workers are either antagonistic or apathetic. They are isolated in small company villages where they have been cut off from trade union traditions; they can only remember previous union defeats. In other mills, however, the response is too enthusiastic. Workers are eager for action, strikes if need be, yet the groundwork of union education has not been completed."[66]

The dilemma the TWOC faced was distressingly familiar to anyone acquainted with trade unionism's unhappy history in the textile industry. In an industry in which unions had consistently failed to achieve real strength and durability, millhands, both North and South, were generally disposed to wait for concrete proofs that the TWOC could deliver on its promises before taking the certain risks that union membership entailed. In both regions, most millhands who had held back early in the campaign did so because they wanted irrefutable evidence that the historic imbalance of power between bosses and workers in the textile industry was being corrected and that the new egalitarian order the TWOC proclaimed was being codified in collective bargaining agreements. In short, they wanted proof in advance of management's willingness to accept labor as an equal partner in deciding the terms and conditions of employment.

In New England and the Middle Atlantic states the apparent success of the labor movement in general, and of the CIO in particular, combined with the TWOC's early triumphs in several branches of the industry to provide the proofs that textile workers wanted before taking the union plunge. In the South, neither the labor movement in general nor the CIO in particular wielded significant power or commanded much respect. There, the TWOC was left to accomplish on its own what the combined forces of trade unionism were striving to achieve elsewhere. Steve Nance and his lieutenants belatedly acknowledged the severe drawbacks of the TWOC's isolation when they implored Hillman, in early October, to seek a commitment from the CIO to undertake a broader campaign of organization in the South. "It would be a tremendous aid to the TWOC campaign if an allied campaign in other industries could be more vigorously pressed," Lucy Mason told Hillman. In the absence of "strong CIO leadership in other fields," she gently complained, the TWOC was obliged to carry "most of the burden" of sustaining industrial unionism's credibility in the South. "A campaign on a wider front," she insisted, "would lessen the concentration of opposition to TWOC and give it moral support."[67]

While the additional material and moral support that a broader-based CIO campaign promised might have enhanced the TWOC's prospects in the South, on its own the organization faltered there. Despite all the upbeat talk and fond hopes, the unhappy truth of the TWOC's record in the Lower South was, as of the fall of 1937, that six months of unprecedented organizing efforts had yielded precious little. In Alabama, Georgia, and the Carolinas, where, organizers boasted, tens of thousands of millhands had signed pledge cards, the TWOC had negotiated only nine contracts covering slightly more than 5,200 workers.[68]

The extraordinary resources it had brought to bear notwithstanding, and despite the almost religious zeal with which its organizing staff had embraced the conviction that, this time, things would be different, the TWOC seemed no closer to unraveling the "mysteries" of the South than the UTW had been. Toward the end of 1937, those who had worked so hard to organize the Piedmont began to entertain the possibility that they might fail. Their apprehension was deepened by the inescapable realization that, unlike the UTW, whose failures in the region had been attributable to its chronic inadequacies—too little money, too few organizers, poor planning, inept leadership—the TWOC had come up short for reasons that raised serious doubts about the future of industrial unionism in the South.

The official public explanation of the TWOC's slow progress in the South continued to be that it was simply too soon to expect the seeds it had carefully planted there to flower. In private, however, the inquiry was more rigorous. Yet even a critical analysis of the planning and implementation of the organizing drive did not disclose obvious causes for its failure. More money and organizers might have helped in some places, but the TWOC's poor results in cotton textile centers in the Carolinas, where it had spared no expense, seemed to indicate that a fatter treasury and a larger staff would not have made much of a difference.

Indeed, what was most disturbing was that the campaign in the Lower South had failed, despite the TWOC's best efforts. Had its setbacks been traceable to particular administrative or operational deficiencies, union strategists could have taken corrective action. Instead, the campaign's overriding dilemma was that it needed the strong support of southern millhands to make real headway in the region, but it needed to make headway before it could hope to attract that support.

The belief, shared by Hillman and Nance, that "enlightened" southern mill owners might be won over to collective bargaining once the benefits of responsible unionism were made evident to them proved to be utterly mistaken. If Nance's gentlemanly rectitude and Lucy Mason's conciliatory press releases fostered a slightly less hostile attitude toward unionism in some elite circles of Piedmont society, nothing that they or anyone else did to paint the TWOC in a kindlier light had the desired effect. Even Miss Lucy, who prided herself on her thorough understanding of the "southern mind," finally confessed that she had grossly underestimated the visceral passion that fueled employer resistance to unionism in the Piedmont. "Even with my intimate knowledge of the South," she told John L. Lewis, "I did not know of the misunderstanding and hostility to the CIO and TWOC in this section." Under such circumstances, she admitted, the campaign's progress was likely to be "infinitely slow."[69]

As their northern counterparts had when they were thwarted by unyielding employer opposition, TWOC officials in the South sought refuge in the Wagner Act. Yet unlike most northern employers, who grudingly complied with the law and bargained in good faith when the outcome of NLRB elections appeared to leave them no other choice, most southern mill owners opted to defy the law rather than to obey it. "No device for slowing up the process of collective bargaining is left untried," Lucy Mason dejectedly informed Hillman.[70] Consequently, the TWOC's success in winning NLRB representation elections among southern millhands, which it did with impressive frequency during the latter half of 1937, led only to further stalemates as obdurate mill owners discovered that technical compliance with the law could be substituted for the real thing. In one of her frequent circulars to southern newspaper editors, Mason complained that mill owners were conspiring to deny textile workers the rights guaranteed to them under the Wagner Act by means of "adroitly staged sit-down strikes" at the bargaining table. "The technique," she explained, "is to obey the letter of the law and not refuse to negotiate, to negotiate week after week, month after month, accepting nothing of importance to the union, but never refusing to continue to negotiate." Such a tactic, she warned, provoked frustrated workers into extreme action. "If employers are not in good faith in negotiating contracts, workers have but one recourse—to withhold their labor. If they can obtain results no other way, they will be compelled to use this method."[71]

While she was always careful in her public comments to suggest that any strikes provoked by employers' tactics would be "unauthorized" or "spontaneous," a precaution that preserved the TWOC's conciliatory image, Miss Lucy's growing private conviction, as she expressed it to Hillman, was that "Only a few successful strikes will offset these tactics."[72] As a practical matter, however, strikes carried risks the TWOC was loath to take, both because of the lingering bitterness at the suffering occasioned by past failures and because a strike would give southern mill owners an excuse to mobilize every strikebreaking weapon in their arsenal. Hillman and Nance had committed to an organizing campaign designed to contradict the cant of southern mill owners and their allies that violence and coercion were the CIO's tactics of choice. The "great fear of a labor dictatorship" was, Lucy Mason acknowledged, something that "even the more liberal papers in the South" were inclined to take seriously as long as the CIO's reputation as a strike-prone movement remained in force.[73] So long as it was preoccupied with image, it seemed, the TWOC could not be the aggressive organization in the South that it was in the North. That did not mean, of course, that strikes were out of the question in the South—the TWOC conducted a very successful ten-day strike against the Hickory and Granite Falls Mills in Hickory, N.C., toward the end of October.

It did mean, however, that the resort to strike action in the region would be limited by the desire to deny critics the ammunition they needed to sustain their fear mongering.[74]

Even at the cautious, plodding pace that Nance and others adopted to allay the fears that unionism excited in the Piedmont, the TWOC might have accomplished more had the circumstances obtained during the initial stages of its organizing campaign endured. Yet, even before Hillman touted the drive's progress at the CIO's October conference, the TWOC's momentum was slowing noticeably. The substantial war chest that had sustained its early efforts was largely depleted by mid-August, and, despite John L. Lewis's pledge on September 1 to lend the TWOC an additional $200,000 over the following six months, its financial situation was growing increasingly precarious.[75] Both expenses and income peaked in August. During September, the TWOC was forced to cut its budget by 30 percent owing to a sharp decline in its revenues, the bulk of which continued to flow from the coffers of the Amalgamated Clothing Workers and other CIO unions. After six months, dues from its own membership still accounted for less than 40 percent of the TWOC's total operating income. Clearly, the TWOC still had a disturbingly long way to go before achieving financial self-sufficiency. As Hillman stood before his CIO colleagues in early October proudly reciting the textile campaign's accomplishments and confidently predicting new victories to come, the TWOC's total cash on hand amounted to $3,987.26.[76]

Because the TWOC's hand-to-mouth financing left it very little leeway when revenues began to shrink, Hillman had already begun to reduce expenses. At a meeting on September 1, the first convened by Hillman since the textile organizing drive began, he and other TWOC members met with regional directors and key organizers to receive what an official press release said would be "reports of progress."[77] Yet, Joe Mayo, a former United Mine Workers official who worked for the TWOC in Rhode Island, promptly reported to John L. Lewis's brother, Denny, that the chief purpose of the meeting was to implement immediate reductions in the cost of the textile campaign. According to Mayo, the meeting resulted in a decision to eliminate as many as 250 of the TWOC's 600 organizers.[78] The TWOC would continue to avail itself of the services of 100 organizers on loan from other organizations, but, by the first week of October, its own payroll had been slashed to well under 400.[79]

With new advances ever more difficult to achieve, especially as the TWOC's finances continued to deteriorate, the CIO's mighty drive to organize the American textile industry was in serious trouble. As bad as things were by early October, however, the already demoralized TWOC staff soon learned that they could get even worse. Before the month was out, the TWOC had suddenly lost its leader. Sidney Hillman, whose personal stature had invested the TWOC with authority and credibility that no labor leader other than John L. Lewis could have matched, fell seriously ill at the end of October and remained totally incapacitated until spring. Although Hillman had not, as he claimed, directed TWOC operations day to day, his illness and long convalescence in Florida left the direction of the textile drive to subordinates who lacked his encompassing perspective. Emil Rieve, an original member of the TWOC, was appointed acting chair in Hillman's absence. Yet, because Rieve remained in Philadelphia, where he continued to run the hosiery workers union, it was Solomon Barkin, the TWOC's self-designated research director, who, "without formal delegation or invitation," assumed responsibility for actual running the union's New York City headquarters until Hillman was well enough to resume those duties.[80]

As much as Hillman's absence and a depleted treasury exacerbated the TWOC's plight, it was the national economy's headlong descent into a withering recession during the latter half of the year that ultimately brought unionism's lurching advance in the textile industry to a standstill. And as the painfully familiar scenario of slumping demand, curtailed production, reduced hours, and soaring unemployment unfolded once again across the diverse terrain of the textile industry, the only solace union officials could salvage from an otherwise bleak outlook derived from their ardent belief that, but for the TWOC, millhands would have been even worse off. "Severely as textile workers are now suffering from short time work and actual unemployment," Lucy Mason informed southern newspaper editors in mid-December, "their plight would be much worse but for the salutary effect the textile workers' organizing campaign has had on wage rates." Those best acquainted with southern textiles, she claimed, agreed "that notwithstanding the very serious slump of recent months, there is little evidence of cuts in hourly rates of pay."[81] Though plainly self-serving, Mason's thesis was endorsed by the *New York Times*, which confirmed that it was the looming presence of the TWOC, more than other forces, that caused mill owners to resist the powerful urge, in hard times, to slash wages.[82]

However instrumental the TWOC could claim to have been in forestalling wage reductions, and despite the modest residual gains its campaign produced in the weeks that followed, when all was said and done the grand undertaking that Hillman announced to the country with such high resolve and evident confidence only a few months before had run its course without achieving victories of the magnitude of those won by CIO unions in other basic industries. The TWOC had performed very impressively in New England and the Middle Atlantic states, where tens of thousands of millhands employed by textile firms previously resistant, or even immune, to unionism had won bargaining rights and their attendant benefits. What was equally apparent, however, was that the TWOC could never be entirely secure in its northern successes as long as the South, where the future of the industry lay, remained beyond the reach of industrial unionism.

In failing to accomplish the ambitious goal it had set for itself, the TWOC also gave its internal critics the ammunition they needed to find fault with its direction and its AFL rivals the encouragement they needed to contest its jurisdiction. And as it struggled during the early months of 1938 to sustain an appearance even vaguely reminiscent of the vigor it had earlier projected, the TWOC found itself confronted, not only by its traditional adversaries but also by opponents advancing from new directions.

CHAPTER 5

Two Steps Forward, One Step Back

In the early spring of 1937, a brief, charmed season when the vast and beguiling possibilities of a truly encompassing workers' movement tantalized otherwise cautious and uninspired American trade unionists as never before, the emboldened activists who gathered in New York to plot the future of the newly christened Textile Workers Organizing Committee seemed justified in their unbounded optimism. The prospects for textile unionism had never been brighter.

A year later, when they paused to assess just how much a year's unstinting effort had advanced their grandiose vision toward practical realization, the exuberant optimism of more innocent days had given way to a somber concern that the TWOC's transcendent promise might not be realized after all.

An extraordinarily difficult task under the best of circumstances had been made harder still by the nation's descent during the latter half of 1937 into an economic malaise that by the following spring had become frighteningly reminiscent of a full-blown depression. Distress in the various branches of the textile industry had become particularly acute. As the threat of hard times chastened employers and millhands alike, the TWOC increasingly devoted itself to holding on to what it had rather than contemplating new initiatives that it had neither the resources nor the will to pursue.

By nearly every measure, the TWOC was in late March of 1938 a substantially less vigorous organization than the one that Sidney Hillman had so grandly described to delegates at the CIO national conference only six months earlier. The TWOC's organizing staff, which had already been reduced by a third when the CIO conference convened, continued to shrink as the organization's operating budget declined sharply in response to dwindling dues revenue and substantial reductions in outside support. By late March, the TWOC employed a staff of only 181 organizers. And even with the 68 organizers still on loan to it from other unions or separately employed by its own larger locals, the TWOC, with little coherent leadership from its national office due to Hillman's continuing absence, was endeavoring to carry on its increasingly difficult work with a staff whose strength was less than half of what it had been only nine months earlier.[1]

The TWOC's difficulties, however, went well beyond those resulting from the country's still severely strained economic condition in the spring of 1938. In the South, its organizing campaign had barely dented the power and authority of resolutely antiunion employers. The TWOC's already dim prospects were further reduced by the sudden death, in early April, of A. Steve Nance, director of its Lower South region.[2] Nance, whose impeccable southern pedigree and comforting respectability were supposed to invest the TWOC campaign with the legitimacy it needed to break through in the South, had proven to be an undeniably impressive representative. "The tributes paid Mr. Nance since his death are unique in the annals of the South," wrote Lucy Mason in a widely distributed eulogy. "Never before has a labor representative here received such widespread and unstinted praise not only from organized labor, but from business executives, professional people, government officials, social workers, ministers and editors."[3] Still, it was clear almost from the beginning that, as impressive and respectable as many elements of the southern establishment found him to be, Nance's gentlemanly airs and elevated stature did little or nothing to win over Piedmont mill owners to the view that unionism and collective bargaining were not such awful, "unsouthern" ideas after all. The familiar characteristics of speech and habit may well have persuaded southern mill owners that Nance was one of them in some ways, but in the ways that mattered most to them he still personified an evil they were sworn to oppose.

Whatever Nance's actual record, an enduring myth of what surely would have been accomplished had he lived quickly took shape. Thus, for years after his death, Steve Nance continued to serve the cause to which he had devoted the final year of his life by providing a palatable explanation of the TWOC's failure to accomplish its mission in the South. This legend was to prove particularly burdensome to his successor, Roy Lawrence, another printer whose service as president of the North Carolina Federation of Labor commended him to TWOC leaders still convinced that someone with solid credentials as a southern craft unionist was best suited to direct textile unionism's course in the Piedmont. As it turned out, Lawrence was a leader of distinctly limited abilities, but, judged in terms of concrete institutional gains rather than on a basis of personal style or civic celebrity, his generally unimpressive record in the South disclosed greater continuity with Nance's brief service than his numerous critics were willing to concede.[4]

As demoralizing as Nance's loss was to those who had depended on his leadership, it only added to the TWOC's woes in the South. Despite dogged efforts to use the Wagner Act and the NLRB to its advantage, the TWOC continued to find in the early months of 1938 that, as beneficial as the new federal labor relations policy was proving itself to be elsewhere in the nation, south of the Mason-Dixon line it was a flimsy and porous shield for workers' rights.

Indeed, long before workers in the rest of the country would be forced to the reluctant conclusion that their rights to organize and bargain collectively were perhaps more illusory than real, southern millhands had learned the hard way that even promises codified in federal law were not guarantees.[5] And because so many southern textile workers were conditioned by past disappointments to withhold their support until the TWOC achieved tangible results, the failure of the NLRB to ensure that election victories would lead to signed contracts was an often insurmountable impediment to unionism's advance in the region.

In the face of so many hardships, the TWOC was hardly in a position to revive its stalled organizing drive. With tens of thousands of its members either unemployed or working sharply reduced hours, the TWOC had its hands full during the spring of 1938 maintaining even the appearance of a viable organization. Staffers who were devoting their energies to organizing new members only six months earlier became de facto social workers as hard times hit every branch of the textile industry. "As the depression deepened," the TWOC's official history later explained, "the union found it necessary to instruct the membership in . . . the functions of the union in time of stress." In this new capacity, the TWOC, through its local affiliates, "enlarged its sphere from the plant to the entire community." In mill towns and villages from Maine to Alabama, TWOC officials who had presumed to speak for textile workers on the job now became their advocates in urging local, state, and federal agencies to provide more and faster relief to those suffering the cruelest effects of the industry's withered condition. "By this type of service, in a host of fields," the TWOC contended later, "each local union developed close bonds with its membership, adapting its services to local conditions." Such activities were also intended "to combat employers who either had attempted to convert distress of unemployment into discontent with the union or had launched company unions."[6]

To an increasing degree, during the winter and spring of 1938, the TWOC also struggled to combat the reflexive tendency of employers in a highly competitive industry like textiles to shift the burden of declining business onto workers by cutting their wages, already the lowest manufacturing wages in the nation.[7] The effectiveness of these efforts to resist wage cutting varied greatly. Where the organization had established itself most securely, it responded to arbitrary wage reductions by shutting down offending mills. In January and February, wage cuts instituted by mill owners in Vermont, New Hampshire, and Maine resulted in fifteen separate strikes, each of which, the TWOC claimed, succeeded in forcing employers to rescind earlier wage reductions. In the South, mill owners were apparently reluctant, at least initially, to risk undermining their generally successful efforts to resist the TWOC by adding wage cuts to their workers' already long list of grievances. Yet as the TWOC ultimately faltered in its efforts to "dike the flood of reductions" in New England cotton mills, southern mill owners were emboldened to implement "wholesale reductions" in wages by the late spring.[8]

Where the political climate was conducive to such efforts, the TWOC sought to enlist community and governmental help in fighting wage cuts that it claimed would only exacerbate the nation's economic woes. Especially in areas and branches of the industry where its lack of organizational strength limited its ability to pursue direct action against employers, the TWOC implored political leaders—mayors, governors and even the President himself—to bring their authority to bear against wage reductions. And even where it had made significant inroads during its organizing drive the previous year, the TWOC was eager whenever possible to augment its own resources through appeals for third-party intervention. When the Bigelow-Sanford Carpet Company, which operated newly unionized mills in Amsterdam, N.Y., and Thompsonville, Conn., unilaterally imposed a 10-percent wage reduction in early May, the affected locals, vigorously assisted by the TWOC's national office, devised a comprehensive plan of defense that ultimately relied as much on community, state, and federal intervention as on traditional forms of union power to win at least a partial victory.[9]

Despite such sporadic moments of triumph, however, the TWOC had neither the influence nor the power to do much more than lament what research director Sol Barkin glumly described as "the tremendous and staggering" wage-cutting trend that swept inexorably across branch after branch of the textile industry during the first half of 1938.[10] Yet in the midst of the troubles it confronted due to the "Roosevelt recession," the TWOC endeavored to carry on where it could. The union continued to petition for NLRB-supervised elections and continued to win many more elections than it lost, including in the South.[11]

The problem of converting an election victory into a signed contract also continued to plague the organization, especially in the South, where antiunion employers abandoned one line of defense only to fall back on another. The evident willingness of textile millhands to cast their lot with the TWOC, despite its limitations, inspired constantly beleaguered and often demoralized organizers to persist in their efforts,[12] but also to interpret developments in the South in ways that sometimes fudged the difference between progress and victory. When TWOC publicists announced in mid-June that an election win at a small cotton mill in Columbia, S.C., marked "the complete organization of the textile mills of Richland County," it deftly skirted the less happy fact that, until and unless a collective bargaining agreement followed, millhands were still denied the fruits of victory.[13] After a year's costly and often heroic effort, TWOC functionaries, in most regions of the Piedmont, were still preparing the ground for textile unionism rather than administering its benefits. "All through the South the process of recruiting new members and building unions through regular meetings and union education goes quietly on," a still hopeful, if noticeably less ebullient, Lucy Mason continued to assure any southerners who would listen. "The foundation is being laid for progress in securing union contracts when the industrial situation improves, and a rapid growth in organization will be apparent with a return of regular employment."[14] Still, it could hardly escape the notice of even the most hopeful forecaster in the late spring of 1938 that the TWOC was going nowhere fast.

The more subdued mood that spread through the ranks of TWOC loyalists as fast-paced action gave way to what one historian aptly described as "hard slogging" was evident at the top of the organization as well.[15] Heralded in the *New York Times* only a year earlier as "the third major offensive of the CIO in the nation's basic industries," the TWOC was an example of the new industrial unionism whose momentum no longer seemed irresistible.

When officials of the Amalgamated Clothing Workers gathered in Atlantic City in mid-May for the union's biennial convention, the great campaign launched the previous year to bring a million and a quarter textile workers into the CIO's burgeoning orbit received remarkably little attention. Although, unarguably, the Amalgamated's, and Sidney Hillman's, most important, costliest, and best publicized undertaking since the union's last convention, the textile campaign was less a feature presentation than a short subject. The recently recovered Hillman, who, John L. Lewis told delegates, was miraculously "back from the valley of the shadow," made no mention whatever of the textile drive in his opening address. Hillman spoke at length and with passion on such topics as the CIO's bruising competition with the AFL, the stellar role of Labor's Non-Partisan League on America's political stage, the Amalgamated's nearly complete organization of the men's clothing industry, and his hopes for the quick passage of the federal fair labor standards bill that had languished in the Congress the year before. Yet on the subject of the textile campaign, the initiative that had propelled him to national prominence and secured a place second only to that of the lordly Lewis in the CIO's pantheon, Hillman said nothing. Apparently unwilling to draw attention to what his foremost biographer later described as the TWOC's ever more "spectral appearance," Hillman, in the resilient fashion of leaders whose best-laid plans had gone awry, simply chose to accent the positive.[16] Even in the official convention report of the Amalgamated's General Executive Board, a document in which at least some mention of the textile campaign was unavoidable, Hillman and his colleagues were hardly disposed to linger over details. "Looking back at the year of this campaign and going over the record of events," they wanly announced, "we feel that we are justified in saying that the results achieved have compensated our efforts in a greater measure than we could have foretold when we undertook this responsibility."[17]

Not until the day before the convention ended did delegates finally receive an accounting of their massive investment in the textile campaign. Yet what they heard from the TWOC representatives selected by Hillman to address the convention were reports more notable for what they obscured or omitted than for what they disclosed. Only rarely, and inadvertently, did the grim reality of the TWOC's actual circumstances intrude on their fulsome reveries of splendid achievements. When Emil Rieve, who had assumed leadership of the TWOC during Hillman's long absence, drew loud cheers from delegates by claiming a dues-paying membership of 176,237, he hastened to add, presumably for the benefit of those not acquainted with the unconventional accounting methods that obtained in the arcane world of textile union, that "many of those I mentioned as dues-paying members are not able to meet their obligations."

Rieve, perhaps, came closest to providing a realistic assessment of what a year's effort had accomplished when he told the TWOC's most generous benefactors, "The foundation for organizing the textile workers has been laid." By asserting in his next breath, however, that the "permanency of textile unionism in the South" was now assured, Rieve left little doubt that his ultimate mission was to deliver good news to the Amalgamated convention whether or not circumstances in the Piedmont or elsewhere justified such optimism.[18]

Of course, Rieve and the other TWOC representatives who spoke can hardly be faulted for doing what union conventions had from time immemorial obliged every speaker to do: herald the good news of labor's inexorable advance without letting an undue concern for accuracy get in the way. It is exceedingly unlikely, however, that even the least informed conventioneers were unaware that the textile campaign's condition was decidedly less robust than its custodians were disposed to confess.

Hillman's interest, which only a year earlier had seemingly superseded every other concern on his crowded agenda, was now merely perfunctory. Whatever hopes he once harbored that the textile industry might become a venue for personal triumph comparable to what steel and autos had been for John L. Lewis, rapidly faded as the TWOC drive bogged down and his health failed. And when, in the spring of 1938, Hillman's health finally permitted him to return from a long convalescence in Florida to the many concerns that awaited his personal attention in New York, active oversight of the languishing affairs of the TWOC was not among them. He would continue to "front" for the TWOC at press conferences and on occasions calling for a ritual personification of the "new" textile unionism's vitality and alleged centrality to CIO interests. After a personal conference with President Roosevelt on July 5, Hillman took advantage of the media attention the meeting attracted to tell the White House press corps that reports of the TWOC's waning prospects in the South were unfounded. Citing the union's role in discouraging wage cuts and its lengthening list of victories in NLRB representation elections, Hillman assured reporters that imminent triumphs in the Piedmont would confirm that the TWOC was anything but the foundering organization that overwrought employers in the region desperately claimed. "If the committee makes as much progress in the next two years as it has in the last year," he grandly said, "I feel sure that the employers will deal with the union on a national basis."[19] Hillman was also willing to be front and center, and to feign active involvement in directing TWOC affairs, when there was especially good news to announce.

For example, it was Hillman, rather than Rieve, the union's foremost spokesperson during the summer of 1938, who informed the press in early July that the American Viscose Company had renewed a collective bargaining agreement covering the 20,000 synthetic yarn workers it employed.[20]

Such increasingly infrequent gestures notwithstanding, Hillman's most pressing concerns lay elsewhere. As a result of his reimmersion in Amalgamated and CIO affairs, in state and national politics, and in the bruising legislative fight to finally enact even an eviscerated version of the fair labor standards bill that had stalled in the Congress the year before, Hillman had a ready reply to those who wondered why he had not also resumed active generalship of the TWOC.

The decision taken at the beginning of the textile drive to entrust TWOC regional directors with authority to run the organizing campaign as each saw fit meant that Hillman had never really exercised the day-to-day control that he tended to suggest. Still, before his physical collapse toward the end of 1937 he had been available both to provide authoritative leadership and to promote the impression that the immediate destiny of textile unionism could hardly be in better hands. The appointment of Emil Rieve to act in Hillman's place until he was well enough to resume his duties fostered the impression that the TWOC would continue to be capably led, but the hosiery workers' president was, in fact, too busy attending to his own duties in Philadelphia to give the faltering textile campaign anything more than sporadic attention.[21]

It is, of course, impossible to determine the extent to which Hillman's absence, and later his remoteness, from the TWOC's helm at a critical juncture may have contributed to the troubles that beset the organization throughout 1938. Certainly, there was strong evidence that the textile drive was in trouble weeks before Hillman fell ill. Moreover, there is no reason to believe that the recession that suddenly reversed the country's, and the textile industry's, economic fortunes during the fall of 1937 would have been less damaging to the TWOC if Hillman's illness had not forced him to relinquish leadership to less able and resourceful surrogates.

Where Hillman's adroit leadership and commanding stature in the industrial labor movement might have made a real difference was in fending off or managing internecine disputes that seriously undermined the TWOC during 1938. Perhaps, if the TWOC had actually accomplished in its first year of operation what Hillman and his supporters promised when they brusquely shouldered aside the UTW's fatigued and aimless old guard in March of 1937, there would have been no need for the deft leadership that the emergent fractiousness of 1938 required. That is not to argue, as the internal battles that convulsed the United Auto Workers at about the same time instructively attest, that greater success in organizing its jurisdiction would have ensured less disharmony within the TWOC. Because of the textile industry's diversity and the cultural chasm that separated its northern and southern branches union solidarity had been an ideal more readily imagined than achieved. Still, both the form and manner of the TWOC's ascendency under Hillman's uncompromising stewardship virtually guaranteed that the UTW veterans who were summarily displaced when his new team took the field would be quick to second guess its disappointing performance.

The first clear evidence that the textile campaign's already weakened condition was in danger of being exacerbated by internal discord appeared in January of 1938, when the New Bedford Textile Council, an organization whose member locals proudly traced their origins to the earliest of days of craft activism in the textile industry, openly defied the authority of the TWOC by agreeing to a wage reduction without seeking its approval. In the historic districts of textile unionism like New Bedford, where the interests of local unions had rarely been subordinated to the broader purposes of national organization even during the most vigorous days of the United Textile Workers, the resentment occasioned by Hillman's preemptory assertion of the TWOC's supremacy was slow to dissipate. And when local leaders in New Bedford decided that the TWOC had fallen far short of achieving what it had promised the previous spring, they plainly felt justified in acting once again on the basis of more provincial, self-serving considerations.[22]

The New Bedford Textile Council's sin—agreeing to a 12.5-percent wage reduction to boost the competitiveness of local cotton mills—was actually one that TWOC affiliates in nearly every branch of the textile industry would commit in one degree or another as the national economy continued to decline in the early months of 1938. What made the situation in New Bedford special, however, was that local leaders there had formally agreed to wage cuts rather than simply acquiescing in the arbitrary actions of employers. Moreover, New Bedford leaders acted before national TWOC officials had resigned themselves to the inevitability of wage cuts and while they were still trying to appease or mollify those local affiliates in other New England textile centers who were vehemently opposed to any wage reductions in the region.[23]

In deciding to suspend the seven locals that made up the New Bedford Textile Council, five of which had chosen to retain their identity as UTW affiliates rather than reconstitute themselves under the TWOC's banner, acting chairman Emil Rieve and his colleagues plainly hoped to prevent the fragmentation of national union authority. The practiced tendency of local unions to walk away from the obligations of national affiliation whenever it suited them had done more to impede the development of textile unionism on an industry-wide basis than anything else. TWOC leaders would have been derelict had they permitted the actions of the New Bedford Council to go unchallenged. Yet in explaining why the seven offending locals had been suspended, Rieve placed less emphasis on their defiance of TWOC authority than on their failure to abide by the constitution of the UTW.[24]

Given that the UTW constitution had effectively been junked as a condition of the TWOC's ascendency, Rieve's reliance on the authority it supposedly conferred to order the suspensions of New Bedford locals was more an act of expedience than of sincere deference to its dictates. His claim that the New Bedford Council had offended the democratic sensibilities of unionists in all branches of the textile industry was similarly disingenuous since the TWOC functioned by design on a basis that routinely sacrificed its members' rights of democratic participation in the interest of centralized authority and control. The essential advantage of an organizing committee over a more conventional trade union structure, after all, was that it was not constrained by constitutional provisions.

Yet, whatever the merits of the claims and counterclaims advanced in the course of the New Bedford dispute, its real significance lay in what it revealed about the rising tide of anti-TWOC sentiment in those New England textile centers where the decision of UTW leaders the previous March to subordinate their union to Sidney Hillman's unassailable authority had engendered more disdain than delight. That the New Bedford contretemps was symptomatic of deeper-seated troubles became evident almost at once, as unreconstructed UTW partisans in Rhode Island mounted an even more direct—and ominous—challenge to the TWOC's authority.

Like the conflict in New Bedford, the simmering controversy that flared into an open dispute in Rhode Island during the spring of 1938 pitted disaffected UTW officials determined to reassert claims of local autonomy against TWOC leaders equally intent on preserving their organization's "top-down" structure. Led by Joseph Sylvia, a veteran UTW functionary whose personal animus toward the TWOC probably had more to do with the abrupt loss of authority and stature he had suffered at the hands of the new regime than with strategic or philosophical differences, the Rhode Island dissidents declared that they would no longer be bound by an agreement to which they had not assented. Beyond denying the TWOC's legitimacy, however, Sylvia and his supporters were motivated in particular by a determination to revive the Woolen and Worsted Federation, one of the semiautonomous, if chronically atrophied, appendages of the old UTW whose abolition Hillman regarded as a necessary prerequisite to textile unionism's successful rehabilitation.[25]

In the absence of further complications, the churlish self-indulgence of Sylvia and his backers might have been just another of the "temporary local disturbances" that the TWOC's official history later claimed. Yet in opening the door to a broader challenge by a more credible and formidable critic of the TWOC's legitimacy, Rhode Island dissidents unwittingly provoked an internal struggle whose consequences went well beyond those of a "temporary local disturbance."

What turned an otherwise minor and mundane localized squabble into a major headache for the TWOC was the decision by UTW president Francis Gorman to exploit the discontents of rebellious Rhode Islanders in the service of his own simmering unhappiness with textile unionism's new order. That Gorman chose to ally himself publicly with an ineffectual careerist like Joseph Sylvia undoubtedly surprised and disappointed those who embraced solidarity as trade unionism's most sacred principle. Yet, for anyone who appreciated the depth of his personal humiliation in submitting to the draconian terms that Hillman and his CIO backers imposed as a condition of their promised goods works in the textile industry, Gorman's determination to vindicate his reputation and redeem his authority, even at the expense of the TWOC's internal harmony, was understandable, especially as the new organization sputtered virtually to a halt in the spring of 1938 with much of its mission still to be accomplished.

To be sure, Gorman was not the only UTW leader who sacrificed status or position in the cause of textile unionism's revitalization. Yet, no one had lost as much. He had been the UTW's leading figure even before he succeeded Thomas McMahon as president at the beginning of 1937. And although his prominence in the wake of the 1934 general strike was probably sustained by his notoriety as much as by his achievements, Gorman was the only UTW leader who could plausibly claim a base of support that extended across the textile industry's several branches. Moreover, he had provided real leadership at the critical juncture in the UTW's history when the promise of textile unionism demanded self-sacrifice. Whatever his personal reaction to the Hobson's choice Hillman offered, Gorman had argued sincerely and persuasively before the UTW Executive Council that the future of their cause must not be threatened by self-interest. Despite Hillman's "drastic" terms, he lectured his colleagues, the time had come "to forget ourselves personally" and do the "best thing for the UTW."[26] Gorman may have hoped that his impending appointment to the TWOC by John L. Lewis would cushion his own personal diminution, but he knew from earlier "negotiations" with Hillman that his role in the new organization would be to impart an impression of continuity rather than to share in its leadership.

For nearly a year after the deal that ceded authority to the TWOC, Gorman had dutifully done what was expected of him: he disappeared into virtual exile. Following his return from Europe, where Hillman had sent him during the early weeks of the TWOC organizing drive to keep him out of the way, Gorman toiled unobtrusively in Washington, D.C., still obsessed with the possibility that he might salvage from the ruins of the Roosevelt administration's original recovery program a workable plan to rationalize the textile industry and, thereby, to facilitate worker organization.

Had Gorman been left alone to tilt at windmills in Washington and accorded at least a modicum of respect by Hillman and his aides, the deepening disaffection that led, ultimately, to his open break with the TWOC might have been forestalled. Instead, during the fall of 1937, Gorman was subjected to new humiliations which, though usually petty in magnitude, combined to further his estrangement from the TWOC. And while most of these new slights were not undertaken at Hillman's express direction—in fact, they continued well after his illness forced him to the sidelines—they nevertheless reflected his undisguised contempt for Gorman.

As a seasoned labor politician who appreciated that personal opinion should not be indulged at the expense of internal solidarity, Hillman knew better than to alienate Gorman gratuitously. The same sensibility, however, cannot be attributed to Hillman's often supercilious major domo in the TWOC's New York City headquarters, Solomon Barkin. A person of formidable intellect, Barkin had first come to Hillman's attention while working for the Labor Advisory Board of the National Recovery Administration. The scholarly, self-consciously intellectual Barkin, who might have pursued an academic career but for an unfinished economics dissertation at Columbia University, was an unlikely recruit to labor's cause. More convincing as technocrat than as partisan activist, Barkin later guessed that he had been recruited to the TWOC in March of 1937 because "he had stood up to Hillman at meetings of the Labor Advisory Board."[27]

Beyond revealing his academic pretensions, the title Barkin appropriated for himself when he joined the TWOC—Director of Research—announced to the veteran trade unionists whose company he had joined that he should not be mistaken for one of them. Indeed, throughout his long career in the labor movement, a career that would establish his preeminence as a union research director, the persona that Barkin found at once most congenial and authentic was that of an intellectual in labor's service. His loyalty and devotion to the cause to which happenstance consigned him were never in question, but his unyielding sense of detachment left him comfortably outside the intimate fraternity of textile unionism throughout his career.

Had Hillman's health not failed suddenly in the fall of 1937, Barkin would no doubt have remained merely an irritant, and an enigma, to Gorman and the other UTW veterans forced to deal with him when union business required interactions with the TWOC's New York office. As it happened, of course, illness did force Hillman to abandon his duties for more than six months, and Emil Rieve, the person who was supposed to assume his duties in New York, was too busy in Philadelphia running the activities of the American Federation of Hosiery Workers to oversee the day-to-day affairs of the TWOC. The result was that, by sheer inadvertence rather than anything even remotely suggestive of conscious design, Barkin was suddenly heir to a degree of administrative authority that made him the effective head of the TWOC during what was destined to become a period of deepening crises.[28]

While acknowledging that Barkin was "the best research director a union ever had," a longtime colleague later observed that his oversight of the organization during Hillman's absence offered ample evidence that "he certainly can't run anything."[29] In Barkin, an obsession with detail combined with a frequently dismissive manner and a seemingly irrepressible pomposity to create what even his admirers conceded was a difficult personality. James Starr, the UTW's Secretary-Treasurer, soon learned that Barkin's naturally overbearing manner could, when reinforced by the open contempt that Hillman and others expressed toward textile unionism's old guard, make him a difficult person, indeed. In dealing with Starr, who had been left to oversee the suddenly moribund administrative affairs of the UTW following its subordination to the TWOC, Barkin never even pretended deference to the older man's seniority. When Starr had the temerity to speculate aloud that the UTW might at some time in the future regain its sovereignty, Barkin, who had spent less than six weeks in service to the cause of textile unionism, curtly informed him that "our probable future plans . . . have not been developed and we cannot as yet indicate them to you."[30]

When, in the early fall of 1937, growing financial difficulties forced the TWOC to slash its staff, Starr found that Barkin could be as callous and insensitive as he was brash and contumely. Without prior consultation, Barkin instructed Starr on September 18 to discharge three of the seven clerical workers at the UTW's Bible House headquarters on Astor Place. Naming one who was to be retained, Barkin told Starr that he was "at liberty to choose according to whatever regulations you wish to follow from those who remain." Expressing confidence that Starr appreciated "the necessity of this curtailment," Barkin gratuitously added, "I know that it will not be any serious handicap to you in the performance of the work which remains to be done."[31] Dismayed by Barkin's instruction and offended by his tone, Starr disputed the claim that there was no longer much to do at the UTW's headquarters and objected to the cavalier manner in which the staff cutback was communicated to him. "I do not think you are in a position to judge . . . just what help will be necessary to carry on the work," he curtly informed Barkin. Moreover, he charged, Barkin was guilty of both bad faith and bad form in his approach to cost cutting. "On more than one occasion since the TWOC drive started," he reminded Barkin, "I took up with you the question of the girls at this office and you assured me, not once but many times, that the girls would be taken care of." He continued, "The question of seniority enters in this matter—an important issue with any union—and one we compel employers to recognize." Insisting that "different approaches" were available to achieve necessary spending cuts, Starr advised Barkin that he would not take any action until UTW president Gorman had an opportunity to discuss the matter with "the proper officials of the TWOC."[32]

With that threat, Starr was deferring to someone who already had his own reasons for thinking that the TWOC Director of Research was overreaching the limits of his authority. When he returned to Washington, D.C., from his European mission Gorman was stunned to learn that, only 24 hours earlier, Barkin had, without consultation or prior notice, "liquidated" the office that the UTW had long maintained there. Despite his protests, and the fact that Hillman had promised at the time of the TWOC's takeover to maintain the UTW's Washington office and retain its two-person clerical staff, Gorman suffered the humiliation and embarrassment of having to conduct the few official duties his union presidency still entailed out of his home.[33]

For Gorman, the abrupt closing of his Washington office was only the first in a series of personal affronts that he came to view over the months that followed as part of a larger campaign engineered by Barkin to further insult, embarrass, and incapacitate him. Throughout the fall of 1937 Gorman fumed as Barkin, who had assumed informal control of the TWOC's financial affairs in Hillman's absence, routinely challenged or disallowed many of the modest travel and other expenses he incurred while carrying out what he saw as the legitimate duties of the UTW presidency.[34] Unable to appeal to Hillman, who remained gravely ill, Gorman had no alternative but to beseech acting TWOC chairman Emil Rieve to put Barkin in his place. Yet Rieve, whose low opinion of Gorman was as old as their association, proved unsympathetic. When Gorman noted in response to Barkin's alleged mistreatment of the UTW clerical staff that unions had an ethical obligation to "set an example for the employers in matters of this kind," Rieve brushed aside his concern.[35] "With reference to the lay-offs that are taking place in this office," he coldly explained,

> I wish to say that this matter lies entirely in the hands of Barkin. As you probably know, the girls in this office are organized and working under a union contract. Should any of them have any grievances, I take it for granted that they are at liberty to take them up with their Union.[36]

By the beginning of 1938, Gorman's alienation was complete. Convinced that his personal sacrifice for textile unionism's advancement had been interpreted by Hillman and his surrogates as weakness rather than selflessness, Gorman resolved to reclaim the authority and prestige he had earlier relinquished. Confiding to James Starr in late January that he would have been content to serve the TWOC by working "to set up an effective legislative program for the Committee" in Washington, Gorman complained bitterly that he had been denied even that modest participation in the new regime. Referring to his perennially unrequited efforts to accomplish the salvation of both the textile industry and textile unionism through legislative enactment, Gorman groused,

> I have been almost insurmountably handicapped in this work from the start by Barkin's interference, which has taken two forms: first, the closing of my office here without consultation or permission from me; and, second, his continuous efforts to harry and embarrass me in my work. I have kept these things to myself believing that eventually he would learn an elementary lesson in psychology, and revise his arrogant and exceedingly inadvisable way of dealing with his coworkers. He has not. Of course, Barkin may be naive enough to believe that these unconscionable insults will go unheeded by me. I should not now be surprised if this is the case.

His ill treatment at the hands of Barkin and others harmed not only him, Gorman told Starr, but textile unionism, whose once bright prospects had begun to dim appreciably as the faith and forbearance of UTW veterans increasingly gave way to doubt and disaffection. Moreover, he claimed, it was just this sort of festering discontent that he might have forestalled if Hillman's shortsighted minions had not conspired to render him impotent. Suggesting that he was uniquely suited to ease such internecine frictions, Gorman wrote,

> I have been receiving dozens of complaints from the field which, in spite of the gravity of some of them, I believe could be adjusted if I were in a position to function normally in my official capacity both as President of the UTWA, and as a member of the TWOC, without interference and with a minimum amount of cooperation.

Instead of enlisting his singular talents to defuse the discord that threatened to derail the TWOC, Barkin, Rieve and, at least implicitly, Hillman were too intent on opposing and humiliating him, Gorman alleged, to consider what was best for the common cause. Now, he warned Starr, things had to change. "Because I have been desirous of seeing the textile workers organized regardless of at what cost it may have been to myself," he declared, "I have attempted to conduct my affairs here without necessary facilities and regardless of nagging interference. I shall no longer do this."[37]

It is possible, as historian Irving Bernstein insists, that Gorman "opted for mutiny" in 1938 because the "dethronement" he had accepted the previous spring seemed likely to become permanent when Hillman tapped Emil Rieve as the TWOC's "crown prince."[38] Certainly, the multiplying difficulties the TWOC faced by the winter of 1937–1938 may well have prompted some of the veteran UTW functionaries earlier pushed aside by Hillman's crowd to conclude that "all bets were off" if the new regime proved unable to do for textile unionism what CIO-backed campaigns had done for industrial unions in autos and steel.

It is not clear, however, that the deepening rift that developed in 1938 between Gorman and the TWOC leadership was unavoidable. If Gorman had been accorded the personal respect he craved and permitted to occupy himself in Washington with his pet project, the National Textile Bill, he might have been content to leave the running of the TWOC to Hillman and his cohorts. Instead, as his wounded pride nourished a deepening conviction that it was, as he vaguely intimated to Starr, nothing less than his manhood that Hillman, Rieve and Barkin were challenging him to defend, Gorman resolved to reinstate his personal stature and authority without evident concern for what damage that might do to the already fragile solidarity of textile unionism.[39]

The opening Gorman needed to launch his challenge to the TWOC's authority was conveniently provided at the beginning of 1938 by the New Bedford Textile Council, whose unauthorized acceptance of employers' demands for a wage reduction had excited fears among New England millhands and union officials that the economic gains they had struggled to win over the preceding ten months were suddenly in danger of being wiped out. Aware that the issue of wage cuts was one that afforded him an opportunity to pursue his personal agenda behind a facade of selfless concern for the welfare of millhands every-where, Gorman wrote to Rieve on February 8 demanding that the TWOC "take a positive and militant stand on the question of wage cuts in the textile industry."

Insisting that he was speaking out only at the incessant urging of "protest-ing locals" and "union representatives" who were "losing members because the workers have begun to feel that the TWOC either can't or won't protect their interests in this critical situation," Gorman assured Rieve that he would have remained silent but for the dereliction of the organization's leadership in not offer "an official and general enunciation of policy" against wage reductions. "I am thoroughly convinced (and I speak with years of experi-ence in the textile industry, as you well know)," Gorman gratuitously observed,

> that unless we take a firm stand immediately, we are faced with the wholesale slashing of wages and a demoralization of many of the gains made by the TWOC during the past 10 months. I am of the opinion that the tide of wage-cutting can be stemmed by a strong stand now by our committee, and that if we do find our-selves faced with a general reduction in wages it is our own fault.

While Gorman was undoubtedly correct in thinking that TWOC members were distressed at the prospect of industry-wide wage reductions, his claim that they were also "emphatically in favor of a forceful program for the pas-sage of the National Textile Act as the only means of aiding the union in its campaign to stabilize the industry" was self-indulgent nonsense. It hardly mattered, however, since he was clearly more intent on crafting a pretext for rebellion than on representing the members' most urgent concerns. The lead-ership's inexplicable neglect of these issues was, Gorman asserted, unsettling evidence of " 'a certain looseness and bankruptcy of authority in the TWOC which . . . is disastrous to the welfare of the organization and must be imme-diately remedied."

In explaining why he had decided that his personal intercession was now imperative, Gorman assured Rieve that it was "not personal matters at all, but matters of policy" that motivated him. And it was with "these pressing matters in mind," he explained, that he was "drawing up a letter to our membership on the question of wage cuts and action on the National Textile Act." The only remaining question, he defiantly informed Rieve, was "whether or not the membership list of the TWOC . . . is going to be made available to me without my having to resort to less pleasant means of getting it."[40]

Despite the provocative message and quarrelsome tone of Gorman's letter, Rieve's response to it, though firm, betrayed remarkably little concern or annoyance. Gorman's claims that TWOC leaders had been negligent in resist-ing wage reductions and derelict in letting the National Textile Bill languish were, Rieve coolly replied, simply without merit. The TWOC was "doing everything possible to stem the tide of [wage] reductions," he told Gorman, and was just "not interested" in the National Textile Bill "at this particular time." As for Gorman's demand that he be supplied with lists of local unions so that he could address his concerns to TWOC members directly, Rieve replied that because such an overture would only "create unlimited confusion," it was best that "all letters to the membership . . . come out of this office."[41]

Although Rieve, and later Hillman, were no doubt correct in believing that Gorman wielded too little influence, even in the surviving remnants of the UTW, to accomplish what he threatened, they probably underestimated just how much mischief he could make, especially as the textile industry's continuing slump during the first half of 1938 fueled new fears and discontents within the TWOC's thinning ranks. Indeed, it was because the organization's progress had slowed so appreciably that Gorman was willing to risk an open challenge. Had the textile drive sustained its early momentum, his complaints, and those of other disgruntled UTW veterans, would have remained irrelevant and probably unexpressed. Moreover, he would have had no ground for thinking, as he did by the beginning of 1938, that the best way to recover his personal dignity was to rescue the practically moribund UTW from its subordination to Hillman and the TWOC.

In his effort to revive the UTW, and so to regain whatever authority and standing the union presidency still conferred, Gorman was inadvertently assisted by Emil Rieve. In justifying his decision, in mid-February, to suspend the New Bedford Textile Council's seven member locals for improperly agreeing to wage reductions, Rieve claimed that the TWOC's specific authority to take such actions derived from provisions in the constitution of the United Textile Workers of America.[42] In truth, he had no alternative, since the TWOC was, by design, an organizational artifice whose essential appeal was that it could function free of the constitutional constraints that a conventional union structure imposed.

For Gorman, now determined to "return from exile," Rieve's invocation of the UTW constitution promised to be useful in two ways. First, it attested to the union's continuing relevance. Second, it meant that whenever the authority of the UTW was invoked its chief executive was also validated. When Rieve told him that the New Bedford locals had been suspended for their unauthorized action, Gorman complained that in presuming to enforce "the laws of the United Textile Workers of America" the acting chairman of the TWOC had himself flagrantly violated them. "I feel," he scolded Rieve,

that I must call to your attention . . . the fact that you yourself have acted in contravention to the laws of the International Union by usurping the powers of the President in the suspension of these charters. Of course, I am well aware that such violations of the UTWA constitution are common practice as far as your office in

New York is concerned, and that, therefore, you very likely gave the matter no second thought.

Indignant that it "should be necessary for me to remind you that I am President of the International Union," Gorman warned Rieve that he intended, "when the time comes," to take his growing list of grievances and concerns directly to the membership.[43]

Although Gorman appeared to be on solid ground in disputing Rieve's legal authority to apply the UTW constitution in the New Bedford situation, the prerogatives he claimed as UTW president simply did not exist as a practical matter. In his eagerness to reestablish the UTW as a discrete organization affiliated with, but no longer subservient to, the TWOC, Gorman appeared oblivious to the fact that precious little remained of his former domain. Of the more than 400 locals affiliated with the TWOC in March of 1938, only 61 retained their UTW charters, and many of those were little more than paper organizations. Even more revealing of the UTW's debilitated condition was the fact that fewer than 2,300 of the 176,000 dues-paying members the TWOC claimed were from unconverted locals still stubbornly clinging to their original charters.[44]

Gorman, however, was undeterred by the bleak reality of his prospects. Convinced that the alienation and disaffection he felt permeated the ranks of UTW veterans likewise insulted by the upstart TWOC functionaries, Gorman believed that he could exploit this seething discontent for his personal resurrection. That they had formally agreed, only a year earlier, to submit unconditionally to TWOC authority was, Gorman reckoned, an impediment that could be overcome by claiming that their purpose was not to subvert textile unionism but to save it.

Gorman sketched the outlines of this dubious strategy in a letter to Sidney Hillman in mid-May. In a tone more deferential than the one he'd used with Rieve and Barkin, Gorman nevertheless insisted that a sweeping overhaul of the TWOC organization must be undertaken if the textile organizing campaign was to regain its momentum. Assuring Hillman that he had arrived at that conclusion "only after mature consideration of the factors involved," Gorman offered recommendations designed, he wrote, to "pave the way for a more fruitful and satisfactory continuation of our textile drive, and provide the basis for a better understanding and a more equitable relationship between the forces involved in the campaign." Moreover, he earnestly confided, "I feel morally certain . . . that the inauguration of these changes in policy will serve to check the increasing loss of unions and membership through secessions, and will eventually result in the reaffiliation of those who have left our ranks." Not surprisingly, the benefits Gorman alleged for textile unionism coincided with his personal preoccupations. Reduced to their essentials, Gorman's proposed "reforms" called for ending, or at the very least relieving, the UTW's subordination to Hillman and the TWOC and seeking solutions to the industry's chronic wage and employment problems through a federal stabilization plan along the lines of the languishing National Textile Bill.

The key to overcoming the organization's deepening malaise, Gorman argued, lay in permitting the "several branches of our industry . . . [to] again function on a departmental basis." Citing the "successful organizational achievements" of the hosiery workers and dyers and finishers, the two federations in the old UTW that had been allowed to retain control over their internal affairs despite the TWOC's nominal supremacy, he expressed confidence that "the same policy . . . applied to carpet and rug, rayon and synthetic yarn, woolen and worsted and velvet and plush, silk, etc." would confer similar benefits. Even cotton goods, the branch of textiles that remained most resistant to union penetration, might be overcome, he thought, if all cotton locals were encouraged to coordinate their operations. "Though it will be a difficult task," he advised Hillman, "it can and must be done, since it is necessary that we spur on the drive to organize the southern branch of the textile industry and thus cement the strength of the entire organization." Beyond having been "unanimously endorsed" by delegates at the 1936 UTW convention, Gorman added, the departmental structure he was advocating had "evolved out of 35 years' experience in searching for the most effective manner in which to handle our far-flung and diversified industry." In the past there were "weaknesses in the manner in which it was applied," he admitted, but these could be remedied "through action by the textile workers at the next convention." It would take the UTW no more than 90 days, Gorman guessed, to put its "machinery in working order." After that, he told Hillman, "we can call a general convention of all textile locals in order that the elected representatives of the textile workers can decide on our future course and policy."[45]

Although he assured Hillman that the new organization would still operate under what he vaguely described as "the supervision of the Textile Workers Organizing Committee," Gorman had proposed nothing less than the restoration of the UTW as a largely self-governing organization. He had tried to express himself tactfully, but his meaning was clear: Hillman and his hand-picked votaries had been given a fair and full opportunity to show what they could do for America's expectant millhands, but, now, with their stewardship called into question both by the inefficacy of their approach and the paucity of their results, the time had come to defer to the judgment of experienced textile unionists like himself. The TWOC could continue to serve the cause for which it was created, Gorman implied, but it should be as the UTW's partner rather than as its master.

Whether because he was too busy with the crush of work to which he had only recently returned or because he was confident that Gorman could safely be ignored, Hillman offered no response. Indeed, as Gorman later complained to John L. Lewis, even when he repeated his proposals to Hillman during a rare face-to-face meeting in July, "they were superciliously laughed off by the Chairman of the TWOC and his aide, Rieve."[46] In disregarding Gorman's insistence that he spoke, not only for himself but for a large number of other UTW officials and members, Hillman had little to fear. Even as concerns mounted, among leaders and members alike, during 1938 that the TWOC was falling disappointingly short of matching the progress of CIO unions in other mass-production industries, they were never disposed to look backward to a brighter future. After nearly a year of hard traveling, the TWOC was no longer the gleaming conveyance of more innocent days, but for the vast majority of those still committed to textile unionism's advance it remained the best vehicle available.

Not for the first time in his career, Frank Gorman had badly misjudged those whose minds and hearts he presumed to know so well. In the end, the only open support he received came from the small band of militant contrarians in Rhode Island whose obstinate crusade to resurrect the defunct Federation of Woolen and Worsted Workers had finally forced exasperated TWOC leaders to expel them.[47] In rationalizing their insurrection, however, Rhode Island insurgents did not co-opt Gorman's argument that it was the TWOC leaders' misfeasance and bad faith that left them no alternative to rebellion. Instead, they challenged the legality of the pact that gave rise to the TWOC, insisting that Gorman had been "tricked" into signing an agreement that wrongly "permitted the President of the Amalgamated Clothing Workers, Sidney Hillman, to seize absolute control of our Textile Union and dictate its policies."[48] Although loath to endorse an argument predicated on assertions of his own gullibility or incompetence, Gorman was willing to indulge the conspiracy theorists among his Rhode Island supporters to the extent of agreeing that Hillman had cunningly engineered a "plot to liquidate the UTW."[49]

Regardless of how artfully he contrived to explain his motives, Gorman could not persuade other UTW veterans, including some who privately harbored many of the same grievances and complaints, to join his threatened crusade to undo the TWOC. Especially disappointing was the adamant opposition expressed by UTW Secretary-Treasurer James Starr, a longtime colleague and confidant who had openly deplored the contemptuous and peremptory treatment accorded him and other old-guard textile unionists by Solomon Barkin and his cohorts. Still, as he bluntly informed Gorman, Starr was not willing to redress his personal grievances at the expense of a cause he had faithfully served all his adult life. When Gorman informed him, in mid-July, that he had called a special meeting of the UTW Executive Council to discuss his plan to regain the union's independence, Starr would have none of it. Taken aback by the vehemence of his old friend's objections, Gorman quickly retreated. "While I had made the arrangements," he sheepishly assured Starr, "I will now communicate with those interested stating that we believe a meeting at this time is untimely."

All he asked in return, he submissively informed Starr, was "that nothing is said to those who will take comfort when the meeting isn't held."[50]

A less resolute, or perhaps more astute, malcontent might have decided, after such forceful rebukes, to defer to the majority. For Gorman, however, there was simply no turning back. To save what remained of his personal pride his ill-conceived insurrection had to go on, even if whatever sense of authentic menace his public opposition to TWOC authority once posed had been neutralized by the emphatic refusal of others to follow his lead.

Scorned by his opponents and rebuffed by his friends, Gorman took his complaints to the industrial union movement's supreme authority, CIO chairman John L. Lewis. On August 2, he informed Lewis of his intention to resign from the TWOC.[51] Two weeks later, apparently without any indication that Lewis was eager to know more, Gorman sent him nine-page letter in which he detailed his reasons for resigning. That he had taken such drastic action, he told Lewis, attested to the depth of his conviction that the CIO organizing drive in textiles was in serious trouble. And, despite what his critics might say in their eagerness to denigrate his motives and to disparage his judgment, he assured Lewis, nothing short of a grave crisis could have caused him to take an action so open to misinterpretation. "If, in the conduct of the campaign to unionize the textile industry it had been demonstrated that such a campaign would be to the best interests of the textile workers," Gorman wrote, "I, for one, might have been constrained to continue to suffer in silence the unspeakable abuse and contumely which has been heaped on me and the organization I represent since the inception of the drive of the TWOC." Yet because "the facts . . . speak very forcefully" that the best interests of textile workers had not been served by Hillman's stewardship, he argued, it was now time to abandon the "tactics, strategy, and policies" of the TWOC and to reconfigure the CIO campaign in the industry "upon a genuinely progressive trade union basis."

In his desire to persuade Lewis that the TWOC was a dysfunctional organization, whose "results . . . have been piddling compared to the possibilities— recession and all—which the campaign offered," Gorman was willing to stretch the truth to the breaking point. His suggestion, for example, that the TWOC had a smaller dues-paying membership in July of 1938 than the UTW had when it delivered itself into Hillman's hands 16 months earlier was patent nonsense. Indeed, Gorman's dogged contention that the UTW was, at the time of its takeover by the TWOC, "no tottering, moribund craft organization, but a lively, progressive union" defied logic and denied history.

Despite his distortion and transparent self-deception, however, the case that Gorman laid out for Lewis made a few points that even the most ardent apologists for Hillman and the TWOC had trouble rebutting. In their determination to distance and distinguish the TWOC campaign from those of its discredited predecessor, the UTW, Hillman and his lieutenants refused to consider the possibility that those most familiar with the arcane culture of textile unionism might contribute to its success. Gorman exaggerated only slightly when he complained to Lewis that

> The textile workers, their elected local representatives and their elected national officers were eliminated at the beginning from strategic positions in the conduct of the drive, where they could be of . . . use or influence in the direction of the campaign. People totally unfamiliar with the industry and thus incapable of administrating the campaign without advice from experienced textile people, were put in charge of almost every locality.

It was also difficult to dismiss Gorman's contention that Hillman's preferred organizing strategy, while appropriate in an industry whose employers were disposed to consider the benefits of "responsible unionism," had little to commend it in the bewilderingly diverse and chronically irrational realms that textiles encompassed. "The fundamental strategy was not emphasis on mass organization of the textile workers as a necessary predicate to negotiation with the manufacturers," Gorman observed of Hillman's approach, "but of organizing the manufacturers on the basis most acceptable to them and at the same time as favorable as possible to the workers. This policy has worked in the garment industry, but, and I have pointed this out time and again, it is not correct in textiles because of the difference in the structure of the industry, the nature of the textile workers and of the manufacturers themselves." Hillman's defenders could plausibly argue that his strategy had paid handsome dividends in relatively coherent branches of the industry like synthetic yarns and carpets and rugs, but in most others, including cotton textiles, which employed by far the largest number of potential TWOC members, overtures to employers did little to diminish their visceral antiunionism.

Finally, and inevitably, there was the South, where, by Gorman's reckoning, the TWOC was actually doing more harm than good to the CIO cause. It was sadly the case, he told Lewis, that:

> Hundreds of thousands of pledge cards in the South have been torn up and hundreds of thousands of workers have become disillusioned [with the TWOC] due to the fact that the organizers poured in in certain territories promising the workers everything, condemning the UTW, and then contributing absolutely nothing in the way of offering an alternative, not even the formation of a local union.

Even more distressing, he added, "Mill after mill has gone over to the CIO in NLRB elections and the number of contracts which have been signed are [*sic*] negligible." So hapless and vexing was its performance in the Piedmont, he concluded, that "A worker from a North Carolina textile mill characterized the TWOC as 'The AFL with a CIO face.' "[52]

Gorman's damning assessment of the TWOC's record in the South, though simplistic and shamelessly self-serving, was not so far from the truth. Hillman's promise that the TWOC would end the degradation of long-suffering southern millhands while simultaneously benefiting the industry seemed naive and fraudulent in light of the harsh realities that obtained throughout the region in the summer of 1938. The TWOC, its once swarming organizing staff reduced by successive cutbacks to an overburdened rear guard,[53] continued to do what it could in the Piedmont, but survival had displaced grander ambitions as its top priority. No one familiar with the historic difficulties involved in organizing southern textile workers, or with the problems that beset the TWOC from late 1937 on, was at a loss to explain why it had lost its momentum. But the fact remained that the "new and improved textile unionism" that Hillman boldly hearlded less than 18 months earlier, now betrayed features depressingly reminiscent of the defective model it had replaced.

In the end, however, Gorman's belabored contention that the TWOC was not all that it had been cracked up to be was pointless. The TWOC had problems, but reinstating the UTW was not the answer to them. Perhaps Gorman actually believed his eccentric boast to Lewis that "the United Textile Workers remains, so far, the only organization which has demonstrated an ability to mobilize and maintain a stable union in textiles." But neither the CIO chief nor anyone else familiar with the UTW's impoverished and consummately discombobulated condition at the time of the TWOC takeover could share that belief. Moreover, it was fanciful in the extreme to image that an inveterate autocrat like Lewis would have presumed to dispute Hillman's authority to rule his domain as he saw fit, even if the disarray that Gorman alleged in his critique of the TWOC was proved. With evidence mounting that the textile campaign had bogged down, Lewis may well have concluded privately that the CIO was not getting its money's worth, but whatever the TWOC's problems, they were for Hillman alone to handle.

Hillman's strategy in dealing with Gorman's increasingly open rebellion followed two tracks. In public, Hillman simply ignored Gorman's fulminations, a tactic undoubtedly intended to convey the impression that they were of too little importance to merit his personal comment or rebuttal. Even when CIO organizing director John Brophy asked Hillman to issue a public statement refuting a Hearst News Service report that Gorman's resignation from the TWOC was proof of an impending split in the organization, he refused.[54] Instead, he had James Starr, whom he cast as the authoritative voice of the UTW, publicly denounce Gorman and his Rhode Island allies.[55]

If in public Hillman behaved as if Gorman's tantrums were for other former UTW functionaries to quell, he was far more concerned and forceful in private. He sought, in particular, to shore up support for the TWOC in the New England mill towns where Gorman was most likely to attract a following. Only four days after Gorman submitted his resignation to Lewis, the TWOC hurriedly convened a special two-day "woolen and worsted trade conference" in Worcester, Mass. Intended to halt further spread of "Gormanism," the meeting was an occasion for Hillman loyalists to remind the 300 local leaders in attendance how much the TWOC had already accomplished and to assure them of even greater progress to come once the business climate in textiles improved. Several "high officers of the old UTW" were on hand to condemn Gorman and Rhode Island secessionist leader Joseph Sylvia as treasonous renegades willing to sacrifice textile unionism on the altar of personal ambitions.[56] After the conference, Starr wrote a letter urging restive woolen and worsted workers in Rhode Island not to be misled by the efforts of secessionists to associate their movement with the United Textile Workers of America. True friends of the UTW, he advised, knew that "Textile workers are now solidly behind the Textile Workers Organizing Committee in its efforts to build a strong unified textile labor movement which will enroll the million and one-half textile workers in this country. Concentrate your efforts on the organization of textile workers under the TWOC."[57]

Beyond taking steps to restore order in the ranks, Hillman was also obliged, in the wake of Gorman's challenge to the TWOC's legitimacy, to address the deeper issue it raised. Under Hillman the TWOC was, in fact, the autocracy Gorman alleged. But, of course, as everyone associated with the its creation, including Gorman, knew, the TWOC's special advantage derived from the increased efficiency that centralized authority afforded. Had the TWOC achieved all, or even most, of what Hillman had promised a year earlier, it is unlikely that its top-down structure would have been cast in any but a positive light. Yet the truth was that its disappointing performance was an invitation to other critics to echo Gorman's charge that its troubles derived from its too centralized organizational structure. Hoping to defuse the issue, which had become the focus of a court challenge to TWOC authority by Rhode Island dissidents, Hillman decided in October to create a seventeen-member Advisory Board. Composed of the TWOC's regional directors and all five elected national officers of the old UTW, including, ironically, its now terminally-estranged president Francis J. Gorman, the board was designed to counter the claim that the CIO drive to organize America's textile workers was a one-man show.[58]

Hillman quickly made it clear, however, that his decision to broaden the TWOC's leadership was more than a mere ploy to defuse Gorman's complaint that the union was run "by dictum, with no voice either encouraged or permitted from below." Long since disabused of his once ardent hope that the textile industry might become the fulcrum of industrial unionism's transcendent power, Hillman ultimately chose to use the opportunity that Gorman's mischief afforded to distance himself from the TWOC. When the members of the new Advisory Board gathered for the first time in early November to learn what Hillman expected of them, they were told that he "had . . . made it clear that this body was set up as an executive council and had all the powers of an executive council until one was elected by the TWOC Convention."[59]

Although he remained TWOC chairman, Hillman was content to entrust the organization's future to a group of loyal subordinates under the immediate authority of Emil Rieve, now its Executive Director. There is no evidence to suggest that in broadening its leadership Hillman intended to transform the TWOC from an organizing committee into a more conventionally governed union. Yet, as the implications of Gorman's campaign to nullify the TWOC-UTW pact became clear, his evident intention to maintain an organizational structure that permitted leaders to lead without effective constraints from below was rendered increasingly untenable.

The clearest evidence that the TWOC was in line for far more drastic alterations came on the last day of November, when the rancorous legal action that the union was pursuing against Joseph Sylvia and a tenacious band of Rhode Island secessionists spun out of control. The legal confrontation, which CIO general counsel Lee Pressman disapprovingly compared to "using a 15- ton gun on a tomato can," arose from sharp differences between local TWOC officials and "the Sylvia gang" over who had the stronger claim to collecting dues and to designating itself a CIO affiliate.[60] In its ardor to teach Sylvia and his followers a lesson, the TWOC unwittingly empowered a Rhode Island superior court judge of suspect leaning to decide whether the agreement that had given it control over the UTW was legally binding on its constituent parts.

The decision of Judge Charles Walsh that the contract between the CIO and the Executive Council of the UTW was invalid because local unions had had no say in the matter—though it was reversed on appeal—gave Gorman the excuse he needed to break from the TWOC. On December 13, in a letter to "all textile locals and textile workers of the United States and Canada," Gorman proclaimed that the "sweeping decision" of the Rhode Island court declaring the UTW-CIO agreement "null and void" meant the effective end of the TWOC. As a consequence, he explained, it was his duty to instruct all union members "to look to the United Textile Workers of America as their sovereign organization." Reiterating his self-serving contention that "the prime mistake [of the TWOC under Hillman] was in the throttling of the democratic participation of elected representatives of the textile workers," Gorman grandly announced that until a special convention could be arranged, he, as "International President," would take the lead in trying "to unite the various factions and departments in the textile industry under one common banner to function democratically under the constitution of the United Textile Workers of America—which the courts have held to be the only legal body through which the organized textile workers can express themselves."[61]

Publicly, TWOC leaders dismissed Judge Walsh's ruling—there was "nothing in the decision of the lower court of Rhode Island which in any way prevents the activities of the Textile Workers Organizing Committee from being carried on"—but, in private, they were less sanguine.[62] Similarly, when Gorman announced that the UTW was now free to reassert itself as the true institutional embodiment of textile unionism, TWOC leaders scoffed in public but worried in private. "Mr. Gorman's attempt is doomed to failure," Hillman assured the press, "because he has no organization and he has no following. He is being repudiated by textile workers in all sections of the country."[63]

Strictly speaking, of course, TWOC leaders correct in their claim that the legal setback the organization had suffered in Rhode Island was very limited in scope. They were also essentially correct, but indecorously vindictive, in characterizing Gorman as "a pathetic little 'Napoleon' without an army."[64] Yet the combination of an adverse legal ruling open to easy misinterpretation and a desperate dissident willing to distort its meaning was too volatile to ignore. The AFL had publicly invited textile workers to "come home" when the first signs of discord surfaced within the TWOC,[65] and with Gorman already gravitating toward the realization that such a reunion was his only hope for professional survival, the CIO's presumptive title to the UTW and its extensive jurisdiction was suddenly in jeopardy.

After months of dismissing or deflecting the threat that Gorman had schemed to mount, Hillman and other TWOC leaders were finally disposed to take forceful action. One day after Gorman declared that the UTW was once again free to chart its own course, Hillman expelled him from the TWOC Advisory Board.[66] The remaining members of the UTW Executive Council (four vice presidents and Secretary-Treasurer Starr) issued a vehement condemnation of Gorman, with the intention to confirm their allegiance to the TWOC and to inform veteran textile unionists unsure where their loyalties properly belonged that only Gorman, among the six elected officers of the old union, was "attempting to foment division in the textile workers' ranks."[67]

The furious contretemps over the next several weeks between Gorman and his erstwhile associates was, ultimately, farcical jousting to expel each other from a defunct organization to which both had equally dubious claims of exclusive authority. Their only real accomplishment was to turn a muddled situation into an utterly bewildering one. The agreement that gave rise to the TWOC had been ratified by UTW leaders under circumstances that came perilously close to constituting duress. So desperate were they for the CIO's help, and so confident were Hillman and his associates of the good works they would accomplish, that not even a rudimentary discussion of future institutional contingencies occurred before the bargain was sealed. Such haste and carelessness might not have mattered had the TWOC's initial promise been more fully realized. As the organization's troubles multiplied during 1938, however, those seeking a way out of an agreement they had rushed into the year before had reason to celebrate its loose construction.

Lawyers for the TWOC concluded that Gorman's claim of authority could probably be challenged successfully in a long and expensive legal battle, but, they warned, as long as the organization's legitimacy remained open to question dissidents would be free to wreak havoc on it. Aware that both Lee Pressman, the CIO's general counsel, and John Abt, the Amalgamated's chief lawyer, believed that Gorman's challenge demanded a forceful response, TWOC attorneys Isadore Katz and Alfred Udoff recommended that the organization would do better to reconstitute itself under its own authority than to rely on the vague mandate derived from the UTW-CIO agreement. To that end, they urged that delegates from all TWOC *and* UTW locals convene as soon as possible. Since Gorman, who intended to lead the handful of UTW locals still loyal to him back into the AFL, had already announced that he would soon call a textile workers' convention of his own, Katz and Udoff warned TWOC leaders that it was "imperative that your convention be called prior to the Gorman convention."[68]

On January 4, 1939, the same day that fifteen members of the UTW Executive Council convened a "trial" that resulted in Gorman's formal expulsion, the Advisory Board of the TWOC (now, unaccountably calling itself the Advisory Council) took the first tentative step toward securing the union's (and the CIO's) jurisdictional primacy in the textile industry. Persuaded that they must clear up the "confusion which exists," thwart Gorman's "splitting tactics," and "bring about solidification of the ranks of the textile workers," board members unanimously adopted a motion calling for a convention of all TWOC and UTW locals as soon as it could be arranged. Anticipating that the convention's principal business would be to dismantle the TWOC in favor of a new organization modeled on more traditional trade unions, some board members worried that the CIO and the Amalgamated Clothing Workers would withdraw their financial support "if we become an independent group." When Hillman finally joined the discussion, however, he pledged that funding from the CIO and the Amalgamated would continue, "even if TWOC became an independent organization." Anxious to distance himself from textile unionism and its chronic difficulties, Hillman nevertheless assured the board: "The ACWA and the CIO consider the textile situation one of our major responsibilities, and will see it through."[69]

While the TWOC limped toward the May convention destined to bring its brief and turbulent career to a close, most of those responsible for administering its tangled affairs preferred to explain the coming change as a natural transition from organizational expedient to mature institution. Beyond any force it had to rebut proliferating press accounts that the TWOC was in serious disarray, such an explanation also spared its purveyors the excruciating discomfort of having to admit that Frank Gorman's defection had forced them to do what they would not have done.[70] Still, explaining to John L. Lewis why the TWOC seemed suddenly compelled to reinvent itself, CIO general counsel Lee Pressman strongly implied that at the heart of Gorman's otherwise ill-advised and regrettable insurrection was a valid complaint. It appeared, he told Lewis, that "the TWOC, unfortunately, in carrying on its administration under the agreement between the CIO and the United Textile Workers did not give sufficient heed to the rights of the United Textile Workers." As a result, he reported, the TWOC now faced the task of "working out a procedure to adjust itself to such rights."[71]

The original agreement between the CIO and the UTW anticipated a time when the TWOC, having served its purpose, would cease to exist. The parties clearly intended, however, that that would occur only after a careful, deliberate assessment of the organizing drive's progress had confirmed that the institutional interests of textile unionism would be best served by restoring the UTW's authority. Without question, those who hastily sealed the TWOC's fate in January of 1939 had not been afforded the luxury of making their decision on that basis. Had they, it is extremely unlikely that they would have decided that early 1939 was a good time to forfeit the special advantages that operating as an organizing committee conferred. Indeed, Solomon Barkin's sobering report to the Advisory Board on the TWOC's generally dismal condition suggested that there could hardly have been a worse time to undertake a reorganization that was bound to reduce the leadership's freedom of action. While noting that there were some industry branches and a few regions in which the organization was actually doing better than simply holding its own, Barkin frankly admitted that, as the TWOC approached its second anniversary, "Very few areas can be truly described as being really free of important problems."

In the South, where the TWOC faced its most rigorous tests, there was almost no good news. Only in the cluster of mills around Huntsville, Al., where the spirit of unionism remained uncommonly strong, did the TWOC have anything to celebrate. Southern workers remained sufficiently enamored of unionism's possibilities to support the TWOC in most of the NLRB-supervised elections that took place in 1938, but the union's continuing inability to win contracts left millhands across the Piedmont deeply skeptical about the future of unionism there. Even more disturbing, Barkin observed, was the TWOC's "equally uninspiring" performance in New England, a region where the union desperately needed to prevail, if only to mitigate the impression of chronic inefficacy imparted by its scant progress in the South. Referring to the special effort the TWOC had undertaken in the hope of rebuilding its momentum in the region, Barkin ruefully noted, "The results of the drive are hardly equal to the attention and efforts which have been devoted." Moreover, he lamented, whatever the union attempted had to be done on a shoestring because of its constant financial woes. "This organization is still not self-sustaining," Barkin told the Advisory Board. The chief reason he cited was that the TWOC, like the UTW before it, could not persuade the low-wage workers who comprised so much of its membership to pay their dues. Even after carrying out drastic staff reductions and requiring organizers and others to work one week out of each month without pay, he reported, income from all internal sources provided only $32,000 of the $45,000 the union spent in an average month. "There is much work still to be done," he glumly concluded, "to really develop a dues-paying organization."[72]

The larger, more daunting reality that TWOC leaders confronted as they began to plan for the sweeping reorganization that lay ahead was that they had yet to prove, either to millhands or to employers, that the better, stronger union they had struggled so mightily to create was, in fact, truly better and stronger than what it had replaced. When the TWOC came into being in March of 1937, it was as a bold innovation, an organization whose modern structure and ethos, as well as its command of large resources, seemingly equipped it to become the forceful instrument of worker power in the textile industry that the fatigued and discredited UTW plainly could not. Yet, only two years later, no suspicion loomed more ominously over the immediate future of textile unionism than that the soon-to-be-discarded TWOC, despite its once fecund possibilities, in the end amounted to just another institutional variation on a depressingly familiar theme.

An early meeting of the Textile Workers Organizing Committee, spring 1937. *Left to right:* ACW vice president Charles Weinstein, United Rubber Workers vice president Thomas F. Burns, UTW president Francis Gorman, CIO organizing director John Brophy (not a member), United Mine Workers secretary-treasurer Thomas Kennedy, TWOC chairman Sidney Hillman, and American Hosiery Workers president Emil Rieve. (United Press International/Corbis)

New York City mayor Fiorello LaGuardia (*seated in the center*) waiting to follow TWOC chairman Sidney Hillman to the microphone at an organizing rally in New England during the spring of 1937. (From the UNITE Archives, Kheel Center, Cornell University)

CIO chairman John L. Lewis waiting to address a TWOC rally in Lawrence, Mass. in May 1937. TWOC chair Sidney Hillman is seated to Lewis's left. (From the UNITE Archives, Kheel Center, Cornell University)

Founding officials of the Textile Workers Union of America in 1939. Sidney Hillman is second from the left, followed by John L. Lewis, newly elected TWUA president Emil Rieve, and TWUA executive vice president George Baldanzi. (From the UNITE Archives, Kheel Center, Cornell University)

Sidney Hillman and Emil Rieve sharing a private moment at the founding convention of the Textile Workers Union of America in 1939. (From the UNITE Archives, Kheel Center, Cornell University)

J. P. Stevens employees in Roanoke Rapids, N.C., marching for a union contract after the TWUA's NLRB election victory in 1974. (From the UNITE Archives, Kheel Center, Cornell University)

TWUA president Sol Stetin addressing somber colleagues at the union's final convention, in the spring of 1976. (From the UNITE Archives, Kheel Center, Cornell University)

The leadership of the Amalgamated Clothing and Textile Workers, the union formed by the merger of the ACW and TWUA in 1976. *Left to right:* former TWUA secretary-treasurer and new ACTWU executive vice president William DuChessi, ACTWU secretary-treasurer Jack Sheinkman, former TWUA president and new ACTWU senior executive vice president Sol Stetin, AFL-CIO president George Meany, and ACTWU president Murray Finley. (From the UNITE Archives, Kheel Center, Cornell University)

Sol Stetin rallying support for the ACTWU's boycott against J. P. Stevens in the late 1970s. (From the UNITE Archives, Kheel Center, Cornell University)

The two "Norma Raes": actress Sally Field, who won an Academy Award for her portrayal of the title character, and Crystal Lee Sutton, whose organizing efforts inspired the character. (From the UNITE Archives, Kheel Center, Cornell University)

At a news conference early in 2000, Pillowtex Corp. CEO Chuck Hansen, seated at left, listens as UNITE secretary-treasurer Bruce Raynor describes to reporters provisions of the historic first contract between Fieldcrest Cannon and its more than 5,000 employees in Kannapolis, N.C. (Photo by Joey Benton, *Salisbury Post*)

CHAPTER 6

The Spoils of War

On May 8, 1939, delegates representing the ragtag following that Francis Gorman had enlisted in his feeble crusade over the preceding year met in Washington, D.C., with delegates representing the even more pitiful collection of would-be textile unions huddled at the "back door" of the American Federation of Labor to reconstitute the United Textile Workers of America under its pre-CIO charter. Explaining to the press that the UTW had only recently returned to the nourishing embrace of the AFL, and, so, had yet to emerge fully from the "state of temporary demoralization" in which "the ruinous and disruptive policies of the CIO Textile Workers Organizing Committee" had left it, Gorman asserted that, once revitalized, "the UTW expected to bring 95 percent of the old locals back."[1]

Gorman also undoubtedly expected that, when the UTW-AFL was revivified, it would be under his leadership. It was, after all, he almost alone who had gathered 132 delegates in Washington for the purpose of reasserting the AFL's jurisdictional claims in the textile industry. Had they had been free to vote their preference, there is no doubt that the delegates would have installed Gorman as their president. The AFL leadership, however, was not yet ready either to forgive or to forget Gorman's past transgressions. As pleased as they were to employ the ammunition Gorman's well-publicized defection provided in their increasingly nasty war of words and wills with the CIO, federation leaders were insistent that his earlier sins demanded an appropriate act of contrition. Gorman's penance, which he meekly accepted without apparent protest, was to decline election to the presidency of the UTW-AFL in favor of C. M. Fox, an obscure 36-year-old textile worker from Georgia whose qualifications consisted of little more than ardent animus toward the CIO. Gorman was allowed to chair the union's executive board, but not until 1941 was he sufficiently redeemed, in the eyes of William Green and other AFL chiefs, to warrant becoming its president again.[2]

Whatever personal gratification Gorman derived from his success in reclaiming at least a piece of the old UTW for his own use, it proved, in the years that followed, to be a largely unrewarding achievement. The UTW-AFL would accomplish enough to sustain a presence on the margins of the textile industry, but never enough to alter the fact, as *Business Week* observed on the eve of its convention, that the CIO continued "to hold all of the cards—and most of the union members." There were, of course, occasions when the UTW-AFL actually bested its CIO rival in the head-to-head competition for the allegiance of textile workers, but its principal roles were those of irritant and spoiler, rather than serious contender. As Gorman, perhaps, knew better than anyone else, the future of textile unionism belonged to the organization he had departed rather than the one he had resurrected.

Less than a week after the UTW-AFL revived itself in Washington, the TWOC and its far bigger share of the old UTW met in Philadelphia to formally consolidate. Following brief conventions at which more than 700 delegates representing the two organizations gathered separately to endorse the plan they would follow in becoming one, they met together to refit and launch the CIO's new vessel in textiles, the Textile Workers Union of America. While it retained the structure that the TWOC had earlier borrowed from the Amalgamated Clothing Workers, one that encouraged the coordination of local unions through regional joint boards and permitted the hosiery workers' and dyers' federations to continue to function as semiautonomous affiliates, the new TWUA operated under the authority of a constitution of its own invention.[3]

The union's transition to a constitutionally based scheme of internal governance silenced those who had earlier faulted its authoritarian structure. Yet, in opening itself to democratic participation, the TWUA risked a return to the internal divisiveness that had been one of textile unionism's historic maladies. Unlike the TWOC, whose top-down structure permitted decision making responsive to the interests of the whole, the TWUA's new democratic structure would foster a political culture in which decision making was increasingly attuned to the desires of the most important parts. And in the textile industry where ethnic heterogeneity, product diversity, and regional antagonisms had long tended to make worker solidarity an idea more compelling in theory than practice, the task of uniting distinct constituencies not always disposed to put their differences aside would test the political skills of TWUA leaders as much as it would their administrative talents.

The leadership of the new organization, chosen through a carefully orchestrated process that guaranteed that not a single office would be contested, was an amalgam of TWOC and UTW veterans whose calculated composition attested to the union's diverse membership. In a gesture of respect to their benefactor, delegates elected Sidney Hillman chairman of the TWUA executive board, but the day-to-day running of the new union was entrusted to the two men who had emerged, by the spring of 1939, as its leading personalities, Emil Rieve and George Baldanzi.[4]

Nearly complete opposites in both style and temperament, Rieve and Baldanzi had established reputations for forceful and effective action in a back-water of the labor movement where leaders of authentic ability were scarce. As the respective heads of the hosiery workers' and dyers' federations, the old UTW's only self-sustaining appendages, Rieve and Baldanzi shared, in 1937, both a strong belief that the TWOC represented textile unionism's best hope for the future and a firm conviction that Frank Gorman's leadership would be a liability, rather than an asset, to the organizational work that lay ahead. When the TWOC's career came to a close two years later, each man—Rieve because of his close ties to Hillman, Baldanzi because of his election to the UTW's presidency after Gorman's expulsion—was positioned to claim a place for himself at the top of the TWUA. Rieve's election as president of the new organization ensured his superior authority, but Baldanzi made it plain from the start that he would be a highly visible and independent executive vice president. The complex (and ultimately adversarial) relationship that developed between the two would not cause significant problems until many years later, but, almost from the first, as one observer noted, Rieve and Baldanzi were "two steering wheels on one machine."[5]

Given the bleak circumstances that obtained in the spring of 1939, leading the TWUA appeared to afford opportunities for nothing but headaches. All who spoke to the convention, from John L. Lewis and Sidney Hillman to the youngest and least experienced delegates, found in the relatively brief record of the TWOC's performance ample reason to praise it. Even the most stirring recitations of its triumphs, however, did little to dispel the air of apprehension that filled Philadelphia's Scottish Rite Temple as leaders and delegates contemplated all the organizing battles and contract fights still to be won before the TWUA could reasonably count itself among the CIO's true successes. Repeating a metaphor rendered threadbare by the frequency of its use over the preceding two years, Rieve solemnly reminded convention delegates that they had "laid a foundation" for durable unionism in the textile industry but that "the structure is yet to be built."[6]

Though there was union building to be done in nearly every branch of the industry, delegates left the convention having agreed that the TWUA's attention was most urgently needed in the South. Hillman, Rieve, and others boldly informed the press that the TWUA, having decided that conquering the South was its "No. 1 task," would shortly embark on a major drive "to complete its program of organizing southern textile workers."[7] What remained unexplained was how the new organization would pay for so costly an undertaking. With only a small fraction of the 275,000 members it claimed to have under contract actually paying dues, the TWUA was almost flat broke. Noting that the TWOC had spent more than $2 million on an organizing campaign that achieved only very modest gains, *Business Week* wondered whence came the money to finance a new drive in the South. The writer also guessed that the new 32½-cent-per-hour federal minimum wage proposed for cotton textiles under the Fair Labor Standards Act might make the TWUA's organizing work in the South even more difficult. "With the coming of the federal wage-hour law," he observed, "the southern workers have in many places been boosted to a wage which, although small, is more than the unions previously had been able to get. With the government's arm around him, will the southern mill worker figure he needs to pay union dues?"[8]

When the newly elected members of the union's Executive Council first gathered in New York after the convention, the blustery optimism they had served up in such large portions both to delegates and to the press was nowhere in evidence. Emil Rieve reported that his first act as president of the TWUA had not been to augment the union's organizing staff but to reduce it further. While acknowledging that "this wasn't the time to curtail our activities," Rieve insisted that the TWUA's desperate financial straits dictated that "no other course could be taken." William Pollock, the former Philadelphia joint board manager who had become the union's new secretary-treasurer, reported that the TWUA was beginning its work with a bank balance of $2,583.75. Yet even that was a "false balance," he explained, "if one took into account the $3,000 the union owed in unpaid Social Security tax." With that accounted for, Pollock told his colleagues, the TWUA's bank balance was "actually showing a deficit of close to $200." Members of the Executive Council agreed that, until they were able to close the substantial gap between its revenues and expenses, the union would have to continue begging or borrowing what it could from the CIO and the Amalgamated Clothing Workers and requiring its staff to work every other week for only half pay.

As the union's nineteen vice presidents took turns assessing current conditions and immediate prospects in their respective industry branches and regions, it became depressingly clear that, in the short term at least, the TWUA was, despite the cosmetic differences between the two organizations, destined to be much more like the old UTW than anyone wanted to acknowledge. In those regions or branches of the industry still awaiting concrete evidence of the economic recovery that the Roosevelt administration claimed was at hand by the summer of 1939, TWUA officials were using their meager funds simply in the hope of keeping a bad situation from getting worse. Where improving economic conditions had boosted business activity enough to warrant new organizing initiatives, dejected union leaders reported that they had too little money and too few organizers to take advantage of the opportunities. Elizabeth Nord, who directed TWUA activity in Connecticut, complained that, with only three organizers at work in the entire state, taking on any new obligations was out of the question. In the lower South, where the TWUA had earlier promised to do more and where the UTW-AFL said it also intended to concentrate, regional leaders saw little reason for optimism with funds and organizers in such short supply. Paul Christopher, whose highly effective leadership in the mills around Huntsville, Alabama, had helped to establish one of the few secure footholds the TWOC could claim in the South, expressed grave doubt that he would make much headway organizing millhands in his new territory, the state of South Carolina, until the TWUA gave him the organizers the task required. As things stood, he glumly confided, only 500 of the state's 87,000 cotton millhands were dues-paying members of the TWUA.[9]

Although the principal underwriters of the TWOC, the Amalgamated Clothing Workers and the CIO, were still willing to assist the TWUA, the patience and optimism of earlier days had been eroded by the inability of textile unionism to break away from its blighted past. The more than $2 million spent to establish a viable union in textiles had undoubtedly been a rewarding investment insofar as some branches of the industry were concerned, but it is unlikely that either Sidney Hillman or John L. Lewis truly believed on the basis of its full record that they had gotten their money's worth from the TWOC. Certainly, neither was disposed to be as generous in supporting the TWUA as he had been in bankrolling the TWOC.

As they struggled during the summer and fall of 1939 to achieve some measure of financial solvency, TWUA leaders discovered that they could expect less support from both the Amalgamated and the CIO and that the terms of that support would be increasingly stringent. Instead of the generous grants Hillman had doled out earlier, the Amalgamated now invited the TWUA to borrow much smaller amounts from its bank at 3-percent interest.[10]

Lewis, who had earlier dipped into the coffers of both the CIO and the UMW to help fund the TWOC, also put the TWUA on notice that his largesse was at an end. That Lewis was no longer willing to coddle the CIO's sickly relation in textiles was made evident in midsummer when he demanded that the TWUA, like other affiliated unions (including some just as financially burdened) begin paying its per capita tax to the national organization. Lewis proposed that the TWUA pay $5,000 per month, and offered to return $4,000 of that as a loan.[11] Rieve objected that such an arrangement would only exacerbate the TWUA's impoverished condition. "You will agree with me," Rieve wrote pleadingly to CIO Comptroller J. R. Bell, "that to borrow money from the bank and sign notes and then send money to the CIO and have part of it returned and sign additional notes, would mean that for the same dollars we would have two obligations to repay." Warning that the CIO's demands might seriously hamper what he (falsely) implied was a new organizing initiative under way in the South, Rieve suggested, in effect, that the TWUA was already paying its dues to the entire labor movement by breaking down barriers to unionism in the region. "We are . . . convinced that if we are to have a labor movement in America," he loftily avowed, "the South must become part of that labor movement. And we are of the firm opinion that there can be no labor movement in the South unless textiles is the foundation for that type of labor movement, so you can see that we are pioneering in the South—building a labor movement and spending a large sum of money at a time when we can ill afford to make such expenditures."[12] The compromise they finally worked out gave Lewis the concession he had demanded and took into account the TWUA's financial dilemma. Beginning in November, 1939, the TWUA began paying CIO dues on behalf of 80,000 members—$4,000 per month. In return, the CIO would contribute $5,000 per month, for four months, to support TWUA organizing work. When this special subsidy ran out in March, 1940, the CIO's affiliate in textiles was, after three years on the dole, finally obliged to pay its own way.[13]

While the promise of an improved business climate in textile gave TWUA leaders reasons to hope that better times lay ahead, especially as the outbreak of war in Europe stimulated production in much of the industry,[14] continued cost-cutting remained the union's strategy for survival in the short run. Between June and September, the TWUA slashed its organizing staff by a third. At year's end, the TWUA was struggling to sustain a presence in 32 states with a national staff of only 84 organizers, most of whom were spending as much time trying to collect dues from current members as they did working to organize new members.[15] Despite its continuing financial troubles, however, the union remained remarkably resilient. It continued to rely on the still uncertain authority of the NLRB to assist it in overcoming the most blatantly illegal opposition of millowners, but it also used its own paltry resources, and the fighting spirit of an unbowed membership, to defend earlier gains, and even to add some new ones. Between the founding convention in May and the end of 1939, TWUA locals conducted strikes in nearly every branch of the industry and every region of the country, including the Deep South. Some were lost, and others ended in settlements that fell short of real victory, but enough were won to persuade millhands and employers alike that the TWUA was still willing and able to fight for what it could not achieve through more peaceful methods.

In recounting for John L. Lewis the strike victories the union had won against mills in Alabama, Georgia, and the Carolinas during the fall of 1939, Lucy Randolph Mason buoyantly commented, "While TWUA has won most of its contracts through conference and negotiation without resort to strikes, it has shown its staying powers in significant ways when strikes and lockouts have occurred." The TWUA's continuing weakness and inefficacy in the Carolinas, the vital center of the cotton textile industry, was deeply disconcerting to anyone concerned with its future welfare, but its slowly growing institutional stability in adjacent regions sustained a fragile hope that the Deep South was not impenetrable wilderness that it often seemed. "It is significant," Mason assured Lewis, "that with one exception every Alabama textile company with which TWUA won an [NLRB] election now has a contract with the union."[16] Even in the Carolinas, the TWUA's new national monthly, *Textile Labor*, reported, there were new signs that once obdurate employers were at last acceding to unionism's inexorable advance. A case in point, it noted, was the large Marshall Field and Company textile chain, which at year's end signed union contracts covering 3,000 North Carolina millhands. Emphasizing that the agreement had been reached "without loss of time either to the firm or the workers," the paper highlighted Emil Rieve's enthusiastic boast that it also constituted "a major stride in collective bargaining relationships in the South," one that shattered "the myth that the South will not open the door to a sound method for reasonable and calm settlement of problems between employers and workers in the textile industry."[17]

Although the union's successful negotiations with the Field chain proved to be an aberration rather than the precursor of a new era of class harmony in the Carolinas, the optimism the agreement sparked was real enough. After enduring more than eighteen months of tumult and hardship, the organization was clearly showing signs of regaining some of its erstwhile vitality. The industry-wide agitation the TWUA launched in late September to promote wage increases had produced results in nearly every branch of textiles by the end of the year. In most cases, the increases only restored wages to the levels that had obtained before mill owners began slashing labor costs during the first half of 1938. Still, the mounting reports of wage increases that appeared in both union and industry publications gave the impression not only that textiles were rebounding from recession but also that the TWUA was vigorously, and successfully, exploiting that recovery on behalf of all workers, union and nonunion.[18] The TWUA had conceived its wage drive, Rieve explained, as a "pointed reminder" to mill owners "that the cooperation of textile workers in recession deserved cooperation by employers in a time of rising business, swelling profit, and spurting costs of living."[19]

Whether or not the perception was merited, *Textile Labor* informed its readers at the beginning of 1940 that the TWUA was "running in high gear." The union claimed that its wage drive had increased the aggregate income of textile workers by $70,000,000 and that the industry's surging prosperity would enable it to double its dues-paying membership before the year was out.[20] Rieve reported to the Executive Council that, during the second half of 1939, the union, despite financial constraints, had signed 64 new contracts covering approximately 16,000 workers. In addition, he boasted, the union had succeeded in renewing nearly 220 existing contracts covering 80,000 some workers. With organizers back on full pay and emboldened by recent successes, TWUA leaders easily persuaded themselves that even bigger victories lay just ahead.[21] In an open letter to the union's rank and file, Rieve boldly predicted the "continued rapid expansion of our organization." The TWUA's future could not be secured "by wishful thinking or by magic," he cautioned, but its burgeoning success attested to the increasing likelihood that it could be secured through determined organizing.[22]

To workers and union officials, who had heard more bad news than good for the past two years, Rieve's sunny forecast was undoubtedly a welcome tonic. Beneath the ballyhoo, however, lingered the less congenial reality that the historical barriers to textile unionism's success, while shifted slightly by political or economic pressures, had not been torn down. The union's financial situation had improved sufficiently by the spring of 1940 that it was finally operating in the black, but, by any reasonable standard of institutional solvency, it remained seriously underfund. Of the more than 225,000 members the union claimed to have under contract, fewer than half paid their dues. William Pollock complained to the Executive Council in May, "Even though we have been successful in negotiating increased wages in practically all branches of the industry," the union's dues-paying membership averaged less than 100,000 per month. "We must organize the textile industry," he groused, "and to do this we must maintain a large staff of organizers, and to maintain such a staff we must have revenue."[23]

Though only about half of the millhands working under union contracts regularly paid their dollar-a-month dues, TWUA revenues steadily increased in the period leading up to Pearl Harbor because of membership gains resulting from rising employment levels and its greater success in negotiating new agreements providing for the check-off of dues.[24]

The easing of the TWUA's financial problems allowed its leaders to plan with greater confidence, but funds were never plentiful enough, before the end of 1941, to permit them to accelerate the union's plodding pace in organizing the eight out of ten textile workers who remained outside its orbit. The national organizing staff slowly grew—to 94 (including six women) by May, 1941 and to more than 120 by the beginning of 1942—but the inability of poorer locals to employ their own business agents meant that organizers on the TWUA payroll were still spending much of their time attending to routine administrative duties.[25]

As prosperity and full employment returned to an industry that lately had had precious little recent experience with either, the TWUA, like most other industrial unions, reaped the institutional benefits the nation's rapid economic expansion conferred on its "strategic" sectors. What unions once had to gain for themselves, often through brutish struggle, now was attainable by riding an economic tide that raised labor's vessels as readily as it raised those of capital. "Almost every day now," *Business Week* reported in October of 1940, "some branch of the military is contracting to buy, or signifying its desire to purchase, large supplies of textile goods." The Army Quartermaster Corps had just placed the largest peacetime orders for textiles in its history, and other branches of the military were close behind. "This," the writer concluded, "adds up to greater employment and bigger payrolls for the largest employer of labor among domestic industries."[26]

It also added up to substantial membership gains for the TWUA. From the middle of 1940 through the end of 1941, the union took advantage of the industry's dramatically improved health to consolidate its position in nearly every branch of textiles. During that time, its leaders claimed to have signed more than 200 new collective bargaining agreements covering more than 65,000 workers.[27] A handful of the new contracts were with large firms that employed more than a thousand millhands, but the vast majority were with mills that had only a few hundred workers. Most also came through negotiations, often after NLRB elections, which the union continued to win handily.

When more forceful methods were necessary to win contracts, and when a victory seemed attainable, the TWUA unhesitatingly resorted to strike actions.

It was still the case, especially in the South, that where mill owners remained unyielding in their opposition to unionism and ruthless in their methods the TWUA was usually powerless to impose its will. And despite the union's continued reliance on the NLRB when its own efforts and authority were not enough, mill owners determined to deny rights accorded workers under the Wagner Act were able to do so with distressing frequency, especially in the South. In its report to delegates to the second biennial TWUA convention in April of 1941, the Executive Council cited more than 50 cases, some dating back to the days of the TWOC, of employers' nullifying the results of NLRB elections by refusing to engage in good-faith bargaining. For tens of thousands of southern millhands, particularly those employed by large, resolutely antiunion chains like Cannon and Burlington, the "revolution" in workers rights sparked by the passage of the Wagner Act more than five years earlier was still only a tantalizing abstraction.[28]

Despite such persistent difficulties, however, the TWUA's overall progress was undeniable. By the end of 1941, approximately 275,000 millhands were working under TWUA contracts, although only some 150,000 regularly paid their dues. The union had nevertheless succeeded in relieving its most acute financial worries. TWUA leaders also found other reasons to be hopeful. The union's campaign to raise wages during the last few months of 1939 was followed by even more successful wage drives in 1940 and 1941. And unlike the initial campaign, which had only restored wages to the prerecession levels, the new drives raised the pay of workers throughout the textile industry to unprecedented levels. When compared to employees in other manufacturing industries, textile workers continued to be poorly paid, but the wage increases the TWUA helped to win, especially during 1941, permitted it to claim, with at least some justification, that the new wealth accruing to the industry was being shared with labor as it would not have been in the absence of union pressure.[29]

Where it had won bargaining rights, the TWUA pursued its wage demands through direct negotiations. In carpets and rugs and synthetic yarns, two branches where the union was securely entrenched—it claimed, in 1941, to have organized two thirds of the workers in each—the wage increases wrung from leading companies were usually conceded by other producers, whether unionized or not.[30] Even though the TWUA represented fewer than a quarter of the country's woolen and worsted workers, the higher wages it negotiated with the giant American Woolen Company soon became the industry standard.[31] In silk and rayon and knit goods, two branches of the industry in which the union's "follow the leader" wage strategy was not applicable, TWUA bargainers adopted a piecemeal approach, winning wage concessions from one organized mill after another until the owners of unorganized mills were pressured to follow suit, if for no other reason than to keep a step ahead of unionism's enveloping embrace.

As always, cotton textiles posed special challenges when it came to forcing wage increases. In the northern branch of the industry, where the TWUA claimed, in May, 1941, to have 40 contracts covering 18,000 workers, companies long had struggled to compete with southern mills that benefited from interregional wage differentials that kept labor costs in the South at levels roughly 20 percent lower than those in the North.[32] As long as the vast majority of southern mills kept unionism at bay, beleaguered producers in New England were understandably reluctant to increase their millhands' wages absent assurances that Piedmont mill owners would, at the very least, boost wages in their region enough to prevent the gap from widening. Yet given its continuing weaknesses in the southern branch of cotton textiles—in May of 1941 the union had 23 contracts covering only 17,000 of the region's more than 400,000 cotton millhands—the TWUA could do little more than plead for comparable wage increases there.[33] In the fall of 1941, the TWUA, with the help of federal mediators, was able to bring an additional 5,500 North Carolina millhands employed by the Erwin Mills Company under union contracts, but the agreements, which provided for exclusive bargaining rights, grievance arbitration, dues check-off, overtime pay, seniority guarantees and procedures to resolve workload disputes, did not provide for general wage increases.[34] In the end, the union's strategy for raising wages in southern cotton mills relied more on its influence in Washington than in the Piedmont. The TWUA was, one historian wrote, "less a trade union than a spectral lobby, haunting the corridors of the Wages and Hours Administration" hoping to achieve through a relentless importuning of federal bureaucrats what it was unable to achieve through feeble threats hurled at heedless southern mill owners.[35]

Finally, by the middle of 1941, the union had something to show for its efforts, but not much. In June the Department of Labor's Wage and Hour Division announced its decision to raise the federal minimum wage for the cotton textile industry from 32.5 to 37.5 cents per hour. Although it left southern millhands earning far less than what the U.S. Bureau of Labor Statistics said was necessary to support a decent standard of living,[36] for workers living in abject poverty the new minimum was not a small victory. "It is estimated," Wage and Hour Administrator Phillip Fleming observed in announcing the new minimum, "that this rise ensures wage-rate increases to about 300,000 workers, which is the largest number of workers to benefit from a single industrial wage order since the enactment of the wage and hour law."[37]

As 1941 came to a close and the nation turned its attention to meeting the challenges of a war destined to transform American life and work as nothing else ever had, the TWUA was as strong and viable as it had ever been. Now absent from its leaders' thinking, however, was the facile conceit of headier days that the textile industry was a prime location for building industrial unionism's grandest edifice. After more than four years of often desperate struggle to erect a union structure capable of withstanding the vicissitudes of a habitually tumultuous industry, TWUA leaders were disposed to relinquish grand designs in favor of objectives at once more modest and attainable.

Still, the TWUA had progressed far beyond the advances of any of its predecessors, and with the war promising both robust economic growth and respite from the ferocious antiunionism of earlier days, the union's immediate future looked uncommonly bright. Within the extended family of CIO unions, where it had always been a poor relation dependent upon the charity and forbearance of its more affluent kin to maintain even an appearance of respectability, the TWUA was, by 1941, enjoying the unfamiliar esteem of self-sufficiency. It had yet to join unions of mine, clothing, steel, and auto workers at the front ranks of the CIO, but it seemed only a matter of time before the TWUA closed the remaining gap between itself and industrial unionism's bellwether organizations.

Given the deteriorating interunion relations within the CIO during the immediate prewar period, it may have been to the TWUA's advantage that it did not hold a leading position in the organization. The union unhesitatingly fell in line behind the Amalgamated when worsening relations between bitterly anti-Roosevelt isolationist John L. Lewis and avidly pro-Roosevelt internationalist Sidney Hillman forced CIO affiliates to choose sides at the end of 1940, but the TWUA's was generally neither a loud nor an influential voice in the increasingly savage debates the confrontation fueled.[38] At the emotionally charged 1940 convention of the CIO, one of the few occasions when TWUA president Rieve was bold enough to speak above a whisper in support of Hillman's position, Lewis angrily lashed back, characterizing the organizing effort in textiles as industrial unionism's biggest flop and suggesting in language dripping with contempt that it ill-behooved the head of a union that was so recently supplicant at the UMW's door to bite the hand that had generously fed it.[39]

Having endorsed Roosevelt's reelection to a third term and backed his efforts to prepare the nation for war, TWUA leaders also tended to sympathize with the administration's efforts to quell labor-management conflicts that swept through the country's heavy industries during 1941. With Sidney Hillman as the president's point man trying to keep the peace on the labor front, the TWUA could hardly have done otherwise, although Rieve and his fellow leaders were also responding to their own burgeoning patriotism.[40]

Rieve readily accepted an appointment as an alternate labor member of the Hillman-conceived National Defense Mediation Board, and proudly informed the Executive Council, in April of 1941, that he had taken a leading role in several of its pending cases.[41] In reporting Rieve's appointment, *Textile Labor* boasted that it was "not only a signal honor," but also an important opportunity "to serve labor and the country . . . by working out settlements to protect labor against the hue and cry in Congress for legislation to curb strikes and the rights of organized labor."[42]

Perhaps because of his close association with Hillman, whose rising prominence in the Roosevelt administration tended to elevate the status of like-minded trade union leaders in his immediate circle, Rieve's personal stature was growing. In a flattering article published early in 1942, *Business Week* portrayed Rieve as virtually the savior of textile unionism. He had performed near miracles in guiding the TWUA's recovery after the "almost fatal . . . body blow" that the recession of the late 1930s dealt. He did the job by concentrating on writing union-shop contracts. The writer gushed,

> He has sacrificed wage demands if, by so doing, he could get the employer's agreement to union membership as a condition of employment. Next time, he might come back for wage increases, but union security always came ahead of economic gains, and that's how TWUA was built to its present strength.

Describing Rieve as a reliable fixture of "the conservative wing of the CIO," the writer approvingly concluded:

> On the whole, the Rieve philosophy of trade unionism is as conservative as any to be found in the CIO. A close associate of Sidney Hillman, he had been characterized as a "dotted line instead of a picket line" unionist. One of his favorite retorts to criticism from left-wingers, who think capitalism has to go, is this: "I'm for the spoils system. I'll fight to protect it. I'll fight just as hard to see that the members of my union get their share of the spoils."[43]

Yet, as keen as Rieve was to present the impression of "responsible unionism" and to support the Roosevelt administration's preparedness program, like other union heads in the volatile industrial climate of mid-1941 he was adamantly opposed to the idea gaining currency in both public and private circles that the national emergency demanded that the government curtail or suspend labor's right to strike. "I recognize the fact that because of the international situation and our own uncertainty," Rieve told delegates to the TWUA's 1941 convention, "labor must put some sound restraint upon itself and avoid all needless and unnecessary strikes." Citing recently strikes against the country's most blatant and notorious violators of the Wagner Act, Rieve insisted that there were still circumstances, even in the midst of national crisis, when labor was honor-bound to fight for its rights. "When big employers . . . believe they are bigger than the government itself and believe they can violate the National Labor Relations Act or any other law that the Government has enacted," he declared, "then I say it is time that labor, if there is no other force, should tell them they cannot get away with it in this country."[44]

Despite its affection for Hillman and allegiance to Roosevelt, the TWUA risked public disapproval by siding with John L. Lewis and the UMW in their widely condemned attempts to force the National Defense Mediation Board to extend the closed-shop provision of the basic coal industry collective bargaining agreement to the "captive mines" owned and operated by the country's biggest steel companies. While conceding that Lewis was a raging "egoist" who was not above pursuing a personal "vendetta" against Roosevelt and Hillman at the nation's expense, *Textile Labor* nevertheless concluded, "The National Defense Mediation Board should include the closed shop in its award."[45] And when the NDMB finally rejected the miners' demand, Rieve very reluctantly followed the lead of other CIO members and resigned from the board.[46]

As long as war was only a threat, the TWUA had not been willing to compromise its freedom of action. Despite growing public pressure to suppress conflicts that threatened defense production, from July through September, 1941, TWUA locals conducted nearly 150 strikes involving more than 30,000 workers.[47] After the attack on Pearl Harbor, however, the TWUA immediately joined the rest of the American labor movement in pledging to make whatever sacrifices the nation's defense demanded. Rieve was one of six CIO representatives who met, under federal auspices, with AFL officials and prominent business leaders shortly after Pearl Harbor to forge an agreement that would ensure peace between labor and management for the duration of the war. The no-strike pledge that American unions formally agreed to on December 23 was perhaps labor's most significant contribution to the war effort. It was also the riskiest.[48]

By surrendering the most potent weapon in its arsenal, labor effectively entrusted its well-being to federal authorities whose commitment to defend the rights and interests of American workers was suspect. The NLRB record in enforcing workers' rights under the Wagner Act had been mixed, at best, and federal bureaucrats were rarely willing to risk the wrath of politically powerful business interests and their congressional allies by appearing too deferential to labor.

By giving up strikes for the duration, unions also risked alienating their members, whose anger and frustration, especially at delaying tactics commonly used by employers to thwart collective bargaining, often could not be relieved by any other means. That was especially true in textiles, where the most determined southern mill owners had refined temporizing to an art. Even when strikes hurt millhands more than their employers, the therapeutic value of a strike was often worth the price, especially when the union's refusal to fight might cost even more.

Realistically, however, unions, the TWUA included, had no alternative to the no-strike pledge. The sense of urgent national purpose the war created resonated as powerfully in union halls as everywhere else, and the reflexive patriotism of workers quickly crowded out narrower preoccupations that had tended to distinguish them as a class apart. Yet, if a common patriotism mitigated some class antagonism, the fundamental causes of workplace conflict remained the same. Throughout the war unions and employers continued to be about what they had always been about. Their diametrically opposed interests ensured that the tension between them would persist even if wartime imperatives temporarily altered the rules of engagement. In announcing the

TWUA's decision to forego strikes while the nation was at war, Emil Rieve emphasized that the union's concession should not be interpreted as a cessation of hostilities between labor and capital. "This does not mean that we shall in any degree relax our organizing drive," he assured millhands. "To the contrary, we shall expand our activity. This means merely that disputes shall be settled by peaceful means. Employers are making tremendous profits, and we shall continue to insist that the workers be given their fair share."[49]

Whether organized labor got its "fair share" during the war would be debated for decades afterward, but it is doubtful that any other national crisis of the 20th century (with the possible exception of the Great Depression) influenced the institutional fortunes of America's trade unions more profoundly. Greater security for unions and higher wages and better conditions for workers, the concerns that had dominated labor's agenda before the war, remained dominant during the war. Labor's progress on those fronts varied from union to union, but, when it was over, the war had had a powerful and lasting impact on nearly every union.

For the TWUA, the war had nearly instantaneous consequences. On February 25, 1942, in the first case it decided involving the critically important issue of union security, the National War Labor Board (WLB), the special tripartite agency empowered by Roosevelt to settle labor disputes during the war, ordered an amendment to the collective bargaining agreement between the TWUA and Marshall Field and Company providing that all employees who had voluntarily signed cards authorizing dues check-off "will, as a condition of employment, maintain their membership in the union in good standing during the life of the contract."[50] The "Marshall Field clause," as the order came to be known, was the first expression of the WLB's maintenance of membership policy, which, in broader form, became the essential foundation for union security throughout the war. Seen by the board's public members as a workable compromise between management's insistence on the open shop and labor's demand for either a union or closed shop, maintenance of membership was deemed necessary "in order to secure increased production which will result from greater harmony between workers and employers and in the interest of increased cooperation between union and management, which cannot exist without a stable and responsible union."[51]

As it did for many unions during the war, the WLB's maintenance-of-membership policy helped the TWUA to achieve a degree of institutional stability far beyond what it could have accomplished on its own. In combination with the benefits conferred by full employment and the rewards of aggressive organizing, the policy was conducive to a dramatic increase in union membership. By March of 1943, the union claimed to have more than 1,100 contracts covering 360,000 workers in every branch of the textile industry.[52] The rate of increase in the number of millhands under TWUA contracts slowed appreciably during the last two years of the war, but it remained impressive nonetheless. By the fall of 1944, union contracts covered nearly 400,000 workers.[53] "Never in the history of unions in the United States" TWUA leaders proudly boasted at war's end, "have so many workers been members of a textile union."[54]

As had always been the case with textile unions, however, membership figures alone were misleading. The TWUA was unquestionably a much larger organization at the end of the war, but its distinctly uneven wartime growth was a disquieting commentary on both its immediate circumstances and its postwar prospects. The TWUA's success in strengthening itself during the war was far more apparent in the North than in the South. In the North, the union took full advantage of the singular opportunities wartime conditions created to consolidate its position in several branches of the industry. By contrast, its persistent, even heroic, efforts to establish an equally strong institutional presence in the South, especially in the all-important cotton textile industry, produced far less impressive gains.

Had the TWUA's fortunes depended only on its success in the textile industry's northern branches, it would have been counted among the unions that derived the greatest institutional advantage from wartime conditions. In woolens and worsteds and carpets and rugs, two northern-based branches of the industry in which it was firmly established before the war, the union gained a commanding influence. By the end of the war, the TWUA had 20 of the American Woolen Company's 24 mills under contract, a circumstance which, given the firm's dominant position, accorded the union the practical authority to bargain for millhands throughout the industry. In addition, it had finally overcome the stubborn antiunion legacy of the 1926 strike to reestablish viable unionism in New Jersey's Passaic Valley, the largest center of woolen and worsted production outside New England. The contracts signed during the war with Botany Mills and the Forstmann Woolen Company, the region's principal employers, helped to extend the union's coverage to approximately 60 percent of the nearly 150,000 U.S. woolen and worsted workers.[55]

In the carpet and rug industry the TWUA's success was almost total by war's end. The Mohawk Carpet Company, the last major holdout, was brought under contract in the late summer of 1942 after an NLRB election in which disgruntled millhands finally ousted an entrenched company union that had served for years as the firm's chief line of defense against genuine collective bargaining.[56] With only a handful of stragglers still eluding its grasp as the war ended, the TWUA represented some 80 to 90 percent of carpet and rug workers.[57]

In other important branches of the textile industry where the TWUA had been established before the war—synthetic yarns, silk and rayon, knit goods, dyeing and finish, hosiery—wartime brought incremental gains that added to the union's overall strength. Only the full-fashioned hosiery industry, once a center of union vitality, failed to keep pace. Battered by the ill-effects of wartime production priorities, the industry's continuing southward migration, and new machine technologies that shifted production to longer-wearing seamless nylon hosiery, the American Federation of Hosiery Workers entered a long period of decline. By 1945, the TWUA represented no more than 30 percent of workers in the hosiery industry.[58]

By far the union's most important wartime growth during the war occurred in the northern branch of cotton textiles. An arena in which the TWUA had earlier achieved only modest gains, New England's cotton textile industry was the union's vital center by war's end. Although long since eclipsed by its southern counterpart, whose lower operating costs and newer, more efficient manufacturing facilities contributed to its dominance in every area except the production of fine goods, the New England branch of cotton textiles was a much better bet for union penetration.

Throughout the war, but especially from late 1941 to the end of 1943, TWUA organizers brought almost every important mill in New England into the union's bargaining sphere. Each advance fortified the union and burnished its previously suspect reputation, but the most meaningful ones, practically and symbolically, were achieved in the two production centers that had been most inhospitable to the TWUA, Fall River and New Bedford. Each boasted a solid tradition of worker activism, but the persistence of often parochial craft sensibilities gave rise to organizations whose defining characteristics—stiffnecked independence, jurisdictional provincialism, ethnic exclusivity, idiosyncratic leadership—made them less than ideal constituents of an industrial union.

In Fall River, where the independent American Federation of Textile Operatives (AFTO) remained the dowdy embodiment of obsolescent unionism, first TWOC and then TWUA organizers were repulsed by local craft zealots disdainful of the CIO's "mongrel" organization. By the summer of 1941, however, the TWUA had launched a new effort to bring Fall River millhands into the fold. Edward Doolan, a TWUA vice president and Fall River native who had gone to work in a local mill when he was only fourteen, supervised the organizing campaign. Its themes were the inherent superiority of industrial (over craft) unionism and the singular capacity of a national organization to preserve New England mills by imposing union standards on their southern competitors. The campaign did not extinguish the AFTO's divisive influence, but, by the late summer of 1942, Doolan and his assistants could proudly report that 12,000 of Fall River's 15,000 cotton mill workers were covered by TWUA contracts.[59]

In nearby New Bedford, where the TWOC's bitter 1938 confrontation with the New Bedford Textile Council had left millhands sorely disaffected, the TWUA faced an equally formidable challenge. When Emil Rieve reported to the TWUA Executive Council, in November of 1942, that he had dispatched six organizers to New Bedford to see what could be accomplished among the area's 12,000 or so millhands, he cautioned that the pace of progress likely would be slow.[60] That prediction proved accurate. The effort was coordinated by executive vice president George Baldanzi, who established himself during the war as the national union officer most intimately involved in its field operations and the New York–based leader who best personified what was for many workers in widely scattered mill towns an otherwise remote entity—the TWUA. Most of the day-to-day work fell to Mariano Bishop and Antonio England, two veteran organizers whose respective ties to the Portuguese and French Canadian communities that supplied most of New Bedford's textile workers eased the work of persuading conflicted local millhands to shift their allegiance from the New Bedford Textile Council and the UTW-AFL to the TWUA.[61]

The New Bedford campaign quickly degenerated into a festival of mutual vilification that dragged on through 1943. The TWUA effort was sustained by mounting evidence that it would succeed, but, as one historian observed, the deep and abiding bitterness the contest engendered "did not bode well for the future" of textile unionism in New Bedford.[62] The competition finally came to a head at the end of March, when more than 11,000 workers from eleven mills cast ballots in an NLRB-supervised election. The result—TWUA victory in all but one mill—constituted the union's greatest triumph in the northern cotton industry during the war. An exultant correspondent for *Textile Labor,* struggling to convey the extraordinary magnitude of the union's victory in New Bedford, gushed that it "brought militant and progressive unionism to an ancient stronghold of do-nothing unionism that has held thousands of cotton mill workers in its grip for nearly half a century."[63]

In fact, the New Bedford victory, while it represented significant progress in an important New England textile center, was hardly the rout that many partisans gleefully claimed. Of the votes cast in the election, the TWUA's share—5,596—amounted to slightly less than half. The UTW-AFL got 5,408 votes, and 238 New Bedford millhands voted against representation by either union. The TWUA had gained the upper hand in New Bedford, but not so decisively that its primacy there was assured.[64]

Still, when the union's wartime progress in the textile industry's northern branches is compared to the relatively modest gains that TWUA organizers made in the South over the same period, its greater vitality in New England and the Middle Atlantic states becomes starkly evident. While it was generally the case that the war fostered an environment more conducive to labor's success, it failed to unleash forces powerful enough to persuade or compel most southern mill owners to desist from their fierce antiunionism. Union pressures and WLB coercion did sometimes combine to force southern employers to make concessions they would not have otherwise, but those mill owners in the Piedmont who remained steadfast in their determination to resist TWUA encroachment regardless of the cost remained largely untouched. The large chains that dominated southern textiles—Cannon, Burlington, Deering-Milliken, Cone—either resisted union inroads completely or made under WLB duress such meager, grudging concessions that the TWUA could not build on them. The management of Burlington Mills was so unyielding in its antiunionism that it shut down mills during the war rather than comply with WLB orders to bargain with the TWUA.[65] Other vehemently antiunion mills in the South resorted to equally extreme tactics. Both the Gaffney Manufacturing Company in South Carolina, and the Mary Leila Cotton Mills in Georgia, were so resolutely defiant of WLB authority that, shortly before the war ended, the U.S. Army was ordered to take over their mills.[66]

Despite such opposition, the TWUA made a number of notable gains in the South during the war, the greatest in 1942, in Danville, Va. The Riverside and Dan River Cotton Mills, which local boosters proudly proclaimed the "world's biggest textile mills," employed 13,500 workers by the summer of 1942. In the aftermath of a bitter confrontation with the UTW in the early 1930s, the company had skillfully exploited the fear and disappointment of its defeated employees to keep unionism at bay for a full decade. The TWOC did charter three locals in Danville during the late 1930s, but they made almost no headway among still wary millhands.[67]

When TWUA organizers led by George Baldanzi launched a new drive to unionize the Riverside and Dan River Mills in the fall of 1941, they found local millhands haunted by the legacy of the 1930 strike. "That was the biggest problem we had," one organizer observed, "the memories of that strike." Still, local workers were dissatisfied enough with their working conditions to listen to union appeals. Encouraged by TWUA Research Director Sol Barkin to approach their work in Danville "scientifically" by employing the psychological and sociological profiles of southern textile workers and their culture that he had prepared after a brief tour of the Piedmont, the young organizers on the scene chose instead to use methods commended by their personal experience.

Joe Pedigo, a young Virginian recruited to the TWUA's organizing staff by George Baldanzi in 1939 following his success in organizing workers at the American Viscose Corporation's synthetic fiber plant in Roanoke, decided that "the whole mess of stuff" Barkin sent from New York "on how to run a campaign" had little practical value in Danville. "I just put it to one side and never touched it," he recalled,

> and Baldanzi asked me if I had got the stuff from Sol and I said, "Yes, and for Christ's sake, if Sol wants to run this campaign, let him come down here and run it, but I don't give a damn about this psychological makeup of the community or any of the sociological background or any of that stuff. I want to know what these people are saying in the pool rooms and the bowling lanes and the churches and everywhere else about this company and about what they need. When I get that all put together and get the right kind of committee, I'll have something. I won't have anything until I do.

Apparently persuaded that Pedigo and the other members of the Danville organizing staff knew what they were doing, Baldanzi let them run the campaign as they saw fit. "So, I was given a completely free hand," Pedigo explained, "and anybody that wanted to butt in, any of the big shots that wanted to butt in, I had an advocate that would tell them to lay off, 'these kids are running their show down there. Let them run it.' We made out all right."[68]

Assisted at times by TWUA Education Director Larry Rogin and publicist Val Burotti, who promoted the campaign so glibly that even the *Danville Bee* grudgingly praised it as "an appeal to reason rather than an appeal to the emotions," Pedigo and his colleagues made such great progress during the early months of 1942 that the union petitioned the NLRB for a vote at the end of May. The resulting election less than a month later, which *Textile Labor* claimed was the largest of any kind in Danville's history, gave the TWUA its greatest single victory during the war. Of the 11,920 valid ballots cast, 7,204, or 60 percent, were in the union's favor. The company announced that it would accede to the "revolutionary change," the vote portended, but its negotiators stalled for almost a year before finally signing a contract, under WLB pressure, in June of 1943.[69]

In reporting the "greatest election victory of the textile labor movement," *Textile Labor* predicted that what the TWUA had accomplished in Danville it would soon accomplish throughout the South. "The greatest fortress of antiunionism in the South has . . . fallen," the paper jubilantly declared. "A wedge has been driven and the whole unorganized section of the Piedmont region down through the Carolinas has been opened to the union."[70] As it turned out, the wedge did not penetrate as far into the heart of Dixie as the TWUA's overheated rhetoric suggested, but the union's subsequent wartime successes south of the Dan River in neighboring North Carolina, though modest, lent at least some credence to its claim that the victory in Danville was doubly important "because of the prestige which the union gained with textile workers throughout the South."[71]

Encouraged by the progress its organizers had made just before the war in winning contracts with two of the state's biggest textile producers, Erwin Cotton Mills and Marshall Field, the TWUA made North Carolina the special focus of its wartime efforts. With more than 200,000 textile workers, North Carolina was the union's biggest challenge and held its richest promise.[72] Despite the magnitude and intensity of the campaign, however, it did not produce the concrete gains the union had hoped for. When organizers did succeed it tended to be in small mills rather than large ones, and in independently owned ones rather than in those operated by the large textile chains, although a drive in Greensboro among workers employed in the complex of denim mills owned by the Cone family did yield a few small victories during the war.[73] The TWUA won another minor victory at Cannon's Amazon Mill in Thomasville, but the resulting WLB-ordered contract remained largely unenforced because of the company's unyielding resistance.[74]

By war's end, the union's efforts in North Carolina had gained it only 13,000 additional members. The increase more than doubled its prewar membership, but in a state with more than 200,000 textile workers by 1945, the 19,000 represented by the TWUA were a fraction of the whole too small to offer either comfort or encouragement to those who had hoped that wartime conditions might facilitate a long-sought breakthrough for unionism in the South. If anything, the union's organizing record in the rest of the Piedmont was even more discouraging. In Alabama, Georgia, and South Carolina, which together employed close to 350,000 millhands, the TWUA was able, despite the best efforts of its organizers and the support of the WLB, to add only 12,000 new members during the war.[75]

While the TWUA's overall success in adding to its membership during the years of World War II attested to textile unionism's increased vitality, the starkly uneven pattern of its progress remained deeply troubling. The Piedmont's dominance in the production of cotton textiles, which was bolstered by both the southward relocation of northern firms and new capital from local sources, was so well established by the end of the 1920s that almost no one who contemplated textile unionism's future imagined it as anything but a southern institution in the long run. And as other branches of the industry moved south, there was even less reason to doubt that textile unionism's survival depended ultimately on its success in doing likewise.

Yet, during the war, a period more hospitable to trade unionism than any before (or any that was likely to follow), the TWUA made no significant headway in accomplishing its relocation to the South. The TWUA was a northern-based union before the war, and it was even more emphatically a northern-based union when the war ended. The assumption that the union would, in the end, have to move south to survive was unassailable, but the practical reality that confronted leaders who had tried and largely failed to do just that was that the TWUA's immediate well-being depended more than ever on its ability to sustain itself in those beleaguered northern precincts of the textile industry where recent experience disclosed that workers could be successfully organized and contracts could be successfully negotiated.

Not surprisingly, regional tensions that had long been present in the TWUA and its predecessors were exacerbated during the war as union dues from the large northern membership subsidized organizing efforts in the South. Given the results, it seemed a poor investment. To keep faith with both southern millhands and northern employers, the union was obliged to keep plugging away in the Piedmont regardless of the rewards, but the logic of that commitment was destined to change, if only subtly, as the perception grew that defending the TWUA's greatly expanded base in the North must become the primary objective of its activities in the South. In the end, of course, that meant eliminating, or at the very least substantially reducing, the wage differential that continued to undermine fair competition between northern and southern manufacturers. And because the competitive disadvantages that northern employers faced were not relieved by the union's organizing successes in the Piedmont unless they translated into pay increases that brought southern labor costs into line with those in the North, which they had not, protecting the TWUA in the area of its greatest vitality required a frontal assault on regional wage differentials.

The union's attempts before the war to standardize labor costs across the textile industry by raising the federal minimum wage had produced a slight, temporary narrowing of the gap between northern and southern wage rates in cotton textiles, but in December of 1941 average hourly earnings in the South remained 20 percent below those in the North.[76]

Almost as soon as the war began, the TWUA launched a drive for both a general wage increase in cotton textiles and an additional increase in the South, to "narrow down" the geographic differential.[77] At meetings in Boston and Charlotte in early 1942, Emil Rieve announced a union push for an across-the-board hourly increase of ten cents for all cotton millworkers "plus an additional amount that will substantially reduce the differential that now prevails between northern and southern wages." It was time he declared, for the TWUA to demand that the wages of southern millhands matched those of their northern brothers and sisters. "The entire South and North," *Textile Labor* reported, "responded enthusiastically to the union's project to reduce the differential."[78]

Predictably, mill owners, especially those in the South, greeted the union's plan with much less enthusiasm.[79] Northern employers, who argued that the union's wage demand was excessive, nevertheless strongly agreed that regional disparities should be eliminated. Southern mill owners, who alternated between denials that a regional wage differential existed and claims that it was justified by lower costs of living in the Piedmont, rejected the union's demands out of hand.[80]

The TWUA's case for a ten-cent per hour increase in northern cotton-rayon mills was presented to the WLB at a hearing in Washington in late April. The union's argument rested on two central claims: first, that textile workers' earnings were far enough below those of workers in other northern manufacturing industries to be considered "substandard" and, therefore, warranted increases beyond those otherwise permitted under the wartime economic stabilization policy; second, that the industry's soaring profits would enable employers to absorb the increases without raising their prices.[81]

While representatives of the 48 northern mills involved in the case called the union's demands excessive, they warmly endorsed the TWUA's arguments in favor of standardizing wages across the industry to eliminate what they, too, claimed was an unfair competitive advantage enjoyed by southern producers. The *New York Times* reported that northern cotton and rayon mills were willing to agree to an increase greater than what they otherwise would "if the North-South differential were removed" by the WLB.[82]

The TWUA's demand for a 20-cent-per-hour wage increase for southern millhands, the amount its spokesmen claimed was necessary to match the proposed increase in northern mills and eliminate the differential, was submitted to the WLB on May 25 and 26. The union's case, *Textile Labor* boasted, was so forceful and compelling that "flabbergasted" southern mill owners were left "hanging on the ropes," so undone by the arguments arrayed against them that they had pleaded for a postponement of the hearings.[83] Any suggestion of faltering resolve among southern mill owners, however, was wishful thinking. The centrality of differential labor costs to the success of southern textiles was too deeply rooted in the economic logic and industrial folklore of Piedmont mill owners to admit of any doubt, and its preservation had become their sacred duty.

Certainly, the political delicacy of the issue was not lost on the members of the WLB. The reports of the panels that heard the cases reflected broad agreement on an industrywide 7½-cent-per-hour wage increase but a deep split on what, if anything, should be done to reduce or eliminate the North-South differential.[84] Members of the WLB found the issue equally nettlesome and divisive. Emil Rieve, an alternate labor member of the WLB and thus privy to its deliberations, later reported to the TWUA's Executive Council that board members "had their hands full in the battle over the differential between the North and South; there had practically been another Civil War over the situation."[85]

The WLB's decision, which was announced August 15, made it clear that the issue of regional wage differentials in the cotton textile industry was one that its members found too hot to handle. The board decided that workers were entitled to a 7-½-cent-per-hour wage increase, but insisted that it lacked the authority to redress the historic disparity in labor costs between the industry's northern and southern branches. Emphasizing that "a North-South differential in wages" was not a product of the industry's recent history but rather "a long-standing relationship" that reflected the "complexities" of its evolution as an industrial phenomenon, the board argued that the issue could not be "satisfactorily approached by the simple expedient of arranging wage rates so that equal average earnings are produced for northern mills and for southern mills." Moreover, the board held, to address the issue as the TWUA and northern mill owners proposed would require that it venture beyond its defined mission, which was only "to stabilize wage rates in conformance with the national wage stabilization program." Having thus set forth the limits of its authority, the board explained, it was bound to find that "stabilizing wages in the light of the national stabilization program precludes a narrowing of the North-South differential in wage rates."[86]

The refusal of the WLB to adjust or eliminate the North-South wage differential in cotton textiles was a major setback for the TWUA. Had the board been willing to bring labor costs in southern mills into line with those in the North it might have slowed or halted the process of erosion that left New Englanders mourning the piecemeal loss of their oldest manufacturing industry and the TWUA wondering if it would ever become in the Piedmont the formidable presence it had lately become in the cotton textile industry's northern domain. The war had afforded the northern branch temporary respite from its dilemma, but the persistence of the regional differential in labor costs ensured that, when peace returned, New England mills would again face the prospect of inevitable decline.

Unable to accomplish its goal by a direct means, the TWUA sought, throughout the remainder of the war, to close the gap between northern and southern wages by pressuring federal officials to raise the minimum wage in cotton textiles. Increasingly, however, the union's leadership was caught between federal bureaucrats determined to keep wartime wages in check and members expecting increases to bring wages in textiles into line with those in other large manufacturing industries. Early in 1943, Emil Rieve complained to members of the Executive Council that, even though wages in most branches of the textile industry had increased by about 32 percent since January of 1941, there was still "terrific pressure from the people in the field" to get them more. Yet, "viewing the picture as it is at the present time," he admitted, there was "no chance" of persuading the WLB to agree to further wage increases for textile workers in the immediate future. "For the time being," Rieve argued, the union had "reached a maximum in wages," and would "have to find other means of contributing to the welfare of the workers."[87]

In exploring "other means," the TWUA established itself during the war as one of the labor movement's most resourceful and innovative promoters of fringe benefits as an alternative to direct compensation. The union had prided itself on its success in negotiating paid vacations for textile millhands even before the war began,[88] but, boxed in by restrictive wartime wage policies, its leaders decided to "try new schemes to get something out of the employers if it is impossible to secure [wage] increases." As a result, the collective bargaining agreements negotiated by the union between 1943 and the end of the war broadened the assortment of "health and welfare" benefits that became a staple of union contracts in nearly every major American industry.[89]

As worthwhile and welcome as they were, however, fringe benefits lacked the ameliorative power of higher wages. And in the face of strong continuing pressure from an aroused rank and file convinced, despite assurances of government economists to the contrary, that higher living costs had long since nullified earlier pay raises, TWUA leaders began, during the summer of 1943, to lay the groundwork for a broad new campaign to increase the wages of textile workers in general and of cotton-rayon millhands in particular.[90]

The new wage demands, formally announced in mid-November, contained something for everybody: a general increase of 10-cent an hour for *all* textiles workers, a 60-cent-per-hour minimum wage in cotton-rayon mills, a 65-cent-per-hour minimum in woolen and worsted mills, and "appropriate minimums in all other branches of the industry." The union further demanded "wage uniformity by occupations within each industry in the textile trade, so that all workers doing the same job in the same industry, whether in New England or the South, the Midwest or the Pacific Coast, will get the same rate of pay." The union's goal, Emil Rieve explained to readers of *Textile Labor,* was a simple one: wage equality for textile workers. "Textile workers are sick to death of being the little stepchildren of American industry," he declared. "America's 1,250,000 textile workers have been exploited from pillar to post, and they're tired of it. The worm is about to turn."[91]

The TWUA's wage fight dragged on into the spring of 1945 and proved endlessly frustrating—for leaders and members. President Roosevelt's "hold the line" order of April 1943 had stripped the WLB of its independent authority over matters of wage adjustments. As a result, the boards "orders" were subject to the approval of the newly created Office of Economic Stabilization, headed first by former South Carolina Senator and Supreme Court Associate Justice James R. Brynes and, then, by another southerner, Fred Vinson. Under great pressure from Roosevelt to keep a lid on wages, Brynes and Vinson were disinclined to listen sympathetically to the chorus of complaints rising from union circles. Moreover, as southern politicians keenly attuned to power relationships below the Mason-Dixon, neither wanted to offend the prickly sensibilities of Piedmont textile barons.[92]

As it had in 1942, the TWUA's campaign for higher wages centered on the cotton and rayon weaving industry, the branch of textiles whose labor standards, especially in southern mills, provoked the most acute discontent. And, certainly, the union's survey of living costs and standards in five "typical" cotton textile centers—New Bedford, Massachusetts; Lewiston, Maine; West Warwick, Rhode Island; and, Henderson and High Point, North Carolina—yielded abundant evidence of the substandard conditions that its spokesmen alleged in their vigorous presentations to special WLB fact-finding boards in Atlanta and Boston during the spring of 1944.

Reporting the union's findings, *Textile Labor* declared, "Whether he lives in the North of the South, the American cotton worker earns wages so low that they bar him from the comfort, health and dignity which are the birthright of every American." As before, however, the TWUA's desire to highlight the egregious inequities of the continuing North-South wage differential in the industry prompted it to focus on the infamously degraded living standards of southern millhands. Using, for purposes of comparison, an "emergency" subsistence budget developed by the WPA during the mid-1930s to fix relief standards, union researchers claimed that a southern millhand paid the prevailing 57-cent-per-hour average wage for 40 hours received only $22.80 a week, an amount so inadequate to his needs that it left him "behind the eight ball . . . even if he lives at the level of a relief recipient in the depths of the depression, even if he works 52 weeks a year and pays no taxes."[93]

In both North and South, TWUA spokesmen sought to buttress their case by linking low wages to declining employment and production in the cotton-rayon industry.[94] First in the North and then in the South, Research Director Sol Barkin told WLB fact finders, tens of thousands of disgruntled millhands had abandoned jobs in the cotton-rayon industry for better-paying ones in other industries. Citing Bureau of Labor Statistics findings "that the cotton-rayon industry is the lowest-paid in the country," Barkin argued that only substantial wage increases would keep workers in the mills. "Neither rationing nor the manpower freeze can hold workers in the textile mills," he insisted. "Wages are at the root of the manpower problem and therefore at the root of the production problem, which is becoming critical." Higher wages for textile workers were a good thing not merely because they would relieve impoverished millhands, but because they served the war effort. "The effective prosecution of the war," he concluded, "requires that the cotton rayon wage scale, which is interfering with production, be remedied without delay."[95]

Although mill owners everywhere vigorously opposed wage increases, the union's case seemed exceptionally strong. "From this array of facts," the editor of *Textile Labor* confidently asserted,

> the Board should have no trouble at all establishing in its own mind the fact that cotton mill workers are sorely in need of wage relief. . . . As we see it, every argument is on the side of the union. Wages are substandard. There is a serious manpower shortage that can be remedied by higher wages. The WLB has the responsibility for remedying low wages. The mill owners can amply afford to meet the increased cost of higher wages.

"In essence," he concluded, "there is the union's case, and the proof is in the record."[96]

Although they had to wait for several months to find out if the members of the two fact-finding panels who had heard their case agreed, TWUA officials, and the 50,000 organized millhands who were the intended beneficiaries of the union pleadings, finally learned in late September that their arguments were, indeed, persuasive. The *New York Times* reported that a majority of each panel had advised the WLB that the TWUA was "correct" in its assertions that wages in the cotton-rayon industry were substandard and that wage increases were necessary to keep workers in the mills. Referring to the wage Barkin had claimed was necessary to sustain a minimally decent standard of living, the panels reported, "We are not able to find any point at which it could reasonably be reduced. Any lower level of living may, we think, reasonably be considered substandard."[97]

Since the panels' charge was only to find the facts, it remained for the WLB to decide on the basis of its own criteria whether the "Little Steel formula," the controversial standard it applied to most union wage demands, should be waved to permit new pay increases for textile workers. The award that the WLB tentatively proposed early in the new year—five cents an hour across the board and a 55-cent-per-hour minimum wage for the cotton-rayon industry—was denounced by the TWUA while it was still only a rumor. "If the public members of the Board, who reportedly are urging a 55¢ minimum wage for cotton workers, are making their proposal in all seriousness," Emil Rieve caustically observed, "they are blind to the cold realities of the situation that now faces the country generally and cotton workers in particular."[98]

As Rieve and his colleagues soon discovered, however, even the modest increases the WLB had in mind were more than southern mill owners intended to permit. At a press conference in Washington on January 23, Rieve disclosed evidence of southern employers' clandestine efforts to persuade several prominent politicians and federal officials, including War Mobilization Director James Byrnes, one of Roosevelt's closest confidants, to pressure Director of Economic Stabilization Fred Vinson into blocking any WLB order that threatened the cotton-rayon industry's North-South wage disparity. Rieve cited in particular a confidential memorandum to Piedmont mill owners from William P. Jacobs, an industry representative on the WLB's southern fact-finding panel. "From conferences which I held," Jacobs wrote, "I know that Justice Byrnes, Senators George, Maybank, Russell, and Governor Gardner and perhaps others have insisted that [Economic Stabilization Director Fred Vinson] do nothing which will wipe out the traditional North-South differential."[99]

Although embarrassed by public disclosure of what *Textile Labor* condemned as "the whole sorry mess of intrigue, connivance, and political high-pressuring" orchestrated by southern mill owners to influence his judgment, Vinson remained cool to wage increases. In mid-February, when the WLB finally issued an order for a five-cent per hour across-the-board wage hike and a 55-cent-per-hour minimum for the cotton-rayon industry, Vinson and Office of Price Administration chief Chester Bowles promptly stayed the order until its impact on prices could be determined.[100]

Already frustrated by the glacial pace of the WLB's deliberations and bitterly disappointed by its "piddling" awards, TWUA leaders exploded with anger when they learned that the wage increases they had been demanding for nearly 18 months would be delayed further while bureaucrats from other federal agencies studied their possible inflationary impact. At a special gathering of the Executive Council on February 19, a meeting which Rieve solemnly described as "the most important . . . since the formation of our Union," TWUA leaders decided it was time to let the Roosevelt administration know that the patience of long-suffering textile workers had finally been exhausted. "When labor gave its no-strike pledge in 1941," Rieve reminded council members, "it was with the understanding that the WLB would adjudicate all of labor's grievances speedily." It was now distressingly evident, he told his colleagues, "Not only does the Board not adjudicate cases speedily, but there are now superimposed upon the Board other personalities which makes the WLB today nothing more than a rubber stamp."

While insisting that TWUA members "were not unpatriotic," Rieve argued that their "terrific unrest" demanded attention. "Telegrams from our locals are daily being received urging us to release them from the no-strike pledge," he reported. And while he was "not unmindful" of his obligations both "as a labor leader and as a citizen," Rieve told the Executive Council, it seemed that nothing short of rescinding the union's no-strike pledge would suffice as a means of convincing the Roosevelt administration that textile workers had finally had enough. At Rieve's insistence, the Executive Council issued a bluntly worded statement condemning the WLB's inefficacy and denouncing other highly placed federal officials who, the union believed, had conspired with southern mill owners to sabotage its efforts to raise wages for "100,000 cotton textile workers directly and at least half a million indirectly." "Whether directly or indirectly," the statement charged, those functionaries, including Vinson and Byrnes, had willingly "lent themselves to the purposes of the cotton manufacturers in effectively preventing the National War Labor Board from handing down any order in this case." As a result, the statement continued, "the cotton textile workers feel that the independent, tripartite nature of the National War Labor Board has been completely subverted and there remains no government agency to which they can turn for justice." Since the "principle of equal sacrifice" had been exposed as "a hollow mockery," the statement concluded, the union was honor bound to accede to its membership's increasingly insistent demand that cotton-rayon workers "be released from the no-strike pledge."[101]

To punctuate its protest, the Executive Council agreed that Rieve should resign as an alternate member of the WLB. In a sharply worded letter to Roosevelt, Rieve explained that, since the WLB had "become little more than a hollow echo of the opinions and authority of other federal agents and agencies," it was no longer deserving of labor's confidence or support. In light of the WLB's sorry record in handling the textile wage cases, he told the president, it was "time for the Board to face the bald fact that it is beating its brains out against a wall of utter futility and that other agencies have in effect taken over its functions and authority."[102]

There is little doubt that both union leaders and members were willing, in many cases even eager, to strike, but the bureaucratic logjam that thwarted WLB orders in the textile wage cases was broken before that could happen. William H. Davis, who as chairman of the WLB had presided over its deliberations in the textile cases, succeeded the embattled Vinson as Director of Economic Stabilization in March. Within six weeks of his appointment, Davis reversed Vinson's decision and authorized the WLB to implement the five-cent across-the-board raise and the 55-cent minimum wage previously approved.[103] Its contempt for the WLB unabated, the TWUA nevertheless promptly informed its members in the cotton-rayon industry that they were, once again, bound by the no-strike pledge.[104]

While they never came easily or quickly, and invariably fell short of what union members and leaders felt was fair, the wage increases won by the TWUA between 1941 and 1945 almost certainly constituted its most significant wartime accomplishment. By its own reckoning, the union did more during the war to lift the oppressive pall of poverty from America's textile towns and mill villages than had been accomplished in the industry's entire history. For workers in the cotton-rayon industry in particular, *Textile Labor* boasted, the TWUA had established, not just for its members but for hundreds of thousands of still unorganized millhands, a standard of living beyond their fondest prewar hopes. Citing the estimate of Atlanta Regional Labor Board Chairman

M. T. Van Hecke that some 350,000 to 400,000 southern millhands would ultimately benefit from the five-cent-per-hour increase won in the "Big Cotton Case," *Textile Labor* claimed that the "all out fight for higher standards of living" would in the end "put between $35,000,000 and $40,000,000 a year into the pay envelopes of workers." Almost from the moment the wage increases were implemented, the paper reported in July, they had

> an electrifying effect upon every textile community. War bond sales jumped. Banks did a land office business. Stores reported their sales way up. In short, the economy of whole communities and whole areas got a lift, as it will also get a lift from the millions of dollars a year that will be added to the annual payrolls of the mills.

The TWUA had tried to get even more for badly underpaid cotton-rayon workers, the writer acknowledged, but even in falling short of its goal the union had won a victory of historic magnitude. "Everything considered—the lifting of the substandard level of pay, the boost to workers' morale, the healthy effect upon the economy of textile communities and the cotton-rayon industry generally—those close to the situation were of the opinion," he pridefully observed, "that the TWUA cotton-rayon case was probably the most important single case that the WLB ever has passed upon."[105]

The TWUA's pride in its wage gains during the war was well-deserved. Textile workers' earnings still lagged behind those employed in other manufacturing industries, but, between the end of 1941 and the middle of 1945, average hourly wages in the industry had increased by more than 30 percent. Improving wages in the cotton-rayon industry was a special focus of the TWUA's efforts during the war, but workers in every branch of textiles saw comparable increases.[106]

The higher wages the TWUA won enhanced its reputation, but in the South they posed potential difficulties for the postwar period. Unlike in the North, where the economic benefits won by the union during the war were accompanied by substantial organizational gains, wage improvements in the South, and particularly in the region's cotton-rayon industry, did little to help the TWUA win new members. The union had successfully exploited its foothold in the Piedmont to secure a somewhat higher living standard for nearly all millhands there, but, even with its wartime organizing gains, it still represented fewer than one out of five textile workers in the South. The discrepancy between economic and institutional progress meant that southern workers who had benefited from union-won wage gains without bearing the risks and costs of membership might, ironically, end up in the post-war period being less, rather than more, inclined to join the TWUA. Certainly, for unorganized southern millhands disposed to judge the value of union membership largely on the basis of the exceptional material benefits it conferred, the relatively large wage increases they received, though mainly the result of TWUA pressures, could as easily weaken the case for unionism as strengthen it.[107]

The union's official outlook in the summer of 1945 as the prospect of reconversion loomed immediately ahead was that the strength it had gained during the war prepared it to prosper even more in peacetime. With more than 600 locals and at least 400,000 textile workers under contract, it was now one of the CIO's biggest unions. Moreover, with the affiliation of 10,000 Canadian textile workers three weeks after V-J Day, it had become an "international" organization in fact as well as in name.[108] Its once desolate bank account was now bulging with savings and its once skeletal organizing staff was again thickly populated by dedicated young activists. And unlike some industries, which faced the prospect of sharply reduced production as the economy lurched and shuttered through the tumult of reconversion, the textile industry, and the TWUA, could look to the immediate future content in the expectation that pent-up consumer demand for its products was likely to keep mills operating at or near full capacity no matter what troubles might beset other business sectors.[109]

Behind all of the self-congratulatory rhetoric and sanguine prophecy, however, lingered the sobering reality that nurturing and defending textile unionism—never easy before—was not likely to be easy in the future. "With the end of the war," *Textile Labor* solemnly cautioned in a front-page editorial published just after V-J Day, "Our union faces a crucial test. An era has ended—and an era has begun." It had taken unexampled valor and resolve to meet the daunting challenges of war, and it would take no less "courage and vision" to confront the different, but equally formidable ones that peace was likely to impose on the TWUA and its members.

"It is true," the editorial writer conceded, "that the textile industry will not suffer the same reconversion pains as many other industries. It is also true that the specter of unemployment probably will not haunt us for a few years because of the backlog of demand." Even so, he warned, "These facts must not lull us into complacency. . . . Our battle has been transferred from Washington to the mill and the collective bargaining table. In short, we are on our own again.[110]

CHAPTER 7

"On Our Own Again"

Despite its many successes, which included organizing victories of unprecedented scale over some of America's largest and most powerful industrial corporations, the CIO was still a vulnerable movement at the beginning of 1941. Its affiliated unions had established themselves in several of the country's leading mass-production industries, but none was so well-entrenched that its future was ensured. The Wagner Act, though hugely beneficial to American workers when the rights and protections it conferred were effectively enforced, had nevertheless proven unreliable in the face of the fanatical resistance mounted by the nation's bitterest corporate scofflaws. Moreover, as public opinion shifted in response to the ceaseless barrage of antiunion fearmongering perpetrated by the National Association of Manufacturers, U.S. Chamber of Commerce, and other business and employer groups during the late 1930s, sentiment in favor of curbing the allegedly excessive power of organized labor in general and the CIO in particular grew both in Congress and in state legislatures. Overcoming such pressure would have been difficult under the best of circumstances, but the beginning of 1941 was anything but a good time for the CIO. Deeply divided by fierce wrangles in its ranks and unable to count on help from the Roosevelt administration, whose ambivalence toward an independently powerful labor movement was never more in evidence, the CIO confronted 1941 without having the means clearly at hand to cope with the dangers arrayed before it.

That its salvation was nevertheless accomplished had less to do with what the CIO did for itself than what was done for it by the capricious exigencies of the coming war. Almost certainly, that, more than any other factor, gave CIO unions *and* the Roosevelt Administration the leverage they needed to bring Ford, "Little Steel," and other brazen violators of the Wagner Act to heel. And once the war was on, the benefits that organized labor derived from full employment and the suspension of capitalism's controlling imperatives was invaluable. The policies of the National War Labor Board, though endlessly assailed and deplored by labor, not only created conditions conducive to spectacular growth—the labor movement nearly doubled in size during the war—but also afforded unions, and especially the still-struggling affiliates of the CIO, the lengthy respite from management counterattacks they needed to consolidate their earlier gains and to attend to their institutional maturation. As a result, by the middle of 1945 CIO unions were bigger and richer, and their members were emboldened by a sense of formidable presence far exceeding what they could have hoped to develop in the absence of the war's nurturing influences.

The war's restorative effects on the TWUA were little short of miraculous. The union had done what it could, in the aftermath of the 1937–1938 recession, to regain the momentum that hard times had so effortlessly destroyed, but its troublingly slow progress had fed fears that it might never recover. Yet the war seemed to change everything. The doubt and gloom that had settled over the union soon gave way under the war's ameliorative influences to a bracing optimism. Textile union leaders who not long before had wondered whether their expectations for textile unionism were unrealistic once again dared to imagine a time, not too distant, when every millhand in America would be recruited into the TWUA fold.

Yet for all the important differences that a post-war membership of more than 400,000 textile workers appeared to symbolize, the TWUA contemplated its return to the maelstrom of renascent capitalism in the fall of 1945 fearful that it might still be vulnerable to its perennial troubles, the ones that had beset it before the nation took up arms. Its spokesmen routinely claimed that the TWUA represented between 400,000 and 450,000 textile workers by the war's end, but its dues-paying membership never remotely approached those numbers. During 1944 Secretary-Treasurer William Pollock reported that the union was collecting dues from no more than 225,000 members despite its success in establishing the check-off as a staple of its contracts.[1] By the middle of 1946, the numbers ranged as high as 250,000, but even then nearly four of every ten members failed to pay dues.[2] Thus, even though the TWUA had more money in the bank at the end of the war than ever before, its leaders faced the prospect of having to finesse more dues increases to meet the higher operating costs that peacetime conditions would soon reimposed. Money problems had always plagued textile unionism, and the inordinate amount of time that TWUA leaders spent in the immediate postwar period trying to solve or manage them suggested that the union, while solvent, still had a long way to go before it could feel secure financially.

The TWUA's future was further clouded by its still evident inability to conquer the South. Wartime opportunities to organize in the Piedmont notwithstanding, the TWUA had not overcome the implacable antiunionism that had always been a defining characteristic of the southern textile industry. The union's vaunted triumphs against Erwin Mills, Marshall Field, and the Riverside and Dan River Mills, and its less spectacular success in opening the door to collective bargaining with the Cone chain in South Carolina were eagerly touted as harbingers of still greater progress in the South. Yet, the far-reaching influence it needed to entrench the TWUA in southern textiles remained elusive.

When the union's leaders assessed its wartime achievements, they found much to celebrate. In an industry long notorious for its "substandard wages and miserable working conditions," the Executive Council declared in its "Statement of Policy on Union Gains," the TWUA had achieved transforming changes. "[B]y raising wages, providing job security and protection against discrimination, establishing the principle of paid vacations and free insurance, and bringing many other benefits to the textile workers," council members boasted, the TWUA had validated itself as no other textile union ever had. Yet, their statement was conspicuously silent on the subject of the South,[3] as was the Executive Council's report to the 1946 convention. It claimed significant progress in the region overall, but the few concrete gains it was able to cite attested to the union's persistent weakness in the South. That the union's advance during the war had been woefully uneven was made abundantly clear in its progress report on cotton textiles. While proclaiming that 85 percent of northern cotton-rayon workers were represented by the TWUA at the close of the war, the report acknowledged that less than 20 percent of those in southern mills were covered by union contracts. Furthermore, the report ignored the not inconsequential fact that the wages and benefits the union negotiated for its southern members continued to be markedly inferior to those that collective bargaining conferred on their northern counterparts.[4]

Organizing the South had been declared the TWUA's "No. 1 task" at its founding convention in 1939. Yet if organizing Dixie was essential to the union's well-being before the war, it was vital to its survival at the end of the war. By reversing the decline in northern branches of the cotton-rayon industry, the war afforded the TWUA opportunities for growth that it would not have had in an atmosphere of continuing southward migration and mill liquidations. In taking full advantage of those opportunities, the union bound its future even more closely to a region whose long-besieged textile industry was living on borrowed time. The "new lease on life" that the war granted to northern textiles had produced a temporary appearance of robust health, but it was an illusion that would last only as long as wartime economic forces sustained it. As powerful as wartime influences had been in reshaping and redirecting the massive forces of national production, including those in the textile industry, their abrupt dissipation at war's end reinstated many of the prevailing influences of America's pre-war economy. There were, to be sure, residual influences of the wartime emergency that were felt in many industries for years to come. In textiles, however, the underlying economic structure remained unchanged, and there was no reason to think that the pressures that had impinged so powerfully (and destructively) on the industry's northern branches before the war would not reassert themselves with equal or greater force after the war.

The threat of peace posed an inescapable dilemma for the TWUA. Uneven growth during the war—large membership gains in New England and the Middle Atlantic states, much smaller ones in the Piedmont—meant that the union's welfare was more closely tied to the fate of the textile industry's northern branches than ever before. And since the TWUA's ability to secure its position in the South seemed even more problematic as a result of its disappointing record in the region during the war, saving the industry's endangered northern branches became the key to saving itself. In anticipation of the textile industry's continuing southward migration, leaders of the old UTW had largely resigned themselves to the likelihood that theirs would, in time, become a southern-based organization, a fact attested to by their decision at the end of 1936 to relocate the union's headquarters from New York City to Washington, D.C. In contrast, TWUA leaders were apparently content to see their organization for what it was at the end of the war: a northern-based union. Thus, when Sidney Hillman informed TWUA officials, shortly after the war, that the Amalgamated's headquarters in lower Manhattan was no longer big enough for both unions, the Executive Council decided, without more than a perfunctory discussion of the issue, to relocate to a building just a few blocks away.[5]

The public rhetoric of its leaders strongly suggested that the TWUA was as determined as ever to organize the South after the war. Promises of new and more vigorous efforts to organize the southern textile industry remained a featured theme of their public pronouncements following the war, but the TWUA's strategy in the South during the late 1940s betrayed an increasingly clear tendency among its dominant northern elements to regard the organizing of Piedmont millhands as a means to an end rather than an end in itself.

A desire to defend the industry's northern branches from destructive southern competition had always been an important motive of the TWUA's organizing work in the South. But its overarching purpose before the war had been to organize textile workers throughout the country and in every branch of the industry, and its sustaining conviction had been that its mission would not be accomplished until the goal of complete organization was realized. Disillusioned by the union's failures in the South and sobered by the pressing need to protect its expanded base in the North, most TWUA leaders abandoned their idealism in favor of a less ambitious, more realistic organizing theory. It was not necessary to organize the entire southern textile industry, they reasoned, but rather just enough of it to ensure that labor costs in Piedmont mills were sufficiently close to those of northern mills to no longer constitute a destabilizing competitive advantage. In short, the TWUA's organizing efforts in the South would be geared to the needs of its larger northern membership rather than to the establishment of an equally strong base among southern millhands.

As it always had been, reducing or eliminating the North-South wage differential in the cotton-rayon industry was the TWUA's best hope of ensuring the viability of northern mills. And during and immediately after the war, the union could point with pride to its success in narrowing the differential from 20 percent or more in the late 1930s to a little over 12 percent by 1946.[6] Still, because wage restraints during the war made it almost impossible to negotiate for higher pay, the union had been forced to concentrate on winning new and more generous fringe benefits. While the workers probably would have preferred fatter pay envelopes, the paid vacations and holidays, sick pay, group health and life insurance, and pension guarantees negotiated by the TWUA had great value nevertheless. They were also costly and more likely a consequence of collective bargaining than of the beneficence of non-union employers. As a result, fringe benefits were far more common in the North. Thus, despite the TWUA's success in reducing the wage gap between the cotton-rayon textile industry's northern and southern branches, a new "fringe-benefit differential" between largely organized mills in the North and largely unorganized mills in the South ensured that the regional disparity in labor costs remained in force.[7]

As TWUA leaders struggled during the latter half of the 1940s to determine how best to secure the union's future, they were responding more to immediate circumstances than to a grand design. As a result, the strategies devised after the war to seize opportunities and address challenges tended to reflect the influence of unfolding events rather than abstract formulations. Those strategies also reflected wartime changes in the internal dynamics of a still diverse organization. Representatives of the New England cotton-rayon and northern woolen and worsted industries, having gained the most members during the war, enjoyed new prestige and authority in union councils. It was after all, in their bailiwicks, where the union shop and dues check-off had become the rule rather than the exception, that the TWUA collected most of the money required to pay its bills and to fund organizing initiatives in the South. The synthetic yarn and carpet and rug divisions had also prospered during the war, but their smaller size and insularity tended to put them on the fringes of TWUA executive power. Thus, to the extent that President Emil Rieve was attuned to the needs and sensibilities of any particular parts of the whole following the war, it was more likely than ever to be to those of the union's northern cotton-rayon and woolen and worsted divisions.

The strength that northern textile workers had forged during the war was also evident in the methodical way they went about enforcing the successive wage demands they made on employers once peace was at hand. The repressed desire among industrial wage earners to claim what they believed was their fair share of the mammoth profits that corporate employers earned during the war manifested itself in an explosion of labor strife almost as soon as the economy and labor relations reverted to private control. Between the fall of 1945 and the summer of 1946 aggrieved workers struck in unprecedented numbers against employers in every mass industry in the United States.[8] Members of the TWUA, who felt as keenly as any workers in America that they had sacrificed inordinately during the war, were prominent both among those making new wage demands and among those walking picket lines when their bosses demurred.

In those regions and industry branches in which the TWUA had strengthened itself during the war, wage increases were generally won without the union's having to do anything more than threaten walkouts.[9] In ominous contrast, its efforts to consolidate its modest wartime gains and extend its reach in the South met with savage resistance from mill owners intent not merely on holding the line against new concessions but on reclaiming what they had grudgingly conceded to unionism under duress from the War Labor Board. The result was that, while northern millhands were bringing their militancy to bear in the service of higher wages and better benefits, their union brothers and sisters in the South were, for the most part, taking extreme action and great risks merely to hold on to what little they had.[10]

Only two weeks after V-J Day, 550 workers struck the Industrial Cotton Mills in Rock Hill, S.C., in the hope of forcing the company to comply with WLB orders that it had willfully defied for months. A week later, on August 29, nearly 700 millhands struck the Athens Manufacturing Company in Athens, Ga., for the same reason.[11] Less than two weeks after that, several hundred more millhands struck the Gaffney Manufacturing Company in Gaffney, S.C. when the company, which had just been returned to private control following its seizure by the U.S. Army three months earlier, continued to defy WLB orders directing it to bargain with the TWUA. Though only three among many conducted by TWUA locals in the early postwar period, the Rock Hill, Athens, and Gaffney strikes provided instructive, and profoundly disheartening, examples of what was in store for union millhands when they dared to take on the southern textile industry's most zealously antiunion employers.

The TWUA began trying to organize workers in Rock Hill during May of 1942. After two years of legal disputes were resolved in its favor, the TWUA handily won an NLRB-supervised election in early 1944 by a vote of 462 to 75. When the company refused to recognize the union and enter into negotiations, the regional WLB in Atlanta began a lengthy bureaucratic process that eventuated more than a year later in decisions upholding its original orders. Still, the company refused to sign a contract, and shortly after the Japanese surrender freed them to do so, the mill's 550 frustrated and impatient workers took matters into their own hands. The strikers never lacked for courage and resolve, but a company that had been willing to defy the U.S. government in the midst of a world war was not likely to relent no matter how resolute the strikers. After a failed attempt to reopen the mill in the strike's seventh month, its frustrated management greatly increased the pressures on strikers by serving eviction notices on those living in company houses. With the striker's morale sinking fast, the TWUA ended the nine-month stalemate by abandoning its demand for a contract containing the union security provisions ordered by the WLB a year earlier. That Industrial Cotton Mills was willing to sign any contract was apparently enough for *Textile Labor*, which described the settlement as "satisfactory." Yet the union's failure to win the security provisions it had sought guaranteed that its position in the mill would remain extremely precarious.[12]

If the Rock Hill strike was by most measures fruitless, its results were dazzling as compared with those of the Athens and Gaffney struggles, which disclosed to interested parties on both sides of the class divide in the post-war South just how improbable unionism was when mill owners brought the full weight of their economic, legal, political, and cultural resources to bear in opposing it. Like so many of the TWUA's actions in the South after the war, the Athens strike was less an act of aggression than of desperation. For two years following its lopsided victory in a representational election held in August of 1944, the union had battled in vain to negotiate a first contract. Even in the face of mounting pressure from the WLB, the company would not budge. And, because the WLB was even less likely to prevail once the war ended, angry workers had little choice but to strike. As the conflict dragged on, for weeks and then months, company lawyers expertly deflected, defeated, or delayed every attempt by the NLRB to enforce the law. And with every success they demonstrated to other would-be nullifiers among the ranks of Piedmont mill owners that, where the will was strong enough and the pockets deep enough, the rights of textile workers to organize and bargain collectively could be effectively revoked. For nearly 19 months, strikers clung steadfastedly to the conviction that the law was the law, but, on March 21, 1947, the TWUA quietly "liquidated" the strike when the patent falsity of that innocent faith could no longer be ignored. When strikers sought reinstatement to their jobs—on whatever terms the company might dictate—they were told no positions were available. Three months later, a federal appeals court finally upheld union claims made nearly two years earlier that the company was guilty of unfair labor practices. As a practical matter, of course, it no longer mattered. In the fall of 1948, the Athens Manufacturing Company used the same law it had earlier defied to win a decertification election that cleared the tangled wreckage of unionism from its mill once and for all.[13]

The TWUA's experience in the Gaffney strike closely paralleled its struggle in Athens. Both companies were adamantly antiunion and willing to do and spend whatever was required to avoid collective bargaining. Yet, the union's two-year long fight against the Deering, Milliken–owned Gaffney Manufacturing Company disclosed the special dangers workers faced when they presumed to exercise their constitutional rights in a company town. The company's management, so flagrant in its lawlessness toward the end of the war that the Army had to be called in, announced to workers on the same day that the mill was returned to its control that it would not bargain with their union. Strikes were a risky enterprise for southern millhands under the best of circumstances, but under the conditions in Gaffney, once the company's power and influence were fully deployed, strikers found it nearly impossible to defend their cause. The forces of local government, presided over by a mayor whose father was a local mill owner, made no pretense of neutrality. Local police harassed and arrested strikers without provocation, a pliant city council enacted special ordinances designed to impede the strikers' efforts, and servile local judges issued one injunction after another to keep the union off balance.[14]

The last major tactic of the company's strategy, which became a template for efficient strike breaking and union-busting throughout the Piedmont during the years that followed, was to raise the threat of permanent closure, a goal that the mill's management neatly accomplished by selling off half of its machinery. As this and other devices sapped their morale and their resources, and as their hope for help from the NLRB faded, the Gaffney strikers finally surrendered to reality and their mounting despair. On July 16, 1947, nearly two years after it began, the strike was formally terminated. The editor of *Textile Labor,* desperate to find a faint flicker of light in the gloom that descended on the local union, pluckily assured unemployed former strikers that, despite having been "soundly licked," theirs "was a defeat without disgrace," one that "added a proud chapter to the history of textile unionism." Certainly, the loss "came hard" to Gaffney workers, he noted, "but it is from such setbacks that ultimate victory is built."[15]

The less fanciful and poetic interpretation of the Gaffney strike, and the one that commended itself most plausibly to its battered casualties, was that it was from such setbacks that the TWUA's continuing fraility in the South could be predicted. The union's harrowing experience in Gaffney, as in other Piedmont milltowns where battles were fought and lost, showed just how high the stakes could be when a strike's outcome not only determined the terms and conditions under which a collective bargaining relationship would proceed, but whether or not such a relationship would continue to exist. Increasingly, when southern mill owners provoked strikes in the late 1940s it was not to gain a temporary contractual advantage but to vanquish unionism for good.

That did not mean, of course, that every strike the TWUA fought in the South during the postwar period was a fight for its survival. Several of the strikes the union conducted in the Piedmont during the first two years after the war, including a bitter struggle that 4,500 union members successfully waged against the Erwin Cotton Mills in North Carolina from October of 1945 through the following February, were fought to force contractual settlements that the parties had failed to hammer out at the bargaining table. Of course, in its dealings with the few southern employers seemingly disposed to give collective bargaining a chance (including Marshall Field and the giant Riverside and Dan River Mills), the union was able to negotiate satisfactory settlements without resorting to strikes or even to strike threats.[16]

Still, the prospect the TWUA confronted in the postwar period, and one that cast an ever darker pall over its future, was that its work in the South would only become more difficult. Early in 1946, however, TWUA leaders and members were given a reason to believe that the region might not remain a graveyard of union hopes after all. Once again, it was supplied by the CIO, which, in February, unveiled its plan to undertake a massive organizing campaign intended to drag the South, kicking and screaming if need be, into the orbit of industrial unionism and collective bargaining.

Touted by the *CIO News* as "one of the greatest organizing drives in labor history," the comprehensive southern campaign that CIO president Philip Murray described to the press following a meeting of the organization's top leadership on February 25 gave concrete dimensions to an idea that had, according to one insider, been "talked about . . . in every convention that the CIO has ever had." Bringing the benefits of organization to the region's powerless and impoverished workers had always been a good idea, Murray explained, but the greatly enhanced reputation that industrial unions had gained in the South because of its wartime successes had created an amenability to unionism among southern wage earners that was simply too inviting to resist.[17] "Reports from CIO regional officers throughout the South reveal the significant fact that the CIO national wage campaign has laid the foundation for immediate organizing," CIO organizing director Allan Haywood told readers of *Labor and Nation*. "In many of these areas during the past few years, the CIO has succeeded in organizing substantial numbers of workers in one or more industries. The new prestige which CIO has gained is stirring the people in the southern areas to concentrated and immediate action." Moreover, he reasoned, southern workers who had experienced unionism's benefits while working in wartime defense industries were not disposed to do without them once peace returned. "Many workers who had their first taste of union organization in some of the CIO-organized shipyards and aircraft plants in the South are leading the call for further organization," Haywood wrote. "As the wartime industries began to curtail operations, many workers returned to their former cities and old jobs, and it was only after they had reexperienced working in unorganized shops that they developed a fuller appreciation of the value of unionism."

But it was not the workers' receptiveness alone that made the spring of 1946 a good time for the CIO to look southward, Haywood declared. The war had not only altered the South's economy, it had weakened those ancient forces of history and habit that had for generations rendered southerners deeply suspicious of "northern" institutions like unionism. The decline of southern parochialism was most evident, he argued, in the postwar attitudes of the burgeoning middle class. "There is growing appreciation, even among some of the so-called middle-class groups in the South, that unionization and higher wages will help pave the way for great advances by all of southern society."

In deciding to launch a major organizing effort in the South, the CIO was not, Haywood pointedly emphasized, presuming to rescue southern workers from indigenous habits of industry that had helped to enslave them so much as it was extending a helping hand to industrial wage earners whose expanding class consciousness led them to demand economic justice. "The CIO believes," he declared, "that, to an important extent, southerners themselves hold the key to the so-called 'problems of the South' in the life of the nation. More particularly, we feel that southern workers, by building their own union organization and by winning a share of economic democracy, can help to alter the depressed picture presented by the greater part of the South."[18]

Although CIO leaders were no doubt sincere in such public declarations, good works were not their only motive. At war's end, they were more keenly aware than ever that their unions' achievements in other parts of the country would not be secured as long as the South remained beyond industrial unionism's reach. As they tallied the wage gains won for their members through raids on overflowing corporate treasuries once peace was at hand, CIO leaders readily agreed with veteran labor journalist J. B. S. Hardman's contention that the time was right "to reduce to as little as nothing the union movement 'differential' between the North and the South."[19] With wage rates "at the highest level in history," the *CIO News* observed, "the southern drive has become even more important. . . . It will not only bring comparable benefits to the southern workers, but will protect the northern, unionized workers from low-pay competition in open-shop areas."[20]

To direct the CIO's "holy crusade" in the South, which was modeled on the historic organizing drive he had personally led in the steel industry a decade earlier, Murray selected his chief assistant in the United Steelworkers, Van Bittner. Aptly described by a CIO colleague as "an experienced old war horse,"[21] the 61-year-old Bittner brought fifty years of trade union experience to his new assignment. A coal miner from the age of eleven, Bittner was elected president of his UMW local at sixteen and thereafter moved up steadily through the mine workers' ranks. Appointed by John L. Lewis to help Murray build the Steel Workers Organizing Committee, he had established himself by 1946 as one of the industrial union movement's most seasoned and dependable functionaries.[22]

For all his experience, however, Bittner's talent was for administration rather than organizing. Responsibility for directing field operations in the twelve-state region encompassed by the campaign was delegated to assistants drawn largely from the leadership of CIO unions that had significant jurisdictional interests in the South. Because the region's most important manufacturing industry, textiles, was due from the outset to be accorded "special emphasis," TWUA executive vice president George Baldanzi, whose work in the Piedmont during the war qualified him as one of the CIO's foremost authorities on southern organizing, was the logical choice to be Bittner's chief aide.[23]

The popular press promptly dubbed the effort "Operation Dixie." CIO officials vainly sought to shake the name, which they feared would raise the specter of carpetbagging in some southern circles. The campaign was designed to function independently of the CIO's affiliated unions, including those that contributed most to its promised million-dollar budget.[24] "The southern drive will be conducted as a CIO enterprise," the *CIO News* explained, "with the organizers directly responsible to the national organization. As locals are established, they will be turned over to the international union in each industry, and the CIO organizing staff will turn their attention to new unorganized spheres."[25] And though the textile industry was singled out for particular attention, other important southern industries would also be targeted, including furniture manufacturing, tobacco, lumber, clothing, rubber, steel, oil, and chemicals.

Anticipating claims by employers and their allies that the drive was yet another effort by Yankee interlopers to impose their ruinous social and racial values at the expense of the South's consensual harmony, Bittner and Baldanzi made sure that the credentials of the more than 250 organizers they recruited were impeccably southern. Reporting that the CIO Organizing Committee would be headquartered in Atlanta, the *CIO News* underscored Bittner's assurance that his staff would be comprised of "CIO organizers already working in the South and . . . new organizers drawn primarily from among the southern workers."[26] Moreover, by making sure that most of the organizers active in the southern campaign were also war veterans, Bittner hoped to blunt the charges bound to issue forth from every venue of antiunionism in the region that the CIO was Communism dressed in trade union garb. In explaining to the CIO convention a few months later why veterans comprised 75 percent of the southern organizing staff, Bittner declared,

> We knew what we were up against. We knew that every charge that has ever been made and some that had not been made would be made in this organizing campaign, so, at least if a young man had spent three or four years in the South Pacific, in Europe or in Asia, certainly nobody could accuse him or them of attempting to destroy America because they happened to be members of the CIO organizing staff.[27]

To persuade the people of the South that the CIO would not be the radical despoiler of all things southern that its most rabid and inventive critics claimed, nearly every official associated with the drive repeatedly articulated its conventional aims. While his somewhat overwrought characterization of its mission in the South as "almost a holy crusade" may have left southerners untutored in union hyperbole wondering just what devilish depredations the CIO intended, Murray, ever the orthodox trade unionist, had in mind what he described in the next breath as "a straight, clean-cut, pure, unadulterated campaign to organize that territory, to establish collective bargaining, and to elevate the standard of living."[28]

Bittner and Baldanzi were even more eager to reassure apprehensive southerners that the CIO was not mounting an invasion, but coming to the aid of workers who wanted nothing more extreme than "an American standard of living." Bittner publicly ordered everyone associated with the campaign to steer clear of anything even vaguely suggestive of political activity for the duration. He rarely spoke in the weeks before the drive without offering fulsome assurances to any southerner who would listen that the CIO was about helping them rather than harming them. At the opening of his new headquarters in Atlanta on May 3, Bittner told the press, "We have one objective—just one, and that is to organize all the unorganized men and women of the South into unions of the CIO for collective bargaining for higher wages and better working conditions." Despite the inflammatory slanders of "greedy southern employers" (who, he hastened to add, were no worse than "greedy northern employers"), Bittner said the organizing campaign would be as American as pecan pie. "The CIO is coming to the South with nothing mysterious, but dedicated to the sole purpose of bringing improved working conditions and economic liberty for the people in this part of the country." He predicted that workers in the South would rush to embrace unionism, not because they had been duped by the sinister, Red-tinged CIO proselytizers caricatured in many area newspapers, but because "southern men and women . . . have the same ideas, desires, hopes, and ambitions as labor in other sections of the country."[29]

For George Baldanzi, whose direct oversight of the campaign from his field office in Greensboro, N.C., would afford an understanding of its strengths and weaknesses that the more isolated Bittner could not have, calming the fears of those who found the prospect of "Operation Dixie" ominous or offensive was an urgent concern. Persuaded by personal experience that unionism's viability in the region ultimately depended on its success in establishing itself as an authentically southern institution, Baldanzi was anxious to correct the implication in the patronizing rhetoric of many northern activists that unions had to be explained to southern workers. Reciting some of the Piedmont place names—Elizabethon, Marion, Gastonia, Danville—that were synonymous with uncommon suffering and sacrifice in the cause of unionism, Baldanzi reminded delegates to the TWUA's 1946 convention, "The pages of American labor history are filled with the stories of the heroic struggle of the southern worker to organize." In resolving to concentrate its energy and resources in the South, he insisted, the CIO was simply committing itself to help southern workers as it had northern workers. "This is not a drive where the northern workers or the northern organizer is going to invade the South . . . This is a drive where the workers of the North, South, East, and West are going to wipe out, within our economy, any low-wage area so that we can rebuild an economy of full employment. We expect that the workers in the American trade union movement will march shoulder to shoulder with every worker who is not now earning a decent living wage, no matter where he may be located."[30]

Baldanzi's concern that the campaign not be viewed by the South's 500,000 unorganized textile workers as a northern "invasion" reflected a belief that its rich potential could easily be squandered by needlessly offending southern sensibilities.[31] No union had more to gain from the success of the southern campaign than the TWUA, and no individual labor leader more than George Baldanzi. "Odd man out" in a union whose constitution granted specific authority to the president and secretary-treasurer but no clear authority or responsibilities to the executive vice president, Baldanzi had been left to stake claims in those realms of union leadership not expressly reserved to Emil Rieve and William Pollock. Had Rieve been disposed to delegate significant authority to the union's second in command, Baldanzi's apparent determination to carve out a niche for himself might have been less pronounced. In Rieve, however, the TWUA had a president whose willingness to listen to the views of the other leaders was not matched by an equal willingness to share his broad presidential authority with them. And because the conspicuously ambitious Baldanzi was not one to concede the superior judgment or ability of any of his fellow TWUA leaders, including the union's elected president, he was increasingly regarded by Rieve as a rival rather than a dutiful subordinate.[32]

Easily the best known and most popular of the union's top officers among the rank and file, Baldanzi established himself during the war as the TWUA's unofficial organizing director. Engaging and articulate, he was one of the CIO's most effective public speakers and most charismatic personalities. Convinced that the union's future lay in the South despite its impressive growth elsewhere during the war, Baldanzi had made the southern cotton-rayon industry the focus of his attention both because it held the greatest possibilities for growth and because it had unmatched potential as a base of personal support in an organization whose leaders tended to rise or fall in stature based on the size and strategic importance of their respective constituencies.

Rieve was neither as well known to textile workers nor as popular. And, because, like Sidney Hillman before him, he tended to regard the South as a place of deep mysteries not readily fathomed by other than its own, he was apparently content to let Baldanzi see what he could accomplish in the region. Rieve's personal uneasiness in addressing the special challenges of the South, where his heavy German accent betrayed that he was, at once an outsider and a "foreigner," had led him to indulge the facile belief that by entrusting the union's affairs there to southerners of respectable background he was doing what he could to promote the TWUA's success. Yet in stubbornly standing by Roy Lawrence, who became the union's top official in the South following the death of Steve Nance in the spring of 1938, Rieve had ensured the continuing authority of a southerner who lacked both the temperament and the talent to be an effective leader in the region.

A former printer whose lingering craft mentality revealed itself in a preoccupation with contractual minutiae and administrative details, Lawrence neither inspired confidence among southern textile workers nor commanded respect among their employers.[33] Disliked and mistrusted by many of his underlings, who found him intolerant of dissent and averse to innovation, he was competent enough to retain Rieve's support but lacked the personal élan to excite the hopes or embolden the spirits of southern millhands. To a region that required, above all else, an indefatigable organizer, Roy Lawrence brought the stolid aptitude of a business agent.

To the extent that the TWUA had been guided by a "strategy" in seeking to organize southern textiles, it was one that relied upon the force of example. Like the Textile Workers Organizing Committee before it, the TWUA had based its work in the South on the assumption that its initial successes in creating local unions and establishing collective bargaining would afford a basis for demonstrating to southern millhands and employers alike the mutual benefits that derived from orderly, contractually governed labor relations. When that approach failed to produce the intended results, union leaders seemed less inclined to doubt the wisdom of their strategy than to question the capacity of both southern workers' and mill owners to appreciate the essential value of collective bargaining: the former because they were supposedly hostage to cultural forces that dictated subservience to authority; the latter because they were steeped in a managerial parochialism that favored individual over collective relations. At its most extreme, this amateur psychologizing, which revealed more about the frustrations of its practitioners than the pathology of its subjects, yielded informal "profiles" of southern workers and employers that cast them as hapless creatures of an aberrant culture.[34]

As a means of explaining the TWUA's ineffectiveness in the South, arguments that emphasized a cultural aversion to unionism among southern millhands were appealing because they tended to minimize the union's culpability. Yet such explanations were strangely at odds with the long history of activism to which southern textile workers were heir. If most southern millhands, like most of their northern counterparts, were more often disposed to accede to the boss's authority than to defy it, there were also too many instances of open and forceful activism in the cause of unionism among those same workers to support easy generalizations about how their preindustrial sensibilities and cultural inhibitions combined to immobilize them. The history of labor relations in the Piedmont, even when rendered unsentimentally, disclosed the immutable fact that textile workers had been willing to endure uncommon suffering and sacrifice in the union cause when doing so was commended by their independent perceptions of what might be gained. If southern history and culture exerted influences that tended to dilute unionism's appeal among workers, the effects were never so powerful that an aroused labor force was unable to overcome them. And if, in the end, northern millhands had more to show for their activism than did their southern brothers and sisters, it was not because they had been molded by cultural forces in the North to be better trade unionists but because their employers had been molded by cultural and other forces to be less resolute and resourceful antiunionists.

Although his approach to organizing southern workers did not differ appreciably from that of other TWUA organizers before the war—they all regarded winning NLRB elections as a necessary prelude to collective bargaining— George Baldanzi adopted the view, following his first extended stay in the South in early 1942, that for the union to secure a place for itself in the region it would have to be more than a means to higher wages and better working conditions. Unlike those who believed that the TWUA's success in the South was conditioned upon its representatives' ability to inculcate values among southern millhands that caused them to think and act more like their northern counterparts, Baldanzi argued that the union would succeed in the region by accommodating the workers' culture rather than transforming it. Impressed by what he saw as their humane and guileless character, which he carelessly romanticized as "the best of what remains of truly American folklore," Baldanzi assured his colleagues in New York that southern workers would be won over to unionism once the union learned to appreciate and to reflect both the secular and religious values that suffused their communities.

Too often, he complained, a "middle class complex" prevalent among TWUA representatives in the South caused them to distance themselves from their working class constituents in textile communities. Successful organizing among workers so attuned to class distinctions, he argued, required "putting oneself at their level and not making them feel inferior in any way." The TWUA was involved in nothing less than "a crusade for the improvement of the lot of the workers," Baldanzi insisted, yet union staffers in the region evinced little in the way of a "crusading spirit." In a comment aimed squarely at Roy Lawrence, the person he thought most responsible for the union's stumbling performance in the Piedmont, Baldanzi fretted that, instead of a "long-range program for permanent organization and stability," the efforts of staffers reflected an inordinate and ultimately counterproductive preoccupation with "more check-off and more dues."[35]

What was needed, Baldanzi concluded, was an entirely new orientation, one that cast the TWUA as an organization at ease among southern workers and unionism as an institution at home in the South. What he did not say, but definitely implied, was that what the union really needed in the South was George Baldanzi. And with his personal reputation on the rise because of what organizers under his direction were achieving in the spring of 1942 among workers employed by such large firms as the Dan River and Riverside Mills in Danville, Va., and the Erwin Mills in and around Durham, N.C., Baldanzi was in a strong position to convince Rieve and other TWUA leaders that he was the person best equipped to take on the singular organizational challenges of the South.

Although Baldanzi's growing prominence and expanding authority in the South constituted a tacit rebuke of Roy Lawrence's conspicuously unproductive stewardship, Rieve's continued devotion to his inept but loyal lieutenant fostered a regional leadership that was increasingly divided and confused. While Lawrence oversaw the activities of the local business agents and joint board functionaries who attended to the day-to-day administrative affairs of the TWUA,[36] Baldanzi, surrounded by a fiercely loyal cadre of highly motivated young activists that included organizers Lew Conn, Joe Pedigo, Joel Leighton, David Burgess, and southern Education Director Margaret "Pat" Knight, busied himself with the work of expanding the union's domain and inculcating among workers and nonworkers alike an appreciation of its authentic "southernness."

That Rieve and members of the union's Executive Council were content to give Baldanzi the free rein he wanted in the South was evident in their decision to grant his demand for more and better union education programs and their willingness to defer to his vision of textile unionism as an integral part of community life in southern mill towns and villages. By the middle of 1943, the union's Education Department reported significant progress in implementing the Executive Council's mandate of "a southern educational program with emphasis on the building of the union as a community center." Describing to the Executive Council how Baldanzi's brainchild had taken shape in Columbia, S.C., TWUA Education Director Larry Rogin explained, "This program led to a development of new activities in the community, which, while initiated by a member of the Education Department, are expected to continue permanently. These were intended to attract the membership to the union, establish ties between the union and the community and educate the community for a better understanding of the union."[37] Baldanzi's notion of community-based unionism continued to enjoy the TWUA's official sanction once the war was over. "On the community front," the editor of *Textile Labor* declared after the 1946 convention,

> we have merely scratched the surface. By and large, local unions and joint boards have not made the influence of the union sufficiently felt in textile towns. Education programs must be undertaken on the local level, and public relations programs, too, so that a social consciousness and a sense of social responsibility may be brought to bear.[38]

Although the union's gains among southern workers during the war fell short of matching his grander claims of what a comprehensive plan of action might accomplish in the South, Baldanzi and his band of like-minded activists had nevertheless succeeded in establishing themselves as the faction best suited by experience and disposition to represent the TWUA when the CIO declared its intention to organize Dixie. The need for a broader CIO presence in the South had been recognized early on by leaders of the Textile Workers Organizing Committee, who complained that their job was made infinitely more difficult because other industrial unions were reluctant to run the antiunion gauntlet there. When the CIO, emboldened by its wartime growth and awakened to the risks that the unorganized South posed, resolved to turn its attention to southern workers, the TWUA eagerly embraced the hope that it might at last accomplish its mission in the Piedmont.

At the union's 1946 convention in Atlantic City during the last week of April, the CIO's still evolving plan to take on the South was a topic of special moment. Delegates cheered wildly at every mention of the campaign and listened with gladdened hearts to the glib assurances offered by Philip Murray, George Baldanzi, and others that, when the smoke of battle finally cleared from the contested terrain of the South, the CIO's shining victory would illuminate the dawn of a new day in Dixie.

Even those guilty of the most extravagant optimism were careful to issue obligatory warning of the special difficulties that breaching the fortress of southern antiunionism presented. Only Emil Rieve's comments, however, verged on a realistic forecast of the hard struggle ahead. Having participated in planning a CIO-led southern campaign, Rieve was always an ardent supporter of the idea. He encouraged the Executive Council to pledge $125,000 to the campaign's initial million-dollar war chest, and was no doubt sincere when he assured delegates, "We have every reason to believe that out of this drive will come many thousands of new members of our union." Yet, whether because of innate caution or fear that the TWUA's apparent need for outside help in organizing the southern textile industry might be construed as impugning his personal stewardship, Rieve warned delegates against unrealistic expectations and against losing sight of what the union had already done, and was still doing, to help itself in the South.

In a tone at once measured and mildly defensive, Rieve warned,

> Much has been said at this convention, and rightly so, about the drive that the Congress of Industrial Organizations is starting in the South. Much enthusiasm has been created because of it. That is all for the good. But let me tell you that resolutions or speeches will not do the job. Every one of us will have to get in and try to do it ourselves.

"Don't expect miracles to happen," he lectured, "The days of miracles are over." What the CIO proposed to do in the South was not all that different, in method or scale, from what the TWUA had been doing there for nearly a decade. "We have pioneered with a great deal of pride in organizing situations in the South," he declared. "At the present time the Textile Workers Union of America has between 80,000 and 90,000 dues-paying members in the South. We now have 86 organizers and business agents operating in that part of the country. So, you see, the 200 organizers that we are talking about are not such a great lot in comparison with what we alone have now. We intend to keep them. We intend to act through them, so they and the organizers supplied by other international unions, plus the ones the CIO can put in, probably will be reasonably sufficient to do the job."[39]

Rieve's caution was well-founded. For all the fanfare attendant to its creation and all the hope nourished by its possibilities, neither the organizing apparatus nor the strategy that Bittner and Baldanzi hastily fashioned during the spring of 1946 offered ideas and approaches that had not been tried before in the South and found wanting. The insistence that winning NLRB elections was an absolute prerequisite to further organizing efforts betrayed nearly total reliance on Wagner Act guarantees. The assumption was strangely ingenuous, given how southern mill owners had exploited or flouted the law to thwart unionism. And, even when elections were won, labor had no assurance, as more than a few TWUA organizers knew from bitter personal experience, that employers would accede to the expressed will of their workers and enter into good-faith bargaining. Yet, from the start, the campaign's progress would be measured almost exclusively by a grossly misleading week-to-week tally of NLRB election wins and losses.

That the southern campaign was likely to achieve less than the profligate rhetoric of its most exuberant champions suggested was further intimated by the trifling resources it commanded. The $1 million that CIO unions had pledged in support of the drive sufficed as a gesture of their solidarity with unorganized workers in the South, but it was not nearly enough to confirm the seriousness of their purpose. Similarly, the legion of organizers the CIO promised to place at the drive's disposal failed to take adequate account of inevitable disparities in the quality and effectiveness of the service they rendered. The TWOC had learned the hard way, in 1937, that numbers alone were no substitute for talent and experience when it came to organizing southern millhands. Nearly ten years later, the CIO was to learn that same lesson. Most of the more than 250 organizers who took part in the southern campaign brought both ability and enthusiasm to what was never other than an excruciatingly difficult job. Many others, according to Joe Pedigo, were "nice young fellows [who] would have made organizers," if only "somebody could have taken them and brought them along." A few he described as simply "[not] worth shooting."[40]

Yet the factor that, more than any other, afforded skeptics a basis for doubt that the CIO drive in Dixie would be a transforming enterprise was that its essential promise was one that southern millhands, the workers who would decide its ultimate fate, already regarded as problematic. In one guise or another, the CIO had been trying to organize southern textile workers for almost ten years. Organizers might not personally have solicited the allegiance of workers in every mill village in the Piedmont, but they had spread their message wide enough (and long enough) to ensure that unionism and its benefits were, by that time, ideas familiar to textile laborers. By emphasizing that theirs was a cooperative venture committed to mustering the experience and resources of America's leading industrial unions to organize every important southern industry, the CIO was, at least technically, correct in claiming that this was something new. Behind the fresh facade, however, were tenets and tactics that, to southern millhands, looked suspiciously like more of the same. What the CIO proposed in 1946 was necessarily informed by what the TWOC and TWUA had earlier attempted. And, if those prior efforts provided a foundation to build upon, they also constituted an additional barrier to winning over those southern millhands who had concluded, on the basis of prior knowledge and experience, that the demonstrated weakness of unionism in their industry made activism an incommensurately risky choice.

Finally, public sentiment ran against the drive in the South. Antiunion forces, held in check during the war by the WLB, now reasserted themselves with a vengeance. And, as war-weary Americans poised at the threshold of an era of frenzied consumerism found their path obstructed by big strikes in the mass-production sector, they began in the early months of 1946 to signal with increasing clarity their willingness to go along with the practiced union-haters who insisted that organized labor had become too powerful for the nation's good. Thus, the timing for bold union initiatives could hardly have been worse. In seeking to establish a new labor stronghold in the South while public opinion was warming to the view that a stronger labor movement was the last thing the country needed, the CIO was unwittingly offering its critics a fresh target.

The myriad difficulties of doing what they promised in the South became evident to CIO officials as soon as the southern campaign got under way. The resolve of southern employers to resist with every weapon and resource at their command was expressed in a torrent of vitriol that gushed from every well-spring of antiunionism in the region. The familiar charges that unions were venal Yankee contrivances with no purpose other than to deceive and defraud honest, hardworking southern wage earners were augmented by scripture-laden harangues from entrepreneurial preachers behind scurrilous publications like *The Trumpet* and *Militant Truth*. Organizers also had to rebut the intimations of professional Red-baiters, including George Googe, the top AFL official in the South, that the CIO was really not a labor organization, but the leading edge of a rapidly spreading Communist menace in the United States. And, as was nearly always the case when the Ku Klux Klan and other accomplished promoters of race hatred sensed an opportunity to ply their singular talents, the CIO was viciously condemned as a sinister aggregation of race-mixers and mongrelizers intent on shattering the racial tranquility of the Jim Crow South.[41]

The CIO had done what it could even before the campaign began to assure southerners that its intentions were entirely conventional and honorable. Once the drive was under way, those who directed its course bent over backward to demonstrate that industrial unionism sought to change nothing other than the feudal labor relations that still obtained to the region's detriment in its mills and factories.[42] The CIO's southern-bred publicist and designated voice of reason, Lucy Randolph Mason, tried to recruit churchmen to attest to the CIO's virtue, but most of those who in private conceded the righteousness of its cause would not do so in public. John Ramsey, vice chairman of the Industrial Division of the Federal Council of Churches of Christ in America and a former staffer of the steelworkers union, also tried to muster support among the religious establishment. Like, Mason, he found that even sympathetic southern clergymen were usually loath to risk alienating wealthy mill owners who ranked among their foremost benefactors.[43]

As it had from the moment of the CIO's founding a decade before, the issue of race posed a dilemma from which there was no easy escape for industrial unionists. The official policies of the CIO and its affiliates were liberally festooned with high-minded endorsements of racial equality and equal opportunity, and the industrial union movement had made a conscious commitment to rise above the racist traditions of organized labor in the United States. At the same time, it was a rare CIO union that had not compromised its egalitarian principles when doing so would produce institutional rewards. No CIO union had been more squarely confronted by that dilemma than the TWUA, and it responded in ways that revealed the ineluctable conflict between abstractions and practical realities. At union conventions and those ceremonial occasions when expressions of high idealism were the order of the day, TWUA officials gave voice to a soaring rhetoric that positively oozed racial tolerance and brotherhood. Yet in the Piedmont, where expressing those same sentiments offended the rawest and most fragile of southern sensibilities, TWUA representatives gave racial issues a wide berth, content in a convenient belief that the virulent bigotry of millhands was best addressed in the fullness of time, through patient education. The nearly universal denial of employment to African Americans in all but a few menial occupations on the fringes of production had long been one of the southern textile industry's defining characteristics, but the TWUA, like the United Textile Workers before it, rarely let the idealism it paraded at a safe distance from the South intrude upon its organizational work in the region. Not even during the war, when a critical shortage of workers in southern textiles combined with emergency federal equal employment policies to create conditions more conducive to change, did the TWUA dare to propose hiring underemployed blacks to replace departing white workers. It took no special olfactory powers to detect the stench of hypocrisy that sometimes wafted from the TWUA's expediency in the South where matters of race were concerned. Even so, the preference among most union officials to regard themselves as trade unionists rather than social engineers when they confronted the rock-ribbed racism of white millhands in the region is not difficult to comprehend.[44]

Except in industries like tobacco, which employed large numbers of black workers, the leaders of the CIO's southern organizing campaign generally adopted the view that the less said about race the better. When backed into a corner, Bittner, Baldanzi, and other leaders recited the CIO's official commitment to racial equality, but rarely did they invite or encourage such inquiry. Bittner's strategy from the first was to emphasize that the CIO drive was about organizing industrial workers without discrimination. Black workers, Bittner insisted, were like all others. To someone who suggested that blacks might present a special challenge to CIO organizers, he answered, "That's nonsense. A Negro gets just as hungry as a white man. And from my experience, I can say that there's no better union men than the hundreds of thousands of Negro workers already in the CIO." Yet, black workers were not being organized because they were black, he quickly added. "We're organizing all the men and women of the South, because they are all God's own human beings. And this campaign means a better Georgia, a better South, and a better United States."[45]

Told that the campaign was likely to face "strong opposition from the rejuvenated KKK," Bittner defiantly declared, "There are not enough sheets made in this country to drive the CIO out of the South." Still, that he and his colleagues understood that racial fears, like land mines strewn across a battlefield, could be detonated by careless handling or a single misstep was evident in their insistence that organizers come from the ranks of southerners familiar with the cultural terrain. Apparently persuaded that the extraordinary perils arrayed before them made the unwavering course dictated by the CIO's expressed ideals too risky to follow, those in charge of the campaign were generally disposed to follow whatever route the region's racial topography left open to it.[46]

In answering the charge that the CIO was Communism in disguise, Bittner and his colleagues endlessly reiterated the campaign's apolitical goals. Because the issue was broached at a time when postwar tensions between the CIO's left- and right-wing factions were reaching a flashpoint, and Cold War animosities were being expressed with increasing vehemence both in national and international debates, the leaders of the southern organizing drive were eager to answer their accusers with deeds as well as words. Both Bittner and Baldanzi were outspoken anti-Communists never reluctant to lambaste their leftist brethren when ideological squabbles arose within the CIO. Once the southern campaign got under way, neither hesitated to flail away at the real or imagined Reds infesting industrial unionism's ranks, especially when by doing so they were also attesting to the purity of their motives in the South. The CIO, Bittner repeatedly explained, had not gone South to spread Communism, as its antiunion critics and their AFL accomplices absurdly charged. Rather, it sought to combat it. "That is one of the fundamental reasons we are so greatly interested in organizing the unorganized workers into the CIO," he declared several months into the campaign. "We know from experience that organized labor and genuine collective bargaining provide the best means of keeping communism from taking over in our country."[47]

As its undisputed boss, however, Bittner was in a position to do more than decry the involvement of Communists and fellow travelers in the campaign. He publicly enjoined campaign organizers from all "political" and "educational" work and privately worked to bar those associated with the CIO's left-wing unions from participating in the drive. Whether this ideological fastidiousness had any effect on the campaign's subsequent fortunes is impossible to say. Certainly, a case can be made that organizers from its left-leaning affiliates were among the most diligent, committed, and effective to serve the CIO cause during the 1930s and 1940s. Yet, given the nature of the formidable impediments the campaign met, it is unlikely that even organizers energized by political faith would have had more than a marginal influence on it, overall. What is equally unlikely, however, is that CIO conservatives improved the campaign's prospects by restricting involvement to those whose bland politics supposedly reduced their vulnerability to Red bating. Neither committed southern antiunionists nor seasoned AFL cynics like George Googe were noticeably constrained by considerations of accuracy or fairness in endlessly alleging the CIO's subversive purposes. If Bittner and his underlings truly thought that the campaign's opponents would desist from further Red baiting once the integrity of its emissaries was established, such thinking was naive and self-defeating.[48]

Whether Bittner, Baldanzi, and their colleagues planned and executed the campaign wisely or foolishly, expertly or ineptly, was rendered largely irrelevant by its seemingly inevitable outcome. From the outset, evidence began to mount that the CIO had taken on a challenge it was unlikely to meet. In the textile industry, where the CIO's battle to organize southern workers would be won or lost no matter how it fared in the region's smaller industries, a forecast of bitter disappointments to come was possible almost before the campaign became fully operational.

With more than 900 unorganized textile mills in North Carolina alone, CIO organizers were never at a loss for battlements to storm. From the outset, however, Baldanzi, who had official responsibility for the Carolinas and assumed informal authority over the textile industry elsewhere, adopted the same follow-the-leader strategy that the TWUA had always preferred in attempting to organize southern millhands. Convinced that its success in organizing small, independently owned mills would count for very little if large chains like Cannon, Burlington, and Deering-Milliken remained unorganized, Baldanzi and his lieutenants, William Smith in North Carolina, and the TWOC veteran Franz Daniel in South Carolina, invested most of their resources in capturing the industry's biggest prizes.[49]

Although no producers in the still highly competitive southern cotton-rayon industry were so influential that their acceptance of collective bargaining could induce smaller mills to follow suit, the companies Baldanzi listed as "immediate objectives" were the most formidable ones. In North Carolina, organizers were dispatched to Kannapolis and Concord, where the giant Cannon chain dominated, to the Greensboro–High Point area, where Burlington and Cone held sway, and to Gaston County, home to more than 100 mills (and the scene of deadly strikes during the legendary millhand's revolt of 1929). In South Carolina, efforts would be concentrated around Greenville and Spartanburg, where mills employed close to 30,000 workers in all. In Alabama, the Avondale chain was targeted, and in Georgia, the Bibb and Calloway chains.[50]

Eager to sustain the impression that the campaign was, indeed, something new under the southern sun, Baldanzi promised that organizers would "utilize every modern organization technique" to put "the Declaration of Independence into action" in the textile industry. Yet, though many of the faces were new and more of the voices betrayed the comforting intonation of a southern upbringing, the message CIO organizers earnestly conveyed to Piedmont millhands during the summer and fall of 1946 was essentially indistinguishable from the one that TWUA representatives had been imparting with little success for close to ten years.[51]

That message—that trade unionism and collective bargaining were the only practical and enduring means by which workers can redress their grievances and redeem their democratic birthright—was the foundation of the organized labor movement in the United States. That it was a compelling message was evident both in the century and a half of struggle and sacrifice American workers had sustained and in the institutional representation they enjoyed at the end of World War II. If neither proof of its abiding appeal was as evident in the South as in other regions of the country, the message had nevertheless stirred the blood and emboldened the spirits of southern workers often enough to refute the myth that they were constitutionally immune to its allure.

Yet, in the summer of 1946, southern textile workers tended to react to the CIO's message more with skepticism than enthusiasm. Mindful of a deepening popular suspicion of unionism, pacified by an enhanced sense of economic well-being, and persuaded by recent history that neither the TWUA nor the CIO was powerful enough to break down the barriers that resolute antiunion employers had erected, most southern textile workers concluded that taking the risks union organizers urged would probably cost them more than it would gain them.

For those determined to interpret this otherwise straightforward and uncomplicated calculation as an expression of the southern industrial worker's immutable antediluvianism, the aberrant history and culture of the South offered a veritable treasure trove of intriguing causalities. Such inquiries, however, yielded little genuine understanding. The problem with southern textile workers was not that they had stayed the same but rather that they had changed. Even when they had nothing else working in their favor, union organizers had almost always been able to count on the southern millhands' brooding discontent at being the lowest-paid workers in America's lowest-paid industry. And, by any standard, the wages of southern millhands were still substandard. Yet, it was perception that mattered, and, as most southern millhands saw it, their economic status had never been higher. Their wages had increased twice as much as the cost of living over the preceding five years, and, by 1946, many of them were, for the first time in their lives, enjoying a standard of living measurably above the abject poverty that was for so long a feature of employment in the cotton textile industry of the South.[52]

Of course, as CIO organizers endlessly reminded Piedmont millhands throughout the summer of 1946, it was unionism, more than any other force, that accounted for their improved standard of living. By means of collective bargaining in organized mills, wage drives in unorganized mills, and relentless pressure on the WLB and other federal agencies involved in wartime wage administration, the TWUA had wrested from southern mill owners far greater increases than they would ever have volunteered. Because it was in the union's interest to keep all southern wages high enough to keep the North-South differential within a tolerable range, the TWUA had been obliged to represent the interests of all textile workers in the Piedmont. "Even where we have no contracts," TWUA southern director Roy Lawrence told staffers in Alabama, "we can help the workers. The bosses fear their employees will organize and to forestall it, give unsolicited wage increases."[53]

Yet, even for the southern millhands who realized that the TWUA was chiefly responsible for their higher wages, the value of union membership remained problematic. The TWUA's success in raising wages during and immediately after the war had a powerfully seductive effect on its leaders, who, from Emil Rieve on down, succumbed increasingly to a temptation to measure the value of union membership on a basis of the material rewards it conferred. Wages and benefits were concrete measures of progress, easily quantifiable and not open to interpretation. And, as long as they were revealing how handsomely unionism was rewarding those in its orbit, neither members nor leaders had reason to question their validity as indices of the value of union membership.

What CIO organizers discovered as they fanned out across the Piedmont, however, was that unorganized millhands, because they were already enjoying the economic and other benefits that the TWUA's exertions in the region had yielded, were often at a loss to understand what additional value union membership might bestow. Leaders of the TWUA had always known that their wage strategy in the South might backfire, but they hoped that unorganized millhands would feel indebted to the union and appreciate, as one official said, that "the only real raises are those they can write into a union contract."[54] "No reasonable person will suppose," a *Textile Labor* editorial insisted after the union's successful southern drive in early 1946, "that the employers who are now rushing in with raises would be willing to grant the smallest concession to their workers. All of which points up an old, old moral—without a union you have no one."[55] Commenting later on yet another increase, which it predicted, "would sweep through the southern cotton industry like wildfire," *Textile Labor* cited assurances from Baldanzi that the TWUA's agitation for higher wages for unorganized workers would soon pay off in new members. "This newest increase," Baldanzi explained, "will stimulate organization rather than otherwise. For if the manufacturers feel that it is necessary to grant this increase at the very outset of our drive, unorganized workers don't need much imagination to figure out the gains that will be possible when every southern textile worker is a member of the union that made these gains possible." When CIO organizers tested that assumption, however, it proved dubious at best. "The workers in many big mills," veteran TWUA leader H. D. Lisk later reported,

> are sold on the idea that they are getting all that the unions have been able to get for the workers in the mills which have been unionized—and without cost. Most of them know that their wages rise according to the pressure that the union puts on the organized mills; but they are getting a free ride, so what the hell.[56]

While many, perhaps most, unorganized southern millhands agreed that they might be better off with a union, than without one, they also made it clear to CIO organizers that, with few exceptions, they were loath to pay the inordinately heavy price that membership was sure to exact. Organizers found that millhands who were initially responsive to their solicitations, perhaps even to the point of signing a union authorization card, backed away from their commitment when employers and their community allies, a group that typically included representatives of every important local institution, apprised them, by word and by deed, of the retribution that continued activism invited. It was, perhaps, a less than flattering commentary on their collective mettle, but in light of the TWUA's historically feeble performance in the region, and in the absence of proof that the CIO was any better equipped to protect them from the bosses' wrath if they persisted in their union zeal, southern millhands could hardly be faulted for their survivalist ethic.

Accounts, in the *CIO News* and other labor publications, of the organizing successes achieved in other southern industries during the first few weeks of the campaign, successes invariably tallied by NLRB elections won rather than contracts signed, raised the hope that the CIO might, indeed, be equal to the task it had set for itself. Yet, as reports of the drive's depressingly slight progress in textiles trickled into Bittner's Atlanta headquarters, grimmer assessments slowly came to the fore. Bittner reported, at the end of July, that 78 full-time organizers were on the job in the Carolinas and predicted that, within a month, there would be enough nascent locals to "keep one man busy just keeping tab on the elections that have just been held or are going to be held soon by the National Labor Relations Board."[57] Such rosy prophesies initially kept those in the field from giving in to their disappointments, but they lost their ameliorative power as the campaign bogged down.

Veteran TWUA organizers knew from personal experience that winning an NLRB election was a hollow victory unless a contract followed, but most consoled themselves with the rationalization that persuading workers simply to declare themselves for collective action still constituted progress. Yet, in the summer and fall of 1946, many of those same organizers discovered that talking southern workers into even tremulous gestures of support for the CIO was distressingly difficult. Early in the campaign, the TWUA did win a lopsided election victory among the 220 employers of the Borden Manufacturing Company in Goldsboro, N.C., but it did not herald greater triumphs to come.[58] In early August, three successive election defeats in mid-sized North Carolina mills that organizers thought would yield union majorities provided a more accurate forecast of what lay ahead.[59]

In the end, however, it was the CIO's dismal failure to engage employees of the textile giants—the companies that strategists said must be won if the southern drive were to be counted a success—that extinguished whatever flickers of optimism remained. In some cases, the ferocity with which employers and their allies reacted to the mere appearance of CIO organizers in their communities was enough to keep even the most receptive millhands from risking a supportive gesture. When workers were openly responsive to the organizers, millowners countered with threats, intimidation, and, if necessary, dismissal. In those circumstances, activism was not an option.

Bibb Manufacturing, the principal target in Georgia, used its suffocating control of the town of Porterdale (all municipal officials, including the police, were on the company's payroll) to enforce a virtual ban on union activities. It enlisted the assistance of local Klansmen and subjected its 8,000 employees to viciously antiunion ravings of *The Trumpet,* a "Christian" hate sheet that eagerly marketed its race-baiting, Jew-baiting, and Red-baiting services to any southern industrialist with the price of a mass subscription. When union representatives filed a formal complaint with the NLRB, they received a sympathetic response but no real assistance. Lawyers for the Bibb Company, like those for other determinedly antiunion companies in the southern textile industry, were well-schooled in legal devices that rendered the NLRB incapable of enforcing workers' rights, and they applied their expertise with ruthless efficiency.[60]

The experience of CIO organizers who solicited support among the employees of the Avondale Mills in Alabama proved equally harrowing. Controlled by the Comer family, whose opposition to unions bordered on fanaticism, Avondale Mills had kept its 7,500 employees beyond unionism's reach by paying them well above the prevailing wage in textiles, manipulating them through a company union, and inflicting brutal punishments at the first sign of "disloyalty." The Comers used the same assortment of legal and extralegal tactics that had been used to advantage elsewhere in the region, racist and religious fearmongering prominent among them. (The Comers found that the viperous smears and imprecations that were the stock in trade of *Militant Truth* fit the bill nicely.) Union organizers scurried for cover. At the CIO's request, the NLRB ordered the Comers to desist from their blatantly lawless conduct. Predictably, they demurred, and the CIO's organizing drive at Avondale Mills sputtered to a halt.[61]

The serious setbacks the CIO suffered in Georgia and Alabama left its textile campaign badly wounded. Its crushing encounter with Cannon Mills in North Carolina left it "at death's door." Charles Cannon's unrivaled stature in the southern textile industry was built on his suffocating paternalism and the daunting personal authority he wielded. He was employer—and patriarch—to nearly 25,000 millhands in and around Kannapolis, in 1946 easily the largest surviving mill village in America. An informal CIO survey of workers during the early weeks of the campaign revealed that good standing in "Uncle Charlie" Cannon's "family" was a relationship that few millhands were willing to jeopardize. Most Cannon employees enjoyed higher than average wages, reasonable workloads, steady employment, and decent, low-cost company housing in an orderly, well-tended community. Indeed, organizers discovered, most Cannon employees so valued those perquisites of staying in their benefactor's good graces that even the thought of what they might lose by defying or displeasing him was enough to discourage any contact with them.

Still, organizers hoped that just beyond the reflexive caution that loyalty and fear inspired was a long-suppressed yearning, among Cannon employees, for the dignity and sovereignty that unionism alone afforded. It was just a matter of time, they believed, that skittish Cannon workers would shed their diffidence. The organizers waited in vain. No doubt, the image of a millhands' union powerful enough to bend any employer to its will was alluring to many workers, but, in their daily lives, where ideals rarely survived head-on collisions with reality, Mr. Cannon's power and the TWUA's weakness contrasted too starkly to be ignored. After nearly five months of effort, which revealed the southern campaign in textiles at both its best and its worst, dispirited CIO organizers quietly added Cannon Mills to the growing list of battles they would fight another day. More out of pride than any realistic hope of future progress there, the CIO maintained a tiny garrison in the Kannapolis area throughout the southern campaign, but no one who understood the magnitude of its defeat at Cannon Mills could regard its future in the South as other than precarious.[62]

Not surprisingly, when those in charge of the southern campaign reported on its progress at the CIO convention (held in mid-November), they carefully picked through the record for whatever evidence of success they might cite. Philip Murray and other top leaders willingly played along, telling the delegates, "This southern campaign is successful, as attested by the fact that . . . the CIO won 150 and lost only 24 NLRB elections." There was, of course, real progress to report on a few fronts. The CIO's food and tobacco workers affiliate had made significant inroads in Virginia and North Carolina, and the woodworkers and furniture workers unions, as well as the Atomic Workers Organizing Committee, claimed at least modest membership gains. In all, however, the southern drive organized fewer than 25,000 workers during 1946. In textiles, which had more than 500,000 unorganized millhands and was the arena most crucial to success, the fact was that fewer than 7,500 workers had voted for the TWUA in 47 NLRB elections.[63]

Van Bittner explained that he was "not going to say too much about what we have done" because there had already been "entirely too much talk in the past few years about organizing the South." He chose instead to recount to convention delegates what had been done to CIO organizers by lawless southern employers and their assorted collaborators. Yet, in Bittner's vivid, if contrived, telling, these outrages somehow became proofs of its progress. Because "we are not in the South to conduct a Sunday School picnic," he explained, "we expect these tyrannical, Tory corporations and employers to be against our Union. To me it is a good sign, because as I say we are building a union of workers for workers and by workers." Warming to his oddly convoluted theme, Bittner declared,

I feel this way—and I am sort of consoled in the fact that we are meeting more opposition each day, and I feel that the reasons the opposition is becoming stronger each day is because we are doing something. If we were not organizing, if we were not doing something, if we were not doing the things that would change conditions for the men and women of labor in the South the opposition would not be so great. So we expect opposition.

"Sure, the fight is terrific," he conceded,

but that is what makes life interesting, that is what makes us like it, that is the reason we are getting a lot of fun out of it, because, my friends, the harder they fight and the bigger they are, the harder they fall, and that is what they are doing and going to continue to do in the South as the months and the days go by.

Bittner was obliged, however, to admit that, despite the mounting tally of NLRB election victories—"a government record that cannot be disputed"—there was a good deal more "fun" to be had before the CIO could fold its tent in the South. To those who had expected a quicker return on their investment in the region, he offered a reminder. "This was no ten months' or no one year's job. We understood that very well. We have been organizing in some sections of our country, in the North, the East, and the West, and even in some parts of the South for more than 70 years, and yet we have this tremendous job of organizing the unorganized before us." Its peculiarities notwithstanding, Bittner concluded, the southern organizing drive was "going along just about the same as any other organizing campaign that has been undertaken by the Congress of Industrial Organizations. We did not expect to complete the job in a day, a month, or a year, and so that there will not be any misunderstanding anywhere, the campaign in the South will be carried on in 1947 to a greater degree than it was in 1946."[64]

George Baldanzi, who had operated closer than Bittner to the front lines, also spoke to the convention. He emphasized what would be lost should delegates let concern over the slow pace of progress in the South undermine their resolve to press on. The CIO's "campaign against Feudalism" in the South was primarily intended to benefit underpaid workers "sick and tired of eating fatback and turnip greens three times a day," Baldanzi reminded delegates. In the end, however, its outcome would affect "every trade unionist throughout the land." Whether CIO members elsewhere realized it or not, he insisted, it was as important to their well-being as to that of southern workers that organizing efforts "go on and on until such time as we establish in this country the kind of bond between workers in every part of our country that there should be, and eliminate substandard conditions wherever they may exist, whether it be in the South, the East, the West or the North."

Baldanzi also warned his listeners against assuming, from the fierce resistance the campaign had met, that southerners in general were antagonistic to it. "No one should get the impression that the southern people as such are opposed to the CIO," he cautioned.

> The only people that are opposed to the CIO in the South are the reactionary politicians, the mill owners and all the corporate powers that exist in the East, and have controlled the lives and the destinies of the people in the South and have not permitted them to really raise their standards of living to the degree you and I, through our unions in this part of the country, have been able to do.

Nor, he added, should anyone worry that southern workers lacked the fortitude to make the most of the CIO's assistance. Recalling the exceptional valor that southern workers had already exhibited, Baldanzi declared, "I don't believe there is a group of people anywhere in the world that are more courageous, more determined, than the people who live in the South."[65]

When convention delegates were asked to adopt a resolution commending "the highly constructive policies and activities" of the southern Organizing Committee and pledging "the full financial support and . . . complete cooperation of the CIO and its affiliated unions to the successful completion of its historic task," they did so enthusiastically. When CIO leaders met behind closed doors to discuss the future of the southern campaign, however, enthusiasm gave way to skepticism. Persuaded that continuing to fund the southern drive at existing levels (nearly $800,000 had been spent by November) was a poor investment, and increasingly disposed to wonder if the money might not be better spent for defensive purposes (the just concluded 1946 congressional elections had provided a chilling forecast of resurgent antiunionism in the country), CIO leaders informed Bittner that whatever he did in the South in the year ahead would have to be accomplished with only half the funds previously available to him. In light of the solemn oaths sworn by Philip Murray and others at the campaign's highly publicized inception only ten months earlier, the CIO could not abandon its commitment to southern workers. But it could—and did—act to ensure that the cost of its subsequent organizing efforts in the South would be commensurate with the very modest gains they were likely to achieve.[66]

Although the work of the CIO's southern Organizing Committee continued on a much diminished scale (it was not formally dissolved until 1953), the promise it embodied as industrial unionism's great postwar initiative quickly dissipated. Efforts in textiles continued to yield election victories from time to time, but they were, inevitably, in smaller mills. The big mills whose organization was essential to the campaign's ultimate success remained beyond its grasp, ringed by defenses that organizers seemed powerless to penetrate. The passage of the Taft-Hartley Act, in 1947, which made the already stupendously difficult job of union-building in the South even more challenging by restricting workers' rights, did equip CIO organizers with a fresh, all-purpose excuse for their ineffectiveness in the region. In fact, the new barriers Taft-Hartley placed in the campaign's path only added to those it had already failed to surmount. The big textile companies that had forced the CIO into retreat were quick to deploy the new weapons that Taft-Hartley placed in their antiunion arsenal, but, as they had demonstrated for the better part of a decade in thwarting the "pro-labor" intentions of the original Wagner Act, their power was neither subject to nor dependent upon the force of federal law. Still, to union organizers in search of a ready exegesis of their poor record in the South, the Taft-Hartley Act, instantly infamous in labor circles, offered an explanation too tempting to neglect. Less than four months from its passage, over President Harry Truman's veto, the law was being blamed so frequently for the southern drive's failure that Van Bittner impatiently told organizers that rather than "crying" about its ill effects and using it as "an alibi for our failure to organize the unorganized" they should instead endeavor "to put more fight into the battle." Only by remaining on the offensive, he insisted, could the frontline troops of the campaign ensure that the CIO would endure in the South "long after Taft and Hartley are dead and in hell."[67]

However it was explained or rationalized, the CIO's failure to establish industrial unionism on a secure footing in the South after the war was both a humbling setback and a disquieting omen of tougher times ahead. Still, in those industries where its leading affiliates had entrenched themselves before and during the war, the CIO had good reason to feel confident that the expanding global hegemony of American enterprise would ensure its continuing vitality, even if a resurgence of antiunionism in the country impeded its advance into new realms. For the TWUA, however, the drubbing it suffered in southern textiles during the late 1940s was more than a mere setback. With the South continuing to attract nearly all of the new capital investment in textile manufacturing in the United States, and with evidence mounting that the temporary respite from decline enjoyed by the industry's northern branches during and immediately after the war was rapidly coming to an end, the failure of the southern organizing campaign could only be seen as an ominous harbinger of the TWUA's future.

CHAPTER 8

Enemies Within

If the TWUA did not face the immediate prospect of returning to a parlous existence on the industry's frayed edges at the end of the 1940s, it was clearly in trouble. Even if it succeeded in both exploiting whatever organizational possibilities the North continued to afford and in maintaining its foothold in the South, textile unionism would remain frail and exposed as long as Piedmont mill owners succeeded in blocking its further advance. While the CIO could walk away from the South with nearly everything but its pride intact, the TWUA could not afford to give up on a region that still held the key to its future.

Yet, if TWUA leaders agreed that the South must remain the focus of their organizing efforts, the evident futility of the CIO's campaign sharpened differences among and between them over the proper scale and objective of future endeavors in the Piedmont. These differences were exacerbated by regional rivalries, strategic disagreements, and personal antagonisms and ambitions among union leaders. During the late 1940s and early 1950s, an ever more rancorous and destructive contest developed to decide not only who would lead the TWUA, but also along what path.

Both because they were its dominant personalities, and because their increasingly divergent positions became the distant poles around which leaders, members, and staffers ultimately rallied when differences of opinion became terminal estrangements, it was, perhaps, inevitable that Emil Rieve and George Baldanzi came to personify the internal struggle that wracked the TWUA in the wake of its organizing failures in the South. Men of starkly different styles and temperaments, Rieve and Baldanzi were, a common trade union philosophy notwithstanding, defined by their dissimilarities almost from the moment in 1939 when they emerged as the TWUA's top leaders. A skilled administrator and astute collective bargaining strategist, Rieve was also a man of deep convictions. Among them was a firm belief that the TWUA's hard-won financial solvency should not be jeopardized by organizing efforts in the South that cost more than they returned. It was a concern shared by his strongest supporters, the conservative, trade union traditionalists who predominated among the union's northern constituencies. Always quick to remind colleagues in the South that it was the dues collected from their members that paid most of the union's bills, including those resulting from its southern organizing efforts, TWUA leaders representing the textile industry's northern branches, especially cotton-rayon and woolens and worsteds, tended to be wary of innovation. Rieve, they believed, could be relied on to attend to the business of trade unionism despite the contrary influences of would-be visionaries bent on changing the organization's direction and ethos.

Rieve was also strongly supported by most of the international union's top staffers, whose admiration for his personal integrity and administrative acumen was exceeded only by a keen appreciation of his willingness to give them virtual free rein in their respective departments. Research Director Sol Barkin, Education Director Larry Rogin, Political Director Al Barkan, and *Textile Labor* Editor and Publicity Director Ken Fiester each found in the style and substance he brought to the TWUA's presidency more than adequate reason for believing that Rieve was the right person for the job. When it was time to choose, none hesitated to take his side against Baldanzi, although Barkin steadfastly held to the view that he and his research department staff must pursue a strict neutrality once hostilities commenced. Among the top staffers, only General Counsel Isadore Katz broke ranks when push came to shove within the union. But because he had personal reasons to oppose Rieve, it was not clear whether his defection expressed genuine support of Baldanzi or personal animus toward Rieve.[1]

Most of the support that Rieve received from union functionaries and staffers spoke to their personal and professional regard for him. Yet, there is little doubt that the extraordinary power conferred on him by the TWUA's top-down structure was a powerful inducement to stay on his "good" side. Although the TWUA was democratic in the fashion of the "one-party democracies" typical CIO unions, its constitution provided the president nearly absolute administrative control. With exclusive authority to appoint those who administered the union's affairs—joint board managers, state directors, regional directors, and industry directors—Rieve effectively controlled the TWUA from top to bottom. Delegates to the union's (biennial) conventions had their say on constitutional issues and elected its officers and executive board members (although even those involvements were usually rendered more perfunctory than truly participatory by the tight control the administration exercised), but it was Rieve who decided whose influence would actually matter when it came to the organization's day-to-day operations.

Of the TWUA's other two general officers (Executive Vice President George Baldanzi and Secretary-Treasurer William Pollock), only Baldanzi's personal stature within the union that came close to matching Rieve's. Pollock's strong base of support in and around Philadelphia, historically a stronghold of textile unionism, had commended his selection in 1939 as the TWUA's first secretary-treasurer, but he remained, despite sporadic attempts to be his own man, firmly within Rieve's sphere of influence. Baldanzi, on the other hand, had the credentials and the broad-based support to make him a credible rival for the union's top post. Before Sidney Hillman selected Rieve as the new point man for the CIO's efforts in textiles, he and Baldanzi had been on roughly equal footing, sharing status as the two veterans of the old UTW best equipped to assume leadership of the TWUA. And, even after Baldanzi settled in to a status one rung below Rieve in the TWUA hierarchy, the attention he gained as a result of his continuing prominence in the Dyers Federation and his expanding celebrity and prestige among the union's rank and file guaranteed that he would not be mistaken for a mere underling.

It was in the South, however, where Baldanzi established the base of support that ultimately did the most to fortify his position and to fuel his ambition. At ease among southern millhands, as Rieve and most other TWUA leaders clearly were not, Baldanzi had resolved, early in the war, to devote his energy and talent to energizing the union in the Piedmont, where lay the greatest potential for institutional growth—and, incidentally, for personal aggrandizement. Alternately bypassing or circumventing southern Regional Director Roy Lawrence, the unpopular and ineffectual Rieve appointee with nominal authority over the sprawling southern cotton-rayon industry, Baldanzi and the ardent young activists he had enlisted in his mission infused the TWUA's organizing work in the Piedmont with energy and enthusiasm not seen in the region since the heyday of the TWOC. He and his disciples were only marginally more successful than their predecessors had been when they sought to plant the union's flag on vigorously contested ground, but the campaign they won against textile heavyweights like Marshall Field, Erwin Mills, Cone, and, especially, the Riverside and Dan River Mills established Baldanzi's reputation as the TWUA's most able, influential, and visionary representative in the South. His reputation was affirmed and enhanced by his appointment as second-in-command of the CIO's post-war organizing campaign in the South, and, despite its poor results, Baldanzi's standing in the region was not much diminished.

It was, however, the failure of the CIO drive in textiles that brought the long-simmering differences between Rieve and Baldanzi (and their respective constituencies) to a boil. The important—and welcome—organizing victories that Baldanzi and his aides delivered in the Piedmont early in the war excited concern among some officials in the North that a southward shift in the union's locus might also shift power within the organization. And, in the South, where the authority wielded by Roy Lawrence and other Rieve appointees was widely resented, the increased visibility and influence Baldanzi gained as a result of his organizing successes and his prominent role in Operation Dixie fostered a growing tendency among union leaders and members alike to situate themselves on either side of a deepening divide. When he arrived in Danville, Va., in 1948 to take up his duties as manager of the Pittsylvania County Joint Board, which coordinated the activities of TWUA locals in the region, most notably those at the giant Riverside and Dan River Mills, Emanuel "Slim" Boggs, a seasoned veteran whose service dated from the founding of the TWOC, recalled feeling intense pressure to take sides, to join either the "pro-Rieve" or "pro-Baldanzi" factions taking shape in the South.[2]

Long since convinced that Lawrence's rigid orthodoxy and low regard among TWUA members and staffers were significant impediments to its success in the South. Baldanzi was spurred by the new defeats that enervated the CIO drive in textiles to undertake a risky and provocative scheme to force a personnel change that Rieve had steadfastly refused to make. At the TWUA's 1948 convention, Baldanzi, in a challenge to the administration leadership slate (of which he was a member), endeavored to block Lawrence's reelection to the Executive Council by backing a rival candidate. Emboldened by his own popularity and Lawrence's low standing among many of the delegates, Baldanzi obviously believed his ploy could succeed. He was, however, running a risk of a backlash from Rieve and his allies, no matter how it turned out. Already disposed to regard Baldanzi as someone whose loyalty to the administration was suspect, Rieve's principal disciples on the Executive Council, a majority faction dominated by northern cotton-rayon Director Mariano Bishop, woolen and worsted Director John Chupka, and synthetic yarn Director Herb Payne, immediately seized upon his bold gamble as irrefutable corroboration of their deepest suspicions: that he "wasn't a team player" and that his naked ambition was to capture the union's presidency. Long fearful that Baldanzi's success, both personally and in building the union's strength in the South, would come at their expense and the expense of the northern strongholds they represented, the Rieve faction defended Roy Lawrence—less because he was capable than because he had become a symbol of a more far-reaching struggle.[3]

In the end, the deep internal schism that the battle over Lawrence's status revealed had less to do with personality clashes and differences of opinion than with a fundamental question: How fully *should* the TWUA commit itself to becoming a southern union? Baldanzi's answer was that the union simply had no choice. He told the convention,

> The future of this union is in the South. Your future in your own little mill, no matter where you are located, is in the South. . . . If we don't build powerful unions in the South—your woolen and worsted industries, that are already beginning to locate plants there—the development of the synthetic yarn industry, the dyeing and finishing industries, every basic textile industry in this part of the country will find itself in that part of the country, too.

As discouraged as they all were by setbacks the union suffered in the South, Baldanzi insisted, turning back was not an option.

> I say to you that this is not the time to be fickle, it is not the time for timid people. We have reached a period in the development of our union, in the development of progressivism in this country, where it is going to be necessary to stand up and be counted. And in this crusade that we have in the South we just cannot and must not and will not in any sense retreat.[4]

As was so often the case when he loosed his exceptional oratorical skills on an audience primed to believe his every word, Baldanzi concluded his speech to "prolonged applause, cheers, and whistles." Yet, the observations and sentiment it contained had, by the late 1940s, become increasingly familiar and perfunctory, and, with each reiteration, a little more hollow, and threadbare. The logic of Baldanzi's argument was unassailable from a theoretical perspective, but to Rieve and his practical-minded northern allies, fiscal conservatives inclined to think that concrete results were the only truly meaningful measure of the union's southern organizing policy, theory ran a poor second to reality. In short, what Baldanzi and his followers continued to see as a critical investment in the TWUA's future, Rieve and his supporters saw as a bottomless pit into which scarce union resources disappeared without yielding anything approaching fair value in return. Moreover, if the wage parity that many northerners considered the essential strategic objective of TWUA efforts in the Piedmont could be achieved by organizing only *some* southern millhands rather than all of them (an apparent possibility given the narrower North-South differential obtained by the late 1940s), the union could limit its activities in the region to protecting what had already been secured.

Had Rieve and his supporters been content with their success in beating back Baldanzi's ill-considered challenge, which they did only with some effort, the bitter and destructive fight that convulsed the TWUA over the next four years might have been avoided. It could also have been avoided, of course, if Rieve had been willing to act upon his own privately expressed criticisms of Lawrence's ineffectual performance as the union's chief administrator in the South. The modest administrative talents Lawrence brought to his work in the South were always more than outweighed by his failure to expand the union's southern base. Moreover, his petty and heavy-handed supervisory style eroded staff morale when it was arguably most important to their success. Educational Director Larry Rogin, a fierce Rieve loyalist, later acknowledged that Baldanzi's dismay at Lawrence's continued authority was well-founded and that the union would have been served if Rieve had fired or reassigned him. Rogin faulted Baldanzi for the provocative means by which he brought the issue to a head, but there was not much to admire in Rieve's failure to act in the best interests of the union.[5]

While Baldanzi's assertedly overweening ambition was an article of faith among his many detractors in the Rieve camp, especially northern leaders like Mariano Bishop who harbored their own poorly concealed ambitions for higher union office, his closest associates in the South attributed his attempt to oust Lawrence to frustration rather than self-interest. Emanuel Boggs had been indoctrinated by Rieve supporters to believe the worst about Baldanzi before he took charge of the Danville headquarters, but he found far more to admire than to mistrust once he got to know him. Boggs was one of those who came to doubt the endlessly repeated claims of Rieve loyalists that Baldanzi was ambitious to a fault. "Baldanzi always said," Boggs recalled more than thirty years later: " 'All I want is for the bastards to leave me alone. I have no ambitions to do anything except what I'm doing.' "[6]

Among those top union functionaries whose opinions mattered most, however, Baldanzi's attempt to oust Lawrence marked him as a menace too dangerous to ignore. For Executive Council members like Herb Williams, a native southerner and former craft unionist who, like Lawrence, already had reason enough to distrust Baldanzi because of the "bunch of . . . long-hairs" he had recruited to the union's service in the Piedmont, the dispute's origins were plainly evident: Rieve supporters were provoked into battle. "Baldanzi began to reach out in all directions," Williams later explained. "Then he began to take just a little more, little more, little more. Finally, they had a run-in."[7]

Rieve's most ardent defenders would later insist that he was a reluctant participant in the effort launched from the union's northern strongholds after the 1948 convention to retaliate against Baldanzi for his alleged disloyalty. If he was ambivalent, it was not enough to keep him from using his presidential authority for baldly partisan purposes during the following two years. Within weeks of the convention confrontation over Lawrence, Rieve was doing his utmost to undermine Baldanzi's base of support in the Dyers Federation. Permitted, along with the hosiery workers union, Rieve's old base, to retain its semiautonomous status in the TWUA, the Dyers Federation continued to be a main source of Baldanzi's personal support long after he moved up to the number-two leadership position in the union. Yet when delegates to the 1948 convention ratified the TWUA Executive Council's expulsion of the Hosiery Workers Federation for refusing to pay higher per capita dues, the dyers' status as the only remaining semiautonomous federation became untenable. The dyers' bitterly disputed transition from a largely self-governing federation to a fully integrated branch of the TWUA afforded Rieve an opportunity to extend his personal influence. His choice of leaders for the new Dyeing and Finishing Division was clearly intended to weaken Baldanzi's position in his old stronghold. Unwilling to risk rebellion in the ranks by immediately entrusting control of the dyers to Baldanzi's chief internal enemies, Rieve picked his fiercely loyal principal assistant, Herb Payne, as the division's director. Payne, a "nondyer" who already directed the union's Synthetic Yarn Division, promptly turned over day-to-day management of the dyers' affairs to William Gordon, who, by his own later admission, was selected for the job mainly because he was one of Baldanzi's most determined opponents.[8]

Rieve was even more blatantly political in attempting to undermine Baldanzi in the South. With the opening of the union's new southern regional headquarters in Atlanta in May of 1949, Rieve informed the Executive Council that two of his closest New England allies in the deepening rift with Baldanzi, northern cotton-rayon Director Mariano Bishop and woolen and worsted Director John Chupka, had been named "assistants to the president" and would assume new duties in the South. Bishop was placed in charge of TWUA affairs in North Carolina, Virginia, West Virginia, and Maryland; Chupka, in South Carolina and Georgia. Furthermore, the post of southern regional director had been eliminated and Roy Lawrence, in addition to becoming the top official in Alabama, Tennessee, Louisiana, Mississippi, and Texas, would also serve as an assistant to the president. Finally, Rieve advised his colleagues, Herb Payne, who had emerged as the chief strategist in the administration's blossoming offensive against Baldanzi, would continue to run the synthetic yarn and dyeing and finishing divisions, and, as yet another special assistant to the president, would "coordinate the activities of the various departments in the International office."[9]

Although Rieve may have gained the personal advantage he sought by undercutting Baldanzi's southern base, the move did not benefit either organized or unorganized millhands in the region. Neither Bishop nor Chupka was particularly well-acquainted with the special challenges the union faced in the South, and neither was well-known to southern millhands. Moreover, with Rieve and his northern allies seemingly more interested, in the late 1940s, in adding to the union's treasury than its membership in the Piedmont, a shake-up in the southern leadership that was not backed by a commitment to more vigorous organizing efforts in the region was an empty gesture at best.[10]

In the end, Baldanzi's position in the South was reasonably secure no matter how artfully Rieve and his supporters conspired to undermine it. During the late 1940s, Baldanzi's prominence in the region owed less to his official standing in the TWUA than to his highly visible leadership of the CIO's southern campaign. When Baldanzi succeeded to head up the drive after the death of Van Bittner in the summer of 1949, his prestige as industrial unionism's leading representative in the South was enhanced despite his increasingly embattled status in his "home" union. Even Rieve's vengeful decision to reassign nearly every TWUA organizer on loan to the CIO, a move that destroyed whatever slight chance the campaign might still have to make a difference in the southern textile industry, probably did little to diminish Baldanzi's standing.[11]

Baldanzi's influence in southern textiles was even more effectively safeguarded, however, by his unrivaled popularity among the rank and file and the esteem of Piedmont millhands for many of his protégés. In contrast to union officials like Roy Lawrence, Julius Fry, H. D. Lisk, and Herbert Williams, who were often mistrusted by its southern members as custodians of the national organization's interests rather than those of the rank and file, the personable young activists Baldanzi recruited were generally popular among the mill-hands they served and led. The outstanding ability of Lewis Conn, Joel Leighton, Joe Pedigo, Emanuel Boggs, Norris Tibbett, and David Burgess, among others, was generally conceded even by Baldanzi's most implacable critics, and whatever vitality the TWUA projected in the Piedmont during the otherwise gloomy late 1940s was largely attributable to the strong rapport these men maintained with the union rank and file. Baldanzi's reputation was similarly served by the idealistic young intellectuals from the TWUA education and political action staffs, who, in working among southern millhands, did little to conceal their ardent conviction that it was Baldanzi's vision of textile unionism rather than Rieve's that would best serve their interests over the long run.[12]

Had Baldanzi's opponents appreciated just how popular he was among the members, they might have planned and executed more skillfully what turned out to be an embarrassingly inept frontal assault on him at the 1950 TWUA convention in Boston. Convinced that nothing short of ousting him would suffice as a solution to the problem of divided leadership within the union, and worried that Rieve's uncertain health—he had a history of heart problems—might permit their nemesis to ascend to the presidency before they could change the order of succession mandated by the TWUA constitution, the northern members of the Executive Council most determined to depose Baldanzi pressed for a convention slowdown.[13]

With the backing of Rieve and Secretary-Treasurer William Pollock and the support of seventeen of the twenty Executive Council members, the dump-Baldanzi faction devised a plan, in the months leading up to the 1950 convention, to install one of their own as the new executive vice president. Cotton-rayon industry Director Mariano Bishop was a trade-union traditionalist whose interest in organizing southern millhands was mainly inspired by his desire to protect the jobs and wages of northern workers. He, too, was ambitious, but also sincerely believed that Baldanzi placed self-interest above loyalty to Rieve and the organization. Considered by administration loyalists and Rieve himself as the person best suited to take the union's reins when the time was right, Bishop was what Baldanzi assertedly was not, a steady, dependable team player whose guiding faith was that the TWUA's solid record of progress belied the whispered complaints of its internal critics. Explaining the "principles" that bound the loyal fraternity that Baldanzi had allegedly forsaken in favor of personal advancement, Bishop declared,

> We believe in loyalty, not to one man, but to our union. We believe in teamwork, in mutual trust and confidence. We believe in a firm and consistent policy in administration and in negotiations. We believe that any officer of this union, no matter what his rank, must be frank and honest with the dues-paying membership

of the organization, even if that means telling them a disagreeable truth at times—even if it means that. We believe that policies and decisions of the convention, of the executive board, of industry conferences must be carried out by the officers who are bound by them, even though they may personally be in disagreement. We believe that the executive vice president of this union should in actual fact be the president's assistant as provided under the constitution. Only then can we go on and be a strong organization.[14]

Apparently confident that the nearly 2,000 delegates who crowded into Boston's Mechanics Hall for the 1950 convention could be persuaded that Baldanzi's ouster was the only sensible solution to a deepening problem at the top of their union, Rieve's forces were unprepared for the vehement opposition that awaited them.[15] They were also undoubtedly surprised that what they intended as a referendum on Baldanzi's fitness to lead became, largely at the insistence of delegates themselves, a referendum on the propriety of an internal structure of governance that, in the minds of many, fell intolerably short of being genuinely democratic.

The case against Baldanzi, made by Herb Payne, William Pollock, H. D. Lisk, Mariano Bishop, and Emil Rieve during a raucous four-hour debate more contentious than anything previously witnessed by delegates to the usually tranquil, well-orchestrated conventions of the TWUA was that he was disloyal to the union in general and to its president in particular. In the end, however, Baldanzi's critics argued that delegates should vote to remove him from office whether or not they believed he was guilty as charged. According to both Pollock and Rieve, the breakdown in relations between Baldanzi and nearly all other national union leaders was irreparable, and that nothing short of his removal from office would suffice if the organization was to restore to its executive ranks the comity and unity essential to effective stewardship, and, thus, to the members' well-being. It did not matter, Pollock told the delegates, who was chiefly to blame for the rift that had developed within the union. It mattered only that they act decisively to end it. "It is my candid opinion," he declared, "that your union cannot afford the luxury of a split right down the middle, where for the next two years we will spend our time and effort in fighting each other instead of organizing the 750,000 workers in this industry that still remain unorganized." Because he personally believed that Rieve was "the most capable individual that we have in this organization to lead us as its president," and because he "could not conceive that all of these other vice presidents could be wrong in the situation," Pollock explained, he was bound to conclude that, in the union's best interest, Baldanzi had to go.[16]

In answering the charges against him, Baldanzi, and those who spoke in his defense, sought not only to rebut specific claims of misconduct, but also to shift the focus of the debate to what many critics of the Rieve administration claimed as its true motive: to silence the chief advocate for those in the union who believed that its leadership had become undemocratic and "monolithic."

The democracy "issue," which Rieve and his allies dismissed as a "gimmick" that Baldanzi cynically hoped to exploit for personal advantage, was plainly of keen interest to many of the TWUA's rank-and-file members.[17] Baldanzi knew, from his contacts with members throughout the textile industry, that rank-and-file participation in union decision making, especially the selection of joint board managers and state and regional directors, excited real passion among them. While his detractors were probably correct in claiming that he was not above exploiting workers' concerns for his own purposes, their attempt to trivialize the issue attested to their failure to recognize the real and legitimate desire of workers to have a larger role in union governance.

Although it was easily overlooked amidst the hyperbole and vitriol to which each side resorted during both the formal debate and the impassioned exchanges that passed for reasoned discussion on the convention floor, the fundamental question that divided delegates to the TWUA's 1950 convention—how much authority and control should members concede to their national union in the cause of organizational order and efficiency—was as old as trade unionism in the United States. More particular to the culture of textile unionism, it was the issue that, more than any other, had bedeviled, and ultimately defeated, earlier attempts to fabricate a union from the insular parts of a notoriously diverse industry. The unwillingness of members both at the local level and in particular branches of the textile industry to entrust enough power to a central authority had been the fatal flaw of the United Textile Workers. And, when UTW veterans mindful of its flawed governance gathered in Philadelphia in 1939 to fashion the TWUA from the remnants of the Textile Workers Organizing Committee, they were disposed by bitter experience to believe that giving the national leadership too much control was a lesser sin than giving it too little. As good an idea as democracy was in theory, it was in the minds of many TWUA leaders a luxury that textile unionism could not afford in practice if it undermined the organization's effectiveness.

In responding to complaints from the convention floor that the effort to "purge" Baldanzi was nothing more than a "power play" that betrayed his own dictatorial tendencies and the union's drift from its democratic moorings, Rieve testily insisted he was "not interested in some kind of monolithic union," and that the TWUA was already "the most democratic union in America." His allies, however, were less guarded in expressing their ambivalence about arguments espousing a more democratic structure. Disputing the view that the rank and file were ill-served by centralized leadership, Mariano Bishop told the delegates,

We have heard a lot of talk about rank and file. There are some in the union who try to spread the impression that they are for the rank and file, while the rest of us are not. . . . The finest thing that the union can do for the rank and file is to make the union administration stronger and [more] efficient.

Herb Payne was even more evangelical about effectiveness being the organizational virtue from which all other blessings flowed. "I happen to be a person who believes," he declared, "that as a trade union policy you can build all the democracies you like on words, but it won't be a damn bit of good unless the people have protection on their jobs, and the job of the union is to keep on building it up—building it up until it's worthwhile, and then they'll have the wherewithal to build democracy, not on words." William Pollock also argued that a governing structure that facilitated effective operation in the short term would foster more democratic policies over the long term. The Rieve administration, he explained, had "taken the position right along that our organization is in the formative state, and that we are in an organizational atmosphere and that we must have sufficient elasticity in our structure so that we can move forward and try different methods to find out the best workable organization for the interests of our work."[18]

The decision made eleven years earlier by Rieve and other leaders, George Baldanzi among them, to dissolve the Textile Workers Organizing Committee in favor of a constitutionally based organization, a step forced in large part by Francis Gorman's rebellion against the TWOC's intentionally undemocratic structure, was recognized at the time as one likely to necessitate a trade-off of operational efficiency for institutional legitimacy. Yet, the culture of top-down control that the older structure fostered and that most TWUA leaders still regarded as essential to textile unionism's progress remained powerful enough to ensure that the accommodations of rank and file participation in union decision making that constitutional governance implied were minimal. The dissolution of the TWOC and the formation of the TWUA marked the formal transition from autocracy to democracy, but a largely unreconstructed devotion to the organizing committee model as the one most conducive to effective operation left those at the top reluctant to contemplate significant changes in how the union was actually run. As long as the union's leaders remained dedicated to a structure that concentrated authority at the top, dissent from below had no effective conduit.

Though they were loath to concede in public that the TWUA was anything less than a model of democratic unionism, the structure that Rieve and his allies described and defended to convention delegates in 1950 subordinated member participation to efficiency. Benignly characterized, the leadership philosophy of Rieve and his allies was one that blended the essential features of internal governance from organizing committee and constitutional structures. Less charitably rendered, it was a mind-set that betrayed mistrust of the rank and file and contempt for their right to decide through direct democratic means where the union should go and who should lead it there.

The conviction of many delegates that the TWUA had the trappings of democracy without its substance was a subtext easily obscured in an atmosphere in which both personal and collective animus frequently shouldered aside substantive debate. Seemingly as eager to defame as to dispute, some Baldanzi supporters claimed that the true devotion of those who sought his ouster, whom they intemperately derided as "porkchoppers" and worse, was not to the members, as they piously declared, but to Rieve and the high union offices that their continuing fealty to him secured. Similarly, their careless characterization of Rieve as a power-hungry "dictator" simplified the issue of internal governance to the point of distorting it.

Yet, when the case against the Rieve administration's proposed expulsion of Baldanzi was thoughtfully stated, as it was by Canadian Regional Director Sam Baron and by Baldanzi himself, delegates found it both powerful and persuasive. Baron, a combative, independent-minded TWUA veteran who was one of only three Executive Council members willing to buck the majority, had his own reasons for believing that Rieve's authority was excessive. His defense of Baldanzi, however, emphasized what he claimed was the dishonesty and arrogance of those who sought to drive him out of the union. In recklessly alleging that Baldanzi was "guilty of the most heinous crimes ever committed in the labor movement," Baron mockingly observed, his accusers were themselves guilty of "the most shameless, ruthless, calculated smear for the purpose of power, unadulterated power in this organization." Taking special aim at the cabal of northern leaders whom he blamed in particular for the attack on Baldanzi, he declared,

> I place squarely on the shoulders of the majority of the executive committee the responsibility for dividing our union from stem to stern. I put the responsibility on the shoulders of the majority in pitting friend against friend, business agent against business agent, local officer against local officer, for only one purpose. . . . The move [against Baldanzi] was conceived in an office, on the part of a handful of people who, in their passion, decided to slight this union and then, after completing it, asked the members of the executive council to go along with that decision.

Having been forced into the open, Baron noted, those who had plotted Baldanzi's ouster were chagrined to find themselves under attack. "The majority is indignant that charges are made about power-hungry people, about porkchoppers, etc. I think the indignation is unwarranted. When you heard some of the speakers here, you might think the majority was on trial and not George Baldanzi." It was the majority's decision to "unleash the Furies," he reminded delegates, and they had only themselves to blame if they were now buffeted by them.

Baron dismissed Rieve's claim that, because *he* could no longer work with Baldanzi, delegates were obliged, in the best interests of the union, to replace him with Mariano Bishop. The real danger to the TWUA's future was not Baldanzi's reelection, he warned delegates, but their willingness to "permit the overwhelming authority of your administration to persuade you that whether you like it or not you must get rid of George Baldanzi." Warning his listeners that they must "not let this thing happen, because I am convinced it is to the detriment of our union," Baron declared,

> I appeal to you—I appeal to you, delegates, that you have the power, for once, to make the decision that will ring through the entire labor movement. You . . . can turn back the powerful machinery of our organization, to the extent that they are so shocked that never again will we have the division that we have here today.

In his own defense Baldanzi was at once combative and conciliatory. Clearly intent on portraying himself as the victim of malicious slanders by a clique of power-hungry business unionists oblivious to any but their own interests, Baldanzi also assured his listeners that he would happily entrust his fate to their judgment. "I don't have any feeling in my heart in this question," he insisted,

> I am not bitter. I am mad as hell, but I'm not bitter at anybody. And when I get all through here, I want you to feel free, absolutely free, and when all of the facts have been told, if you want to vote me out of office . . . you go right ahead and God bless you. I will have no ill feeling about it. That is your right.

Yet, while he was willing to submit to the will of the membership, Baldanzi told delegates, he was not willing to be run out of a union that he had faithfully served from its inception by opponents who were themselves contemptuous of the right of the rank and file to choose their leaders. "They say it's not a purge. You have got to have unity. I believe in unity, too, but I don't believe in unity by extermination." It was not for Rieve or Pollock or any of the other top functionaries of the union who had spoken against him to decide whether he was worthy of reelection, he argued. That authority rightly belonged to the delegates alone. "I maintain," Baldanzi declared,

> that the delegates in this convention have a right, by democratic vote, either to defeat me, in which case there is no problem, or reelect me; and if the delegates to this convention should, in their own wisdom, elect me to office, then they must achieve unity up here, because that's the wish of the membership of the union, and if we believe in democracy, we will accept that mandate from the people.

By insisting that the real issue before the convention was not his future but the future of democratic choice in the TWUA, Baldanzi was employing a strategy that his opponents were hard pressed to counter. It was not the Rieve administration, he reminded delegates, but he and the three members of the Executive Council who had rallied to his defense who had fought to place before the convention a resolution requiring that presidential appointees to state, regional, or industry directorships be approved by the members under their authority. And, "so that there might be no misunderstanding about my own position, about my desire to succeed President Rieve as the president in the event of his death," Baldanzi announced to the applause of delegates, he had proposed "a resolution which removes the succession clause from the constitution, and [provides] that in the event of the death or removal from office of the president, that rather than the executive council appointing someone, there should be a special convention called, and the people could elect whomever they wanted as president."

Rejecting as dangerously short-sighted Rieve and Pollock's contention that unity should be the delegates' overriding concern in deciding who would lead the union, Baldanzi urged them to consider a more "fundamental question" in deciding his fate. "I think there is another important issue that even transcends the importance of complete unity of the officers," he declared, "and that is that you must have complete unity of the organization if an administration at any time it sees fit can wipe out an officer without any reason for it at all. You don't build unity on that basis." It was not merely for his own sake that he was imploring delegates to "fight against any attempt on the part of the administration to utilize its power to mobilize a convention for the purposes of carrying on a purge," Baldanzi passionately insisted. If his opponents succeeded in purging him, he warned, other victims were sure to follow. "[I]f it can happen to me today," he grimly cautioned, "it can happen to somebody else tomorrow, and it should not be practiced in the labor movement of America, not the kind of labor movement that I think we have."[19]

When it was finally their turn to have a say in the matter, the delegates rejected Rieve's argument that Baldanzi was no longer fit to serve as the TWUA's second-in-command. By a vote of 1,038 to 742, a surprisingly wide margin given the extraordinary pressure the administration had exerted to achieve its aim, delegates reelected Baldanzi to a sixth two-year term. They dealt Rieve's forces a further stern rebuke in deciding the composition of the union's Executive Council. Sam Baron, Philadelphia Joint Board manager Joseph Hueter, and New Jersey State Director Charles Serraino, the only three members of the Executive Council to oppose the administration, were, far and away, the most popular nominees. Baron, Baldanzi's most ardent defender, received almost 300 votes more than the top vote getter from the Rieve camp. Delegates wanted especially to punish those who had been most outspoken in their attacks on Baldanzi. H. D. "Red" Lisk lost his seat on the Executive Council to a Baldanzi supporter, and Herb Payne, perhaps Rieve's closest associate and confidant, barely retained his seat on the basis of support from fewer than half of the voting delegates.[20]

Rieve and his supporters should not have been surprised by the strong support that Baldanzi commanded among convention delegates. As the most visible and best-known of the TWUA's top leaders and the only representative of the national union whose contacts with the rank and file at rallies and protests, on picket lines, and in other intimate settings were frequent and memorable enough to give them the impression that he was truly one of them, Baldanzi was someone who had earned the benefit of the doubt. In the absence of personal knowledge of the truth or falsity of the allegations hurled at him by suspect accusers, most delegates concluded that they should act in Baldanzi's favor. Norris Tibbetts, a young Harvard sociology graduate and education director with the TWUA's showcase joint board in Danville, in the late 1940s, recalled that most delegates seemed genuinely shocked that Baldanzi, of all people, should have been the target of a purge. Explaining the delegates' refusal to accede to the administration's wishes, Tibbetts later observed, "They had a great deal of confidence in [Baldanzi] . . . as a person who was close to them . . . who appeared to be a person who would support you through thick and thin, a *skilled* negotiator, and a person who seemed to understand what I think was a real difference between the way you organize in the South and in the North. . . ."[21]

It was also possible, as the *New York Times* hinted before the convention, that the attack on Baldanzi was best explained, not by his failure to be a team player but by his emergence as the "team's" star performer. Noting that he "long has been regarded as one of the ablest and most effective organizers in the CIO and one of its most persuasive orators," the *Times* repeated the suspicion later expressed by some delegates "that Mr. Baldanzi's forceful personality, as well as his boldness and imagination, had made him unpopular with the union leadership." That less than compelling reasons had inspired the Rieve forces to risk "a man-sized revolt" by pushing for Baldanzi's ouster was also implied in a *Times* report before the convention that the top leadership of the CIO, "deeply disturbed by the development, . . . had attempted to dissuade Mr. Rieve from his present course."[22]

Beyond rejecting Rieve's claim that Baldanzi's removal from office was in the union's best interests, delegates expressed their displeasure with the administration in other ways as well. They lustily shouted down a proposed amendment to the union constitution that would have blocked Baldanzi's automatic succession to the presidency in the event of Rieve's death or incapacitation. They also made it abundantly evident that they favored a resolution offered by the Baldanzi camp providing for rank-and-file ratification of the president's appointments of state, regional, and industry directors, although according to the *Times,* "the Rieve forces rallied enough strength" to derail the effort "by having the issue referred to the Executive Council, thus forestalling action until the next convention, in 1952."[23]

At the close of what *Textile Labor* breezily described as "the most turbulent, colorful and exciting convention in the TWUA's 11-year history," bruised and bloodied combatants on both sides dutifully called upon their supporters to let bygones be bygones in the interests of future solidarity. Baldanzi urged that his listeners "not go home with the feeling that we are a Rieve man or a Baldanzi man, but that we go home with the feeling that we are union men." Even though the "debate and arguments became somewhat heated," he observed, the time had come to "march back to our respective organizations in complete unity" and "rededicate our energies, our skills and our cooperation . . . to the welfare of the Textile Workers Union of America."

In his final remarks to the delegates, Rieve also expressed the hope that divisions within the union could be reconciled. "This convention has been a difficult one," he conceded. "People's nerves were frayed, wounds were inflicted, and all of those things happened which happen to mankind under stress." Nevertheless, he added, "I am one who believes that the scars on these wounds will heal." Declaring that he did "not care about being president of this organization if we are going to have a Baldanzi faction and a Rieve faction in the organization," Rieve insisted that "whatever factions there may have been prior to the election—those factions must go out of existence."

Still, for those who listened closely to Rieve's comments at the end of the convention, as well as to his remarks following Baldanzi's reelection the day before, there was reason to doubt that he was, in fact, prepared to accept defeat. While promising delegates that he would "bow to your decision and to your mandate," and that he and his allies would "try our damnedest" to "work together with George," Rieve was less emphatic about his differences with Baldanzi being a thing of the past. In the immediate aftermath of Baldanzi's reelection Rieve had pledged to "do my best to comply" with the delegate's decision. He also let them know, however, that he could not guarantee a unified leadership in the future despite their desire for such a denouement. "The delegates have made their decision," he announced,

> I, for my part, will do everything humanly possible to work with George Baldanzi and see whether or not the team can be reestablished, but I would not be honest with myself or with you if, in the event I come to the conclusion that the team cannot be reestablished, I did not make a decision for myself as it affects me.

He was not speaking out of "any spirit of bitterness, or anything of that kind," Rieve assured his listeners, but neither did he appear to be speaking as someone who was sincerely disposed to subordinate his judgment to the delegates'.[24]

His pledge to the convention to at least try to work with Baldanzi notwithstanding, Rieve made no real effort to do so. Their plan to purge Baldanzi had blown up in their faces, but neither Rieve nor his supporters seemed to have doubted the legitimacy of their cause. And, to the extent that the episode occasioned regret in their ranks, it was not because of what they had done, but because they had done it clumsily and failed.

According to *Textile Labor* editor Ken Fiester, who was privy to its deliberations, an informal "strategy committee" comprised of the "Rieve men" who had been most active in trying to get rid of Baldanzi met soon after the convention to devise a new and better plan of attack.[25] Presumably secure in the conceit that, as long as they had the best interests of the union at heart they were justified in using whatever means they thought necessary, the strategy committee, which included William Pollock, Herb Payne, and Mariano Bishop, set in motion, with Rieve's full knowledge and assistance, a plan that would eventuate two years later in Baldanzi's banishment, though at a cost that a union of the TWUA's singularly vulnerable character could ill afford. And, while they were probably correct in thinking that Baldanzi would have acted with equal disregard for fraternal and procedural niceties if he, rather than Rieve, had been in control of the union's institutional apparatus, by far the largest share of responsibility for the harm that the anti-Baldanzi campaign inflicted on the TWUA belonged to those in the administration camp who recklessly concluded that nothing short of full-scale war would decide, once and for all, who would lead it in the future.

Fiester, who later recounted with evident pride both how cunningly the strategy committee laid its trap for Baldanzi and how cleverly he, personally, used the pages of *Textile Labor* to further its work,[26] recalled that planners in Rieve's camp were, from the outset, determined to devise a battle plan that would negate any advantage conferred by his popularity with the union rank and file. At the 1950 convention Rieve supporters had learned the hard way, according to TWUA Education Director Larry Rogin, that getting rid of Baldanzi "wasn't as easy as it looked" once his personal popularity came into play.[27] When they "returned to the drawing board," it was with heightened appreciation that they could not afford to let Baldanzi play David to their Goliath again.

The strategy the Rieve forces adopted during the latter half of 1950 was one whose viability depended upon their success in goading Baldanzi into a convention fight that forced him to field his own full leadership slate in opposition to that of the incumbent administration. Through such a maneuver, they hoped, Baldanzi's popularity would be undercut while their support remained at maximum strength. To make their plan work required a provocation so extreme that Baldanzi, otherwise reluctant to confront the Rieve faction head to head, would have to accept their challenge or risk losing credibility.

Rieve and his advisers decided to bait their trap with the person who had emerged as Baldanzi's foremost ally on the Executive Council, Canadian Regional Director Sam Baron. In nearly every way, Baron was an ideal candidate for such a role. A Spanish Civil War veteran whose strongly held views and feisty nature led him to attack rather than retreat when threatened, he had been fearlessly combative at the 1950 convention, fervidly defending Baldanzi's integrity and service and refuting his accusers with undisguised contempt both for their arguments and their motives. In speaking out so forcefully, Baron endeared himself to convention delegates, but he also caused hardliners in the Rieve administration to conclude that he, too, had to go. Finally, Baron was a suitable foil because his personal base of support in Canada, relatively small and isolated from the TWUA's mainstream, was a group that might be offended without igniting an unmanageable firestorm.[28]

For reasons that Fiester later characterized as "purely political," Rieve began, toward the end of 1950, an escalating campaign of harassment for the express purpose of provoking Baron into words or actions that would constitute grounds for dismissal as the union's Canadian director.[29] As his antagonists expected, Baron had become, by early 1951, accomplice to his own undoing. In response to several sudden and arbitrary changes that Rieve ordered in the union's structure and governance in Canada, each plainly designed to undermine his authority and weaken his support among its 20,000 members, Baron intemperately lashed back just as his tormentors hoped he would. Disputing Rieve's claim to Canadian members on February 11 that he had ordered the structural and operational changes for the purpose of "improving the efficiency and effectiveness of our union's program in Canada," Baron claimed in his own letter to the member that it was actually the president's burning obsession to get even with him that had prompted the sudden reorganization. Insisting that no other interpretation was possible, Baron declared, "Since the convention of our union in Boston, in May, 1950, at which an attempt was made to purge George Baldanzi . . . I have been subjected to a continuous campaign designed to harass, undermine and, if possible, force me out of the organization because I opposed the purge." Dismissing the changes that Rieve had ordered as "merely another broadside in the war upon me," Baron complained to his members that he was "virtually helpless in bringing these attacks to a halt" because the "administration is bent upon carrying out what it failed to do last May in the highest body of our organization, the convention of TWUA."

Rieve lost no time seizing the opportunity that Baron's insubordination provided. Citing as an immediate cause for action Baron's letter to Canadian members, which "bristled with slanderous attacks on me and the administration of our union," Rieve dismissed him on March 6. "Seldom, if ever," an appropriately shocked and appalled Rieve told Canadian members, "has a more disgraceful and unprincipled document been circulated in the labor movement." Yet, as terrible as it was in and of itself, Rieve continued, the letter was merely "the climax of a long series of disruptive, arrogant and insubordinate acts by Baron during the last 10 months." From the moment the 1950 convention ended, Rieve charged, Baron, emboldened by his success in helping to reelect Baldanzi, had conducted a reckless "political campaign" aimed at "disrupting and discrediting the administration." Despite his own best efforts to calm the situation, Rieve insisted, Baron would not be dissuaded from his willful misconduct. "In accordance with my responsibilities as general president," Rieve reported,

I called upon Baron to discontinue his political conniving and attend to his duties. He was deaf to my warnings. Drunk with power, he demanded the right to conduct the union's Canadian affairs without direction or supervision by the general officer of the executive council.

As a Baldanzi supporter, Baron apparently felt immune from the normal obligation of any employee of the international union. He insisted that he had the right to ignore and to attack publicly any program, policy, or decision of the union which did not meet with his personal approval.

Pausing momentarily to note "the similarity of Baron's tactics with those of the Communists," Rieve, unwittingly revealing a compulsion to Red-bait even when denouncing a fellow anti-Communist, confessed to be at a loss to know what choice he had other than to sack such an intractably disobedient and disloyal scoundrel.[30]

The plausibility of Rieve's charges against Baron, which were not documented in the records of Executive Council meetings before his dismissal, depended upon the willingness of TWUA members and leaders who knew his reputation for pugnacity and headstrong behavior to believe that he was capable of such recklessly self-destructive conduct. Yet, even Ken Fiester, whose loyalty to Rieve was unwavering, later acknowledged that Baron was plainly more victim than victimizer in the nasty contretemps that culminated in his dismissal.[31]

As the Rieve faction knew it would, the highly publicized firing of Baron, linked as it was to the union's escalating internecine conflict, placed Baldanzi in an exceedingly difficult position. Because he well understood the power of incumbency in an organization where the authority that mattered most flowed from the top down, Baldanzi had ignored taunts by Rieve and others to field his own opposition slate at the next convention if he did not like the way the union was being run. Having personally benefited from that structure and having joined fellow leaders in maintaining and defending it before his estrangement from them, Baldanzi must have known that a challenge from below had little chance of success, even with substantial rank-and-file support. Yet his failure to risk such a challenge in the wake of Baron's baldly political dismissal would say to his supporters at every level within the TWUA that he lacked the courage or resolve to defend those who had placed themselves in jeopardy by openly siding with him.

Baldanzi was not long in realizing that he had no choice except to meet his opponents head on. On March 8, the day Baron's dismissal was made public, Baldanzi issued a strongly worded denunciation of Rieve that caused *New York Times* correspondent Stanley Levey to conclude that "civil war has broken out among the top leaders" of the TWUA. Despite a "perfunctory truce" after the 1950 convention, he reported, disagreements between the Rieve and Baldanzi factions had escalated to the point that they could no longer be hidden from TWUA members—or the public. Recalling that Baron had been "the leading convention spokesman for Baldanzi," Levey noted that administration critics believed that his dismissal could only be "viewed as an open declaration of a war carried on silently since the convention by Mr. Rieve and his supporters." According to the Baldanzi camp, Rieve had been quietly "chipping away at them" since the 1950 convention and had discharged at least a dozen union officials who had openly opposed Baldanzi's ouster and had coerced other TWUA staffers who doubted the wisdom or justice of the move into resigning.[32] "Mr. Baldanzi asserted that Mr. Baron's discharge was part of the policy of arbitrary transfers, intimidation, coercion, and harassment carried on by Mr. Rieve since the convention," Levey wrote. Moreover, he reported, the dismissal of someone of Baron's stature had caused those in the Baldanzi camp to conclude, "No one who did not 'swear personal loyalty' to the union president was safe."

While noting that Rieve's "constitutional powers are wide" and that he was backed by three quarters of the Executive Council. Levey nevertheless observed that the contest's outcome remained in doubt because, "the struggle is expected to be carried to the rank and file, where the Baldanzi strength is great." Noting that there appeared to be no obvious ideological conflicts between them, since "both are in the anti-Communist camp," Levey hinted that the rift between Rieve and Baldanzi was, in the end, best explained by differences in personal style and generational outlook. Noting that he was, at 43, considerably younger than the 57-year-old Rieve, Levey described Baldanzi "as being in the school of Walter Reuther, president of the United Automobile Workers."[33]

Although he continued to repeat his complaint that Rieve was "engaged in a ruthless campaign to wipe out any independent thinking" in the TWUA, Baldanzi was, at first, unwilling to confirm his intention to run for union president in 1952. Asked if he would run against Rieve at the union's next convention, Baldanzi was coy: "The issue is broader than that. Maybe I am a fool, but perhaps Rieve will awaken to the error of his ways and realize that no one can run a union as though it were his personal affair. The issue is not one of office but of carrying out the needs and interests of the membership." Condemning Baron's dismissal as "a sickening demonstration of what can happen to a man [Rieve] intent on using his power to capture an organization completely," Baldanzi did pledge that he would "stump the country speaking to locals and circularize the members with the 'facts' of the controversy." And, citing what he claimed was the members' "indignation" over such a blatant injustice, he promised to press the TWUA's Executive Council to countermand the firing of Baron. That declaration was clearly more a public relations gambit than something he hoped to achieve, given the council's emphatically pro-administration majority.[34]

Although Baldanzi had proven willing to conduct a war of words against Rieve and his supporters, he remained reluctant to commit himself to the all-out battle for control of the TWUA that some of his more headstrong and incautious backers wanted. At what the administration denounced as an "illegal rump conference" of Canadian union officials in Toronto at the end of March, Baldanzi encouraged TWUA members in Canada to retain Baron as their leader, no matter what Rieve said. He also intimated that he was prepared to do what was required to advance his goal of a more democratic organization, but refrained from threatening a full-blown convention showdown. The "demonic" Baldanzi portrayed by his detractors—a man so consumed with ambition and so emboldened by his triumph at the 1950 convention that he was willing to wreck the TWUA to wrest the presidency from Rieve—was hardly confirmed by his timorous, temporizing behavior in the weeks after Baron's dismissal. Emanuel Boggs, manager of the joint board in Danville, had worked with him as closely as anyone in the union. He later recalled that it took hours of argument to persuade Baldanzi to challenge Rieve for the presidency and that, even after he reluctantly agreed, it was "against his will." According to Boggs, Baldanzi continued to insist that he had no desire to become president and to feel (as Boggs did) that they had been drawn into a fight they could not reasonably expect to win.[35] Philadelphia joint board manager Joe Hueter, one of the four members of the Executive Council who consistently sided with him as the battle lines were drawn, also recalled Baldanzi's reluctance, even in the face of ever bolder provocations from the Rieve camp, to commit himself to fielding a full opposition slate at the 1952 convention. When he finally did, Hueter contended, it was only because the administration's relentless goading left him no alternative.[36]

When the TWUA Executive Council formally approved Rieve's firing of Baron by a 16 to 5 vote, on June 9, Baldanzi was finally obliged to risk decisive action.[37] At a meeting of like-minded administration opponents convened in New York in late July, Baldanzi announced that, in the interest of building a union "where a man has the right to speak without getting fired," he would run against Rieve at the next convention. Backed by a pledge of $100,000 from the 400 TWUA dissidents at the conference, money that the *New York Times* said would support a drive to promote "greater democracy in the internal affairs" of the union, Baldanzi and his supporters admitted that they were now resigned to the inevitability of an all-out battle for control of the TWUA. Rieve's ceaseless machinations, he said, had reduced his own position "to little more than a janitor's job" and had infested the TWUA with "more intra-union spies . . . than they have in Russia." There was simply no alternative to fighting back. He emphasized, however, that, rather than being the "dual movement" that administration spokesmen claimed it to be, the "insurgent movement" he intended to lead "would be carried on within the framework of the organization and would not be a threat to the union."[38]

Although Rieve and other leaders were quick to issue statements professing shock and bewilderment over what they claimed was Baldanzi's brazen attempt to rend the TWUA for the sake of his personal ambition, the declaration of hostilities they so deplored in public was just the response they had hoped to provoke. Apparently convinced that any organizational costs incurred in the short-run would be repaid many times over by the unity their success would bequeath over the long run, Rieve and his allies ran risks that, in a union more solidly grounded and securely situated, might have been reasonable. Yet, in the TWUA, which could not feel truly secure in the North or truly hopeful in the South, the gamble of full-scale, internecine war was anything but prudent. And, in an atmosphere increasingly more conducive to sanctimony and self-indulgence than to altruism and restraint, the best interests of the union, the conveniently murky and malleable ideal in which each side found refuge when its motives were questioned, would be jeopardized as never before.

CHAPTER 9

Self-Inflicted Wounds

Had Emil Rieve been content to pursue his vendetta against George Baldanzi only through political manuevers aimed at influencing the choices made by delegates to the TWUA's 1952 convention, the resultant harm to the union, though by no means inconsequential, probably would not have left it in a permanently weakened condition. By permitting their desire to discredit Baldanzi influence the TWUA's collective bargaining strategy in the southern cotton-rayon industry, however, Rieve and his northern-based allies inflicted an injury from which the union would never fully recover.

Although the decision to undermine Baldanzi where he was strongest rested on the same political expediencies that had driven their calculated attacks on his competence and fortitude at the 1950 convention, the strategy of Rieve and his advisors—to hold Baldanzi accountable for the union's lagging performance in the South—was also inspired by genuine concerns. Having achieved its long-standing goal of reducing the historic North-South differential in industry labor costs immediately after the war, the TWUA watched the gap slowly widen once again during the late 1940s as southern wage gains resulting from bargaining with organized mills and wage agitations against unorganized mills consistently fell short of those negotiated with northern employers.[1] The resurgent differential in labor costs was neither the only nor the most important reason for the northern textile industry's steady deterioration in the late 1940s, but it was one of the few contributing factors that TWUA leaders felt was within the limited compass of their influence.[2]

Under usual conditions, those in the North seeking to place blame for the failure of southern wages to keep pace with northern increases would have been content to excoriate the usual suspects: greedy employers, faint-hearted federal officials, feckless or frightened millhands, and one or another among the fraternity of opportunistic labor-haters to which nearly every institution in the South contributed representatives. In the rancorous aftermath of the 1950 convention, conditions were certainly not "normal," and anyone in the North who was looking for someone to blame for the resurgence of a regional wage differential had the perfect candidate in George Baldanzi. He was personally identified with both the union's progress—and lack of progress—in the South, and when the good news of the early and middle 1940s gave way increasingly to the bad news of the late 1940s, it was Baldanzi, more that any other official in the region, who was expected to account for the reversal of fortune. That he was never the lone architect of either its triumphs or its failures in the South meant little to his most determined opponents, who happily subscribed to any conclusion that promised to facilitate his downfall. And, in their eagerness to accomplish their political goals, Rieve and his allies recklessly permitted their animosity toward Baldanzi to dictate the bargaining strategy the union followed in addressing complex wage issues in the South.

The opening the administration exploited to denigrate Baldanzi's performance at the bargaining table came in the late summer of 1950, when, largely owing to the capricious influences unleashed by the Korean conflict, the union's problematical contract negotiations with the bellweather Dan River Mills afforded an opportunity for some politically inspired second guessing of his handiwork. Considered the TWUA's greatest asset in the South, Dan River Mills was also the wartime prize that had secured Baldanzi's reputation as the union leader best equipped to solve the singular riddle that southern organizing posed. The joint board in Danville was, arguably, one of the most successful in the entire TWUA, an impressive showcase of efficient and effective unionism in a region notoriously short of examples of dynamic worker organization.[3] The TWUA's operation in Danville was even more notable because of the relatively large number of black workers the union enrolled. With blacks constituting between 10 and 15 percent of its total workforce, Dan River Mills was a company that had long distanced itself from the nearly lily-white employment policies typical in the southern textile industry. At Dan River, however, as throughout the industry, black workers were, with few exceptions, segregated from white millhands and relegated to the worst jobs. Their sheer numbers, however,—between 1,000 and 1,500 during the late 1940s—gave blacks a presence and authority in union affairs in Danville that they enjoyed nowhere else. Determined to choose their own leaders and acutely aware, as one white union official later noted, that "it was impossible for black workers to have anything approaching equality within the union unless they had their own structure within the union," African-American millhands at Dan River maintained a segregated local to keep from being submerged in an organization dominated by a white majority. The ingrained bigotry of their white "brothers and sisters" ensured that black TWUA members would remain less than fully equal, but whenever union officials were bold enough to broach the topic of biracial unionism to white millhands elsewhere in the South, the accommodation at Dan River Mills was cited as a model of workplace solidarity beneficial to both races.[4]

Although Dan River Mills had vigorously resisted the TWUA when it became an organizing target early in war, its managers opted for a cool but civil relationship with the union once a substantial majority of its more than 11,000 workers declared for collective bargaining. Negotiations with the company were always exacting but invariably conducted in good faith on both sides. The resultant contracts gained members at Dan River Mills wages and conditions that matched or exceeded the best the union won anywhere in the southern textile industry.[5]

In formulating their bargaining objectives before contract talks with the company in the summer of 1950, union negotiators in Danville were bound by a strategy the national union had devised in response to the severe economic problems that plagued the textile industry. After several years of robust growth, production in the industry was in steep decline by early 1949. By the middle of 1949, the TWUA research department claimed that a quarter of a million textile workers were out of work and that most of those still on the job were working reduced hours.[6] In New England, where both the cotton-rayon and woolen and worsted industries were showing ever more ominous signs of permanent decline, nearly every textile production center soon found itself on the federal government's list of "distressed areas," and some, such as New Bedford, reported unemployment rates among millhands verging on 40 percent.[7]

In the face of the industry's slump, which *Textile Labor* blamed on "the folly of its own management," TWUA leaders decided "with great reluctance" to adopt appropriately modest goals for the immediate future. In advance of what Emil Rieve described as "perhaps the gloomiest peacetime Labor Day in our union's history,"[8] *Textile Labor,* pointedly reminding its readers in a front-page editorial that bargaining, like politics, was "the art of the possible," reported that with no sign of an industry upturn in sight, the TWUA would be "unable to win general wage increases" in upcoming contract negotiations. "It's not pleasant to report such news," the editorial glumly concluded, "but it is better to face the facts than gloss them over. Our only present alternative would be industrywide strikes, many in violation of contracts, which might well wreck the union, the organized segment of the industry, or both."[9]

That union leaders remained pessimistic about the prospect of winning higher wages was made evident by their decision, early in 1950, to renew contracts covering 90,000 workers in the northern cotton-rayon industry without even attempting negotiate wage to increases.[10] The influence of the industry's continuing slump was also apparent in the unanimous decision of the Executive Council, a week later, to make pensions "the union's No. 1 goal in the 1950 bargaining campaign."[11] Even as late as the beginning of July, when the union formally decided against reopening contracts covering northern cotton-rayon workers, Rieve and other top officials insisted that new wage demands would have to await improvements in the industry's still feeble condition. In light of the northern industry's precarious situation, Secretary-Treasurer William Pollock told cotton-rayon delegates the TWUA would do well "to look beyond the immediate question of wages to the broader problems" that confronted it in the North.[12]

In focusing on issues other than wages when they began bargaining with Dan River Mills in the early summer of 1950, the union negotiating team, which included Baldanzi, local joint-board manager Emanuel Boggs, Virginia State Director Boyd Payton, and various representatives from the company's three mills, were following the mandate of the national organization. With employment still more than 20 percent below what it had been when the company's production peaked, early in 1948, it is unlikely that wage advances could have been won at Dan River Mills in any case. And, because workloads had become a source of grating discontent among workers, the bargaining committee's emphasis on negotiating new productivity standards was one that local members heartily endorsed.[13] The one wage-related demand negotiators did contemplate, which grew out of North Carolina State Director Lew Conn's suggestion that a cost-of-living increase be sought, was, according to negotiating committee member Norris Tibbetts, disapproved by Rieve personally on the grounds that any effort to raise pay should wait until the following spring, when a wage-reopener clause would permit the union to revisit the issue.[14]

After protracted negotiations, which were especially difficult because of the complex issues of workloads and productivity, the bargainers reached an agreement just before the August 1 expiration of the previous year's contracts. In addition to establishing a more equitable basis for gauging productivity, one that Emanuel Boggs later praised for affording workers at Dan River Mills "a degree of control over the assignment of workloads" that they had not previously enjoyed, the new one-year contract provided modest improvements in grievance handling and seniority protections and, through the inclusion of a wage reopener, held out the hope that, six months down the line, pay increases might be negotiated.[15]

While the absence of a general wage increase in the new contract ensured that neither union leaders nor rank-and-file members in Danville were likely to regard it as a signal advance, they could not have predicted the immediate political use to which Rieve and his allies would put it in prosecuting their campaign against George Baldanzi. On August 5, one day after the formal ratification of the Danville contract, the Pittsylvania County Joint Board received a letter from Rieve, dated three days earlier. It informed local officials that the union would be seeking wage increases in all southern contracts after all. *Textile Labor,* in an article published the same day, explained that Rieve had adopted the new southern wage policy "because of the changed economic situation brought about by the Korean crisis," which had begun less than six weeks earlier. According to Rieve, a new southern wage policy was justified by "the sharp, general rise in prices (and) the rise in prices, demand and profits in the textile industry."[16]

While the most innocent explanation of Rieve's timing was that negotiators in Danville had simply been caught on the wrong side of fast-breaking events, the unprecedented attack the union administration launched against the contract and its authors shortly thereafter left little doubt that it was politics rather than policy that informed decision making in the New York headquarters. Beneath a headline announcing "New Language but No Dough in Danville," *Textile Labor* published a front-page story, on September 2, that revealed, beyond any question, that the Rieve administration intended to use the Dan River Mills contract to support a charge they had failed to prove at the TWUA convention a few months before: Baldanzi and his supporters could not be trusted to defend workers' interests at the bargaining table. Repeatedly noting the absence of "money benefits" from the contract and coyly belittling the value of the procedural and other improvements that addressed issues other than wages, the article emphasized that the disappointing end result of the union's bargaining with Dan River was largely Baldanzi's handiwork. It hinted that millhands in other organized southern mills could likewise expect to be ill-served by him. "As indicated by Baldanzi during negotiations," the paper reported, "the agreement probably will be a southern pattern for the time being. While disappointed in not obtaining additional paid holidays (one is now in the contract), better company-paid insurance and a pension plan guaranteed to yield a minimum of $100 a month, the negotiators expressed the hope that the new language would lead to a better relationship with the company. No general wage increase was sought."[17]

Surprised and embittered by what they saw as an unfair and dishonest assault on their professional competence and personal integrity, leaders of the Pittsylvania Joint Board complained bitterly to Rieve and denounced *Textile Labor* editor Ken Fiester. Not surprisingly, Rieve stoutly defended Fiester, a dutiful member of his get-Baldanzi strategy committee, disparaged the Danville contract for failing to include a wage increase, and captiously accused joint board officials of letting anti-administration partisanship get in the way of their duty to represent TWUA members at Dan River Mills.[18] Rieve and his allies were in an even stronger position to denigrate Baldanzi and the Danville settlement when, in mid-September, leading employers in the northern cotton-rayon industry conceded to union pressures for a ten-percent wage increase. Shortly thereafter, unorganized southern mills, in the hope of preempting a threatened TWUA wage agitation in the region, voluntarily instituted an eight-percent increase.[19] That action was particularly damaging to the reputation and morale of Baldanzi loyalists in the South, because it placed them in the humiliating position of having to entreat organized mills like Dan River, with which the union had already signed contracts without pay raises, to voluntarily match the wage increases granted by their unorganized counterparts.[20]

Once put on the defensive by the administration, whose scruples seemed to be in abeyance when there was an immediate political advantage to be exploited, Baldanzi and his supporters in the union's southern strongholds saw their authority almost entirely usurped by Rieve loyalists. In place of the ill-conceived organizational scheme he had contrived to limit Baldanzi's authority by delegating responsibility for the union's southern affairs to various "special presidential assistants," Rieve announced in October that James Bamford (previously the assistant director of the woolen and worsted division) would take charge of all TWUA activities in the South.[21] A former Philadelphia hosiery worker who had no substantial experience or standing in the South, Bamford was, nevertheless, a veteran trade unionist of the type that Rieve preferred. Indeed he was, in Rieve's view, someone who would give the TWUA's negotiating efforts in the Piedmont the hard edge they assertedly lacked under Baldanzi and those of his apostles tending toward a similar faintheartedness at the bargaining table. Increasingly hostage to a firm conviction that the union's immediate charge in the South was to protect its base in the North, Rieve and the New Englanders who had become his foremost constituents tended to regard the reappearance of a regional wage differential as proof that that all-important obligation was being neglected. Because the South was also where Baldanzi's influence was greatest, it required only the right political motivation to conclude that the "modern" community-based unionism he had espoused in Danville and other southern bastions was a wan imitation of the genuine article—one that undermined, rather than strengthened, the TWUA's position elsewhere.[22]

Declaring that "the wage differential between North and South . . . is grossly unfair to the southern workers, and is a constant threat to our union," *Textile Labor* informed its readers during the fall of 1950, that, when re-opener clauses in the union's southern contracts permitted the issue of wages to be revisited in the spring, the negotiations would be in different hands. The collective bargaining policy governing those negotiations, Rieve announced in mid-November, would be determined at a special national cotton-rayon industry conference to be held in Washington, in December. Rieve conceded that a national conference was a departure from the union's usual method of setting bargaining goals, which permitted northern and southern cotton-rayon workers to act independently. He insisted, however, that it was not without precedent, since the TWUA had employed a similar industrywide strategy in pressing wage demands before the War Labor Board in 1943.[23]

Without doubt, Rieve and his northern allies were sincerely concerned that the 5- to 10-percent North-South wage differential that had reappeared in the cotton-rayon industry by late 1950 would exacerbate the TWUA's difficulties in New England, where mill closings were occurring with distressing frequency.[24] Neither was there much doubt, however, that the Rieve faction's enthusiasm for a "coordinated" approach to bargaining also reflected their desire to deny Baldanzi and his southern cadre a significant role in future negotiations. With Rieve, cotton-rayon director Mariano Bishop, and new southern regional director James Bamford firmly in control of the process that determined the union's southern bargaining strategy, Baldanzi and company were little more than interested bystanders.

Even before the Washington conference convened, the Rieve administration undertook to persuade southern members that only though more muscular and aggressive bargaining was the union likely to achieve wage equality for them and job security for their northern brothers and sisters. Insisting that the need to "close the gap" between regional wage rates was becoming ever more urgent, Bamford and Secretary-Treasurer William Pollock cajoled delegates to a statewide meeting of TWUA locals in Georgia to declare themselves for a policy aimed at eliminating substandard wages and conditions from southern contracts. Conspicuous by their absence from the Georgia meeting (and from all but one of those held in other southern "textile states"), were Baldanzi and the regional leaders who had assisted him over the preceding decade in establishing the TWUA in the South.[25] Only in North Carolina, where Baldanzi's influence was so pervasive that a meeting without his supporters in attendance was unthinkable, were administration spokesmen obliged to share a platform with the opposing camp.[26]

Yet, given the adroitness of Rieve and his chief lieutenants' manipulation of the union's internal debate over wages during the weeks leading up to the Washington cotton-rayon conference, anyone reluctant to shout a hearty amen to the administration's boisterous call for a more virile and intrepid bargaining posture risked the appearance of timidity verging on cowardice. For Baldanzi and his southern partisans, whose toughness had been called into question by Rieve and others when the Dan River Mills negotiations failed to yield a general wage increase, affecting a stoutheartedness that matched or exceeded that of their critics was suddenly *de rigueur*, even though the belligerence it implied was at odds with their sense of what a realistic approach to labor relations in the South permitted.[27] It was, as TWUA Education Director Larry Rogin observed 25 years later, a circumstance in which the institutional obligation of all TWUA leaders to exercise prudence was increasingly subordinated to a perceived political need to be "macho."[28]

By the time that 700 delegates from the northern and southern branches of the cotton-rayon industry crowded into the ballroom of Washington's Shoreham Hotel in mid-December, the decision to give what *Textile Labor* described as a "new direction to TWUA's collective bargaining program" was a foregone conclusion. Assured by Rieve, Pollock, and Bishop that higher profits and increased productivity made possible a fairer division of the industry's wealth, the delegates readily endorsed the administration's call for more of everything employers had to share.[29] Just what and how much the union would ask of southern mill owners was decided by the national cotton-rayon policy committee in mid-January of 1951, when its members, dependable Rieve loyalists almost to a man, invaded the inner sanctum of the Baldanzi camp, Danville, Va. Determined to make the point that theirs was an approach to dealing with Piedmont mill owners that rejected all claims of southern exceptionalism, the northerners who dominated the policy committee's deliberations proclaimed the elimination of regional wage differentials to be the union's foremost objective when contracts were reopened in the South. In addition to an immediate 12-percent general wage increase, the committee announced that it would seek the establishment of uniform job rates throughout the cotton-rayon industry, a plan that *Textile Labor* lauded as "a means of attacking the North-South differential on the most fundamental basis—equal pay for equal work, job by job."[30]

Although the Rieve administration called on Baldanzi and Danville joint board manager Emanuel Boggs to help sell the policy committee's bargaining strategy to local union leaders at Dan River Mills, neither was to have a direct role in the subsequent negotiations. Headed initially by southern Regional Director James Bramford, and later by Rieve, something he had never before done in the South, the negotiations with Dan River were supposed to set the pattern that other organized mills in the region would follow. From the beginning, however, they were strained and unproductive. Used to bargaining with Baldanzi and local officials like Boggs, whose deference to southern sensibilities bespoke good faith and good will, Dan River executives were offended by the unadorned bluntness with which Bamford and Rieve argued the TWUA's case and by their quick resort to threats when negotiations bogged down. The company's managers prided themselves on a labor relations policy that met the TWUA halfway. In return, they expected the union to appreciate the fact that Dan River had not opted for the diehard antiunionism so typical of its southern competitors. Moreover, Dan River bargainers knew of the fierce internal battle going on in the TWUA, and they bitterly resented what they soon came to believe was an effort by Rieve's camp to exploit the negotiations for partisan political advantage.[31]

Yet, at the core of the disagreement that emerged when negotiations progressed to their most serious stage was a fundamental difference over the standard against which wages at Dan River should be measured. Long steadfast in the congenial belief that the wage rates the union negotiated in New England should be the industry standard, Rieve and his team insisted that wages at Dan River were deficient as long as they were lower than those in the North. Moreover, TWUA negotiators sanguinely argued that, as the "pattern-setter" in the southern cotton-rayon industry, Dan River Mills could afford to meet union wage demands without placing itself at a competitive disadvantage, since other Piedmont mills, organized and unorganized, would dutifully follow suit. Predictably, company negotiators found almost nothing in the union's argument and analysis with which they could agree. Rejecting the union's contention that the wages paid in New England mills were the truest measure of labor's value in the cotton-rayon industry, Dan River spokesmen insisted that it was labor costs in the South, where 80 percent of the industry's spindles and most of their competitors were located, that should set the standard. As long as 85 percent of southern cotton-rayon workers were not organized, they repeatedly insisted, it was hardly reasonable for the TWUA to expect that Dan River and other unionized mills in the region could concede substantial wage increases absent credible assurances that their nonunion competitors would do likewise. Long of the opinion that New England mill owners had, by ignoring competitive realities, abetted the northern textile industry's piecemeal "liquidation," Dan River managers were determined that *they* would not succumb to any such tendency.[32]

Hoping to find refuge in a dubious claim that recently promulgated wartime inflation restraints limited the company's freedom to increase wages, Dan River negotiators proposed only a 2-percent raise. They added that they would be prepared to up that offer by as much as 4 percent if the Wage Stabilization Board, the federal agency created to control wage inflation, approved. Insisting that the Wage Stabilization Board had been rendered defunct the moment its labor members, including Rieve, resigned in late February to protest an announced "wage freeze," union negotiators stoutly maintained that the only genuine restraint on the company was its own niggardliness.[33]

Negotiating under a strike deadline that heightened tensions and inflamed tempers on both sides of the bargaining table, union and company representatives increasingly postured, staking out positions from which retreat became less likely with each restatement of what a settlement had to incorporate. As the strike deadline, April 1, drew closer, Rieve's personal involvement in the negotiations increased. By nearly all accounts, however, his participation made a settlement even less likely. Claiming that only a "mopping-up operation" was required in Danville after the union won a 7½-percent wage increase from strike-wary New England mill owners on March 15, Rieve took personal charge of the Dan River negotiations, apparently confident that the company would, at the very least, match the concessions gained in the North.[34] Instead, by resorting to the tough talk and table-pounding histrionics that had worked to the union's advantage with northern employers, he angered and offended the Dan River officials far more than he intimidated or unnerved them, and only made matters worse. It may well have been that company negotiators would not have budged, regardless of the union's conduct at the bargaining table, but participants on both sides seemed to think that Rieve's ill-advised attempt to bully company officials into a settlement instead caused them to resolve, as one later recalled, that "if we are going to have a strike at Dan River, we are going into it on the basis that we're going to do our best to win it."[35]

Although Dan River's management was not guilty, as the union later charged, of willfully provoking the strike that began on April 1, their refusal to better the wage offer of two percent now (and perhaps, four percent more later) left TWUA leaders no real choice but to make good on a threat they had been recklessly brandishing for more than a month. Having assiduously inculcated in the union's southern members a righteous conviction that striking was the only honorable course of action open to them if negotiations failed, TWUA leaders were hardly in a position to argue, when employers called their bluff, that something short of an all-out battle might suffice. Because the union's tense and constraining political climate cowed into silence those leaders who best understood the extreme dangers that a strike in the South posed, second thoughts were too risky for anyone to openly entertain. With no real choice other than to follow the lead of Rieve's national cotton-rayon policy committee, whose decision-making procedures were both "undemocratic . . . and impractical" according to Emanuel Boggs, local union officials and members were more pawns than participants in the process that led to the most disastrous strike in the TWUA's history. Once the negotiations with Dan River Mills and with other southern firms had collapsed and no other option was available, local union officials and members were extended the "courtesy" of participating in a strike vote. The sad truth, however, was that the "life-and-death contest" that loomed was the destructive by-product of opportunistic political maneuvers that had neglected to take into account the workers' interests, or the future well-being of textile unionism in the South. Expressing a view that many on both sides of the Rieve-Baldanzi divide later came to share, Boggs insisted that striking Dan River and the other major southern mills with which the union reopened contracts in the spring of 1951 was "a political decision." "If there had not been this internal strife within the union . . . ," he argued, "then negotiations would have been handled as they'd been handled in the past. And, in my opinion, people would have reached an agreement in most of the situations. . . . This general strike in the South would never have occurred, except for this political situation."[36]

Although the 1951 strike involved all of the other major southern firms that the TWUA had struggled for more than a decade to organize—Erwin Mills, Marshall Field, Cone Mills, M. Lowenstein and Sons—it was the bruising battle with Dan River that determined its overall outcome.[37] Only Dan River Mills, among all of the companies struck, deployed the full arsenal of strike-breaking weapons available to the South's largest employers. In doing so, it reminded TWUA leaders and members in ways too painful and ruinous to soon forget that, in the singular arena of southern labor relations, strikes were more often the resort of the foolhardy than of the strong.

For the first few days of the strike, the more than 40,000 millhands who manned picket lines in Virginia, the Carolinas, Georgia, and Alabama had reason for hope.[38] Most struck mills, whose bulging inventories made a temporary loss of production a not altogether intolerable prospect, seemed content to outlast strikers who lived from paycheck to paycheck, and the two companies that had resolved to keep their mills in operation, Dan River and Cone, were not immediately able to do so. Yet the disaster the TWUA had invited by picking a fight it had no realistic chance of winning was not long in coming. At Cone Mills in Greensboro, N.C., where the union's strength had long been suspect despite management's tepidly professed willingness to give collective bargaining a chance, the solidarity apparent during the first days of the strike soon dissipated under the weight of forceful company efforts to resume production.[39]

It was in Danville, however, that the full calamity of the 1951 strike unfolded. Determined to impress upon the TWUA the magnitude of its folly in striking a company that had accommodated collective bargaining, managers at Dan River left no possibility unexplored in planning for victory. Unlike the union, whose strenuous campaign to build a fighting spirit among untested millhands was not matched by equally diligent preparations to conduct the fight once it had started (the TWUA had done little, either at the national or local level, to amass a strike fund), Dan River officials crafted a comprehensive plan whose effectiveness was revealed at every stage of the ensuing battle. The company's effort to recruit replacement workers was a model of careful planning and logistical genius. Dan River agents, confident that even the appearance of business as usual would be enough to crush the morale of many strikers, scoured the countryside for scabs without regard for their ability to do the work once they were installed in the mills.[40]

With the expert help of a New York public relations firm, Dan River also succeeded in putting and keeping the TWUA on the defensive in the equally important arena of public opinion. Piously explaining that strict adherence to the announced wage restriction policy of the Wage Stabilization Board was, in wartime especially, an obligation of good corporate citizenship that no employer should conspire to shirk, Dan River spokesmen depicted the TWUA's demand for pay increases, beyond what they said the "law" allowed, as a naked act of grasping—as unwarranted on economic grounds as it was indefensible on patriotic grounds. Fisher and Rudge, the "high-powered, high-priced" public relations firm that Dan River hired to conduct the war of words and images waged against the TWUA was, Harry Conn noted in the *New Republic,* demonstrating through a well-tested formula based on "as much personal smear as the traffic will bear" that "their fine art of psychological strike-breaking" could be practiced as effectively in the South as elsewhere.[41]

For the most part, the union fared no better in the general press, which, to the gloating delight of industry publicists, quickly fell into the lazy habit of according the self-serving releases of Dan River and other employers the authority of holy writ. Overmatched and outwitted union spokesmen did what they could to present the strikers' case in the best possible light, but what artful management flacks put forth as the simple "facts" of the case were not easily disputed, given the public's impatience with explanations that hinged on understanding the conflict's complexities.[42]

Yet, as skillfully as they connived to win over public opinion, Dan River and the other textile companies affected by the walkout provided ample evidence that, when potent and well-aimed words were not enough, they were willing to use the less sophisticated strike-breaking methods that had been the stock in trade of southern mill owners in past labor wars. Throughout the strike, TWUA spokesmen complained that union pickets were subjected both to violent assaults from thugs acting at the employers' instigation and to legal harassment from state and local police, prosecutors, and judges disposed to include strikebreaking among their official duties. "Led by the giant Dan River

Mills . . . ," a dispatch from the frontlines informed the readers of *Textile Labor,* "the employers launched a full-scale strike-breaking campaign against the workers, including gunplay, police violence, mass arrests, and the inevitable court injunctions." The pattern of abuse and mistreatment was depressingly familiar throughout the strike region, a union editorial lamented. "Knock the strikers around, throw them in jail, spare no effort to safeguard the sacred company and the dupes who have turned scab. For these strikers are challenging the whole structure of the South; they treasonably believe that southern workers should live as well as northern workers, and that southern wages should keep pace with the cost of living."[43]

As diligently as employers worked to break it, however, the strike suffered most from the union's inability to retain the support of its own members. At Danville, where all concerned believed the strike's ultimate fate would be decided, the resolve of millhands to persist in their struggle with Dan River was seriously doubted by at least some local leaders even before it began. But, according to TWUA Education Director Larry Rogin, "The internal fight in the union prevented people from telling honestly what they thought would happen when the strike was called." The only "real honest statement" of the danger that lay ahead, Rogin noted, was by Danville Joint Board Manager Emanuel Boggs, an ardent Baldanzi supporter who felt compelled because of the "political atmosphere" within the union to go along with the strike, but not before warning TWUA leaders that Dan River millhands would probably begin to break ranks as soon as the financial strains caused by missed paychecks started to mount. "We'll get our membership and a little more for a week," Boggs purportedly told TWUA leaders, "and after that they'll start going back. And if you want to strike under those circumstances, I'll lead a strike."[44] Other Baldanzi supporters in southern leadership positions were apparently convinced that Boggs was correct in his grim assessment of the situation, but, as one later confessed, a fear of being derided by Rieve loyalists as "a bunch of creampuffs" kept them from openly expressing their doubts that the strike could succeed.[45]

Because the union had done almost nothing in advance to build a war chest, financing the strike was an ad hoc enterprise that did little to reassure strikers whose own resources were nearly nonexistent. Wealthier locals and joint boards throughout the union were reasonably generous with financial aid to their beleaguered southern brethren, but, with more than 40,000 millhands on strike, passing the hat did little to meet their needs.[46] The national union claimed to be spending $250,000 per week in strike relief, but Norris Tibbetts, whose duties put him at the center of the conflict in Danville, complained that financial support from New York came "in bits and dribbles," and always fell woefully short of meeting the strikers' needs or reassuring them that the TWUA was prepared to spend whatever it took to sustain their fight. "I think if TWUA had put a million dollars in a local Danville bank . . . and said 'that's a starter;' . . . if we had met the basic needs of everybody, I think we could have held it," Tibbetts later commented. "I think people were driven back in because they couldn't stand it financially."[47] In the spring of 1951, the TWUA was as well off financially as it had ever been, but the Rieve administration remained conspicuously reluctant to spend enough to ensure that strikers felt adequately supported in their struggle. Some Rieve loyalists later insisted that more generous support from the national union would not have influenced the strike's outcome, but the apparent unwillingness of its leaders to risk its financial solvency, even to sustain a struggle so crucial to its future, cast serious doubt on the soundness of their priorities.[48]

In the end, however, the leaders' critical failure was not in misjudging the level of material resources the strikers required, but in misjudging their capacity to endure the daunting array of emotional and psychological pressures that a strike in Danville was likely to generate. Although only the most senior employees at Dan River, those directly involved in the UTW's challenge to the company in 1930, knew firsthand the special angst and suffering attendant to a strike, it should have been clear to TWUA leaders that the memory of that calamity informed worker culture in Danville at the level of myth. It also colored the thinking of management strategists at Dan River in 1951. Convinced that its employees were "not trade unionists in the true sense of the word," Dan River managers believed that by keeping the mills in operation even on a limited basis they would reawaken visceral fears among enough strikers to fracture their solidarity. Union bargainers were correct in asserting, before the strike, that workers at Dan River and other unionized southern mills were not treated well, as compared with textile employees in the North or with workers in mass-production industries like autos and steel. Mill managers, however, were confident that most Piedmont millhands, whose frame of reference was distinctly regional, understood only too well that the better jobs to which TWUA spokesmen glibly referred were, for reasons both practical and cultural, beyond their reach.[49]

That Dan River managers had not misjudged their strike adversaries was soon apparent. Just as Emanuel Boggs had predicted, the resolve of the strikers to stand their ground began to weaken noticeably as the dispute entered its second week. Exaggerated reports of the company's success in recruiting replacement workers were cynically crafted to erode the strikers' morale, and, as their meager financial resources melted away, so did their fortitude. By the union's own count, nearly 2,500 of the 11,000 millhands who had originally supported the strike were back on the job by April 9.[50] And even if most of those who first crossed the picket lines were not among the 8,000 Dan River employees who belonged to the union, the psychological effect of so many defections was felt by all. "All available facilities are used to thicken the air of portending menace to each worker and his family," a *New Republic* reporter wrote. "Several times a day company radio programs try to make the striker feel alone, to accentuate his insecurity, to convince him that the strike is already lost and keep impressing him with the fact that available jobs are rapidly running out." For those still not convinced that the company meant business, the same writer reported, "strikers were told that those who failed to report to work by April 23 would never work at Dan River again."[51]

Although the union continued to issue press releases attesting to the strike's effectiveness, in private whatever thoughts of success TWUA leaders once entertained had vanished. As early as April 16, while 6,000 Dan River workers were still honoring the union's picket lines, TWUA leaders met in Greensboro to discuss what might happen if they decided to "liquidate" the strike in Danville. In the end, those in attendance agreed with Baldanzi and others who argued that abandoning strikers in Danville would hasten the union's demise throughout the South. Yet, the belief shared by Rieve and his closest associates that the strike there was a lost cause revealed itself in their stubborn refusal to authorize the additional financial assistance that those closest to the Dan River situation claimed was needed to forestall total defeat.[52]

As conditions in Danville deteriorated steadily during the last two weeks of April, TWUA leaders were increasingly preoccupied with finding what Rieve baldly described as "some kind of face-saving device" the union might employ to extricate itself from a situation that could only get worse. For Rieve, who had gleaned from the TWUA's wartime experience a conviction that it was most likely to gain its ends when the federal government lent its support, the most attractive way out of the union's dilemma lay in finding an appropriate agency in Washington to cover its retreat. In an effort reminiscent of Frank Gorman's frantic scramble a decade and a half earlier to terminate the 1934 general strike in a way that would allow a resounding defeat to be passed off as something less decisive, Rieve beseeched the Truman administration to offer a credible pretext for ending the strike. With nearly 9,000 workers back on the job at Dan River by early May, and the company content to let the strike die a slow, public death that left the union humiliated, Rieve finally succeeded in getting Federal Mediation and Conciliation Service Chairman Cyrus Ching to request an end to the walkout on the basis of a vaguely worded proposal that a special three-member panel mediate the parties' differences. Rieve's caveat that there was "no promise or . . . hint of a promise" that anything would come of the arrangement notwithstanding, members of the national cotton-rayon policy committee readily agreed at a meeting in Charlotte, N.C., on May 5, that an opportunity to camouflage the union's surrender as an act of good citizenship was the best they were likely to get.[53]

Apparently in the grip of the same fanciful logic that inspired Frank Gorman's ludicrous attempt to unearth the "good news" beneath the rubble of the 1934 disaster, *Textile Labor* editor Ken Fiester assured readers that the 1951 strike was destined to reside in the annals of the union's history as a triumph of the spirit. "We certainly didn't win the southern strike," Fiester observed, "yet neither did we lose the South." The strike had ended, he declared, at a juncture equidistant from victory and defeat. "To sum it all up," he wrote, "the strike was a disappointment in terms of results. It was not a disappointment in the way it was fought. The gallantry of the strikers proved again that justice is sure to triumph in the South. One battle has ended in a stalemate, but the war will go on until the final victory is won."[54]

Had the strike ended in a draw, TWUA leaders and members would have been justified in looking back on it as an episode attesting to the union's strength as much as to its weakness. Yet, by any conceivable standard, the 1951 southern strike was an unmitigated disaster, one that wreaked permanent devastation on the TWUA in the region that was the key both to its institutional viability and to the future of textile unionism in the United States. Before the strike, there had been outposts of labor-management accommodation seemingly secure enough to justify the hope that still more of the southern textile industry might, through patient and persistent effort, be brought within the union's orbit. After the strike, there was wreckage so vast and despair so powerful that even its most devoted supporters were compelled to discount the TWUA's prospects in the region. Leading southern mills that had earlier been willing, if only grudgingly, to concede the legitimacy of the union's role in representing their employees' interests became unyielding adversaries after the strike. Initially angry that the strike had been called, and then emboldened by their victory, Dan River, Cone, Erwin, Marshall Field, and others hardened their outlook toward the TWUA—in some cases to the point of practically erasing the once significant difference between their attitude and that of the southern industry's confirmed union-haters. Dan River Mills signaled its intention to take a harder line by refusing to renew a dues check-off clause when its union contract expired at the end of July. Almost instantly, that turned what had been the best-funded TWUA joint board in the South into a financial basket case.[55]

Even more disheartening and debilitating was the alienation the strike produced among the union's southern members. Reeling from their disappointment and often confronted by bosses intent on punishing them for their activism and impertinence, most of the more than 40,000 millhands who had answered the strike call gravitated, once it was over, toward the suspicion that union leaders had goaded them into a battle that the national union then refused to support *to the end*. Rieve had worried, when the union decided to end the strike, that southern members would "think they were sold down the river," and their abiding disillusionment with the organization in the sullen aftermath of defeat proved him correct.[56]

As the scope of the debacle became apparent, TWUA leaders sought explanations wherever they could find them. Their initial conclusion was that the TWUA had fallen victim to the antiunion conspiracy that other southern mill owners had long relied on to thwart worker organizing, and which union witnesses had detailed in their testimony before a subcommittee of the Senate Labor and Public Welfare Committee only months before.[57] The escalating political battle in the union also ensured that the search for explanations would quickly descend into partisan finger-pointing. During a contentious postmortem conducted by the union's Executive Council in late June, Rieve and his most ardent New England allies sought to attribute the breakdown of strike support in Danville to the Baldanzi faction's preoccupation with "community relations" and its concomitant inattention to building a fighting spirit among local members. Those in the Baldanzi camp favored an analysis that explained the union's calamitous setback in Danville as the product of Rieve's destructively misguided attempt to use contract negotiations with Dan River as a means to discredit his political opponents. Rieve was hellbent "to come in and demonstrate how a good negotiator could perform," Baldanzi supporter Emanuel Boggs insisted, and, in his ardor to expose the alleged ineptitude and faintheartedness of those who had negotiated earlier contracts with the company, he recklessly maneuvered the union into "a senseless strike."[58]

Even as the faultfinding continued in the weeks and months after the strike, leaders and staff on both sides of the TWUA's political divide were troubled by a nagging belief that the crippling injuries the union had suffered had been self-inflicted. By permitting the union's internal political squabbles to contaminate its collective bargaining policies, TWUA leaders did a grave disservice to the more than 400,000 textile workers to whom they owed their primary allegiance. And, in expressing the view, as so many later did, that the strike would not have occurred if the union had not been embroiled in a consuming battle for partisan political advantage, they validated that damning judgment.

To the extent that the southern strike was a by-product of the leadership battle in the TWUA, it illustrated with distressing clarity the destructive momentum that the fight between Rieve and Baldanzi had gathered by the spring of 1951. Combined with the fierce invective unleashed by Rieve's politically inspired firing of Canadian director Sam Baron, which had occurred just before the strike began, the animus that festered in the wake of the southern defeat imparted to those on the outside looking in a stark impression of the TWUA as a organization careening toward institutional suicide.

It was, perhaps, their ever more urgent sense that the union's internal battles were jeopardizing its existence that caused so many otherwise sincere devotees of democratic unionism in the majority camp to support or acquiesce in the increasingly high-handed and undemocratic methods Rieve and his top aides employed in the months leading up to the 1952 convention to ensure Baldanzi's demise. Having exclusive power to hire and fire most union staffers and to decide which of its elected officials would wield real authority, Rieve was in a position to reward loyalty and punish dissent. With the compliant backing of a comfortable majority of Executive Council members, he exploited his advantage with callous efficiency. Determined to accomplish at the 1952 convention what they had failed so spectacularly to accomplish two years earlier, Rieve and his allies shamelessly manipulated the process of delegate selection to minimize Baldanzi's support. They added to their own delegate count by chartering new locals that were little more than administrative fictions. In June of 1951, the Executive Council, over the vehement objections of its badly outnumbered pro-Baldanzi members, chartered more than thirty new locals in Fall River alone. Although union membership had actually declined significantly from what it had been two years earlier in Fall River, the seat of Rieve loyalist Mariano Bishop's power, the new charters increased its representatives' influence at the 1952 convention.[59]

Given the skill and thoroughness with which they had crafted their strategy and dominated the field of battle, the lopsided victory that Rieve and his allies achieved at the 1952 convention was a foregone conclusion. Overmatched and outmaneuvered long before the convention was called to order on April 28 in Cleveland's Public Auditorium, Baldanzi and his supporters never had a chance. Those in the Baldanzi camp who had naively hoped that the 1952 convention would afford the same opportunity for free and open debate that the 1950 conclave had, found themselves powerless to do much more than watch as the formalities of their practical obliteration were attended to by the efficient Rieve machine. In firm control of every facet of the convention, from deciding which delegates were seated to who among them spoke and for how long, Rieve endured the torrent of insults and wails of protests from his frustrated and enraged opponents on the convention floor with the smug equanimity of someone secure in the knowledge that he had nothing to fear.[60]

When the time finally came for delegates to decide who would lead the union out of the convention, Rieve's masterful orchestration of its proceedings paid off in an easy victory over Baldanzi for the TWUA presidency by a vote of 1,223 to 720. Beyond his own triumph, Rieve could savor the equally decisive victories of his full slate of candidates over the hapless and mostly unknown Baldanzi nominees.[61] When the gavel came down at the convention's adjournment early on the afternoon of May 2, the problem of divided leadership at the top of the TWUA was a thing of the past. For two years, arguably the most critical period in the union's history, it had jostled aside or taken precedence over every other issue on its agenda. Convinced that getting rid of Baldanzi was necessary for the union's greater glory, Rieve had spared no effort to gain his victory. It was, however, a victory won at a ruinous cost to the union.

At a convention that *New York Times* correspondent A. H. Raskin said "bordered on the riotous," Rieve had used his vastly superior authority ruthlessly and expertly, and, when he was finished, no one in the hall, including George Baldanzi, could any longer doubt that the TWUA was Rieve's to run as he saw fit. After the 1950 convention, Rieve and his allies on the Executive Council had feigned interest in proposed reforms to democratize the selection of union leaders. Once their opponents were vanquished and they were free to express their true feelings about decentralizing the leadership structure, they emphatically reiterated their preference for unionism "from the top down."[62] Even some of those otherwise pleased by Rieve's triumph wondered whether he and his supporters were not being shortsighted in their doctrinaire insistence that a chief executive with absolute power was, as one put it, "necessary in order to insure an efficient organization that will pursue a uniform policy laid down by the international union." Even if an organization whose functionaries operated in lockstep was "a completely desirable thing," Rieve partisan John Cort observed in *The Commonweal,* it was not a goal worth achieving at any cost. "If the test of a policy," he wrote shortly after the convention, "is going to be pitched on the plane of 'Look, it works, doesn't it?' then the answer has to be . . . 'No, it doesn't work.' It doesn't work because it fails to recognize the fact that the best way to create loyalty in an organization is to give members a direct stake in that organization, which means, above all, to give them the power to pick their own leaders."[63]

Yet, in the end, it was not the triumph of the organizational philosophy espoused by Rieve and his top lieutenants that cost the TWUA so dearly in the turbulent aftermath of the 1952 convention. Rather, it was their deeply aggrieved adversaries' disdain for the less than honorable way they had gone about securing their victory. Utterly certain from the moment of the opening gavel that the convention was "packed and rigged," Baldanzi and his hopelessly outnumbered confederates seethed as their challenges and protests were drowned out by the derisive rebukes of opponents secure in their unassailable majority. Those who had watched the confrontation build in the months before the convention thought it likely, as *Business Week* predicted, that it would "be a bitter one, and TWUA very likely will suffer for a long time." But even those who understood the depth of the enmity the Rieve-Baldanzi conflict fostered must have been shocked by the destructive passions it unleashed in the end.

Even before the convention was adjourned, secession was on the minds of more than a few Baldanzi supporters. Immediately after his defeat, Baldanzi met with them to discourage secession, and CIO president Philip Murray, who had abandoned his erstwhile neutrality to support Rieve, earnestly preached unity to those in the minority faction still willing to listen. In language more threatening than magnanimous Rieve likewise sought to head off talk of secession, pledging that there would be no reprisals against union staffers in the Baldanzi camp as long as they agreed "to stop their politicking." For at least some, however, appeals for unity and promises of fair treatment in the future were simply too little too late. Jack Robinson, manager of the TWUA's joint board in Hamilton, Ont., informed reporters while the convention was still in session that he intended to recommend immediate secession to his 5,000 members. Already deeply unhappy over Rieve's firing of Sam Baron and bitter about the crude methods the new director, Harold Daoust, used to stifle and discredit Baldanzi supporters in Hamilton and elsewhere in Canada, Robinson was not disposed to let bygones be bygones when the indignities inflicted by the convention were added to his catalog of discontent. Almost certainly egged on by Baron, who had been promoting secession since he had been fired a year earlier, Robinson told reporters that on his return home he would press his followers to seek affiliation with the Canadian branch of the AFL's United Textile Workers.[64]

When emotions other than anger informed their judgment, most Baldanzi supporters were sufficiently astute trade unionists to know that secession offered no guarantees of more congenial surroundings, especially given the UTW's well-earned reputation for inefficacy and malfeasance. Yet with the memory of their humiliation and mistreatment too vivid to permit judicious reflection, repaying their tormentors for their misdeeds was an urge that many Baldanzi loyalists found too powerful to deny. The veteran southern organizer Joe Pedigo later explained that the experience of the Cleveland convention had "disillusioned so many people" that doing nothing was unthinkable. "A lot of us at that time had never seen a really rigged convention before," he recalled. "We were new at it and I think that's the one big thing that caused the degree of bitterness. I think that if we had been older hands and seen a few more things, and I have seen them rigged since and I have never got too excited about it. But that was the first one, and the conventions before that, there is always a certain amount of rigging, but they had been pretty open and you could have your say up until that convention. Nobody was able to take it in stride . . . on Baldanzi's side, they were all just so goddamn mad, they were ready to go anywhere."[65]

For those who had trouble deciding what, if anything, they should do to register their unhappiness with what had gone on in Cleveland, Rieve made the decision easier by almost immediately violating his pledge not to seek reprisals against those union officials who had opposed him. As word spread through the ranks of Baldanzi supporters that such prominent dissidents as North Carolina state director Lew Conn had been purged by Rieve, secession suddenly became for some a duty rather than an option. Still, it was not until Baldanzi himself jumped to the UTW that the magnitude of the secession crisis facing the TWUA became fully evident. Insisting that he was forced to act in response to Rieve's expanding purge of the union officials who had backed his insurgency, Baldanzi announced on May 15, not quite two weeks after the convention closed, that he was signing on as the UTW's national organizing director.[66]

Almost from the moment Baldanzi made his intention known, others in his camp rushed to follow his lead. The residual unrest among leaders and members in the large southern locals and joint boards that had suffered most from the disastrous strike a year earlier needed only to be channeled, and, once Baldanzi pointed the way toward the UTW, large numbers of them fell in behind him. On the same day that it reported Baldanzi's defection, the *New York Times* reported that estimates of the total loss of membership facing the TWUA ranged from 25,000 to 75,000. The *New Republic* reported a few days later an unnamed "Baldanzi spokesman's" prediction that "a minimum of 100,000" disgruntled millhands were likely to abandon the TWUA in favor of the UTW.[67]

Although the success of the secession movement would be measured in terms of how many TWUA members Baldanzi brought into the UTW, his first contribution was in recruiting some of the best and brightest organizers and administrators in the service of textile unionism. Indeed, virtually every experienced TWUA organizer in the South went over to the UTW in the weeks after Baldanzi's defection.[68] Most took the step willingly, out of personal loyalty to Baldanzi and disgust with the TWUA; others did so because Rieve's seemingly irrepressible desire for vengeance against those who opposed him, left them no alternative. Joe Pedigo, who initially declined Baldanzi's offer to join the UTW organizing department because he was put off by the union's unsavory reputation, changed his mind a few days later when he was abruptly fired by a Rieve emissary. "I would have quit TWUA," Pedigo later explained, "but I would never have gone with UTW if I had not been fired the way I was fired. That made me so damn mad, I didn't know which end was up." Pedigo, whose organizing triumphs included Dan River Mills, the largest prize the TWUA would ever capture in the South, was not long in deciding what to do as he angrily departed the union's small office in Kannapolis, N.C. "I walked out," he recalled,

and went down to the closest phone booth and picked up the telephone and called George Baldanzi and said, "Are you still looking for some staff people?" He said, "They haven't fired you, have they?" "Yes." He said, "Damn right. I want you to go up to Marshall Field right away." So, I was out of a job about five minutes there.

Bitterly resentful that his many years of service to the union in the South seemed to count for nothing with the TWUA leaders in New York who summarily fired him, Pedigo lent his talents to the UTW more out of spite than conviction. "I wouldn't have gone if I hadn't been so goddamn mad," he admitted, "I wouldn't have gone. I just forgot all about the CIO and thought, 'Goddamn it, I've organized more plants for this goddamn union than any damn man they've got in this country and they don't even give me a notice.' That was what got me."[69]

With the assistance of Pedigo and most of the other young activists he had recruited to the TWUA's southern organizing team over the preceding decade, Baldanzi had little trouble persuading thousands of alienated union members in the South that they would be better off in the UTW. In the days after his defection, one after another of the TWUA's largest locals in the South switched to its grateful, if slightly bewildered, rival. Workers at Dan River Mills, the TWUA's "showcase" of textile unionism in the South, voted overwhelmingly to switch allegiance to the UTW, as did disaffected millhands at other major unionized firms in the region, including Cone, Erwin, and Marshall Field. The TWUA was able to hold on to the Lowenstein chain's massive finishing plant in Rock Hill, S.C., but employees at the company's mills in Rockingham, N.C., and in New Orleans bolted to the UTW.[70] Emanuel Boggs, also purged after the 1952 TWUA convention, no doubt expressed the satisfaction other ousted veterans felt when he cheerfully confided to a friend, two months after the secession began, that the loss of the large mills that "traditionally set the southern pattern" meant that "Rieve is pretty well washed up in the South. . . ."[71]

While North Carolina was a particular disaster for the TWUA when it came to holding its members, the union fared much better elsewhere in the South. Although workers at several organized mills in Alabama, including Dwight Mills in Gadsden, the state's biggest local, were ardent Baldanzi supporters, TWUA officials succeeded in blocking secession. It took everything they had, however. Herbert Williams, one of the TWUA's top functionaries in the South, recalled that persuading millhands in Gadsden and elsewhere not to follow their hearts was a daunting challenge. "People down South are very emotional," he later explained, "and Baldanzi could lift you out of your seat making a speech. And I think that had a whole lot to do with the way the people felt . . . towards George Baldanzi." Relying mainly on hastily printed flyers that detailed the supposedly horrific consequences of secession, Williams and his assistants worked tirelessly to hold on to several wavering Alabama locals. "We worked our cans off," he remembered. "We was [*sic*] at the gates every morning, noon and night, passing out them damn leaflets. I hate them damn things." Still, Williams reported, making the union's case at the mill gates proved a good deal safer than doing it at workers' homes, where, on more than one occasion, TWUA staffers were forced to retreat at gunpoint.[72]

Yet, if the TWUA succeeded in defending its position in some regions of the South, it failed to keep some supposedly rock-solid northern strongholds. Leaders of the 2,500-member carpet and rug local at the Bigelow-Sanford Company in Thompsonville, Conn., were among the earliest to board the secession bandwagon, and, when TWUA authorities tried to seize its treasury, the defiant officers of Local 2188, who had pledged to "fight to the bitter end" against the Rieve administration's efforts to bring them "back into line," donated nearly $60,000 to the town's hospital construction fund rather than see it fall into enemy hands. The national union had more success when it acted preemptively. The *New York Times* reported on May 22 that Rieve had abruptly suspended 35 local union officials in Massachusetts and Rhode Island "in an attempt to halt a bolt to the American Federation of Labor."[73]

A potentially far more serious threat to the TWUA's institutional integrity arose in Philadelphia, where 9,000 members of the local joint board, one of the largest and most influential in the union, voted to go over to the UTW. Too powerful and independent to be bullied back into the fold, as some weaker constituents had been, the Philadelphia joint board was instead gently enticed back. Rieve personally invited Joint Board Manager Joseph Hueter, a strong Baldanzi backer and the rebel faction's candidate for executive vice president at the 1952 convention, to state his terms for sticking with the TWUA, and when he did so they were met without objection. While anti-Rieve feeling remained strong among the union's Philadelphia members, the secession vote was overturned and Hueter remained in his leadership position, the only prominent Baldanzi ally to do so.[74]

In New Jersey, among the concentration of dyers' locals that had been his original power base, Baldanzi might have reasonably anticipated much greater support than he actually received. Leaders and members of both the Passaic and South Jersey joint boards and those in other locals in Freehold and Belleville, expressed immediate interest in joining the secession movement, but the ultimate losses the TWUA suffered were minimized by the aggressive administrative and legal action taken by the national leadership and New Jersey state CIO president Carl Holderman to oust Baldanzi supporters and to seize the records and assets of the rebel bodies. The TWUA also benefited from many members' concerns about the personal financial costs of secession. William Gordon, a Rieve loyalist who had earlier been appointed second in command of the dyers division so that he might dilute Baldanzi's influence, recalled that a large number of dyers otherwise disposed to bolt the TWUA ultimately declined to do so because it would have cost them their pensions.[75]

By the time the secession movement finally lost its momentum in early June, the TWUA's lost members numbered nowhere near the 100,000 millhands that Baldanzi and his supporters had predicted. The exact number of TWUA members who had transferred their fortunes to the UTW proved impossible to calculate, but it was certainly not more than 25,000 to 35,000. In light of the UTW's inability to generate the money or to sustain the institutional will required to make the most of its sudden windfall, it is likely that many of those who opted for secession in a moment of high emotion later regretted it. Indeed, most of the former TWUA leaders and many of the former rank-and-file members who joined the UTW were not there for long. In time, the leaders migrated to other unions or dropped out of the labor movement altogether when the UTW's true nature was revealed. Their followers either straggled back to the TWUA or melted into the nonunion majority in southern textiles.[76]

Although Rieve and the now uniformly like-minded members of the union's Executive Council expressed great satisfaction at having beaten back the secession movement without suffering the huge membership losses that their opponents predicted, there were, in fact, no good reasons for anyone to be happy with the state of affairs confronting the TWUA after its willful descent into fratricide. In the South, the region that even New Englanders now agreed was most important to the union's future, the devastation the TWUA had suffered left it with barely enough strength to hold on to what little remained of its once substantial assets in the region. Those rushed into the area to fill the leadership void created by the loss, through purges and defections, of the TWUA's most able and experienced organizers, typically lacked both the training and the aptitude to serve the union in any capacity other than caretaker or salvager. Scott Hoyman, whose experience as a labor educator in Maine afforded little relevant preparation for the salvage work ahead of him when he was suddenly ordered south to Greensboro in May of 1952, later acknowledged that trying to keep the union from deteriorating even further was a full-time job. "The first three or four years that I worked in the South," he recalled, "I worked entirely on either holding . . . locals, getting them back where they belonged, or trying to repair the damage."[77]

The TWUA's profoundly weakened condition in the South also had disturbing implications for its future in the North. In combination with the 1951 southern strike, which had severely undermined the union's bargaining power with southern mills, the total incapacitation of its organizing apparatus in the Piedmont ensured that the competitive predicament of New England textile firms would persist. That, in turn, meant that northern mills that had previously conceded higher wages and better benefits in anticipation of the TWUA's forceful endeavors to reduce the North-South wage differential or keep it from getting any worse would be far less likely to do so. "For the northern manufacturers," *Fortune* said of the TWUA's diminished capacities in the South, "the result has been the unhappy assurance that, with new southern organizing postponed, the North-South wage differential will keep New England at a serious competitive disadvantage."[78]

Easily overlooked in assessing the union's two-year political battle was the serious damage inflicted on its service departments. As a direct result of the Rieve-Baldanzi upheaval, the TWUA lost its able general counsel Isadore Katz and his chief assistant David Jaffe, both of whom were immediately retained by several of the dissident locals and joint boards bent on secession. Even more harmful to field operations, however, was the gutting of its extremely effective education and political action departments. The idealistic young activists who conducted the TWUA's educational and political work in the field had been among the first to protest administration moves against Baldanzi, whom they regarded as the union's most forward-looking leader, and they were among the first casualties once hostilities commenced. The TWUA's respected research department survived intact, largely because Director Sol Barkin enforced a policy of strict neutrality, but its value was nevertheless diminished by the union's subsequent inability to make the most of the voluminous data it collected.[79]

In an interview with *Business Week* at the close of the 1952 convention, when secession was still only a vague threat, Rieve promised that the benefit of a fully united leadership would immediately become evident. He and his lieutenants, from Executive Vice President Mariano Bishop and Secretary-Treasurer William Pollock down through the ranks of the Executive Board to its newest members, were now of one mind, and prepared to "account for our stewardship as a united administration" by working "to serve our members better." At last free of the distractions that disunity had created, the TWUA was once again in a position, he insisted, to "go ahead to better contract terms [and not] to take any backward steps." That surely meant, the reporter noted, "that TWUA can be expected to go after substantial wage gains" and that "employers in the South must expect new organizing drives. . . ." Moreover, he reported, as much as some in the Rieve camp wanted to make their opponents pay for their disruptive and disloyal conduct, "cooler heads prevailed" in arguing that the winners must be magnanimous enough in victory to acknowledge that "[m]any of those supporting Baldanzi are recognized throughout TWUA as among the best and most aggressive of the young leaders in the union" and that "[a] purge . . . might split the union wide open—especially in the South, where Baldanzi had a lot of strength."[80]

Assessing textile unionism's prospects less than two months later, *Fortune* saw only trouble ahead. "For the next years at least," the writer observed, "further organization in the textile industry will be at a standstill, and total union membership may even decline." That bleak state of affairs, he predicted, would be "the chief consequence of the fratricidal warfare that has broken out between the CIO Textile Workers Union and the AF of L United Textile Workers."[81]

Notwithstanding the personal satisfaction Rieve and his allies derived from the success that capped their more than two-year-long campaign to depose George Baldanzi, for the fragile organization in whose interests they claimed to be acting, the resultant harm far outweighed the alleged benefit. To be sure, the goal of completely unified leadership had been achieved, perhaps even to the point of compulsory consensus, but the cost left many to wonder for years thereafter whether it had been worth it. Even if Baldanzi had been deficient in all the ways his detractors alleged—shallow, vain, ambitious, unprincipled, self-seeking, inconstant—the means by which Rieve and his confederates ousted him could hardly have been more destructive to its future well-being. The no-holds-barred strategy they adopted after their failed effort to cashier him at the 1950 convention was responsible, directly or indirectly, for most of the devastation that followed, including the 1951 southern strike, whose origins can be traced to their reckless passion to discredit Baldanzi in the region where his popularity and reputation were the strongest.

As the crippling effects of these self-inflicted injuries became even more evident during the mid-1950s, Rieve and his close associates found refuge in the conviction that the TWUA's decline was inevitable and that any mistakes they may have made were more properly classified as effects, rather than causes, of the union's deepening malaise. It was, however, a belief to be valued more for the absolution it promised than the understanding it afforded. In an organization long adept at blaming its chronic troubles on what others had done to it, a new challenge was suddenly at hand, one that beckoned those with the courage and candor to do so to contemplate and explain what the TWUA had now done to itself.

CHAPTER 10

Surviving the Future

For those acquainted with the history of textile unionism in the United States, the self-destructive and exhausting slugfest that raged between the terminally estranged factions of the TWUA during the early 1950s was distressingly familiar. The frustrations attendant to building and sustaining a viable union in America's textile industry had always been wearing and unnerving even under the best of circumstances. Yet, when a tough job became a seemingly impossible one as already daunting impediments took on the appearance of insurmountable barriers, those brooding discontents expressed themselves in ways that undermined the TWUA's historically fragile unity. And it required no special insight to conclude, based on the perpetually beleaguered condition that seemed to be textile unionism's inescapable destiny, that the culture of misfortune that enveloped the TWUA in the early 1950s was simply the latest manifestation of that unhappy providence.

To be sure, the labor movement in general, and other CIO affiliates in particular, had good reasons to believe that the climate of economic uncertainty and political conservatism that had descended on the nation by the early 1950s boded ill for all trade unions. Yet if the generic hardships awaiting unions in general threatened to exacerbate the TWUA's situation, its essential dilemma appeared to be anything but transient or commonplace. The TWUA's own exegesis of that dilemma—one that emphasized the textile industry's schizophrenic structure and inherent irrationality, that implied its inexorable decline, that presumed the immutable antiunionism of southern mill owners and posited the chronic cultural incapacitation of southern millhands—lent credibility to the argument that its deepening misfortune was exceptional, a fate that ran counter to the general experience of the CIO's other (momentarily afflicted, but still vibrant and resilient) affiliates in the mass-production sector. The next generation of industrial unionists would understand all too well that the troubles that plagued the TWUA in the early 1950s were harbingers of postindustrial lassitude destined to blight the future of unions across the spectrum of American manufacturing. In the moment of the organization's unfolding predicament, however, the most plausible interpretation at hand was that textile unionism was, yet again, in the throes of congenital misfortune.

Certainly, in the weeks and months after the 1952 convention, there was little evidence of the institutional revival that Rieve and his allies had predicted once they were securely and exclusively in control of the union's affairs and operations. With the UTW-AFL abruptly roused from fitful somnolence by an influx of energetic TWUA defectors and outcasts intent on gaining revenge against their former comrades, an industry that had been a largely uncontested CIO domain was suddenly up for grabs. It was true enough, as *Textile Labor* would insist for years thereafter, that the TWUA quickly got the upper hand when the UTW's structural frailties and repellent ethics became known to the Baldanzi followers who temporarily swelled its ranks. But the union's piecemeal restoration came at an exceedingly high cost given the resources it expended and the critically important work it neglected while repelling its rival.[1]

In June of 1953, the TWUA announced—prematurely as it turned out—that the year-old secession movement sparked by George Baldanzi's expulsion was over, an "infamous failure" that attested to its own abiding strength and to the UTW's institutional bankruptcy. Fewer than 30,000 millhands "formerly under TWUA contract" had switched to the UTW, *Textile Labor* declared, and only half of those were "dues payers."[2] Even those numbers exaggerated its actual loss, the TWUA maintained, since the defectors' deepening disillusionment with the UTW was causing more and more of them to reverse course. In a gloating editorial that glossed over the real damage that the secession movement continued to inflict on the TWUA, *Textile Labor* editor Ken Fiester observed that, while the pitiable circumstances in which disenchanted defectors found themselves was "in some respects . . . a very sad story," they had only themselves and George Baldanzi to blame. "Consider what has happened to the men and women who, in impetuous defiance of their own best interests, set out some 16 months ago to destroy TWUA-CIO and raise in its place a 'new' and sanctified UTW-AFL." He smugly mused,

> They have sacrificed the workers who followed them; for they have been unable to negotiate workable contracts in many mills, and they are utterly without research, administrative or organizational assistance. . . . They have failed to rebuild UTW in the image which dazzled them so fatally in May 1952. They have found no "democracy" in UTW, nor any purity either. . . . They are pariahs in the labor movement, scorned by all in CIO as traitors, distrusted by the AFL as all turncoats are distrusted. They are subjects of UTW but are treated as aliens even in this miserable principality. After all, self-proclaimed "idealists" are hardly welcome to full citizenship in a regime devoted to the fast buck.

"Most of them," Fiester concluded, "are as good as dead in the labor movement."[3]

If Fiester and others on the "winning" side of the union's wrenching civil war delighted in the mounting distress and disillusionment of those among the losers who had gone over to the UTW, there was precious little genuine comfort to be found in the transparent fiction, ballyhooed in the pages of *Textile Labor*, that no lasting harm had been done to the TWUA. Even as TWUA spokesmen parroted the official line, "Our union has come through the . . . ordeal . . . of political 'secession' without basic loss of strength," evidence mounted, in the North and the South, that its self-destructive detour into fratricide would make a daunting mission even more difficult to accomplish.[4] Indeed, against the melancholy backdrop of the textile industry's stricken economic condition throughout the 1950s, the TWUA took on a sickly pallor that caused even its most indefatigable champions to wonder whether its best days were not behind it.

Despite the TWUA's best efforts to shore up its support among the southern locals and joint boards that had rejected secession, even loyal members in the region tended to be far from passionate in their embrace of Emil Rieve and those who represented him in the South. To the extent that southern members identified with leaders beyond their local officers, far more had felt affinity for Baldanzi and his disciples than for the Rieve appointees who directed the TWUA's administrative affairs. Once Baldanzi and his most ardent followers decamped to the UTW, the stolid functionaries left to replenish the TWUA's depleted assets in the Piedmont had their hands full just keeping its standing from becoming even more tenuous. Though competent, sometimes even accomplished, in tending to routine matters of collective bargaining and contract administration, James Bamford, Boyd Payton, Herbert Williams, H. D. Lisk, Julius Fry, and the other officials to whom Rieve gave responsibility in the South possessed few of the singular talents required to design and direct the massive rebuilding project that confronted the TWUA. Organizing southern millhands took on a special urgency in the sobering aftermath of its strike debacle and secession crisis, but at no time in its history had the TWUA wanted more for skilled and experienced personnel. In time, some of those who had been pressed into service exhibited a talent for organizing that established them as worthy successors to the experienced organizers who had defected to the UTW, but, on balance, they were probably less able than their predecessors. The TWUA would continue to benefit, during the mid-1950s, from the UTW's inability to retain many of the secessionists who had joined its ranks, but winning back members was not really regaining strength.

The TWUA's diminished presence in the South was actually most evident in the North, where mill owners who had hoped that the union would expand its influence in the textile industry's southern branches increasingly gave in to their doubts. The willingness of northern mill owners to concede higher wages and more generous benefits during the late 1940s was sustained by a fragile faith that the union's bargaining strength with the handful of influential southern mills it had organized would be enough to keep regional differences in labor costs from returning to destructive prewar levels. Only the most sanguine of northern mill owners believed that the union could, in fact, completely eliminate the regional cost differential. Nevertheless, before the abrupt reversal of fortune the union suffered as a result of its twin calamities in the Piedmont—the 1951 strike and secession—only the most pessimistic among them would have guessed that their survival plan would soon be rendered hopelessly inoperable. And, once resigned to the somber reality that they could no longer rely on the TWUA to do its part in trying to ensure that labor costs in the South kept pace with those in the North, New England mill owners, reeling from the immediate effects of a worsening industrywide slump and facing the looming prospect of irreversible decline, resolved to fend for themselves.

The inexorable withering away of the northern textile industry, a disheartening reality confirmed throughout the early 1950s by more frequent mill liquidations and transfers of production to the South, was dictated by an economic logic whose essential thrust the TWUA was powerless to parry. Yet, to keep faith with its members in the northern cotton-rayon and woolen and worsted industries, still the union's most important constituencies, the TWUA was obliged to persist in the belief that textile manufacturing in New England was not the doomed enterprise its would-be eulogists too readily assumed. The northern textile industry's investors could, perhaps, afford to be fickle or faint-hearted in reacting to its faltering performance. The TWUA, however, could not concede the industry's demise without raising serious questions about its own viability, especially given the fact that union leaders had by the middle of 1952 new reason to wonder whether penetrating the South was really possible.

The TWUA's dilemma was made starkly evident when northern mill owners, their confidence in the union's ability to influence southern labor costs now shattered, decided in 1952 to reverse a decade-long trend by pursuing wage reductions as a means of easing the competitive disadvantage they faced. Having concluded, as one northern textile executive said after the collapse of the 1951 southern strike, that the TWUA was likely to retain "little or no strength in the South, and that as a factor in preventing the widening of the [North-South] differential it will not be important," New England mill owners took the matter of labor costs into their own hands less out of aggressive intent than deepening despair.[5] And, as evidence mounted that the Korean conflict would not provide the economic stimulus the textile industry's northern branches desperately needed to keep them out of recession, New England mill owners generally agreed, by the beginning of 1952, that when they next bargained with the TWUA they would seek to reduce wages.

With its resources diverted to stemming the tide of secession, its dues-paying membership shrinking as industry layoffs and mill liquidations reached alarming levels, and its leaders unable to offer much more than empty declarations of moral outrage in response to the disarming logic of resolute employers, the TWUA could lament the wage reductions in New England during the spring and summer of 1952 but it could not prevent them. When the union rejected the Maine-based Bates Manufacturing Company's demand that the 7,000 workers in its five mills accept a large wage cut, the issue was referred to an arbitrator, who, though unwilling to give the company all the cost relief it sought, did order a pay reduction of seven and one-half cents per hour. Moreover, in explaining his award, the arbitrator, University of Pennsylvania Professor William Simkin, emphasized that the growing North-South wage differential, and the TWUA's ever more evident inability to do anything about it, weighed especially heavily in his decision. Ignoring the union's absurdly optimistic claims that the northern cotton-rayon industry was in the midst of "a healthy recovery" from recession and that pending negotiations would restore wages in the South "to a sound competitive level," Simkin found greater merit in the company's argument that a wage reduction was the only realistic means of closing the gap between its labor costs and those of southern mill owners.[6]

"No amount of angry words can really express the shock felt throughout the TWUA at the arbitrator's decision in the Bates case," *Textile Labor* indignantly declared. As events soon made clear, however, what union officials hoped would be only an isolated setback in Maine quickly became an insistent, region-wide clamor for wage reductions. At an emergency meeting convened in Boston just after the Bates decision was announced, Rieve, Mariano Bishop, and other officials passionately urged the 400 union delegates in attendance to adopt a "resist-all-down-the-line" policy. Repeating the Executive Council's formal declaration that the Bates decision was "a shocking miscarriage of justice" inspired by "the outrageous conception that industry should be assured of uninterrupted profits even if they must be squeezed from the blood and bone of the workers," Rieve announced, "If the employers want a wage cut, they will have to jam it down our throats."[7]

To the union's deepening dismay, that is precisely what northern mill owners succeeded in doing in the summer of 1952. The same arguments that had carried the day in the Bates case persuaded a sympathetic arbitrator to alleviate the Fall River and New Bedford mills' purported economic distress by ordering wage reductions comparable to those granted in Maine. That defeat forced the TWUA to abandon further efforts to hold the line on wages. Since a "decisive proportion of our membership in the northern cotton-rayon mills" was affected by the Bates and New Bedford-Fall River awards, the Executive Council explained, the union had no option but to concede identical wage cuts to other employers in the region, including those operating under contracts not otherwise subject to renegotiation. "The workers in each case agreed it would be unrealistic," union leaders asserted, "to force these few mills to pay wages which were out of line with competitors in the same area and in some instances in the same communities."[8]

Although for the most part the TWUA resisted equally vociferous demands for wage cuts from hard-pressed employers in the northern woolen and worsted industry in 1952, the variety and magnitude of its troubles during the latter half of the year sapped the union's spirit as much as its resources. The union's perdurable faith that it could be the chief architect of its destiny had always been at odds with a discordant reality, but, during the 1940s, not even the most disheartening difficulty textile unionism faced could quell the sauguine expectation that the future would bring progress. Yet, confronted by the grim prospect that the union's future in the branches of the northern textile industry most critical to its survival was anything but promising, *Textile Labor* embraced the consoling belief that the TWUA's troubles in New England, as in the Piedmont, were largely attributable to the folly and maleficence of others.

"New England mill owners are shedding crocodile tears by the gallon as they predict the extinction of the northern textile industry," an editorial mocked, as wage cutting became the rule, in the summer of 1952.

> Low-wage southern competition is driving them to the wall, they sob; and their beloved New England will never be the same. Still sniffling, they stuff their New England–earned profits into their carpetbags and set out, low in spirits but high in assets, for the promised land of Dixie. The whole performance deserves a mighty high hypocrisy rating. It's time it was given the recognition it deserves.
>
> Who created the southern textile industry? New England mill owners, who sought out a low-wage area 30 years ago and have been building plants there ever since. Who created a North-South wage differential? New England mill owners, who started out by paying their southern workers only a fraction of northern rates.
>
> Who could wipe out the North-South differential? New England mill owners, simply by raising their southern workers to northern wage levels. There are more than enough New England–owned mills in the South to set an effective wage pattern for all the rest.

"We in the TWUA concede," the editorial concluded, "that the New England industry has problems in addition to those it has created for itself. But we insist that sincere effort by management could ease many of them, while wage cutting will only make them worse."[9]

The diversion of personnel and of financial resources that the secession crisis caused from the middle of 1952 onward kept the TWUA from doing much more than talking about what it might do to protect the fruits of ten years' struggle. Union leaders were more acutely aware than ever that organizing southern millhands remained textile unionism's only hope of salvation.[10] But, with every able-bodied official and staffer working full time to fend off a resurgent UTW and the union running large deficits every month because of a 30-percent decline in dues payments, new organizing initiatives were out of the question for the foreseeable future. Nevertheless, the Executive Council agreed in mid-1952, that they should at least plan for such an eventuality.[11] This decision also afforded Emil Rieve an important opportunity to enhance the visibility and bolster the stature of his new "principal assistant," and heir apparent, Executive Vice President Mariano Bishop.

In replacing George Baldanzi, Bishop was almost immediately obliged to demonstrate that the high price the organization had paid to accommodate his ambition was worth the result. The person with the most to gain among those who led the long campaign to oust Baldanzi, Bishop had exhibited a talent for savage infighting. After his victory over Baldanzi, he needed to demonstrate an equally impressive talent for constructive leadership. Certainly, his record gave his allies and supporters reason to believe that he was up to the job he had worked so tirelessly to win. Born in the Azores of Portuguese parents who relocated the family to Fall River before he was a year old, Bishop grew up to do what most immigrants did in one of America's leading textile centers. Working at first in cotton mills and later in a Fall River dye shop, Bishop became a union activist at an early age. Elected president of his local union while he was still in his twenties, he advanced steadily, if unspectacularly, during the mid-1930s in both the UTW and the dyers' federation. When the TWOC was launched, he was among its charter functionaries. Although elected in 1938 to the Executive Council of the dyers' federation, where he toiled without particular distinction in Baldanzi's expansive shadow, Bishop did not achieve real prominence until Rieve assigned him a leading role in consolidating the TWUA's position in Fall River and New Bedford during the early 1940s. In time, he was appointed director of the northern cotton-rayon industry, and so spokesman for the 90,000 millhands who comprised the TWUA's largest and most influential constituency. His induction into the top echelon of union leadership was formalized by his election in 1946 to the Executive Council.[12]

The solid and steady, if unremarkable and uninspiring, qualities that Bishop brought to the union's number two position in the wake of the 1952 convention were, to those who had found fault with Baldanzi's style and orientation, just what the TWUA needed. Described by TWUA Education Director Larry Rogin as "a very narrow trade unionist" more in the "AFL mode [than] a social trade unionist," Bishop made up in steadfastness and persistence what he lacked in vision and verve.[13] Always more in tune with Rieve's thinking than with those like Baldanzi who questioned the organization's devout adherence to traditional practices, Bishop had become the union's unofficial president-designate by striving to be nearly indistinguishable in outlook from the leader he aspired to succeed.

Rieve selected Bishop shortly after the 1952 convention to head a special committee formed to systematize TWUA policies on organizing, the critical union activity with which Baldanzi had been most closely associated. This was Bishop's opportunity to prove himself. The ideas that Bishop brought to the committee's initial deliberations, however, suggested that, under his leadership, strategic innovation would take a back seat to administrative decorum.[14] Instead of focusing the union's attention and scarce resources on the all-important southern cotton industry, Bishop and his fellows opted instead to target unorganized workers in the synthetic yarn industry. Hoping that the morale of TWUA organizers could be boosted by new advances in a branch of the industry that had proven more amenable to unionism than others, the committee urged that special attention be given to organizing the southern operations of producers who already had contracts with the union in the North.

The committee also suggested that better record keeping might enhance the union's organizing prospects by providing a more objective basis for determining when and where its limited resources might most profitably be deployed. "This emphasis on a more factual and detailed analysis of organizing problems . . . may not have been necessary in the days when there was a general sweep toward unionism," the committee noted, but the "increasing difficulties" the organization faced made it imperative that, in the future, "judgments be based upon facts and not on hunches." Looking at its organizing efforts more objectively, the committee argued, might also help the union to decide when it would be better to cut its losses than "to go through with NLRB elections which we are certain to lose by a large margin." Too often, the committee insisted, the union had unwisely persisted in a losing cause because of "the staff's unwillingness to face the facts of the campaign." Certainly, there were times, it acknowledged, "when commitments to local committees and circumstances seem to require that the union participate in elections in which there is no doubt we shall lose." Even so, they concluded, doing the *right* thing must be balanced by an equal resolve to do the *prudent* thing. "Extreme care should be taken to avoid such commitments," they warned, "for the general effect is much more harmful to the union than the local benefit which is gained." Whereas initiative at the local level would help to "rekindle the crusading spirit which made possible many of the successes in the early days of our union, . . . the importance of closer supervision of all organizing activities" had to be recognized.[15]

It is hardly surprising, given its shrinking treasury and the multiplying diversions that the UTW's raiding created, that the TWUA only talked about future organizing during the latter half of 1952. Some progress had been made in developing better procedures for reporting the activities of organizers, Bishop noted in late November, but "the search for some way to reach the minds of textile workers with the message of unionism" had yielded very little. "Our committee has made but a small start in aiding TWUA to solve the problems of organizing the unorganized," Bishop admitted. "There have been no great successes. Unfortunately the employers continue to best us in important elections. And the Republican control of our nation will make the job more difficult rather than easier." Even so, he concluded, building union membership was so important that it rises beyond all other problems. . . . "If the old methods are not successful we must experiment with new ones."[16]

It is impossible to know whether Mariano Bishop had the skill and imagination required to reenergize the TWUA's moribund organizing apparatus and thus to redeem the faith of those who had backed him in his relentless campaign to replace George Baldanzi. On his way to a meeting with union officials in Passaic, N.J., on January 2, 1953, Bishop, only 46 years old, collapsed and died of a massive heart attack. Like others who advanced through the ranks to top leadership positions in the TWUA, he had commended himself to his fellow unionists largely by his administrative talents and political dexterity. He had established his credentials as an organizer during the TWUA's push into Fall River and New Bedford during the early war years, but because conditions there were probably more conducive to the union's success than those in any other center of cotton-rayon production in the country, it is difficult to assess the true extent of his organizing prowess. Certainly, once he became director of the northern cotton-rayon industry, there was little in the record of his day-to-day performance that distinguished him from the other able but stolid national leaders. And, like Rieve, on whom many believe he had consciously modeled himself, Bishop's priorities reflected the values and sensibilities of a leader more at home attending to the business of unionism than rallying the rank and file.[17] His tenure as de facto organizing director was too brief to do anything more than suggest how he intended to conduct the TWUA's most urgent business, but nothing in that scant record attested to special aptitude or commitment or confirmed an ability equal to Baldanzi's when it came to extolling the union's cause among the unorganized.

Perhaps because his accession had come at such a terribly high cost to the organization, Bishop's death had a profoundly dispiriting impact on those who believed he was qualified to succeed Emil Rieve as no other union leader was. "It looked like here you've gone through all this internal mess in the union," Larry Rogin later said of the gloom that descended following Bishop's sudden demise, "and you thought you had the future solved for a while."[18] Rieve was especially distressed by the loss. Having subjected the union to a wrenching internal fight in order to ensure that the person to whom he entrusted the TWUA's future shared his outlook, Rieve reacted to Bishop's death with grief that bordered on despair. It was that grief, his apologists later maintained, that explained Rieve's rigid insistence on settling the leadership succession issue that Bishop's death had suddenly unsettled literally before the flowers on his grave had begun to wilt.[19]

For Rieve, whose determination to bequeath the TWUA presidency to someone of his mind verged on an obsession by the early 1950s, Bishop's death was a doubly cruel blow that robbed him of the continuing counsel of a like-minded ally and of the serenity he had gained when his successor of choice was at last in place. It also increased Rieve's sense of personal isolation. With the death in late 1951 of Herb Payne, the longtime associate to whom he had entrusted control of both the dyeing and finishing and synthetic yarn divisions of the TWUA and on whom he had relied to do much of the dirty work in the bare-knuckles campaign to oust George Baldanzi, Rieve lost his closest confidant in the union. When Bishop died, Rieve lost the person he most trusted to keep the TWUA on the path he personally had charted for it.

As the entire elected leadership and top staff gathered in Fall River on January 7 for Bishop's funeral, most apparently believed that designating a successor, while obviously an important matter, was not urgent. Yet Rieve, for reasons that were baffling to even his closest aides, insisted the question be settled at once. The resultant scramble among union leaders to arrange on short notice a succession they could live with in the long run turned an otherwise solemn gathering into an unseemly frenzy of political maneuvers. Secretary-Treasurer William Pollock, the one union leader who openly coveted the position, had few supporters in the Executive Council. Pollock's loyalty to Rieve had been unwavering, and he was generally regarded as a competent and honest functionary. Few in the union hierarchy, however, believed that he was the person best suited to succeed Bishop as president in waiting. As the keeper of the union's seldom bulging purse, and the final arbiter of the expense accountings of all of those on the international's payroll, Pollock had come to be regarded by many Executive Council members as an officious penny pincher. It might be forgivable in a chief financial officer, but, to the Executive Council, it marked him as distinctly unsuited for a leadership position that demanded subtlety and vision. "Pollock was a difficult man to work with," publicity director Ken Fiester recalled. "He certainly didn't have . . . anywhere approaching the breadth of view that we were accustomed to with Rieve. . . . He was picky, he was petty; he would fuss about little things." Pollock was "a nice man basically, in a personal way," Fiester conceded, "But as a man to deal with on an issue of substance he was especially smallish—the issues of small substance. Perhaps it was the years he had spent as secretary-treasurer and he was conscious of the treasury situation, of every nickel." Union Education Director Larry Rogin, another unswerving Rieve loyalist, characterized Pollock as one of those "honest, hardworking, narrow trade unionists" better suited to follow than to lead. "He was honest. No question about that. And he was dedicated, no question about that. And had demonstrated some competence," Rogin later said. He had fallen victim, however, to an occupational hazard to which secretary-treasurers of unions were peculiarly vulnerable. "The character of the work seems to make you petty and lose sight of the broad issues," Rogin concluded.[20]

In truth, Pollock probably had more in common with Bishop, an equally narrow trade unionist, than his detractors were willing to acknowledge. In the end, however, it was perception that mattered most. Because Pollock wanted the job and made it plain that he was willing to fight for it, those who opposed him were suddenly obliged as a result of Rieve's impatience to recruit an alternative candidate. The paucity of leaders in the TWUA made that choice disturbingly simple. Only woolen and worsted director John Chupka, the one remaining member of Rieve's inner circle in the anti-Baldanzi campaign, seemed a viable alternative to Pollock.

Described by an admiring colleague as "an absolutely charming man . . . a good companion and a fun guy to be around," Chupka was both well-liked and respected by other union leaders. Most regarded him as a far better candidate than Pollock to replace Bishop and, ultimately, to succeed Rieve. Unlike either Bishop or Pollock, however, Chupka was neither ambitious for higher office nor anxious to give his life totally to union service. Somewhat more cerebral than most of his colleagues, Chupka made time to pursue interests that ranged from music and theater to gambling—"the best poker player in the union"—and his desire to maintain some balance in his life prompted him, according to both Rogin and Fiester, to resist the urgent entreaties of the Executive Council.[21]

Undoubtedly aware that the motives of his suitors fell seriously short of being entirely pure or selfless, Chupka simply could not be persuaded, in the end, to stand in Pollock's way. As a result, when the Executive Council met in an emergency session in Fall River on January 8, less than 24 hours after Bishop's interment at Notre Dame Cemetery, its members meekly acceded to Rieve's demand. Without debate or open dissent, they unanimously, if half-heartedly, elected Pollock as the TWUA's new executive vice president. Though he would not agree to become Rieve's successor, Chupka did agree to replace Pollock as secretary-treasurer.[22]

For those union leaders who would look back on Pollock's elevation as a move than weakened the organization more than it strengthened it, explaining Rieve's role proved difficult. The most appealing explanation, which had the advantage of granting absolution to everyone involved in the decision, was that the shock and grief occasioned by Bishop's sudden, unexpected death had momentarily robbed them all, including the usually inerrant Rieve, of their judgment. Less credible were the suggestions, later advanced by Rieve's most indefatigable apologists, that Pollock was elevated against his wishes. It may well be that Chupka was Rieve's first choice, but, given the power he wielded on the reconstructed Executive Council, it is exceedingly unlikely that Pollock would have been elected without at least his tacit approval. Both Rogin and Fiester, who looked back on Rieve's role in the affair with bewilderment, claimed that while he almost certainly could have persuaded Chupka to succeed Bishop had he been forceful in the effort, he made no such effort. As secretary-treasurer since the TWUA's founding, Pollock had always been a dependable, loyal, and obedient subordinate. And it was not unlikely, Fiester later conceded, that Rieve accepted Pollock as the union's new second-in-command because he felt confident that he could influence or control him.[23]

Whatever their explanation of Rieve's supposed diffidence toward designating a new heir apparent, those who observed the process sensed, in his subdued manner and reluctant involvement, an attitude of resignation. His demeanor suggested to many, as Larry Rogin later commented, that Rieve "had given up," that he had concluded after Bishop's death and in the face of the increasingly bleak prospects that textile unionism faced, both in the North and the South, that "it didn't matter" who succeeded him as president of the TWUA.

"The death of Bishop had an impact on his total thinking," Rogin said of

Rieve, and his acceptance of Pollock as his likely successor was evidence that dejection had clouded his usually good judgment. Certainly "if he thought it would have made a difference," Rogin loyally insisted, "he might have done something else." It pained him, Rogin confessed, to believe that Rieve's judgment had "gotten so bad that he made it inevitable for Pollock to become president"; yet, he concluded, no other explanation seemed plausible.[24]

Certainly, if Rieve's attitude betrayed deepening pessimism, he had good reasons for believing that the TWUA's best days were behind it. During the late 1940s, the union was collecting dues from perhaps as many as 325,000 of the 400,000 to 450,000 members it claimed to have under contracts. It was solidly entrenched in every major branch of the textile industry with the exception of southern cotton, though, even there, it was able in most cases to influence wages and conditions. Yet, even at the height of its success, the TWUA was beleaguered. The National Labor Relations Act had never achieved sufficient force in the South to call the most determinedly lawless mill owners to account for their flagrant trampling of workers' rights. After the passage of the antiunion Taft-Hartley Act in 1947, if southern millhands were free to exercise their "legal" right to organize, it was usually because their bosses did not care enough to stop them. It was that dynamic, perhaps more than any other, that explained why the union could win NLRB elections and even contracts when it took on small mills but continued to fail dismally against the large, powerful chains.

By the early 1950s, it was more painfully evident than ever that the cost of the TWUA's impotence in the South would come at the expense of its well-being in the North. The disastrous setback the union suffered in the 1951 southern strike was compounded by the institutional damage the anti-Baldanzi campaign inflicted across the region a year later. Given that situation, there was no longer any assurance that Rieve could offer northern mill owners, no matter how artful its construction, that could disguise the reality of the TWUA's virtual incapacitation in the South. The TWUA could, and did with increasing regularity throughout the 1950s, cooperate with employers in the various strategies they devised to shore up New England's cotton and woolen industries through political maneuvers in Washington and productivity initiatives in antiquated northern mills. Even so, the North-South differential in labor costs, the competitive disadvantage from which northern producers most needed relief, was a problem they could no longer expect the union's help in solving.[25]

With the fortunes of the union he had devoted himself to building and leading at the mercy of economic and political forces the union was increasingly powerless to influence, Rieve can perhaps be forgiven for retreating into a gloomy passivity after Bishop's death. He seemed content to relinquish to Pollock, Chupka, and others more and more of the day-to-day leadership responsibilities to which he had once personally attended with proprietary zeal. Rieve was increasingly an *éminence grise* in the TWUA, still fully capable of being forceful and authoritative when circumstances required him to be, but disengaged from the routine business of the union to an ever more noticeable degree.[26] Lacking the resources and the institutional vitality to dispel the lethargy that descended on it, the TWUA by 1953 was well on its way to becoming what Ken Fiester later described as an "administrative" union, an organization whose focus had shifted from organizing the majority of mill-hands in the country who remained outside its orbit to "servicing" and collecting dues from the continually shrinking minority of textile workers that it did represent.[27]

Although the TWUA was generally supportive of efforts launched in 1953 to reunite the estranged branches of the American labor movement, its relations with the UTW—even after Baldanzi and other defectors had moved on to new affiliations and many of its southern members had reconsidered the wisdom of secession—remained too strained and embittered to permit reconciliation. The two-year "no-raiding" agreement negotiated in late 1953 by labor's new chieftains, AFL president George Meany and CIO president Walter Reuther, was hailed in *Textile Labor* as "a bright new page of American labor history." The TWUA Executive Council unanimously endorsed it, although William Pollock made it clear that support of the pact was more a grudging gesture than a sincere commitment. "We have plenty of reasons for not supporting this resolution," he told reporters at the CIO's convention, "but we realize that the forces of reaction are in charge of this country and we must do a service for all workers so they can march as one toward labor's common goals." In private, he advised his colleagues that, when the agreement went into effect at the beginning of 1954, the union "should taper off raiding and devote more time to new organization." Neither the TWUA nor the UTW was, however, so fastidious in honoring the terms of the pact that it refused to exploit its rival's vulnerability whenever an opportunity arose.[28]

With the textile industry mired in a deep recession throughout the early and middle 1950s, neither the TWUA nor the UTW could do much more than hang on for dear life as continued mill liquidations and relocations, corporate consolidations, and a rising tide of imported goods took their toll. Synthetic yarn, carpets and rugs, and dyeing and finishing escaped the worst effects of its faltering, but evidence was mounting that in the future they, too, were unlikely to be the relatively stable and prosperous bastions of the TWUA they once had been.[29]

In the northern cotton-rayon and woolen and worsted industries, where fully half of the TWUA's dues-paying members were concentrated, the spreading ruin (in New England in particular) meant that, even when the veil of economic adversity that had descended over the industry finally lifted, the gloom would remain. John Chupka, who continued as director of the woolen and worsted division even after his election as secretary-treasurer, glumly informed the Executive Council in early 1954 that, because of "liquidations and mill closings," the number of woolen and worsted mills under contract had declined from 161 to 106 during the last four years. Even in the (unlikely) event that those that remained operated at full capacity, he observed, an industry that, as recently as 1950, accounted for 60,000 union jobs could not hope to sustain more than 40,000 in the future.[30]

At the union's 1954 convention, the textile industry's depression was palpable. Intended as an occasion for celebrating the union's success in weathering the tempest that followed George Bandanzi's banishment two years before, it was instead an occasion for reflecting on its many troubles. Describing the two years since the last convention as "the most difficult we have ever endured as a union," Rieve had little good news for the delegates. In two years, he reported, the number of textile workers covered by TWUA contracts had dropped from 400,000 to 325,000. And, because of the frenzied cost cutting that had swept through the industry's northern branches, many of those still covered by collective bargaining agreements had seen the material rewards of union membership whittled away by profit-starved employers. The union's "liquid resources" had dried up as its dues-paying membership shrank, Rieve reported. Despite having cut its operational and administrative budgets to the bone, the continuing "month-by-month" decline in revenues made it clear that fiscal solvency could be restored only by persuading those who were still contributing to its coffers to pay more.

While expressing the hope that "in the course of the next two years we will reach a turning point, the point when the tide will begin to flow in our direction," Rieve reminded his listeners that struggle and sacrifice had always been the price of keeping the faith. "Even at best, our life is not easy or comfortable, whether we are working in the mill or working for the union." If his report had "not been a cheerful one," and if there were more reasons to despair than to hope when they imagined the future, he told the delegates, they should nevertheless be heartened by the knowledge that,

> A cause that can inspire devotion such as this will always live. We may suffer defeats; we may be forced backwards; there may be times when it appears that all is lost. But we will never quit; and the time will come when we will regain the lost ground, and move forward to new and greater success.

"Do not be dismayed, do not lose heart," he concluded. "We, and those before us, have built a movement too strong to be destroyed. We, and those who come after us, will once again move ahead. Like truth, our cause is mighty and shall prevail."[31]

Whether the delegates still believed it once Atlantic City's Convention Hall had emptied and they were back at their posts confronting the grim reality of the union's plight, the forecast of better times ahead that Rieve volunteered was one that the TWUA's front-line troops no doubt longed to hear. Yet, for Rieve, who knew better than anyone that the TWUA's malaise might not be transient and curable, there was neither comfort nor hope in the rosy scenarios he concocted for the benefit of others. In the months after his perfunctory re-election as president, his involvement in the day-to-day affairs of the union continued to decline. Spending more of his time in Florida and on labor and political issues of broad scope that afforded respite from the tribulations of the union, Rieve was increasingly an absentee leader. At the quarterly meetings of the Executive Council, over which he had once presided with an overweening authority that, at times, seemed proprietary, Rieve steadily became more observer than participant. He was content to let Pollock attend to the routine business and administrative concerns that crowded the agenda. That Rieve's gradual disengagement from the routines of union leadership was a prelude to more decisive action finally became evident in April of 1955, when he informed the Executive Council that, for reasons of failing health, he would not stand for re-election to the presidency at the 1956 convention.[32]

Had it come when the TWUA's fortunes were still on an upward trajectory, Rieve's decision to relinquish the control he had exercised over the union since its founding sixteen years before doubtless would have been hailed as selfless labor statesmanship. Yet coming as it did well after the organization had begun its descent into perpetual misfortune, his abdication conveyed a suggestion of surrender, a painful, grudging acknowledgment that the union he had labored so long to build would never be in the textile industry what its CIO counterparts had become in steel and autos.

If dispassionate outsiders leaned toward a conclusion that Rieve, though an honest and able servant of the union cause, had compiled a record of leadership too flimsy and unexceptional to confer greatness on him, those in the TWUA who were closest to him, who had followed his lead through triumphs and defeats, accepted his greatness as an article of faith. Whether out of sincere conviction, loyalty, or a desire to defend their complicity in a record of stewardship that conferred little distinction and even less glory on those whose service it encompassed, Rieve's most zealous champions could not bring themselves to doubt his mastery. Too often united in the cultish belief that devotion to the man was also devotion to the cause, they remained steadfast in their shared faith that Rieve's leadership had been the essential source of the TWUA's accomplishments, but had in no way contributed to its failures.

That so many of those whom Rieve led esteemed him is, of course, not an unimportant commentary on the quality and efficacy of his leadership. The admiration he inspired in his subordinates attested to an uncommon aptitude for effective trade union leadership. His talents as a negotiator and bargaining strategist were generally conceded, even by critics of his leadership style. There is little doubt that the TWUA's success in keeping workers from the several branches of the textile industry under a single tent was, in no small degree, a function of his political acumen. It is also likely that the disproportionate influence the TWUA enjoyed in the CIO and the wartime federal bureaucracy was largely due to Rieve's personal force and cunning in navigating the corridors of political power.

For all of his strengths, however, there were offsetting weaknesses in Rieve's leadership. Judged by how successfully he addressed the most critical impediments to the TWUA's achievement of enduring institutional viability, Rieve's leadership was not particularly effective or praiseworthy. Indeed, in the South, the region that everyone knew was the key to the union's future Rieve was probably guilty of doing more harm than good. Always at a loss to understand the South and southern millhands, and never wholeheartedly committed to the dogged and costly organizing effort that was essential to the TWUA's progress there, Rieve stocked the union staff in the Piedmont with plodding functionaries who were typically as incompetent as organizers as they were capable as business agents.

It was, however, Rieve's reckless compulsion to oust Baldanzi without regard for the institutional damage he was inflicting that left the most indelible stain on his reputation. Both the 1951 southern strike and the nearly total collapse of the union's organizing apparatus in the South after the 1952 convention were direct consequences of Rieve's self-indulgent insistence that the TWUA's top leadership be all of one mind. The combined effect of those twin disasters was to so weaken the union's position in the South that it could no longer reasonably expect to have any but a marginal influence on the terms and conditions of employment that obtained in the southern textile industry.

Rieve also placed personal interest above the union's well-being by insisting that the end of his tenure did not end his influence over union affairs. On the eve of the 1956 convention, where he was scheduled to relinquish his office to William Pollock, Rieve prevailed upon members of the TWUA's Executive Council, all of whom had benefited from his patronage, to provide the formal means to that end. Created at the TWUA's founding to reward Sidney Hillman for his service to textile unionism, the post of Executive Council chairman was never intended to be move than an honorific. When Hillman resigned not long afterward, the post was promptly abolished. At Rieve's instigation it was restored, at the 1956 convention, for the sole purpose of perpetuating his influence. His decision to resign the presidency meant that he no longer wanted the burden of directing its affairs, he told the convention, but it did not mean that he wanted to give up his leadership role entirely. "[I]t is still possible for me to make a contribution to our union, and to the welfare of the textile workers," he told the delegates. If it was their desire that he do so, they had only to elect him chairman of the Executive Council.[33]

Although he assured the delegates, after they had endorsed his proposal, that he was "happy that we have new leadership . . . and willing and ready to offer my services in any capacity that may be asked for by the newly elected officers," Rieve was not the deferential type. He no longer had a desire to run the union, but neither was he disposed to let his successor run it with the same unfettered authority and unrivaled preeminence that, as president, he had demanded for himself. He insisted, for example, on remaining principal TWUA liaison to the newly merged AFL-CIO. By refusing to step aside and permit his successor to emerge fully from his long shadow, Rieve gave "aid and comfort" to the members of the Executive Council who still regarded William Pollock as unworthy of their confidence and support. Had Pollock been more confident in his own abilities, the natural tendency among his subordinates to compare the substance and style of his leadership to that of his highly visible predecessor might have been only a harmless aggravation. Pollock, however, was anything but secure in his intellectual gifts and leadership talents. Having to work in the oppressive atmosphere of Rieve's "respondent" record tended to bring out the worst in him. Too often, he was inclined to think that colleagues who questioned his judgment were actually disputing his authority. He was prone to let petty differences over trifling issues escalate into confrontations that were resolved only by brusque resort to the powers of his office.

Pollock's behavior might have been the same even if he had not been forced to discharge his duties in Rieve's shadow. It seems likely, however, that had he been given a chance to lead the TWUA in an atmosphere more conducive to the flowering of his better qualities, his detractors might have had fewer reasons to persist in their suspicions of his worthiness. A majority of Pollock's peers on the Executive Council had grudgingly acquiesced in choosing him to be Mariano Bishop's successor only because they could not recruit another candidate on short notice. Now, they were generally loath to give him the benefit of the doubt. Union leaders and staff functionaries who had been content to explain the TWUA's decline during the early 1950s as a fate it was largely helpless to forestall despite Rieve's exemplary stewardship were inclined following Pollock's ascendency to interpret the same phenomena of institutional decline as a function of uninspired leadership at the top. And, it was these same leaders, many of whom had demanded the ouster of George Baldanzi for his alleged infidelity to the union's president, who would, with Rieve's encouragement and support, instigate a deeply divisive effort to force Pollock from office in 1964.[34]

Perhaps inevitably, the frustration that textile unionism's principal emissaries felt when things went from bad to worse was expressed in a facile deduction that better leadership would produce better results. To be sure, the TWUA, like most American trade unions, was never so well administered that it could not have benefited from more astute and imaginative leadership. Yet critics who attributed the TWUA's plight to its officers' failure to be good leaders or its members' failure to be good trade unionists overstated the union's capacity to control its own fate and understated its vulnerability to forces beyond its control. The serious problems the TWUA faced had sometimes been exacerbated by poor leadership, but, by the mid-1950s, the forces that figured most decisively in the union's decline were not reversible by even the ablest leader. The disestablishment of the northern textile industry, which proceeded with every new mill liquidation or relocation; the slow shrinking of the domestic industry overall (as a result of global competition); and the impenetrable barriers to unionism erected by the southern textile industry's dominant chains were the chief causes of the TWUA's deterioration. And, William Pollock, whatever his personal shortcomings, was probably as well-equipped as any of the union's top functionaries, including Rieve, to lead a rear-guard effort that could only slow the pace of decline.[35]

"Bargaining from weakness," the aptly named policy the union concocted in the mid-1950s to impart the impression of strategic purpose to its impotence in the South, conveyed with brutal clarity how fruitless its efforts were likely to prove. Acutely aware that its greatly weakened position in the South left it unable to increase the wages of approximately 40,000 members there, TWUA leaders devised a strategy that relied on various agitation techniques to pressure the region's largest mills, all unorganized, into granting pay increases.[36]

Given that southern cotton-rayon workers had not received a wage increase for nearly five years, the union could feel confident, when it began to put its agitational strategy into effect in 1955, that fomenting unrest among unorganized workers would excite genuine worry among their employers. When Burlington Mills, then the nation's largest textile chain, announced a five-cent hourly wage increase soon after union agitators began inciting discontented southern millhands, union leaders were emboldened to expand and formalize the campaign with Burlington's more than 30 Piedmont mills as its main focus.[37]

Although nominally under the control of William Du Chessi, the new director of the union's carpet and rug division, the Burlington campaign was directed in the field by TWUA education director Larry Rogin, who increasingly devoted his attention to organizing after his department was permanently disabled as a result of the Rieve-Baldanzi fight. Although the effort was initially intended as nothing more than a "leafleting" campaign, Rogin and his colleagues recognized that the union "needed to do a little more" to remain a credible presence in the region. As a result, Rogin later recalled, "the Burlington campaign started as a pretense to organize" even though its real purpose was less ambitious. Because they had decided that they would only "pretend to organize," he explained, "We did it in violation of all the rules, in the sense that we didn't start by building in-plant committees and so on and so forth." Yet, if those in charge of the campaign had not taken it seriously as an organizing drive, many Burlington millhands had. "We started with a public campaign with mail-back cards . . . ," Rogin recalled, "and much to our surprise, we got some response from some mills. We knew that we had to go widely if we were going to have any impact on the company at all, to make them think that we were serious about it, and so we did thirty-four mills. . . ."

Generating wage pressures in the South remained the main goal of the Burlington campaign. The belief that it might blossom into a wholehearted organizing drive, however, inspired many of those involved in day-to-day operations to propose a more ambitious aim. Impressed by the risks that many Burlington millhands were willing to take in the cause of unionism, Rogin urged a shift in their emphasis. "I conceived the notion," Rogin recalled, "that if one went long enough in the campaign . . . and we could make enough progress in the organizing—looking at it from a five-year period—that you could organize." Supported by Pollock, who gave him "more money than I could use intelligently," and assisted by nearly two dozen organizers on loan from the AFL-CIO, Rogin steadily shifted the focus of the Burlington campaign toward organizing during the latter half of 1956. His plan for a long-term effort, however, proved impractical. As the cost of the campaign increased, so did the impatience of union leaders who wanted concrete results. When Rogin left the TWUA in the spring of 1957 (ultimately to become education director of the AFL-CIO), the pressure for "quicker results" led his successors to rush into NLRB elections that the union was still too weak to win. Dismayed that the $300,000 the union spent on it had failed to yield a single organizing victory, TWUA leaders decided, in September of 1957, that the nearly two-year-long Burlington campaign, though "an interesting experiment," was simply not "profitable" enough to continue.[38]

Although the Burlington campaign, and the more conventional wage agitations the union subsequently conducted, afforded TWUA leaders grounds for claiming at least partial credit for pay increases granted by southern mill owners, it also revealed that the transcendent dilemma of textile unionism in the South remained the same, despite twenty years' effort to solve it.[39] The scores of TWOC organizers who fanned out throughout the Piedmont during the spring and summer of 1937 had found that the abundantly evident enthusiasm of most southern millhands for the benefits that organization promised was often tempered by an equally keen resolve to defer the real risks that open activism entailed until the union had demonstrated its power to defend and reward them. That the TWOC could provide those assurances only after southern millhands had rallied to its support became the defining conundrum of the CIO's prewar organizing drive, and it remained a primary impediment to the building of a viable union in the region thereafter.

For the better part of a generation, TWUA organizers in the South had been frustrated by the knowledge that the genuine interest southern millhands exhibited in organization and collective action rarely expressed itself in a commitment durable enough to withstand the antiunion fear mongering that was the employers' weapon of choice. There was no doubt, southern director Boyd Payton told delegates to the 1958 convention, that "the great majority of [southern] workers realize that in unionization lies their only hope of improving their own lot in life and their only hope of making a contribution toward leaving a better world for their children."

"Evidence of this realization," Payton insisted,

is found in the fact that, in almost any textile mill, we can quickly sign up 30 percent of the employees if it is done before the employer learns of the organizing activity. However, it is usually at about the 30 percent point that the company becomes aware of the organizing activity and begins its counter-campaign of coercion and intimidation through brainwashing and spreading of false stories designed to create fear and confusion in the minds of the workers. Further signing of cards becomes almost impossible and, in fact, those who have signed become fearful and refuse to be identified further with the organizing campaign.

"So, really," he explained, "it becomes a contest between a worker's desire for organization and his fear of the consequences." On an institutional level, Payton observed, the struggle between the union and its management adversaries in the South had assumed the character of an interminable "tug of war." The unrelenting antiunionism of most southern mill owners was rooted in the simple conviction that "he must continually keep the line tight" and that "if he allows the rope to become loose, the desire of his workers for organization will pull the line out of his hands and take it forward to their goal of winning the benefits and protections of a union contract." That was the TWUA's inescapable predicament in the South, Payton declared, and it dictated that,

[W]e, too, must play the game of tug-of-war. We, too, must realize that if we relax for one moment and allow the rope to become loose, the employer and his cohorts will pull the line from our hands and take it forward to their goal of not only preventing new organization, but of weakening and eventually destroying the established local unions.[40]

Payton's characterization of the union's main challenge in the South, which reflected the consensus that had emerged among its leaders, was an unwitting revelation of how drastically the TWUA had scaled back its expectations there. No longer able to sustain the hope that it was just a matter of time before southern employers gave in to unionism, TWUA leaders were, by the late 1950s, willing to consider nearly any outcome short of full retreat from the South a victory, including prolonged stalemate. That mind-set offered little to those in search of inspiration, but it permitted union leaders to contend that the value of failed undertakings like the costly Burlington campaign lay in the effort and commitment they demonstrated rather than in immediate results. In place of the self-reliant ethic they had earlier espoused—that independent means and methods were superior to all others—TWUA leaders gravitated, increasingly, toward solutions that the union could neither devise nor implement on its own.

Indeed, when leaders surveyed the principal causes of the union's continuing decline, the remedies that appealed to them most emphasized what government and the industry must do rather than what the union could do for itself. That the union was at a loss to take matters into its own hands, synthetic yarn division director Wesley Cook told the 1958 convention, was not because its leaders or members had lost their nerve or fighting spirit. Rather, it was because the future of American manufacturing was increasingly precarious, and the textile industry, and thus the TWUA, had the misfortune to be the first to confront the new perils of the post industrial order. "It is a stark and inescapable fact," Cook declared,

> that, because of the peculiar situation of the textile industry, the very existence of unionism is more closely related to legislative and political developments than is the case in any of the other basic American industries. This has little to do with the kind of individuals who work in textile mills; we have demonstrated beyond any question or doubt that we have the gumption, the brains and the idealism to build and maintain whatever kind of union the economic characteristics of our employers make necessary during any period or at any place.

In the absence of other handicaps, Cook suggested, the union might have successfully contended with the vehement opposition of southern employers, even though that opposition was buttressed and supported by the full force of political, economic, civic, and religious institutions in the South. Yet, he noted, employer opposition was only one of many impediments to the TWUA's success. The Taft-Hartley Act had effectively "robbed" textile workers of their right to organize, and the NLRB, which reflected the pro-management orientation of President Eisenhower's conservative appointees, had further hamstrung the TWUA. These, however, were not the union's only problems. "In addition to all of these major obstructions in the path of our efforts to organize the unorganized," Cook explained,

> the textile industry is caught up in a worldwide depression which relates to the problems of international trade, international economic reconstruction, tariffs, quotas, and a host of other complex difficulties which even the strongest union cannot master without the aid of Congress and the Administration. And the present government in power in Washington, far from giving needed aid and attention to the economic problems of textile employers—let alone the problems of textile workers—appears to have made up its mind that our industry is expendable and too bothersome to cope with.[41]

Persuaded that the union was severely limited in what it could expect to accomplish on its own through organizing and other conventional activities, TWUA leaders saw government action as the answer to its most serious problems. During the late 1950s and early 1960s, they formulated a legislative program intended to remedy problems that the union alone seemed incapable of solving. Thus, wages would be advanced by regular increase in the federal minimum wage, organizing would be facilitated by repealing or reforming Taft-Hartley and reconstituting the NLRB, New England textile mills would be saved through government-backed revitalization schemes, and the textile industry as a whole would be protected from foreign competition by new tariff barriers. Twenty years after many of them had ridiculed UTW president Francis Gorman for championing legislative action as the best way to guarantee textile unionism's future, members of the TWUA Executive Council were earnestly beseeching the federal government "to restore textiles to the ranks of our dynamic and expanding industries" via the same route. Only by establishing a "permanent federal Textile Development Agency to stimulate and promote the industry's revival," union representatives told members of the Senate Interstate and Foreign Commerce Committee in mid-1958, could they provide "a comprehensive and enduring solution to the problems of the textile industry and of textile workers." That TWUA leaders also expected such a policy to solve the problems of textile unionism went without saying.[42]

Given how the union had faltered in confronting its problems directly during the 1950s and how fondly many veteran leaders recalled the safe haven that wartime labor-relations policies afforded, it is not surprising that TWUA leaders were willing to sacrifice self-reliance for the right reward. The union's official position remained that organizing was its first order of business, and its leaders could always point to some ongoing effort that attested to that commitment. Behind the resolute words and sporadic deeds, however, was deepening suspicion that, under existing conditions, organizing the southern textile industry was impossible.

It was, to be sure, a well-founded suspicion. Almost from the moment the textile industry was established in the Piedmont, millhands in particular and southerners in general were repeatedly warned by nearly every authoritative voice in the South that unionism was an idea so inimical to their shared values—and likely so toxic in its effects on their cultural heritage—that it could be accommodated only at the cost of their collective identity. In the emergent socioeconomic theology of the "New South," trade unionism might be a transgression too recent in derivation to qualify as original sin, but in the adamantine catechism of southern industry it was an evil that the truly righteous were commanded by all that was holy to renounce and oppose with biblical fervor. Yet, because mill owners had learned through experience that their employees could not always be relied on to recognize or acknowledge unionism's inherent malevolence, they had, by making a mockery of workers' rights, effectively arrogated to themselves a decision that, even in the era of Taft-Hartley, was intended to be the millhands' alone. Indeed, far more in the South than elsewhere in the United States, the choice for or against unionism was made not by workers but by their bosses. It was their willingness to obey or defy the law that determined whether a vote in favor of organization and collective bargaining actually meant anything. And, it was this unhappy fact, more than any other, that impelled union leaders toward the disheartening realization that collective bargaining in the southern textile industry was likely to exist only where employers permitted it, rather than where workers wanted it.[43]

Yet, what TWUA leaders might have admitted in private they were bound to dismiss in public as defeatist propaganda. Caught between institutional imperatives that dictated prudence and southern millhands, members and nonmembers, who expected militancy, TWUA leaders performed a delicate balancing act. They had to validate the union's fighting spirit without taking on costly battles it had little or no chance of winning. And, as always, strikes posed a particular dilemma. Following the pivotal 1951 southern strike, which shattered many of the TWUA's illusions and most of its strength, mill owners in the Piedmont no longer feared them and the union no longer believed it could win them. Yet banning strikes was never an option for union leaders. They discouraged strikes when doing so threatened no loss of face, but, backed into a corner, either by employers or their own members, they recognized that fighting and losing was sometimes preferable to not fighting at all. As long as the few strikes it authorized were reasonably short-lived, and not unreasonably expensive, TWUA leaders generally agreed that the benefits outweighed the cost, even when the effort ultimately failed.

As the drawn-out and costly Harriet-Henderson strike made painfully evident, however, persuading striking members that enough was enough could be an exceedingly tricky business. Launched in November of 1958, when the management of the Harriet and Henderson Cotton Mills in Hendersonville, N.C., demanded a grievance arbitration provision be dropped from its contract with the TWUA, the strike fell into that category of battles that had to be fought no matter what the realistic prospect for victory. Neither the company nor its more than 1,000 striking employees would take a backward step. The contest quickly became a test of wills, as each side waited for the other to tire of the struggle. After nearly three months of stalemate, however, the company, whose desire to weaken the union had become an obsession to destroy it, took steps to reopen both of its mills using strikebreakers recruited from the surrounding region and the handful of former strikers who had returned to work rather than risk permanent job loss.

With the company's decision to reopen its mills, a conflict that had been largely limited to harangues in the local press and heated public exchanges immediately took on the familiar character of a southern textile strike. Local and state police placed themselves at the company's disposal for strikebreaking duty, judges promptly issued injunctions restricting the freedom of strikers to defend their interests, local politicians and businessmen condemned the union for alienating the community's biggest employer, clergymen from "respectable" churches preached the gospel of class obedience to the insubordinate millhands. Prompted by recurrent episodes of picket-line violence and a sporadic bombing campaign that each side blamed on the other, North Carolina Gov. Luther Hodges personally intervened to broker a settlement. When the company immediately reneged on the agreement, the governor bowed to political reality and deployed the forces at his command to facilitate the reopening of the mills.[44]

Although the strikers' solidarity prevailed even as their setbacks multiplied, the company's ultimate success in reopening the mills meant the union's defeat. The strikers, however, were not inclined to abandon their cause, even as evidence of its futility mounted, and their expectations of financial assistance from the national union posed an increasingly difficult problem for the TWUA. The two striking union locals had received assurances, before the strike began, that the international was prepared to lend financial support. TWUA leaders in New York honored that pledge, not only by feeding strikers and their families but also by paying their bills, including mounting legal expenses some incurred for violating court orders. Yet, union officials never intended their support for the strike to be open-ended. As long as the outcome remained in doubt, strikers were entitled to financial assistance, and, even after the mills resumed operation with nonunion labor, the TWUA Executive Council put an additional $100,000 into the Harriet-Henderson strike fund. The national union was still funding a commissary for strikers when the first anniversary of the struggle came, in November of 1959, but it was also more active than it had been in soliciting support from outside sources and in helping strikers who realized the strike was futile to find other employment.[45]

Although the strike was lost long before it was a year old, the unwillingness of several hundred strikers and local leaders to admit defeat was costing the national union $10,000 a week that it could not afford. The TWUA was running a monthly deficit of more than $25,000 in the summer of 1960, but, as the conflict entered its twentieth month, the union was still contributing $7,700 a week in direct relief to more than 400 members in Hendersonville who continued to regard themselves as active strikers.[46] Not until the spring of 1961, by which time the international had supported the strikers for almost thirty months to the tune of more than $1 million, did TWUA leaders finally summon the resolve to "strongly urge" local union officials to "seriously consider officially calling off the strike." Acutely aware that common sense was in short supply among the diehard strikers, TWUA officials added a pointed warning: "If the local unions do not call off the strike by May 31, 1961, the International Union will be compelled to do so." All their suffering notwithstanding, TWUA officials told local leaders, the time had come to accept the hard truth: "Through no fault of our membership or the International Union the status of the strike is such that the continuance of it is meaningless and would be sheer folly." The several hundred bitter-enders who refused to abandon a lost cause rejected the international's ultimatum. When the May 31 deadline passed, President Pollock promptly invoked his authority to terminate the strike.[47]

Although the remarkable solidarity they exhibited throughout the conflict provided fresh evidence that southern millhands were as willing as textile workers anywhere to fight for their rights, the chief lesson of the Harriet-Henderson debacle, from the point of view of TWUA leaders, was that strikes in the South, even when conducted with courage and generously financed, were far riskier for the union than for the mill owners. In combination with the other factors that militated against an overly combative strategy in the region, the Harriet-Henderson strike reinforced an already pronounced preference among TWUA leaders to deploy the union's shrinking resources along legal and political battlefronts where the odds against victory, though still daunting, were not so overwhelming as to be hopeless.

CHAPTER **11**

Where There's a Will

Increasingly from the late 1950s onward, the bitter confrontations between the TWUA and the southern textile industry took place, not across picket lines or outside mill gates, but in NLRB hearing rooms, in federal courthouses, before House and Senate committees, and in the offices of Washington bureaucrats. Represented by a legion of lawyers who had turned the negating of workers' rights and the thwarting of federal law into an art that the whole of the U.S. antiunion establishment would in time practice, southern mill owners proved to be no less resolute and resourceful in opposing textile unionism in these arenas. Possessed of the added strength that industry consolidation tended to confer—*Fortune* reported at the end of 1957 that only 26 companies employed nearly half of the country's 650,000 cotton-rayon millhands—dominant chains like Burlington, Cannon, Deering-Milliken, and J. P. Stevens had little trouble mustering the resources or sustaining the will required to keep the TWUA at bay. "With their plants widely dispersed throughout the South," *Fortune* observed, "these firms, if they lose one mill to the union, can simply shut it down and transfer its operations to another mill."[1]

The claim that a vote for collective bargaining was a vote against their jobs had been used by anti-union mill owners to instill fear in southern textile workers from the moment the Wagner Act went into effect. "If an employer fails to remind workers that shutdowns may be the fruit of a union victory in an NLRB election," the *New Republic* noted, "the local paper will probably do it for him." During the late 1950s, however, the fear that winning a union could mean losing your job was reinforced when Deering, Milliken & Company, one of the industry's leading firms, closed its mill in Darlington, S.C., to punish its more than 500 employees there for giving the TWUA a narrow NLRB election victory. Engineered by company president Roger Milliken, whose fierce opposition to collective bargaining was typical of the intractable antiunionism of the southern textile industry's biggest chains, the plan to close the mill was set in motion within a week of the election. On October 17,

1956, only five weeks after Darlington millhands had exercised their legal right under federal law to declare themselves for unionism, the closure was announced. "Two days later," the *New Republic* reported, "the first employees were laid off, and a month later the entire force of more than 500 workers was jobless. The 80-year-old mill, biggest employer in town, was shut down. Machinery was moved out, the mill and remaining equipment sold at public auction."[2]

An angry South Carolina politician publicly predicted that "Mr. Milliken's actions will return to haunt him."[3] It proved to be a poor guess. The openness with which Milliken expressed his motive for closing the mill ought to have left the NLRB little choice except to find for the workers when the TWUA filed an unfair labor practice against the company. The Darlington case would bounce back and forth between the NLRB and the federal courts for more than 20 years before it ended in a hollow victory for the union. Perhaps more clearly than any other legal dispute between labor and management in the post–Taft-Hartley era, if demonstrated that guarantees of workers' rights duly sanctified as the public policy of the United States could be virtually nullified by employers committed to that end.[4] For the labor movement in general, the 1960s were a time of renewed hope, but the prospects for textile unionism could hardly have been bleaker. Saddled with a federal labor relations "policy" that permitted collective bargaining but no longer encouraged or facilitated it, and obliged to petition for what little help the law provided before NLRB functionaries whose sympathies ebbed and flowed with the changing political tides in Washington, the TWUA was an organization in perpetual motion, but getting nowhere.[5]

At the beginning of the 1960s, the TWUA had no more than 150,000 dues-paying members.[6] It had suffered a staggering 60-percent decline over the preceding ten years and was unable to replenish its membership in the region where the industry was concentrated. Even to its well-wishers, the TWUA seemed at the threshold of becoming the industrial labor movement's most conspicuous relic.[7] The American Federation of Hosiery Workers, which had left the TWUA in 1947 in a dispute over dues increases, quietly returned to the fold in 1965. With fewer than 7,000 members and no prospects, however, it was a frayed remnant of the vigorous organization that had, in the late 1930s, contributed so much to labor's revitalization in the textile industry. The long-discussed merger of the TWUA and the 40,000-member United Textile Workers of America, which constituted textile unionism's one real hope for internal fortification, remained an idea that both organizations endorsed in theory but that neither was eager to implement. The impediments to amalgamation left over from their bitter rivalry in the early 1950s were compounded by evidence of corruption in the UTW that had come to light in the late 1950s. Yet it was George Baldanzi's return to the UTW as its president in 1958 that dashed whatever fugitive hope of merger the TWUA still entertained.[8] As *Business*

Week reported, Baldanzi was "still persona non grata" with TWUA leaders, and his election as UTW president, though seen by most outsiders as an effort to restore the union's probity, erected an apparently insurmountable barrier to reunification. "Other reasons may be given by TWUA for holding back on unity," *Business Week* noted, "but Baldanzi's emergence in UTW now looms as the key one."[9] The willingness of TWUA leaders to let their festering enmity toward Baldanzi block a merger whose benefits to both unions were otherwise unarguable attested to the sad reality that the best interests of textile unionism were not always their top priority. Indeed, the inability of TWUA leaders to manage dissent in their own ranks, a failing that produced such destructive consequences during the early 1950s, would wreak further harm during the early 1960s.

Though clearly a clash of two powerful personalities, the fierce conflict that had raged between Emil Rieve and George Baldanzi was also fueled by substantive differences over union policy and governance. In contrast, the escalating squabbles that came to a head at the 1964 TWUA convention were rooted in petty animus, personal ambition, and the firm belief among a majority of the Executive Council that their long-standing doubts about William Pollock's fitness to lead had to be acted on. Led by cotton-rayon director Victor Canzano, woolen and worsted director William Belanger, synthetic yarn director Wesley Cook, and dyers director William Gordon, the anti-Pollock majority, which commanded the unwavering support of twelve of the twenty-two members of the Executive Council, coalesced in 1961. After the union's 1962 convention, the faction became increasingly open and aggressive in challenging Pollock's authority. Although they had endorsed the idea that the TWUA needed a powerful chief executive as long as Rieve held the post, they expediently abandoned that conviction in the early 1960s in favor of a shamelessly self-serving assertion of the Executive Council's primacy. They were egged on by Rieve, embittered because his influence in the union was much reduced when, in 1960, Pollock forced him out of the chairmanship of the Executive Council and gave him the honorary position of "President Emeritus." The majority exploited for their own purposes nearly every issue of policy, personnel, and finances that occupied the leadership between 1962 and 1964.

Had Secretary-Treasurer John Chupka, perhaps the union's most respected leader, responded to entreaties from the anti-Pollock faction to join them they might have succeeded in their insurgency. Whether out of loyalty to Pollock or contempt for his suitors' motives—their case against the union's duly elected president rested largely on vague allegations that he was insufficiently dynamic and excessively frugal—he rejected their overtures. Because Chupka would not board the anti-Pollock bandwagon, those influential Executive Council members like New Jersey state director Sol Stetin who were inclined to follow his lead also remained loyal to the administration.[10]

Although Wesley Cook later insisted that the two-year effort of the dissidents to force Pollock from office did no appreciable harm because the TWUA was already at a "standstill," the nearly total paralysis the Executive Council suffered as each side tirelessly plumbed the depths of vitriol and invective to discredit the other left those who witnessed the carnage from afar bewildered and disgusted.[11] Expressing chagrin that became general throughout the ranks as the battle raged, Julien Cloutier, president of Local 462 in Lewiston, Me., implored both "warring factions" to respect "the feelings of the backbone of our Union, the dues-paying members," and stop their fratricidal madness at once. Having despaired "that men of your caliber would come to your senses and stop behaving like children," Cloutier explained, he and his colleagues were obliged to demand that their elected leaders put union interests above their personal political agenda. While "[a]n attack upon our union from the outside pulls us together and makes us stronger," he wrote, "internal strife of this type is like a cancer, slowly weakening and finally consuming the whole body." Despite the passion and certitude with which each side had argued its case, Cloutier warned, both were derelict in failing to see that the union was bound to be the big loser in the end, no matter how the fight came out. "It is almost criminal," he angrily observed,

> to realize how far this thing was allowed to go. Do all of you realize the great harm you are doing to our Union? We have lost enough ground already. What's become of all your high-sounding phrases on unity and solidarity?

With the union reeling from the body blows it had suffered, he complained, "I shudder at the thought of our future when the employers discover how divided we have become."[12]

The increasingly debilitating struggle for control of the union could have been shortened by as much as a year had Pollock prevailed in his efforts to convene a special convention in spring of 1963. He failed because his opponents, fearing that they could not win a head-to-head confrontation with the incumbent administration, used their control of the Executive Council to ensure that they had as much time as possible to gird themselves for the winner-take-all struggle that lay ahead.[13] In the end, however, delaying did them little good. With nothing more substantive than a low opinion of Pollock to justify their palace revolt, the majority faction faced an uphill battle in persuading TWUA members that only by sweeping the incumbent administration from office could the union be saved.[14]

The majority's principal allegations against Pollock—that he was somehow personally responsible for the union's deterioration and was a would-be "dictator" bent on running "a one-man show"—proved impossible to sustain when delegates finally gathered in New York in June of 1964 to decide which claimants to supreme authority had the stronger case. Most delegates knew well that the union's decline had begun long before Pollock became president and suspected that the insurgents cared less about the principles of democratic governance than about grabbing political power. A solid majority of the delegates quickly concluded that, if one faction or the other had to go to restore internal peace, it was the dissidents who should be sent packing. By a nearly two-to-one margin, they rejected the insurgent slate headed by William Belanger and Wesley Cook, and which included many of the best-known and longest-serving functionaries, in favor of one hastily assembled by Pollock and Chupka from a pool of administration loyalists whose leadership experience in most cases had been gained at the local level.

From the opening gavel, the convention was a rowdy and indecorous affair whose proceedings were, the *New York Times* reported, repeatedly interrupted "by taunting, shouting displays of factional bitterness and, at one point, by fisticuffs." Such fractiousness demonstrated the depth of acrimony to which otherwise reasonable and well-intentioned trade unionists could descend after two years of nearly incessant political strife.[15] Even Emil Rieve, who apparently anticipated the continuing veneration of those he had led, suffered the delegates' scorn when he petulantly presumed to question their judgment in rejecting his protégés in favor of Pollock's faction. Placed on the program at the insistence of the insurgent Executive Council majority, Rieve came to the convention to promote his personal agenda rather than to bind the deep political wounds that fratricide had inflicted. He was 72, a disappointed and embittered man whose skewed and self-serving interpretation of the TWUA's postwar history alleged the nearly unqualified success of his own stewardship and the dismal failure of Pollock's. Rieve addressed the convention with no evident purpose other than to vent his spleen. In a speech that grew more inflammatory and hypocritical with every sentence, Rieve alternately excoriated Pollock as an aspiring autocrat determined "to murder democracy in our union" and belittled him as a mere "bookkeeper" who was hopelessly out of his depth in any more responsible position. An organization that under his stewardship was widely extolled for its "spirit of militancy" and "sense of dynamism," he claimed, had "lost its spark" under Pollock. "Listlessness, insecurity, unimaginative thinking have become our trademarks in the past few years." Even worse, he added, a union once celebrated for its tolerance of all points of view and willingness to accommodate critics and contrarians had become, under his successor, a nascent dictatorship determined "to stifle the opposition and all dissident voices."

Offended by Rieve's mean-spirited and self-indulgent diatribe against an administration they had just returned to office, and outraged by his sanctimonious attribution to Pollock of crimes he had himself committed against George Baldanzi and others only a dozen years earlier, delegates who were initially disposed to let the old man have his say quickly became a vengeful, taunting chorus. When Rieve persisted in his claim that Pollock had attempted to purge his critics, exasperated delegates answered with catcalls and cries of "How about Baldanzi?" and "You started this thing." When he catalogued Pollock's inadequacies, one delegate shouted, to the hearty applause of his colleagues, "He's a better president then you ever were." When he informed the delegates that he was "most likely" attending his last TWUA convention, they responded not with murmurs of regret but with prolonged, raucous cheers.[16]

Although Rieve assured his listeners that he was too old and too firm in his convictions to worry about the consequences of expressing "what is on my mind and in my heart," it is doubtful he appreciated the great injury he was doing to his reputation. "Everything I had in the way of devotion, intelligence, energy and health was given to the labor movement and, more particularly, to the Textile Workers Union of America," he reminded them. When he concluded his remarks a few minutes later to the derisive boos of indignant and disillusioned delegates, he had tragically forfeited most of the respect and goodwill his long service to textile unionism had earned him. He also became accomplice to Pollock's efforts to bar him from any further participation in leading the TWUA.

When he answered Rieve's attack, near the close of the convention, Pollock spoke more out of sorrow than anger. Although he had clearly been a disappointment to his predecessor, Pollock told the delegates, it was not because he had proven incompetent to run the TWUA. Rather, it was because he had refused to run it in obedience to Rieve's wishes. "Instead of playing the role of elder statesman and trying to bring unity and keeping our organization on the move," he noted, Rieve, first as chairman of the Executive Council and then as president emeritus, had stubbornly persisted in "sticking his nose into the operation of this union. . . ." It was beyond dispute that Rieve had given valuable service to the union, Pollock conceded, but it was likewise indisputable that "just because you made a contribution to the organization it shouldn't give you a license to keep interfering with its operation and mischievously causing trouble." Many people on both sides of the union's internal struggle had had a part in keeping it going, he observed, but it was Rieve who had been chiefly responsible for starting it. "He was in the forefront of this fight that started two years ago . . . ," Pollock charged. "Don't make any mistake about that." As long as the TWUA remained hostage to Rieve's divisive influence, he warned, it could not achieve the unity and harmony essential to future progress. The time had come to heal the deep division that had paralyzed the union for the better part of two years, "and we can do that only by removing the cause." Rieve could continue to collect the generous salary and pension he had enjoyed, Pollock declared, but "in the interest of our organization" the convention should act "to eliminate this president emeritus clause from our constitution so we can serve notice on people that when they retire, they ought to retire and keep their noses out of the organization." With Rieve's churlish speech only two days before providing more then enough evidence to validate Pollock's judgment, the convention voted decisively to bring the twenty-five-year career of the TWUA's foremost leader and dominant personality to an inglorious end.[17]

Although the fight between Pollock and his opponents between 1962 and 1964 did considerably less permanent damage to the union than the internal conflict that convulsed it in the early 1950s, the TWUA clearly suffered for its leaders' inability to settle their political differences through means short of fratricide. It had incapacitated the leadership, exacerbated the demoralization of rank-and-file members, and added another unsightly blemish to the public image of an increasingly beleaguered and disreputable labor movement. It also contributed to the arsenal of antiunion arguments mill owners in the South cited to persuade skeptical textile workers that unionizing was more trouble than it was worth. "If anyone thinks that this is going to help our union to organize . . . anyone down there," John Chupka lamented, "they are sadly mistaken."[18]

As wrenching and debilitating as it was, the conflict had had at least a few therapeutic effects. A leadership that had been divided to the point of paralysis was reactivated once the convention had its say, and the sudden elimination of the entire antiadministration faction from the Executive Council speeded the advancement of younger leaders who were closer than most of the veteran functionaries they replaced to the rank and file. That is not to say that the abrupt departure of many of the TWUA's most experienced leaders came at no cost to the organization. The loss of bright and effective leaders like Wesley Cook, for example, was keenly felt. But if there were able servants of the TWUA's cause among the conflict's casualties, there were probably as many self-seeking time servers who had mastered the administrative routines of trade-union leadership for no reason except personal advantage. It helped that the largest turnover of leadership in the union's history came at a time when its efforts were devoted to holding the line more than to pursuing new initiatives. In most cases, however, the duties of those who left the Executive Council in the wake of the 1964 convention were performed as well by their successors.[19]

Above all, however, it was William Pollock, who had endured two years of relentless calumny, who emerged from the ordeal better and stronger for the experience. The personal pettiness and insecurity that had undermined his effectiveness while he remained in Rieve's shadow and surrounded by colleagues who doubted his competence was less evident once the cloud over his leadership was finally lifted. As if to prove that he was not the congenitally niggardly and timid leader his detractors had portrayed, Pollock demonstrated, during the remaining years of his presidency, a greater willingness to take risks. His personal limitations ensured that he would never be the inspired and innovative leader the TWUA might have used to good advantage, but, according to Sol Stetin, the invigorating ordeal of fending off his opponents "provoked him into a greater degree of activity" once peace was restored.[20]

So beleaguered was the TWUA in the mid-1960s, however, that only a miracle worker would have presumed to remedy its chronic miseries. It was stymied in the South by what its leaders claimed was a vast antiunion conspiracy expertly crafted by the region's dominant textile chains and dutifully supported by every pillar of the southern establishment. In the North it had been eviscerated by mill closings that left the region's once-robust woolen and worsted, cotton-rayon, and rug and carpet industries gasping for life. The TWUA looked, for all the world to see, like an organization too debilitated by its afflictions and so overmatched by its adversaries that it could do little except plan for a graceful demise. The union's abiding hope that its prospects would brighten once liberal Democrats were restored to power in Congress, withered in the face of mounting evidence in the 1960s that even labor's "friends" in the White House and in the Congress were not keen to shift the balance of power in its favor. Both the Kennedy and Johnson administrations enfolded organized labor in a ritual embrace, but neither was seriously committed to righting the wrongs of Taft-Hartley even if each did encourage the NLRB to be more forceful in defense of workers' rights. As long as conservative southern Democrats in Congress were willing to break party ranks to help antiunion Republicans keep labor's legislative desires moldering at the bottom of the congressional agenda, pro-union liberals in Congress who wanted to help could only lament their impotence.[21]

In the face of seemingly insurmountable obstacles, the TWUA did what it had always done: it endured, battered and disheartened, but stubbornly unbowed. Time and again in the postwar period, the TWUA engaged the southern textile industry in battle, and time and again it was beaten. Yet the outcome of the war remained inconclusive. In their recurrent battles with the TWUA, southern employers almost always landed the heavier blows. Frequent and punishing though they were, they were never enough to bring the contest to a final conclusion, never enough to persuade the union, once and for all, that its struggle was futile.

In a curiously paradoxical way, the chronic misfortune and hardship that beset textile unionism almost from the moment of its conception had instilled in those who served its cause a resilience and doggedness that rendered them oblivious to the possibility of ultimate defeat. That building a union in southern textiles was as difficult and wearing a challenge as the American labor movement would confront was immediately and indelibly impressed on all of those either bold or naive enough to accept it. Yet, the crushing weight of the endeavor caused remarkably few of them to conclude that the task was impossible. Though many of them were loath to confess it, the men and women in the service of textile unionism were oddly inured to misfortune and failure. As a result, they seemed more willing than was otherwise reasonable to persist in their struggle to build in the South what those more mindful of the lessons of the past believed could not be built there. Of course, in moments of despair, even the most indefatigable unionists probably contemplated the respite that surrender would afford, but, in the end, most decided that abandoning the fight was an indulgence they were honor bound to deny themselves.

That disposition to endure was evident in the excruciating enterprise that dominated the last chapter of the TWUA's history as an independent organization, the campaign to organize the J. P. Stevens chain. Formally begun in early 1963 under the auspices of the Industrial Union Department of the AFL-CIO [IUD], which had reluctantly responded to the TWUA's persistent pleas for help once again in tackling the southern textile industry, the drive to organize J. P. Stevens would become, by the mid-1970s, a defining confrontation between labor and capital in the United States. At the outset, however, there was little to distinguish it from previous attempts to achieve an organizing breakthrough in the South—and no particular reason to believe that it would succeed where earlier efforts had conspicuously failed.

Described by one admiring business writer as "the world's oldest diversified textile company," the Stevens firm, in one or another corporate incarnation, had operated in New England for more than a century before it belatedly followed the lead of its competitors and relocated to the South just after the end of World War II.[22] As a northern-based company, Stevens had accommodated the TWUA and collective bargaining in at least some of its mills, and there was nothing in its labor relations history before or during the war that forebode the rabidly antiunion policy it would adopt after relocating to the Piedmont and emerging during the 1950s as one of the industry's dominant chains. Indeed, by the time the TWUA and IUD decided that it was their best bet, J. P. Stevens, with 36,000 workers in more than fifty mills, had established itself as the nation's second largest textile manufacturer.[23]

Stevens was targeted by the TWUA for a variety of reasons.—its earlier accommodation of unionism in the North; its relatively small mills and their concentration in the Carolinas; the anticipated restiveness of its workers; the fact that other big chains had already beaten back organizers. It proved to be anything but a reluctant adversary. The southern textile industry had never been known for the subtlety of it methods in combating unionism, but the brazen lawlessness of Stevens managers in countering the influence of union organizers plumbed new depths. Members of the Stevens family, who continued to lead the company even in its 150th year, had decided in 1946 to move its manufacturing operations to the South to escape unionism. At the first appearance of organizers outside its mills in the Carolinas, they swore a solemn oath, from their New York headquarters, that the scourge of collective bargaining would never impede them again. "Our positive intention," the company sternly advised the employees of its half-dozen mills around Roanoke Rapids, N.C., when union organizers showed up there in mid-1963, "is to oppose this union and by every proper means to keep it from coming here. It is our sincere belief that if this union gets in here, it would operate to your serious disadvantage." As one commentator later observed, the vehemence of the company's antiunion declaration "led the supervisors on the plant floor to conclude that they were expected to get tough," and with a studied indifference to whether they were employing only "proper means" in enforcing dictates from above, local managers got very tough indeed.[24]

Although almost no method of intimidation or coercion was off limits to Stevens supervisors, firing known union supporters on one transparent pretext or another became a favored tactic, because of the unnerving chill it sent through the ranks of the millhands who had yet to decide where they stood on the issue of unionization. The company's crudely illegal tactics sent union lawyers scurrying to the NLRB with the first of what would become, over the next fifteen years, an avalanche of unfair labor charges. So many were they, in fact, that the money, time, and effort of waging legal battles tended to starve the campaigns of the attention and resources organizers needed to remain credible.[25]

The opposition of southern mill owners to unionism had long rested on the strategic calculation that the immediate advantages to be gained by violating federal law were well worth any of the mild penalties the NLRB might assess against them years later when their opportunities for legal appeals finally ran out. In the hands of Stevens management, however, any subtlety that had earlier attached to such a strategy was quickly lost. "It was like nothing we ever had at the board," one NLRB official in the Piedmont recalled. "Every day the union was filing a new charge of unfair practices—you know, discriminatory firings—against Stevens. Hell, this company was firing people the same day they signed the union card. Doing it blatantly."[26]

For TWUA leaders, the proliferating crimes of J. P. Stevens management were a reminder that, ultimately, the union was helplessness against employers bent on "nullifying the labor policies of the United States and denying to southern textile workers the right to organize which is ostensibly guaranteed to them in the law." As the number of Stevens employees discharged for union activity mounted, TWUA leaders could do little more than repeat the demands for labor law reform that they had been making for the better part of three decades. The Stevens company's open contempt for its employees' rights was "not new to the textile industry in the South," the union's Executive Council bitterly observed, but "simply the most aggravated example of a condition that has continued to exist despite our most strenuous efforts to protect the southern worker and afford him the opportunity to seek economic advancement through self-organization." Workers' rights during the Stevens organizing drive had been abrogated "on a scale so vast and so widespread," the TWUA declared in mid-1965, "that they could only be explained as part of a carefully calculated, cynical plan of deliberate law breaking designed to smash the campaign before it got started." And, why wouldn't southern mill owners persist in their craven lawlessness, the union wondered, after having "learned that the penalties imposed upon guilty employers by the NLRB under Taft-Hartley are so innocuous and so long delayed that they can thumb their noses at the law with impunity."[27]

What made the company's flagrant misconduct especially reprehensible, of course, was that it worked so well to dissuade millhands otherwise inclined to support the union from doing so. It hardly mattered to the average millhand that union supporters illegally fired by the company might, in the fullness of time, have their jobs and lost wages restored. What did matter, and what became infinitely more relevant as the time for deciding the issue of union representation drew near, was that standing up to the boss invited immediate risks most could ill afford. The force of that simple calculation was depressingly evident in the results of representative elections, which the company won with relative ease, despite earlier indications of union support among Stevens millhands. Subsequent investigations of the company's transparently coercive conduct before the elections would lead the NLRB to set aside the results in several cases, but the harm to the union's cause was never undone by ineffectual bureaucratic reprimands quietly issued months or years after the fact. Even when the union won an election, as it finally did at the complex of mills in Roanoke Rapids in 1974, the refusal of Stevens managers to negotiate in good faith left the 3,600 workers in the bargaining unit no closer to realizing the benefits of organization than they were when the drive had begun eleven years earlier.[28]

What made the TWUA's protracted hostilities with J. P. Stevens especially exasperating and discouraging was that the succession of lopsided victories the union won both before the NLRB and the federal bar, not to mention the clear edge it enjoyed in the court of public opinion, counted for little when it came to advancing the goal of worker organization. On the basis of the "facts" alone, the union's case against the Stevens company had been proven beyond a reasonable doubt. "Stevens has been engaged in a massive multistate campaign to prevent unionization of its southern plants," the U.S. Court of Appeals for the Fifth Circuit bluntly concluded. "This campaign has involved numerous unfair labor practices, including coercive interrogation, surveillance, threat of plant closing and economic reprisals for union activity. Moreover, the threats have been made good by extensive discriminatory discharges." The same court ruefully admitted that nothing that had been done by either the NLRB or federal judges to curb the company seemed to have any effect. "Neither the passage of time nor the admonishments of judicial tribunals," the court observed, "have caused the company to alter its now all too familiar pursuance of full-scale war against unionization." A federal judge in the Second Circuit who had also tried, in vain, to bring the Stevens management to heel, observed that the company's unabated obduracy "raises grave doubts about the ability of the courts to make the federal labor laws work. . . ." Describing the legal drubbing the company had invited during the late 1960s and early 1970s, one sympathetic commentator wrote, "Stevens was like a man flipping a coin for high stakes, hearing his opponent forever cry, 'Heads,' and with unbelieving eyes seeing the coin come up heads every time." Yet the fact remained that the nearly unbroken string of legal defeats Stevens suffered in NLRB hearing rooms and federal courthouses did not appreciably diminish the overwhelming practical advantage it gained from its lawlessness. The company had "coldly decided" that it had nothing to fear by committing "massive unfair labor practices as part of its conscious, carefully calculated, union-busting scheme," the TWUA angrily declared, and the abject failure of both the NLRB and the federal judiciary to deconstruct that cynical calculation exposed the grim, inescapable reality that guarantees of workers' rights embodied in American law were "only a hollow promise."[29]

As they had so many times when the law failed them, TWUA leaders sought redress through political means. With the backing of the AFL-CIO, union representatives beseeched friends of labor in the Congress in the mid-1960s to afford them a public forum for exposing the brazen lawlessness of J. P. Stevens. When Democrats on the House Labor Committee obliged by convening hearings on the alleged inefficacy of the NLRB, first in 1965 and again two years later, spokesmen from both the TWUA and the IUD vividly detailed the company's profligate misconduct.[30] On another political front, the TWUA, again with the nominal support of the AFL-CIO, sought to persuade officials of the Johnson administration, throughout 1967 and 1968, that the situation warranted an executive order barring Stevens from doing business with the federal government as long as it persisted in violating workers' legal rights. It was an affront both to reason and justice, the TWUA and its allies repeatedly complained to administration officials, including the president personally, that a corporation found guilty of gross violations of federal law by one government agency should remain eligible to profit handsomely from business it did with other agencies of the same government. "This peculiar and incomprehensible practice . . . wherein government purchasing power is expended in support of scofflaws," the union protested, "is disgraceful, outrageous, immoral, and reprehensible." Both the NLRB and the federal courts had ruled that J. P. Stevens had "flagrantly violated the law," TWUA leaders reminded the administration, yet "as the company goes on defying and flaunting the law, the U.S. Defense Department keeps on awarding lush contracts," the value of which "in 1966 and 1967 alone . . . totaled $130 million."[31]

As always, however, labor's friends in high places were quick to express sympathy but slow to take forceful remedial action. When William Pollock and a delegation of top labor leaders including AFL-CIO boss George Meany petitioned President Johnson directly for forceful action early in 1967, he gave them "a very sympathetic hearing." Yet a few weeks later, when Pollock returned to Washington for "a follow-up meeting," Johnson's aides advised him "that the President would not issue an executive order to accomplish what we were seeking." "When I inquired whether this was the end of the Administration's efforts to help," Pollock told his TWUA colleagues, "I was assured that it was not." Nevertheless, he glumly concluded, "I strongly doubt that we will hear anything more about this."[32]

Confronted by the ultimate indifference of their political friends and the vastly greater influence of their political enemies, those who had hoped that the field of battle with J. P. Stevens could be leveled through government action were left, once again, to their own feeble devices. Of course, it was precisely because the TWUA had lost confidence in its independent agency that, from the early 1950s onward, it was forced to look to others for help in reversing a decline that it could not successfully reverse on its own. The union's repeated attempts, during the postwar period, to enlist the federal government's help in creating economic, political, or legal circumstances more conducive to its well-being had failed, leaving those in its withered compass to watch at a lengthening distance as other industrial unions of the old CIO continued to advance undaunted and confident into an apparently secure future. While their disappointments and frustrations were never so keen that they could no longer muster the resolve to sustain their hopes, TWUA leaders sometimes submitted to the seductive delusion that the more congenial environment they seemed powerless to forge might simply evolve in the fullness of time.

The union's reaction to the growing prominence of black workers in the southern textile industry during the 1960s was illustrative of a tendency among its leaders to believe that some changes should be patiently awaited rather than actively promoted. Like other former CIO unions, the TWUA prided itself on the courage and forthrightness of its official support of racial justice and equal employment opportunity. Yet, like most of those other "officially" egalitarian unions, where matters of race were involved the TWUA tended to be bolder in theory than in practice. The relegation of black workers to the least desirable jobs on the periphery of production was standard practice in all but a few precincts of the southern textile industry from its earliest days. At critical junctures, when the white "hill folk" who constituted all but the tiniest fraction of their laborers became restive or unruly, Piedmont mill owners readily threatened to hire blacks to frighten them back into line. Only when the civil rights movement finally addressed the industry's racist hiring practices in the 1960s did the integration of southern textile mills seem a realistic prospect. Leaders of the TWUA recognized early on that as young blacks steeped in the activist philosophy of the civil rights movement entered southern mills in ever larger numbers, they were likely to be more welcoming of unionism than white millhands had been. While they hoped to benefit from the integration of "southern textiles," TWUA leaders were, for the most part, not noticeably eager to associate the union with change that most white millhands viewed with deep apprehension at best and outright abhorrence at worst.[33]

Race was the most volatile issue that the industrial labor movement confronted in the South, and most unions, including the TWUA, were not above deferring to the racist sensibilities of white workers when they could do so without risking the appearance of gross hypocrisy. As other CIO unions had, the TWUA accomplished the balancing act by coupling its emphatic, unequivocal public endorsement of racial justice with a willingness to skirt the issue when its immediate interests dictated circumspection. At the 1956 convention, champions of racial equality among the union's leadership were understandably proud of their success in winning adoption of a resolution condemning the militantly racist White Citizens Councils that proliferated across the South after the Supreme Court's landmark 1954 school desegregation decision. However significant as a declaration of principle, however, the resolution had no apparent, or intended, impact on the TWUA's day-to-day operations in the South. The union's leading functionaries in the Piedmont strongly opposed the resolution, and, because they, rather than the northern liberals who supported it, personified the TWUA in southern mill towns, the racial attitudes associated with the organization were usually neither provocative nor intrepid. As long as the convention's formal condemnation was not accompanied by efforts to pressure the large number of TWUA members in the South who belonged to white citizens councils to quit them, the symbolic blow for racial justice struck by well-intentioned northern delegates only momentarily chagrined their southern brethren.[34] Throughout the fierce civil rights struggles of the 1960s, the TWUA's handling of racial issues was notably schizoid.

Top TWUA leaders overwhelmingly favored unequivocal support of racial equality. They gave modest financial support to front-line civil rights organizations like Dr. Martin Luther King, Jr.'s Southern Christian Leadership Conference and assisted in federal Equal Employment Opportunity Commission investigations of hiring practices in the southern textile industry.

At the local level, however, where the union's representatives remained acutely sensitive to the risks it ran in the predominantly white workforce by endorsing integration and racial equality, the TWUA, like the labor movement in general, was not in a hurry to join the uncrowded ranks of southern institutions willing to champion civil rights regardless of cost. The prospect of blacks working in mill jobs once open only to whites was one that most TWUA leaders sincerely welcomed, but also one they thought more prudent to await than to promote.[35]

Both leaders and members were bound to acknowledge that, when it came to the issue of racial equality, the union's professed ideals sometimes required more than they were able or willing to give. That was hardly an unfamiliar dilemma to anyone acquainted with the institutional culture of textile unionism. On those rare occasions when circumstances afforded them the luxury of doing "what was right," the leaders and members of the TWUA had generally been as respectful of their principles and as mindful of their ideals as any trade unionists. Yet, in the postwar period as membership plummeted, resources dried up, and the TWUA's future dimmed, it became increasingly an organization whose only option was to make the best of a bad situation. To the profound disappointment of leaders and members alike, the TWUA had become a union inescapably preoccupied with its own limitations, and, thus, one constrained by a deepening conviction that it could afford to take risks only up to a point.

That sense of limited capacity had been very much in evidence when the TWUA persistently importuned the Industrial Union Department of the AFL-

CIO to lead the way in the J. P. Stevens campaign.[36] Sensitive to a perception current in labor circles that theirs was a union unequal to its task, TWUA leaders had nevertheless believed that an IUD-led organizing drive in southern textiles was the best of its limited options. If the campaign succeeded, the union would reap the organizational benefits; if it failed, the IUD would bear the largest share of responsibility, and those who doubted the TWUA's mettle would be reminded, again, that organizing the southern textile industry was a singularly difficult job. It had seemed, at least in the beginning, an ideal arrangement. The TWUA would provide half of the twenty-four organizers who initially staffed the Stevens campaign and contribute a modest $5,000 per month to its operating budget. It would remain free to conduct routine administrative affairs in the South content in the knowledge that the IUD was attending to the more arduous work of winning new millhands to the union cause.[37]

Their optimism aside, however, TWUA leaders never had good reason to believe that an IUD-led organizing drive against the Stevens chain was more likely to succeed than any of the union's earlier campaigns against the industry's big companies. The theoretical benefits of a coordinated, company-wide organizing effort had always been difficult to realize in practice, and the Stevens campaign was no exception. Scott Hoyman, the top-ranking TWUA representative assigned to the Stevens drive, quickly discovered that the IUD's approach—"bringing a whole collection of people together" in a common effort—was not predicated on "a capable staff." Still, despite the difficulties that had beset previous large-scale southern organizing campaigns, TWUA leaders were not easily disabused of the idea that bigger was better or any more inclined to think that "a more step-by-step, less grandiose approach" might produce superior results.[38]

As fervently as they had hoped that the IUD would solve their organizing problems in the South, by the late 1960s TWUA leaders could no longer ignore the haplessness of the Stevens campaign. Because they had talked themselves into believing that the IUD's supposedly more robust agency would gain them what seemed otherwise unattainable, the stumbling progress of the Stevens campaign left TWUA leaders deflated and profoundly discouraged.[39] Disclosures of Stevens managers' overtly illegal methods had mustered considerable sympathy for textile unionism's cause in labor circles and among the American public, but none of the residual benefits of that sympathy obscured the fact that not one of the company's tens of thousands of employees in the Carolinas had been added to the TWUA's rolls. The costly and time-consuming legal battles touched off by Stevens's flouting of the law had undermined the campaign by forcing much of its staff to forego organizing to document unfair labor practices. Ironically, they also provided the only reason for hope in what otherwise appeared to be a hopeless situation. As Scott Hoyman recalled, the brazenly illegal conduct of Stevens management "was the only powerful thing we had going for us," since it allowed battles that would have ended in conclusive defeats to be fought anew before NLRB hearing officers and federal judges.[40]

Because of the extraordinary publicity that attached to the Stevens campaign as a result of the company's reckless endeavors to thwart it, it became, more by inadvertence than design, a contest of such practical importance to the future of textile unionism in the South—and such symbolic importance to the viability of organized labor in America—that the TWUA simply could not abandon it, no matter that a hard look at its prospects commended retreat. Certainly, if Stevens had been less brutish and conspicuous in its methods, the TWUA (and its IUD surrogates) would have been left the option of doing what it had done when other big southern textile chains had proven too tough to crack: retire from the field of battle with a vague, parting threat to resume hostilities at some more propitious time. Yet, hell-bent on demonstrating beyond any doubt that unionism would never gain a foothold in its mills, Stevens forced the TWUA to be more doggedly resolute than it would have been had the path of honorable retreat been left open. Explaining why the confrontation with Stevens ultimately developed into one that the TWUA could not afford to back away from, Scott Hoyman later remarked, "It became such a spectacle and challenge, that there was no way you could get off the tiger's back."[41]

Though it had become practiced at calculating risks in light of its limited wherewithal, the TWUA was obliged, during the late 1960s and early 1970s, to accommodate to the disquieting realization that prudence was not an option in meeting the challenge that J. P. Stevens posed. In the interests of preserving its already precarious credibility in the South and defending the honor of a larger labor community disposed to regard the outcome of the Stevens fight as one destined to impinge upon the prestige of all unions, the TWUA was forced to contemplate bold actions. And, as union leaders despaired that the feeble alliance they had forged with the IUD would never be strong enough to contend with J. P. Stevens on an equal footing, they reluctantly concluded, in the mid-1970s, that reinvigorating their cause was worth any concession, including sacrificing the TWUA as an independent organization.

The unenviable task of leading the TWUA to institutional extinction fell to one of its most experienced and devoted servants, Sol Stetin. Hardly more than a boy when he joined the UTW in Paterson, N.J., in 1933, the Polish-born Stetin was a natural for trade unionism. Small in stature but enormously energetic, Stetin advanced steadily through the ranks of the Dyers Federation, the Textile Workers Organizing Committee, and the TWUA, performing his assigned tasks with competence and enthusiasm, but always mindful of whose patronage might further his union career. He had been a close personal friend and admirer of George Baldanzi early in his career, but he quickly lined up behind Emil Rieve when political differences split the union during the late 1940s and early 1950s. Undoubtedly sincere in his belief that Rieve was better qualified than Baldanzi to lead a union that clearly could no longer accommodate both, Stetin, like most veterans on the Executive Council, was also attuned to the commanding fact that Rieve's control over the internal apparatus of the TWUA was so secure that not even a rival of Baldanzi's force could challenge it successfully.

In the early 1960s, when the Executive Council majority coalesced to seek William Pollock's ouster, Stetin again exhibited a keen instinct for self-preservation. He agreed that Pollock had many of the shortcomings his detractors alleged, but he hesitated to declare his position until the union's second in command, Secretary-Treasurer John Chupka, made his intentions known. When Chupka, perhaps the TWUA's most respected leader, refused to support the anti-Pollock forces, Stetin likewise declined to do so. His loyalty to the administration was handsomely rewarded at the end of 1967, when, after Chupka retired for health reasons, Stetin was elected secretary-treasurer of the TWUA. That promotion virtually ensured his succession to president on Pollock's retirement.[42]

During all of his sixteen years as president of the TWUA (a tenure only one year short of Emil Rieve's), William Pollock had presided over a union in decline. Unlike Rieve, who had known the personal satisfaction and basked in the professional acclaim attendant to building an organization that, for a time, ranked as the third largest in the CIO,—the TWUA had enrolled approximately 325,000 dues-paying members and was bargaining for over 400,000 textile workers by the late 1940s—Pollock was the chief custodian of a union that seemed in inexorable decline. His tenure at the top had afforded precious few opportunities for even momentary exultation and none at all for personal glory. And, when he announced at the 1972 convention that he would not seek reelection, the news relieved his colleagues and followers more than it disappointed them. Pollock's detractors had never believed that his talents and temperament were equal to the special challenges of leading a chronically besieged union. They welcomed his stepping down and criticized it as long overdue.[43] Yet, even his supporters, who never doubted his honesty and devotion and who generally believed that he had done as well as could be expected under the circumstances, had no reason to regret Pollock's departure. He had held the TWUA's top job long enough to become the unwitting personification of its sadly conspicuous incapacitation, and, for that reason alone, his resignation was seen as serving the union's best interests.[44]

Sol Stetin's unopposed election as Pollock's successor continued the TWUA's tradition of rewarding longevity and familiarity. It also underscored the dilemma of a union whose deteriorated condition and bleak prospects made its top job as much a burden as an opportunity. His ebullient demeanor and congenital optimism notwithstanding, it was, as one of his nominators emphasized at the 1972 convention, Stetin's "vast capacity for duty" that made him the right person to take on the union's presidency. Certainly from the point of view of institutional knowledge, Stetin was exceptionally well-prepared to take the reins. For forty years he had faithfully and ably served the cause of textile unionism in nearly every organizational and leadership capacity. At critical junctures in the TWUA's history, when others hopeful of advancement let their ambition and impatience get the better of them, Stetin remained patient and steadfast, content to wait his turn to move up in the union. Yet, if Stetin was a known quantity when his turn finally came, in June of 1972, his determination to make a difference ensured that he would not be a mere time server as the TWUA's third, and last, president. It was his dedication and enthusiasm, more than his intellectual gifts or political acumen, that had commended his elevation, but, at a crucial point in the TWUA's troubled passage when actions were destined to speak louder than words, Stetin would prove to be the right person at the right time.

The effectiveness of Stetin's leadership derived not from his ability to see or to understand what others could not, but from his willingness to commit himself to decisive action once the union's essential dilemma was apparent. Even at the height of its prosperity in the late 1940s, the TWUA did not rank among the industrial labor movement's most affluent unions. As its dues-paying membership went into free fall at mid-century (declining from about 325,000 in 1947 to not much more than 100,000 by the early 1970s[45]), the union's ability to finance its routine operations, not to mention the special burdens imposed by its costly struggles against J. P. Stevens and other well-heeled corporate adversaries in the South, became its most urgent challenge. At once "old" and "new" business on the agenda of virtually every Executive Board meeting from the early 1950s onward, it had, perhaps more than any other factor, deflated the confidence of union leaders who, in a more innocent time, had indulged the thought that organizing the textile industry was an achievable goal. As secretary-treasurer of the union, Stetin was impressed by how severely an anemic bottom line limited its capacity to both advance and protect its institutional interests. As the new president, he was forced to conclude that, in the absence of decisive action to remedy its financial predicament, a serious problem would in time become an impossible one. The strategy of retreat urged by many among the TWUA's northern constituencies was inspired by a deepening conviction that continuing to pour desperately scarce resources into southern misadventures like the decade-old J. P. Stevens campaign was a folly that would ultimately bankrupt the union without having benefited it. But, though a northerner himself, and one who had earlier harbored his own regional biases, Stetin clung doggedly to his belief that textile unionism could not be viable anywhere in the nation if it could not establish a viable presence in the South.[46]

That Stetin was not averse to risking the TWUA's limited resources in what he considered a good cause became apparent almost at once. Scott Hoyman, director of the union's southern operations, recalled that Stetin did not hesitate, in the first year of his presidency, to risk the TWUA's scant resources or his own prestige when southern mill owners provoked head-on confrontations. Both in mid-1972, when the Chatham Manufacturing Company tried to decertify the union at its large Elkin, N.C., mill and, a few months later, when 700 newly organized millhands in South Carolina were forced to strike Oneita

Knitting Mills to get a first contract, Stetin willingly committed the international's resources in support of the actions. Ultimately the union won both fights, but might not have, according to Hoyman, if Stetin had followed the more cautious example of his predecessor. Referring to the Oneita struggle, which dragged on for nearly six months, Hoyman insisted that the union's victory "would have been impossible without the willingness of Stetin to really throw his weight behind the strike." Moreover, Hoyman added, Stetin had placed his personal prestige on the line, knowing full well that "if the strike had been a failure, it would have been . . . embarrassing to [him]." It was, Hoyman concluded, an episode revealing of Stetin's understanding that risks had to be taken, given the precarious position of textile unionism in the South. "He's quite an experimental type of person," Hoyman said of Stetin. "He's the opposite of what you would say was the traditional way of making decisions in the labor movement. Doing what you did yesterday or last year, you do that again this year. He is not too much in favor of that. He's happy to try things."[47]

While he was anything but happy about taking the extreme step that he ultimately decided he must if textile unionism was to endure except in feeble attenuation, Stetin did what he had to. The notion that the TWUA's redemption, if not its salvation, lay in merger had begun to circulate in the union and in the broader labor movement at approximately the same moment when its decline began to seem irreversible. The TWUA's most likely merger partner, especially after the Rieve-Baldanzi contretemps in the early 1950s fueled a destructive competition between the two organizations, was the UTW. From the late 1950s onward, representatives of the two unions met sporadically to discuss a possible merger, but personal animosities, and both sides' unwillingness to make the concessions that a workable agreement required, ensured their continuing estrangement. Even if a merger of the TWUA and UTW had been forged, it would have done little more than tidy up the jurisdictional disarray in the textile industry. Above all, the TWUA needed to avail itself of new resources, and that was something that the small and chronically indigent UTW could not offer.[48]

At the urging of AFL-CIO president George Meany, TWUA leaders briefly considered a three-way merger with two other former CIO unions that by the late 1960s showed signs of faltering: the United Rubber Workers and the Oil, Chemical and Atomic Workers. Except in Canada, however, where the TWUA's political work in support of the labor-friendly New Democratic Party had fostered close relations with both unions, the proposed three-way merger of parties with so little in common initially failed to excite much interest.[49] Leaders of the TWUA briefly entertained the idea again in the mid-1970s. They even held a series of meetings with representatives of the two unions, but, when Stetin had trouble advancing the discussion beyond questions of who would lead the merged organization, he soon abandoned the venture.[50]

Both from the point of view of prior associations and jurisdictional proxim-

ity, the two unions that came to mind most plausibly as potential merger partners with the TWUA were the Amalgamated Clothing Workers and the International Ladies Garment Workers. Despite serious setbacks in the postwar era,
each union remained under the control of elderly, fatigued leaders more concerned with hoarding institutional assets than with mounting an aggressive
defense of its domain. When TWUA leaders proposed various initiatives aimed
at instituting both coordinated bargaining and organizing programs in the
South, as they did repeatedly throughout the 1960s, they discovered that neither union could be coaxed out of its defensive shell.[51]

The Amalgamated, however, began, in the early 1970s, to exhibit clear signs
of emerging from its languorous repose. In 1972, the same year that Stetin
replaced Pollock, 77-year-old Jacob Potofsky, who had presided over the
Amalgamated since Sidney Hillman's death in 1946, finally retired. His successor, 50-year-old Murray Finley, was typical of a new generation of labor leaders. Armed with an undergraduate degree from the University of Michigan and
a law degree from Northwestern, Finley had risen in the Amalgamated's leadership, in only fifteen years, from regional staff attorney in Chicago to manager of the union's affairs in the nine-state area encompassed by its Midwest
joint board. And, when he was elected to the union's presidency, he brought
not only impressive credentials and experience but also a youthful sensibility
largely free of the Amalgamated's traditional preoccupations. The union was
further invigorated by the simultaneous election of an equally energetic and
forward-looking new secretary-treasurer, Jack Sheinkman. Educated at Cornell University, where he earned degrees both in industrial and labor relations
and in law, Sheinkman had drawn attention because of his exceptional talents
and passionate commitment while serving as the Amalgamated's general counsel. Impressed by his character and ability, and mindful that he was a New
Yorker (and thus someone who could provide regional balance at the top of the
union), delegates to the Amalgamated's 1972 convention installed Sheinkman
as Finley's chief collaborator in charting its future course.[52]

For Sol Stetin, who had come to know and admire him through routine contacts between the two unions, Sheinkman's new stature in the Amalgamated
was another reason to favor it as a possible merger partner. Because Stetin did
not know Finley nearly as well, once discussions between the unions began in
earnest, he looked to the more accessible Sheinkman to smooth the strained
relations that his tough head-to-head negotiations with the Amalgamated's
president sometimes created. Indeed, it was Sheinkman, according to Stetin,
who was largely responsible for moving the idea of an ACW-TWUA merger
from the realm of idle conjecture to that of purposeful dialogue. To the degree
that Stetin's willingness, in 1975, to prod his colleagues toward an ACW-
TWUA merger derived from his faith in the integrity of the ACW, Sheinkman's
influence proved critically advantageous.[53]

As a potential merger partner, the Amalgamated clearly had much to offer.
In addition to a membership twice as large as the TWUA's and a bulky portfo-

lio of institutional assets that included the nation's only union-owned bank, the Amalgamated offered the further advantage of a still serviceable reputation for "responsible unionism" that had carried over from Sidney Hillman's days. Yet, however much the Amalgamated's resources and reputation might facilitate textile unionism's advance in the South, neither Stetin nor his colleagues were willing to accomplish a merger at any cost. They were resigned to the fact that a merger would come at the expense of their union's sovereignty, but they were unwilling to concede that it must, of necessity, also cost them their distinctive identity as textile unionists or oblige them to discard the organizational culture that nurtured that identity.

Stetin also insisted that the terms of the merger should guarantee inclusion of the TWUA's full complement of officers—both executive officers and all twenty vice presidents—in the leadership of the new organization. As for himself, however, Stetin had decided early on that he would not let considerations of his personal stature in the new organization become an impediment to reaching a merger agreement. Though not immune to the conceit that he was every bit as able and energetic as Finley or Sheinkman to run the merged organization, Stetin nevertheless readily accommodated himself to the reality that the larger party to the conjoining would, and should, decide who took the helm. It was probably an accommodation that neither Emil Rieve nor William Pollock could have brought himself to make. Each had defended his position and authority with a single-minded zeal that was, at times, heedless of the ruinous institutional consequences that followed, and it is unlikely that either was ever disposed to regard selflessness of the type evident in Stetin's gesture as a true measure of devotion to the TWUA's well-being. Still, Stetin had resolved to do something quite extraordinary. "Sacrifice for the cause" was a sentiment blithely bandied about to the point of meaninglessness in leadership circles, but Stetin's was that rare act of authentic selflessness that rehabilitated the ideal.[54]

Finally, the TWUA's sine qua non throughout the merger negotiations was an ironclad guarantee from the Amalgamated that the new union would commit itself body and soul to the subjugation of J. P. Stevens. It was more than anything else a growing belief that the TWUA could not overcome Stevens on its own that caused Stetin and other leaders to pursue a merger, and nothing short of an irrevocable pledge of support in bringing that triumph to pass could have justified surrender of the union's autonomy. What complicated matters, however, was that the TWUA wanted the Amalgamated to do more than help to defray the escalating costs of its interminable legal battles with J. P Stevens. The frustrating inability of both the NLRB and the federal courts to force company managers to desist from lawless opposition to organizing efforts and refusal to bargain in good faith at its Roanoke Rapids Mills, where in 1974 the union had won its only representation election, left TWUA leaders to devise another means of forcing the issue. And the means they settled on by the beginning of 1976—an all-out, no-holds-barred national boycott against the Stevens Company—caused the cautious leaders of the Amalgamated to wonder whether their more militant and headstrong TWUA counterparts were asking them to pay an exorbitant price for a merger agreement.

Yet, as difficult and contentious as the negotiations between the two unions were to become by the early months of 1976, the compelling logic of a merger remained powerful enough to overcome all of the financial, staffing, and organizational conflicts that might have impeded it. It also helped enormously, of course, that the principals to the negotiations commanded respect and confidence among their respective constituents sufficient that they were free to speak and to act authoritatively. The agreement finally hammered out by late spring was clearly a product of compromise—on both sides—but Stetin had achieved his major goals. It provided, as expected, that Finley and Sheinkman would be the new president and secretary-treasurer respectively, and that Stetin would be senior executive vice president. More pertinent to the concerns of Stetin and his colleagues, the agreement also provided that he would have authority over a separate textile division that was, a few cosmetic touches notwithstanding, merely the TWUA by another name. Its structure, personnel, and organizational culture were almost wholly intact, and its full, twenty-two-person leadership contingent were safely ensconced on the executive board of the new Amalgamated Clothing and Textile Workers Union (ACTWU). Finally, and perhaps most important, the agreement stipulated that once the merger was in effect, the new union would endeavor by every available means to bring J. P. Stevens to its knees.[55]

As measured by their stated goals when merger discussions began, TWUA negotiators had succeeded admirably. Each of the bargaining goals essential to a merger agreement had been met, and Stetin and his colleagues had reason to be optimistic that it could be "sold" to TWUA leaders and its rank and file. Yet given the magnitude of the change that surrender of the TWUA's independence portended, the merger proposal did have to be "sold." The most serious misgivings of TWUA officials and members were rooted more in emotion than in concern for the particulars of the agreement. Stetin could not take for granted that the seemingly irrefutable logic of merger or the impressive fruits of his bargaining were, by themselves, enough to carry the day.

The feeling of many TWUA loyalists—that a merger was little more than a thinly disguised act of surrender—was difficult to counter, no matter how artfully Stetin and others were in the attempt. Similarly, the widespread concern of TWUA leaders and members alike that their identity as textile unionists would be eroded, even under terms that allowed them to carry on within the insular confines of a separate division, could be addressed but not allayed. Because the TWUA's internal culture had always reflected the diversity of the textile industry and the tensions that arose from regional differences, an answer that was satisfactory to one constituency was not always satisfactory to others. In Canada, for example, where the TWUA was already contending with the centrifugal tendencies attendant to rising nationalism, neither leaders nor members of the union had much enthusiasm for a merger with the Amalgamated, whose political image was well to the right of what most left-leaning Canadian textile workers considered respectably "progressive." Although a frank and forthright exposition of the difficulties that lay ahead for the TWUA if it spurned the Amalgamated went a long way toward persuading many doubters that the merger made good sense, others ultimately took it on faith that Stetin knew what he was doing. Canadian director George Watson, who was acutely sensitive to the fact that his constituents "weren't wildly enthusiastic about it," decided, despite his personal reservations, to defer to Stetin and then dutifully persuaded others in Canada to put their doubts aside and do likewise.[56]

By the time of the TWUA's 19th biennial convention—the occasion for the most momentous decision in its brief, turbulent history—the merger agreement was assured adoption by an overwhelming margin. Former union president William Pollock, who enjoyed the luxury of no longer having to live with the consequences of his actions, could persist in his effortless certitude that forsaking the TWUA's independence was a crime against both reason and honor,[57] but those still accountable for their deeds as textile unionism's active custodians were committed to the merger as the best course open to them. Given the top-down structure of the Amalgamated, a durable legacy of Sidney Hillman's influence, the decision of its executive board to proceed with the merger was, practically speaking, the only endorsement it needed. Yet merging with the TWUA under the conditions that Stetin had insisted upon was something that the Amalgamated's secondary leadership had to be talked into by Murray Finley and Jack Sheinkman. According to Stetin, both men were convinced that the merger constituted the Amalgamated's best hope "to become a more outstanding union," but the TWUA's militant reputation and its leaders' proclivity to let internal political wrangles devolve into fratricide excited more than a little unease among clothing worker officials steeped in an organizational culture that counseled circumspection and decorum at all times. Equally troubling to Amalgamated leaders was the knowledge that, by agreeing to the merger, they were also agreeing that the fight against J. P. Stevens would become the new organization's first and most important order of business. Having recently concluded a long, costly boycott of their own against the Texas-based Farah Manufacturing Company,[58] ACW leaders were reluctant to commit to what was likely to be an even longer and costlier boycott campaign against Stevens. In the end, however, the prospect of increasing the size of their organization by more than 100,000 members and gaining title to a jurisdiction that still included at least 600,000 unorganized textile workers outweighed their reservations. Influence had always been a function of size in trade union circles in general and the AFL-CIO in particular, and the leaders of the reinvigorated Amalgamated were acutely aware that securing a place in the front rank of the American labor movement was an ambition to which only a dynamic, growing organization could plausibly aspire.[59]

When delegates to the TWUA's final convention gathered in Washington on May 31, 1976, they brought with them all of the conflicting emotions that the bittersweet occasion evoked. Many of them had served the TWUA since its inception, but nothing in their long experience prepared them for the wrenching task of disestablishing the dilapidated but still cherished union that embodied textile unionism's past in order to break ground for the new organization designed to secure its future. Although many more might have done so if they had spoken their hearts rather than their minds, only a handful of delegates argued for preserving an independent TWUA. The overwhelming majority of delegates—at least 95 percent by Stetin's estimate—recognized that it was time to acknowledge that the struggling organization that had had first claim on their fealty for close to four decades was terminally incapacitated. Now, in the interests of sustaining the cause it was built to serve, they were obliged to swear a new allegiance.

What one speaker described as the palpable "sense of sadness" that weighed on delegates during the first day of the convention was prelude to an outlook more buoyant and hopeful than TWUA veterans could have managed while their old union was still in service. And the gloomy ritual of bidding farewell to the past only momentarily diminished the excitement of imagining the future. "This is not a funeral service," Stetin reminded delegates in his final address as president. It was instead, he insisted, an occasion for celebrating their success in devising the new institutional means by which they could continue their service to textile unionism "in a way that guarantees the preservation of the traditions, the principles and the ideals that have made all of us proud to be part of the TWUA." The decision to merge with the Amalgamated was "a practical step" taken under circumstances that afforded the TWUA no other commensurately viable option. Yet it was, he added, also a constructive step that strengthened their cause: "Operating as a textile division in the new union . . . we will be able to apply our own knowledge more effectively by linking it to the expertise and resources of the Amalgamated. Together we will be greater than the sum of our parts." Yet to understand the full significance of their decision, Stetin concluded, was to appreciate that it was "far more than a practical step" dictated by expediency. "It is," he passionately declared,

> the historic union—even, in a sense, a reunion—of two organizations whose common commitment to the highest principle of the labor movement, and to the cause of human freedom everywhere, has never faltered. It will forever be a milestone in labor history and perhaps in the history of social progress on this continent. This week we have an appointment with destiny—one that we will remember with pride for the rest of our lives.[60]

The necessary preliminaries behind them, delegates from the TWUA and the Amalgamated came together on June 3 in the ballroom of Washington's Hilton hotel for the inaugural convention of the Amalgamated Clothing and Textile

Workers Union. The doubts and regrets of the immediate past no longer pre-occupying them, they happily gave themselves over to what was more a two-day pep rally than a typical union convention. The succession of well-wishers included AFL-CIO president George Meany and former Vice President and labor favorite Hubert Humphrey. The new union's triumvirate—Finley, Sheinkman and Stetin—described how they intended to deploy the greater strength and bolder spirit that unity conferred on the 500,000 members that the ACTWU claimed. In keeping with the commitment that finally sealed the merger, delegates were solemnly assured that bringing J. P. Stevens to its knees would be their primary mission. Emboldened by George Meany's bellicose declaration that Stevens had stupidly picked a fight with the entire AFL-CIO "when it chose its lawless path in labor relations," and trusting that the com-bined strength now at their command was as great as the merger's chief archi-tects claimed, ACTWU delegates lustily resolved to undertake what one of them predicted would be "the greatest boycott the labor movement has ever seen."[61]

Although it never became the overpowering juggernaut that its champions imagined when they set it in motion in mid-1976, the ACTWU campaign against J. P. Stevens was the most innovative and comprehensive union assault ever launched against an American employer. It combined the familiar tech-niques of an organizing drive and product boycott with the bold and endlessly inventive methods of a corporate campaign—a tactic devised by zealous young ACTWU provocateurs to embarrass and harass nearly anyone and everyone linked to Stevens. The crusade was, as *New York Times* labor correspondent Abe Raskin noted, one destined to have "important implications for the future balance of strength between all American labor and management in a period when most of the nation's economic growth is concentrated in the Sunbelt states of the South and Southwest."[62] As organized labor's cause célèbre dur-ing the late 1970s, the campaign won support not only from other unions, but also from the diverse array of activist groups that had coalesced in the 1960s in support of civil rights and the war on poverty. In 1979, the campaign even got an unexpected and very effective boost from Hollywood when the feature-length motion *Norma Rae* was released. Loosely based on the exploits of Crystal Lee Sutton, a young union activist employed at a J. P. Stevens Mill in Roanoke Rapids, N.C., the film was both a popular and critical success—actress Sally Field won an Oscar for her performance in the title role—and brought to the attention of large and generally sympathetic audiences the injustices that southern textile workers faced when they tried to organize. "Unless the moviegoers happened to be charter members of the National Right to Work Committee," a *New York Times* editorialist wrote of the film's impact, "chances were better than good that he or she would emerge from the theater cheering for Norma Rae and the Union and against the Big, Powerful, Impersonal Company."[63]

The campaign against J. P. Stevens would never achieve the unqualified success that its creators and supporters had envisioned, yet it was anything but the failure that some observers later claimed.[64] Its corporate reputation in tatters and the lineup of NLRB cases and lawsuits arising out of its illegal conduct stretching into the future as far as the eye could see, a weary Stevens management was eager, by the fall of 1980, to reach an accommodation with the union. In return for a promise to call off the corporate campaign and boycott and to stop targeting the company in its organizing efforts, Stevens agreed to sign collective bargaining agreements covering workers at the few locations where it had lost NLRB elections and to desist from its illegal opposition to future organizing efforts the ACTWU might undertake.[65]

Although union publicists tried to put the best face possible on the Stevens pact, its meaning remained in dispute. The company had clearly retreated from the extreme doctrine it had earlier embraced, but, just as clearly, it had not renounced its antiunion faith. And, among those who thought that nothing short of total capitulation to the union constituted real victory, both the settlement's limited scope and its subsequent failure to generate a domino effect throughout the rest of the Stevens chain fed the fear that the campaign's actual gains were grossly disproportionate to the massive effort it had entailed.

Yet, if there were reasons to be disappointed about how little the Stevens campaign had yielded, there were at least as many reasons to be heartened and inspired by what it revealed about textile unionism's enduring nature. Its failures notwithstanding, the tumultuous confrontation with J. P. Stevens demonstrated that the spirit of textile unionism was as strong and resilient as ever and that its willingness to persevere in the midst of exhausting adversity had not been undermined by the merger.

The company's decision to sue for peace was followed up three years later with an agreement to "wipe the slate clean" by settling all remaining NLRB charges in return for a $1.2 million payment to the union.[66] Yet, the deeper significance of the Stevens fight became fully apparent only when it was recognized as being just one episode in a serial drama. Stevens had bowed to the union only slightly, but even a partial capitulation caused leading employers in the southern textile industry to question their long-held assumption that unionism would, at some point, collapse under the crushing weight of the disappointments heaped on it.

As the 20th century approached its end, the American textile industry would continue to suffer the ill effects of global competition and the other chronic threats to its vitality, and the union (which was *again* reconstituted as the Union of Needletrades, Industrial, and Textile Employees [UNITE] when the ACTWU merged with the International Ladies Garment Workers Union in 1995) would continue to confront its perennial impediments. A "union free environment" remained the keystone of the southern textile industry's labor relations policy, but fissures of the type revealed by the Stevens compromise would continue to undermine that policy even as employers generally succeeded in preserving it. Individually, most of these episodic proofs of textile unionism's abiding tenacity would be too small and too easily lost in a welter of contradictory evidence to have more than momentary significance. In combination, however, they attested to the possibility that its trajectory was not inevitably downward.

That fragile optimism was greatly strengthened in June of 1999 when the more than 5,000 employees of Cannon Mills, a company that symbolized the seeming immutability of antiunionism in the southern textile industry perhaps more than any other, decided in an NLRB-supervised election to entrust their collective interests to UNITE. Cannon was at once legendary and notorious for the overweening paternalism it enforced at its sprawling complex in Kannapolis, N.C. During the 1940s, as many as 25,000 compulsorily grateful millhands lived and worked in a rigidly controlled family fiefdom that some said was the largest unincorporated town in the United States. Organizing Cannon had been the object of union desires for more than half a century, yet, until 1999, attempts produced only bitter disappointment. It was the forbidding shoal on which the CIO's Operation Dixie sustained irreparable damage to its prospects in 1946. And, on each of the four separate occasions from the mid-1970s to the mid-1990s when first the TWUA and then the ACTWU challenged Cannon's hegemony in NLRB elections, the union cause had come out on the short end of the vote.[67]

In the summer of 1999, however, a historic reversal of fortune would finally occur. Though only a withered vestige of the incomparable behemoth it had been in its heyday, Fieldcrest Cannon Mills, as the company came to be known after passing out of family hands, might still have been a formidable adversary had it resorted to what a U.S. Court of Appeals called the "scorched-earth, take-no-prisoners approach" to opposing unionization ruthlessly employed by its previous managements. Yet, when the company was acquired by the Pillowtex Corporation in late 1997, it not only got a new management, but also a new outlook on labor relations. Although Pillowtex had nine mills in the United States and Canada that were already organized by UNITE, it resolutely opposed the union's efforts to add six Fieldcrest Cannon mills to that total. Unlike the mills' previous owners, however, Pillowtex was not willing to frighten or intimidate its employees into doing what it thought best. As the southern regional director during several of the earlier assaults on Fieldcrest Cannon, UNITE secretary-treasurer Bruce Raynor knew firsthand how powerfully fear intruded upon the judgment of millhands when their bosses contrived to spread it. He readily acknowledged that Pillowtex's uncommon restraint in the weeks and months leading up to the election had made more than a little difference to its outcome. "The campaign was the cleanest of the five," he told the press. "There were no discharges, no trampling of workers' rights."[68]

Given the American textile industry's blighted condition and the still fierce resolve of many of its leading companies to oppose collective bargaining for what they gravely claimed were reasons of economic survival, only an unregenerate Pollyanna would have concluded that UNITE's end-of-the-century conquest of Fieldcrest Cannon was enough to secure textile unionism's future. What the union's victory did affirm, however, was that the desire of textile workers to have an equal role in deciding issues of workplace fairness and justice was likely to be as strong and persistent in the new century as it had been in the old. Misfortune might forever challenge the faith of those who endured in textile unionism's cause, but never enough, it seemed, to extinguish it entirely.

Notes

Chapter 1

[1] Selig Perlman and Philip Taft, *History of Labor in the United States, 1896–1932,* vol. IV (New York: The Macmillan Company, 1935), pp. 265–266.

[2] Robert R. R. Brooks, "The United Textile Workers of America," (Ph.D. dissertation, Yale University, 1935), pp. 8–16.

[3] John R. Commons, et al., *History of Labour in the United States,* vol. II (New York: The Macmillan Company, 1918), pp. 301–305. See also: Brooks, "The United Textile Workers of America," pp. 25–29.

[4] Melton McLaurin, *Paternalism and Protest: Southern Cotton Mill Workers and Organized Labor, 1875–1905* (Westport, Conn.: Greenwood Publishing Corporation, 1971), p. 68. See also: Brooks, "United Textile Workers of America," pp. 29–36.

[5] Brooks, "United Textile Workers of America," p. 36.

[6] The fullest treatment of the NUTW is in McLaurin, *Paternalism and Protest,* pp. 120–177. See also: George S. Mitchell, *Textile Unionism in the South* (Chapel Hill: University of North Carolina Press, 1931), pp. 27–31; Brooks, "United Textile Workers of America," pp. 36–39; and, Herbert J. Lahne, *The Cotton Mill Worker* (New York: Farrar & Rinehart, 1944), pp. 184–189.

[7] Lahne, *The Cotton Mill Worker,* pp. 13, 102–103, 175–179; Robert W. Dunn and Jack Hardy, *Labor and Textiles: A Study of Cotton and Wool Manufacturing* (New York: International Publishers, 1931), pp. 84–86; Melvin Thomas Copeland, *The Cotton Manufacturing Industry of the United States* (Cambridge: Harvard University Press, 1923), pp. 54–111; Brooks, "United Textile Workers of America," pp. 17–25, 42.

[8] Brooks, "United Textile Workers of America," pp. 40–49.

[9] The increased competition felt by northern workers as a result of the dramatic growth of the cotton textile industry in the South after 1880 is readily explained by a comparison of the number of cotton spindles in each region:

	Cotton Spindles (millions)							
	1880	1885	1890	1895	1900	1905	1910	30-Year Increase
North	10.1	12.2	12.6	13.7	14.5	15.3	17.4	7.3
South	.5	1.1	1.7	2.4	4.5	8.8	11.2	10.7
Total	10.6	13.3	14.3	16.1	19.0	24.1	28.6	18.0

Source: Copeland, *The Cotton Manufacturing Industry of the United States,* p. 34.

[10] Brooks, "United Textile Workers of America," pp. 39–49; McLaurin, *Paternalism and Protest,* pp. 178–186; James Duncan, "Textile Workers Conference at Boston," *American Federationist* (June 1901), pp. 203–205; James Duncan, "Textile Workers' Amalgamation," *American Federationist* (October 1901), p. 410; Lahne, *The Cotton Mill Worker,* pp. 187–188.

[11] Brooks, "United Textile Workers of America," pp. 50–51.

[12] On the composition of the UTW's membership at the time of its founding and thereafter see: Brooks, "United Textile Workers of America," chapter II.

[13] Ibid.

[14] McLaurin, *Paternalism and Protest,* pp. 178–195.

[15] Thomas McMahon, *United Textile Workers of America: Their History and Policies* (New York: The Workers Education Bureau Press, 1926), p. 25.

[16] The conflicts arising from the national union's efforts to increase the per capita tax are detailed in Brooks, "The United Textile Workers of America," pp. 83–95.

[17] Robert W. Dunn and Jack Hardy, *Labor and Textiles: A Study of Cotton and Wool Manufacturing* (New York: International Publishers, 1931), p. 183.

[18] Brooks, "The United Textile Workers of America," p. 182.

[19] In 1920, the organization changed its name to the American Federation of Textile Operatives.

[20] On the challenges to the UTW from the right see: Brooks, "The United Textile Workers of America," pp. 182–214; and Dunn and Hardy, *Labor in Textiles,* pp. 183–184, 201–203.

[21] See the report of President John Golden in: Convention Proceedings of the United Textile Workers of America (1912), pp. 60–80; Brooks, "The United Textile Workers of America," pp. 224–228.

[22] "Minutes of an Informal and Confidential Conference of Independent Textile Unions Held in New York City, May 21 and 22, 1921," in Box 674, Third Installment, Textile Workers Union of America Collection, Wisconsin State Historical Society. (This collection is hereafter referred to as TWUA Coll.) See also: Dunn and Hardy, *Labor and Textiles,* pp. 203–204, 220–221; Matthew Josephson, *Sidney Hillman: Statesman of American Labor* (New York: Doubleday and Co., 1952), p. 198; Steven Fraser, *Labor Will Rule: Sidney Hillman and the Rise of American Labor* (New York: The Free Press, 1991), pp. 154–160; Brooks, "The United Textile Workers of America," pp. 232–245.

[23] Brooks, The United Textile Workers of America," pp. 215–249; Dunn and Hardy, *Labor and Textiles,* pp. 197–199, 201–206, 218–221.

[24] Brooks, "The United Textile Workers of America," pp. 197–202.

[25] The debilitating structural problems of the textile industry, both during the 1920s and generally, are informatively detailed in: H. E. Michl, *The Textile Industries: An Economic Analysis* (Washington, D.C.: The Textile Foundation, 1938).

[26] McMahon, *United Textile Workers of America,* p. 38.

[27] Brooks, "The United Textile Workers of America," pp. 151–157. For a detailed analysis of the most significant experiment in labor-management cooperation undertaken by the UTW, see: Richmond C. Nyman and Elliott D. Smith, *Union-Management Cooperation in the "Stretch Out,"* Institute of Human Relations (New Haven: Yale University Press, 1934).

[28] Dunn and Hardy, *Labor and Textiles,* pp. 221–222.

[29] On the Passaic strike see: Brooks, "United Textile Workers of America," 261–265; Dunn and Hardy, *Labor and Textiles,* pp. 222–225. See also: Albert Weisbord, *Passaic: The Story of a Struggle Against Starvation Wages and for the Right to Organize* (New York: AMS Press, 1976).

[30] The New Bedford strike is described in: Brooks, "The United Textile Workers of America," pp. 265–269; Dunn and Hardy, *Labor and Textiles,* pp. 225–227.

[31] Dunn and Hardy, *Labor and Textiles,* pp. 206–207; Brooks, "United Textile Workers of America," pp. 260–261, 269–271.

[32] On the surge of labor activism in the southern textile industry during and after the war, see: Mitchell, *Textile Unionism and the South,* pp. 35–57. On the unique circumstances of southern millhands and the special features of the work culture of the textile industry in the South, see: Jacquelyn Dowd et al., *Like a Family: The Making of a Southern Cotton Mill World* (New York: Norton, 1987); Jennings J. Rhyne, *Some Southern Cotton Mill Workers and Their Villages* (Chapel Hill: University of North Carolina Press, 1933); Lahne, *The Cotton Mill Worker,* pp. 34–202; Harriet Herring, *Welfare Work in Mill Villages: The Story of Extra-Mill Activities in North Carolina* (Chapel Hill: University of North Carolina Press, 1929); Ben Lemert, *The Cotton Textile Industry of the Southern Appalachian Piedmont* (Chapel Hill: University of North Carolina Press, 1933); Cathy McHugh, *Mill Family: The Labor System in the Southern Cotton Textile Industry, 1880–1915* (New York: Oxford University Press, 1988); Myra Page, *Southern Cotton Mills and Labor* (New York: Workers Library Publishers, 1929); Marjorie Potwin, *Cotton Mill People of the Piedmont: A Study in Social Change* (New York: Columbia University

Press, 1927); William H. Simpson, *Southern Textile Communities* (Charlotte: Dowd Press, 1948); Robert S. Smith, *Mill on the Dan: A History of Dan River Mills, 1882–1950* (Durham: Duke University Press, 1960), pp. 3–327; Douglas Flamming, *Creating the Modern South: Millhands and Managers in Dalton, Georgia, 1884–1984* (Chapel Hill: University of North Carolina Press, 1992), pp. 79–187; Bryant Simon, "Choosing Between the Ham and the Union: Paternalism in the Cone Mills of Greensboro, 1925–1930," in Jeffrey Leiter, Michael D. Schulman and Rhonda Zingraff, eds., *Hanging by a Thread: Social Change in Southern Textiles* (Ithaca, N.Y.: ILR Press, 1991), pp. 81–100. For a superb historiographical essay on the large body of scholarship that addresses various aspects of worker activism in the southern textile industry, see: Robert H. Zieger, "Textile Workers and Historians," in Robert H. Zieger, ed. *Organized Labor in the Twentieth-Century South*, (Knoxville: University of Tennessee Press, 1991), pp. 35–59.

[33] At the height of the labor troubles that engulfed southern textiles in 1929, some otherwise antiunion elements in the region did express support for AFL unionism as a last resort in combating the threatened rise of Communist influences among textile workers. See: "Labor's Battle Shifts Southward," *Literary Digest,* April 20, 1929, pp. 11–12; Louis Stark, "The Meaning of the Textile Strike," *New Republic,* May 8, 1929, p. 324; "Union Labor's Drive in the South," *Literary Digest,* August 3, 1929, p. 10.

[34] Paul Blanchard, "How to Live on Forty-Six Cents a Day," *Nation,* May 15, 1929, pp. 580–581; Louis Stark, "The Meaning of the Textile Strike," *New Republic,* May 8, 1929, pp. 323–324; Paul Peers, "Cotton Mill," *American Mercury,* (May 1929), pp. 1–9; M. L. Batey, "One American's Story," Ibid. September, 1929, pp. 1–7; Margaret Larkin, "Tragedy in North Carolina," *North American Review,* December 1929, pp. 686–690; Mercer Evans, "Southern Mill Hills," *The Survey,* April, 15, 1929, pp. 140–141; Marion Bonner, "Behind the Southern Textile Strikes," *Nation,* October 2, 1929, pp. 351–352; "What's the Matter in North Carolina?," *Business Week* October 12, 1929, pp. 22–24. For an alternative explanation of the industries' economic troubles, see: Gavin Wright, "Cheap Labor and Southern Textiles, 1880–1930," *Quarterly Journal of Economics* vol. 96 (November 1981), pp. 605–629.

[35] The general uprising among southern textile workers at the end of the 1920s is very ably chronicled in: Tom Tippett, *When Southern Labor Stirs* (New York: Jonathan Cape & Harrison Smith, 1931). See also: "Sinclair Lewis on North Carolina's Labor War," *Literary Digest,* November 9, 1929, pp. 36, 38, 43–44, 46, 48.

[36] The Elizabethton strike is described in: Tippett, *When Southern Labor Stirs,* pp. 54–75; Sherwood Anderson, "Elizabethton, Tennessee," *Nation,* May 1, 1929, pp. 526–527; Paul Aymon, "Rayon Workers Strike," *American Federationist,* May 1929, pp. 547–548; Jacqueline Dowd Hall, "Disorderly Women: Gender and Labor Militancy in the Appalachian South," *Journal of American History* September 1986, pp. 354–382; Brooks, "The United Textile Workers of America," pp. 313–314.

[37] "Fifty-Six to One," *Nation,* June 12, 1929, p. 690; Mitchell, *Trade Unionism and the South,* pp. 63–65; Tippett, *When Southern Labor Stirs,* pp. 1–34; Irving Bernstein, *The Lean Years* (Boston: Houghton Mifflin Company, 1960), pp. 1–13; Lewis Stark, "On to the South," *The Survey,* January 15, 1929, pp. 508–510; "Labor's Battle Shifts Southward," *Literary Digest,* April 20, 1929, pp. 11–12. A good overview can be found in: Charles A. Gulick, Jr., "Industrial Relations in Southern Textile Mills," *Quarterly Journal of Economics* 46 (August 1932), pp. 720–742.

[38] Albert Weisbord, "Passaic–New Bedford–North Carolina," *Communist* 8 (June, 1929): pp. 319–320; Fred Beal, *Proletarian Journey* (New York: Hillman-Curl, 1937), pp. 17–109; Paul Blanchard, "Communism in Southern Cotton Mills" *Nation,* April 24, 1929, pp. 500–501; Dunn and Hardy, *Labor and Textiles,* pp. 206–208.

[39] Tippett, *When Southern Labor Stirs,* p. 80. For a broader analysis of the character and values of Gastonia's millhands, see: Liston Pope, *Millhands and Preachers: A Study of Gastonia* (New Haven: Yale University Press, 1942). See also: John A. Salmond, *Gastonia, 1929: The Story of the Loray Mill Strike* (Chapel Hill: University of North Carolina Press, 1995).

[40] Mary Heaton Vorse, "Gastonia," *Harper's Monthly,* November 1929, pp. 700–710; Stark,

"The Meaning of the Textile Strike," pp. 323–325; Mitchell, *Textile Unionism and the South,* p. 71; Blanshard, "Communism in Southern Cotton Mills," pp. 500–501.

[41] Tippett, *When Southern Labor Stirs,* pp. 83–84.

[42] Bernstein, *The Lean Years,* pp. 40–41.

[43] Details of the Gastonia story are available in: Tippett, *When Southern Labor Stirs,* pp. 76–108; Salmond, *Gastonia, 1929;* Pope, *Millhands and Preachers: A Study of Gastonia;* and, Robin Hood, "The Loray Mill Strike" (Unpublished master's thesis, University of North Carolina, 1932). Newspaper accounts are abundant in both the regional and national press. See especially the *Charlotte Observer, Raleigh News and Observer, Greensboro Daily News,* and *New York Times.* The official Communist view is reported in the *Daily Worker.* Also very interesting and illuminating is the firsthand account of the Rev. James Myers, who toured the strike area in behalf of the Federal Council of Churches. A copy of his field notes, document 80–5829, is in the Gaston County Public Library, Gastonia, N.C.

[44] Benjamin Stolberg, "Madness in Marion," *Nation,* October 23, 1929, p. 463. The mill villages surrounding the Marion and Clinchfield mills were described by another source as being "among the worst examples of company towns in the South." See: Brooks, "The United Textile Workers of America," 315.

[45] Tippett, *When Southern Labor Stirs,* p. 116. See also: A. J. Muste, "The Marion Massacre," *The Canadian Forum* (December 1929), pp. 81–82; Mitchell, *Textile Unionism and the South,* pp. 75–78.

[46] For details of the Marion strike, see: Tippett, *When Southern Labor Stirs,* pp. 107–155.

[47] Norman Thomas to the Editor, *New Republic,* October 9, 1929, pp. 207–208.

[48] Muste, "The Marion Massacre," p. 82. For contemporary reports on the Marion tragedy, including an eyewitness account by the writer Sinclair Lewis, see: "Sinclair Lewis on North Carolina's Labor War," pp. 36, 38, 43–44, 46, 48; Mary Herton Vorse, " 'Waitin' with the Dead,' " *New Republic,* October 30, 1929; Stolberg, "Madness in Marion," pp. 462–464; Tippett, *When Southern Labor Stirs,* pp. 109–155.

[49] Tippett, *When Southern Labor Stirs,* pp. 142–143.

[50] On the Danville strike see: Smith, *Mill on the Dan,* pp. 241–327; Tippett, *When Southern Labor Stirs,* pp. 210–269; Louis Adamic, "Virginians on Strike," *New Republic,* December 24, 1930, pp. 163–164. The UTW, whose impoverishment was chronic, formally decided on November 22 to end its financial support of the Danville strike, even though the union's Emergency Committee had been informed only two weeks before that "the strike was in a healthy condition and that the workers were just as determined as the day they came out." The union voted on January 29, 1931, to end the strike on terms dictated by the company. See: UTWA, Minutes of the Emergency Committee Meeting, November 7, 1930, November 22, 1930, and January 30, 1931, in File 4A, box 1, mss 129A, TWUA Coll.

[51] W. J. Cash, "The War in the South," *American Mercury,* February 1930, pp. 167–168 (italics in the original).

[52] Bernstein, *The Lean Years,* p. 33.

[53] Ibid., pp. 34–36; American Federation of Labor, *Proceedings of the 49th Annual Convention* (1929), pp. 60, 265–283; Tippett, *When Southern Labor Stirs,* pp. 173–176; Jean Carol Trepp, "Union-Management Co-operation and the Southern Organizing Campaign," *Journal of Political Economy* 41 (October 1933), pp. 602–624, "The AFL Goes South," *Literary Digest* October 26, 1929, p. 10; George Sinclair Mitchell, "Organization of Labor in the South," *Annals of the American Academy of Political and Social Science* 153 (January 1931), pp. 185–186.

[54] Tippett, *When Southern Labor Stirs,* pp. 179–181.

[55] Quoted in Bernstein, *The Lean Years,* p. 35.

[56] Tippett, *When Southern Labor Stirs,* pp. 181–182. For the AFL's decidedly more upbeat assessment of Green's tour, see: Paul J. Smith, "Southern Organizing Campaign," *American Federationist* (April 1930): pp. 408–409.

[57] "Southern Campaign," *American Federationist* (April 1930): p. 402. American Federation of Labor, *Report of the Executive Council to the 50th Annual Convention,* (1930), p. 56.

[58] UTW Vice President Francis Gorman reported to the union's Emergency Committee in May of 1930 that "thousands of textile workers could be organized if we had the men to do the organizing work." See: UTWA, "Minutes of the Emergency Committee Meeting, May 21, 1930," in File 4A, box 1, mss 129A, TWUA Coll.

[59] Tippett, *When Southern Labor Stirs,* p. 183.

[60] Brooks, "The United Textile Workers of America," p. 114.

[61] Ibid., p. 349. For an astute biographical sketch of Thomas McMahon, see: Richard Kelly, *Nine Lives for Labor* (New York: Frederick A. Praeger, 1956), pp. 65–88.

[62] " 'Lawrence Can Take Care of Herself,' " *New Republic* April 1, 1931, 166–167; Edmund Wilson, "Lawrence, Mass.," *Ibid.,* November 25, 1931, pp. 36–39; Robert A. Bakeman, "Lawrence Decides," *Nation,* April 15, 1931, pp. 404–406; George Soule, "Class War in Rhode Island," *New Republic,* August 5, 1931, pp. 308–312.

Chapter 2

[1] Irving Bernstein, *The Lean Years,* (Boston: Houghton Mifflin, 1960) pp. 508–512.

[2] For a more detailed analysis of the antiunion bias inherent in the Roosevelt recovery plan see: Cletus E. Daniel, *Bitter Harvest: A History of California Farmworkers, 1870–1941* (Ithaca: Cornell University Press, 1981), pp. 167–173.

[3] UTWA, Minutes of the Executive Council Meeting, June 1–3, 1933, in File 4A, box 1, mss. 129A, TWUA Coll.

[4] "Code of Fair Competition for the Cotton-Textile Industry," *Monthly Labor Review* 37 (August 1933), pp. 265–272.

[5] Fleta Campbell Springer, "The N.R.A. Goes into Action," *Harper's Monthly* (October 1933), pp. 595–608.

[6] *News-Week in Business,* June 2, 1934, p. 26.

[7] George A. Sloan, "First Flight of the Blue Eagle," *Atlantic Monthly,* June 1933, pp. 321–325; "Laying the Cornerstone," *Business Week,* July 1, 1933, pp. 7–8.

[8] Irving Bernstein, *Turbulent Years* (Boston: Houghton Mifflin Co., 1970), pp. 300–301; James A. Hodges, *New Deal Labor Policy and the Southern Cotton Textile Industry, 1933–1941* (Knoxville: University of Tennessee Press, 1986), pp. 43–78. On the dominant role played by the Cotton-Textile Institute, see: Louis Galambos, *Competition and Cooperation: The Emergence of a National Trade Association* (Baltimore: The Johns Hopkins Press, 1966), pp. 173–256.

[9] Leo Krzycki, "The Upsurge of Textile Workers," *World Tomorrow* November 9, 1933, p. 609.

[10] UTWA, Minutes of the Executive Council Meeting, September 14–16, 1933, in File 4A, box 1, mss. 129A, TWUA Coll.; Brooks, "The United Textile Workers of America," pp. 349–350.

[11] Hodges, *New Deal Labor Policy,* pp. 60–78.

[12] UTWA, Minutes of the Executive Council Meeting, December 7–8, 1933, in File 4A, box 1, mss. 129A, TWUA Coll.; Bernstein, *Turbulent Years,* pp. 302–304; Hodges, *New Deal Labor Policy,* pp. 69–78; Galambos, *Competition and Cooperation,* pp. 230–232.

[13] "Production Control in Textile Industries," *Monthly Labor Review* 38 (February 1934), p. 295. Also see: Hodges, *New Deal Labor Policy,* pp. 57–58; Galambos, *Competition and Cooperation,* pp. 248–250.

[14] Galambos, *Competition and Cooperation,* pp. 257–258.

[15] *New York Times,* May 20, 1934, p. 3.

[16] Ibid., May 29, 1934, p. 3.

[17] *Business Week,* August 11, 1934, p. 15; Hodges, *New Deal Labor Policy,* p. 87; Galambos, *Competition and Cooperation,* p. 259.

[18] *New York Times* June 1, 1934, p. 1; Ibid., June 2, 1934, p. 5; Ibid., June 3, 1934, p. 1;

UTWA, Minutes of the Executive Council Meeting, June 14–15, 1934, in File 4A, box 1, mss. 129A, TWUA Coll.; Galambos, *Competition and Cooperation*, pp. 259–260; Hodges, *New Deal Labor Policy*, pp. 87–88.

[19] *New York Times*, June 3, 1934, p. 1.

[20] Hodges, *New Deal Labor Policy*, p. 89.

[21] The 1934 strike wave is instructively, and entertainingly, detailed in Bernstein, *Turbulent Years*, pp. 217–317.

[22] Interview with Eula McGill, February 3, 1976, p. 54, Southern Oral History Program, southern Historical Collection, University of North Carolina at Chapel Hill (hereafter cited as SOHP). For a detailed account of the Alabama strike see: Debbie Pendleton, "New Deal Labor Policy and Alabama Textile Unionism" (unpublished master's thesis, Auburn University, 1988), pp. 16–37. See also: Alexander Kendrick, "Alabama Goes on Strike," *Nation*, August 29, 1934, p. 233.

[23] Oliver Carlson, "Why Textiles Vote to Strike," *New Republic*, September 5, 1934, p. 96; Hodges, *New Deal Labor Policy*, pp. 97–98; Kendrick, "Alabama Goes on Strike," p. 233; Bernstein, *Turbulent Years*, p. 306.

[24] UTWA, Minutes of the Meeting of the Emergency Committee, July 18, 1934, in File 4A, box 1, mss. 129A, TWUA Coll.

[25] UTWA, Minutes of the Executive Council Meeting, August 11, 1934, in File 4A, box 1, mss. 129A, TWUA Coll.

[26] *News-Week at Home,* August 25, 1934, p. 9. See also: *New York Times*, August 14, 1934, p. 33; and, J. W. "The Textile Strike," *Nation*, September 5, 1934, pp. 273–274. See also: UTWA, *Proceedings of the Sixth Biennial and Thirty-Third Annual Convention (Condensed Form),* August 13–18, 1934.

[27] *News-Week at Home,* August 25, 1934, p. 9; *New York Times*, August 14, 1934, p. 33; Ibid., August 15, 1934, p. 32; Ibid., August 16, 1934, p. 6; Ibid., August 17, 1934, p. 2; Ibid., August 18, 1934, p. 1.

[28] Transcript of interview with Francis J. Gorman, August 8, 1973, part 2, p. 1, Southern Labor Archives, Georgia State University (hereafter cited as Gorman Interview).

[29] *New York Times,* August 18, 1934, p. 1.

[30] Jonathan Mitchell, "Here Comes Gorman!", *New Republic*, October 3, 1934, p. 204.

[31] Ibid., pp. 203–205; Gorman Interview, parts 1–3.

[32] *New York Times*, August 18, 1934, p. 1.

[33] Hodges, *New Deal Labor Policy*, p. 100.

[34] "Strike Realities," *Business Week*, September 22, 1934, p. 5.

[35] Mitchell, "Here Comes Gorman," p. 203. Copies of the mysterious "sealed orders," which, for the most part, contain nothing more than Gorman's hackneyed entreaties to strikers to persevere in their struggle, are in File 4A, box 1, mss 129A, TWUA Coll.

[36] *New York Times,* September 14, 1934, pp. 1–2. The most detailed account of the 1934 textile strike is Janet Irons's "Testing the New Deal: The General Textile Strike of 1934," (unpublished Ph.D. dissertation, Duke University, 1988). Much briefer but still useful accounts can be found in: Hodges, *New Deal Labor Policy,* pp. 104–118; and, Bernstein, *Turbulent Years,* pp. 306–315. The *New York Times* gave the strike extensive coverage, as did other newspapers up and down the Atlantic region.

[37] *News-Week,* September 23, (1934), p. 7. See also: Hodges, *New Deal Labor Policy,* p. 110; John E. Allen, "Eugene Talmadge and the Great Textile Strike in Georgia, September 1934," in Fink and Reed, eds., *Essays in Southern Labor History,* pp. 233–239.

[38] Margaret Marshall, "Textiles: An NRA Strike," *Nation*, September 19, 1934, pp. 326, 328.

[39] On the continuing regional disparities in labor standards within the textile industry, and northern perceptions of southern millhands, see: Lahne, *The Cotton Mill Worker,* especially pp. 11–174; Hall et al., *Like a Family,* pp. 289–357; Michl, *The Textile Industries: An Economic Analysis,* pp. 142–161; Glenn Gilman, *Human Relations in the Industrial Southeast: A Study of the Textile Industry* (Chapel Hill: University of North Carolina Press, 1956); H. M. Douty,

"Recovery and the Southern Wage Differential," *Southern Economic Journal* 4 (January 1938), pp. 314–321; A. F. Hinrichs, "Historical Review of Wage Rates and Wage Differentials in the Cotton-Textile Industry," *Monthly Labor Review* (May 1935), pp. 1170–1180; Mercer G. Evans, "Southern Wage Differentials Under the NRA," *Southern Economic Journal* 1 (January 1934), pp. 3–13; Oliver Carlson, "The Southern Worker Organizes," *Nation,* September 26, 1934, pp. 353–355; Robin Hood, "Some Basic Factors Affecting Southern Labor Standards," *Southern Economic Journal* 2 (April 1936), pp. 45–60.

[40] On strike violence in the North, see: Mary Heaton Vorse, "Textile Trouble," *New Republic,* September 19, 1934, pp. 147–148; Carl Knudsen, "Embattled Rhode Island," *Christian Century,* October 3, 1934, pp. 1239–1240; Carl Johnson, "Two Sides of the Barricades: Bloody Rhody," *New Republic,* October 10, 1934, pp. 237–238; James F. Findlay, "The Great Textile Strike of 1934," *Rhode Island History,* 42 (February 1983), pp. 17–29. *The New York Times* also reported extensively on the strike in New England, as did the major newspapers in the region.

[41] UTWA, Minutes of the Executive Council Meeting, September 22, 1934, in File 4A, box 1, mss 129A, TWUA Coll.

[42] Gorman confided to members of the UTW Emergency Board on October 26 that Sidney Hillman "was responsible for much of the features in [the] Winant report." See: UTWA, Minutes of the Emergency Board Meeting, October 26–27, 1934, File 4A, box 1, mss 129A, TWUA Coll.

[43] UTWA, "Additional Notes on Meeting of Executive Council," September 22, 1934, File 4A, box 1, mss 129A, TWUA Coll.

[44] "The Textile Strike is Ended," *Christian Century,* October 3, 1934, pp. 1227–1228.

[45] *News-Week,* September 29, 1934, p. 10.

[46] *New Republic,* September 26, 1934, pp. 172–173.

[47] Ibid., October 3, 1934, pp. 200–201. Chester Wright, Gorman's ever loyal paid publicist, took issue with the *New Republic*'s pessimistic assessment, claiming that he had never known of a strike "terminated with the positive brilliance of achievement with which this strike was terminated under the remarkable leadership of Francis J. Gorman." Chester M. Wright, to Editor, *New Republic,* November 14, 1934, p. 19.

[48] "The Textile 'Victory,' " *Nation,* October 3, 1934, p. 367.

[49] Mary N. Hillyer, "The Textile Workers Go Back," *Nation,* October 10, 1934, p. 414.

[50] On the reactions of southern millhands to the UTW's decision to end the strike on the basis of the Winant Board's recommendations, see: Irons, "Testing the New Deal: The General Textile Strike of 1934," pp. 478–486; Hodges, *New Deal Labor Policy,* pp. 117–118.

[51] Hillyer, "The Textile Workers Go Back," p. 414.

[52] "The Price is Too High," *Nation,* October 10, 1934, 398.

[53] On the variety of workers' complaints, see: UTWA, Minutes of the Greenville [South Carolina] Meeting, November 20, 1934, File 4A, box 1, mss 129A, TWUA Coll.

[54] UTWA, Minutes of the Emergency Board Meeting, October 26–27, 1934, File 4A, box 1, mss 129A, TWUA Coll. Other estimates of the number of former strikers denied employment were much higher. The *New York Times,* in what was almost certainly a gross exaggeration, estimated, on September 26, that more than 70,000 former strikers had been blacklisted. See: *New York Times,* September 26, 1934, p. 4. See also: Irons, "Testing the New Deal: The General Textile Strike of 1934," pp. 478–484.

[55] Hodges, *New Deal Labor Policy,* pp. 119–126.

[56] *New York Times,* October 6, 1934, p. 5; Ibid., October 9, 1934, p. 9.

[57] Hodges, *New Deal Labor Policy,* pp. 127–130.

[58] UTWA, Minutes of the Executive Council Meeting, March 21–23, 1935, File 4A, box 1, mss 129A, TWUA Coll. Frank Gorman, whose personal renown was never greater than when he was in Washington directing the textile strike, suggested that the UTW ought to consider moving its headquarters there. See also: *New York Times,* May 28, 1935, p. 17; Ibid., June 6, 1935, p. 12; Ibid., June 11, 1935, p. 2. On the UTW's role in the drafting and promotion of the Ellenbogen Bill, an ultimately futile legislative initiative designed to regulate the textile industry on a basis presum-

ably favorable to labor, see: UTWA, Minutes of the Executive Council Meeting, September 12, 1935, box 674, mss 396, TWUA Coll.

[59] UTWA, Minutes of the Executive Meeting, September 12, 1935, box 674, mss 396, TWUA Coll.

[60] On the UTW's increasingly fractious internal relations, see: UTWA, Minutes of the Executive Council Meetings, September 12, 1935, March 12–14, 1936, and September 10–12, 1936; and, UTWA, Minutes of the Meeting of the Executive Officers, June 17, 1936, all in box 674, mss 396, TWUA Coll.

Chapter 3

[1] UTW President Thomas McMahon assured members of the UTW's Executive Council, after the CIO's first formal meeting, that "it made no difference" that their union was unable to contribute financially to the cause of industrial unionism. According to McMahon, Lewis and other CIO leaders made it clear that despite the UTW's impoverished condition "they wanted us as members of their Committee." See: UTWA, Minutes of the Executive Council Meeting, December 5–6, 1935, box 674, mss 369, TWUA Coll.

[2] UTWA, Minutes of the Executive Council Meeting, September 10–12, 1936, box 674, mss 396, TWUA Coll. See also: Thomas McMahon to William Green, February 20, 1936, and Thomas McMahon to George M. Harrison, May 21, 1936, Reel 1, General Files of the CIO (a microfilm copy of this collection is in the Labor-Management Documentation Center, Catherwood Library, School of Industrial and Labor Relations, Cornell University).

[3] UTWA, Minutes of the Executive Officers' Meeting, June 17, 1936, and Minutes of the Executive Council Meeting, June 18–20, 1936, both in box 674, mss 396, TWUA Coll.

[4] Hodges, *New Deal Labor Policy,* p. 130.

[5] UTWA, Minutes of the Executive Council Meeting, December 5–6, 1935, and September 10–12, 1936; Minutes of the Executive Officers' Meeting, June 17–20, 1936, all in box 674, mss 396, TWUA Coll.

[6] UTWA, Minutes of the Executive Council Meeting, September 12, 1936, box 674, mss 396, TWUA Coll.

[7] UTWA, Proceedings of the Seventh Biennial and Thirty-fourth Annual Convention, September 14–19, 1936, p. 10.

[8] Ibid., pp. 9, 29–33, 37–38, 79, 81–83; UTWA, Minutes of the Executive Council Meeting, September 12, 1936, box 674, mss 396, TWUA Coll. The delegates also endorsed a proposal by UTW leaders that the union's headquarters be moved from New York City to Washington, D.C. The move made good sense, according to Gorman, because "It places our headquarters at the seat of the Government with the other great International Unions and the Committee for Industrial Organization," and "places us in the position of reaching all parts of the textile industry and gives us a closer contact with the South." Francis J. Gorman to Vice Presidents and Organizers, September 29, 1936, Reel 15, General Files of the CIO.

[9] Walter Galenson, *The CIO Challenge to the AFL* (Cambridge: Harvard University Press, 1960), p. 326.

[10] UTWA, Proceedings of the Convention (1936), p. 23.

[11] John L. Lewis to John Brophy, September 10, 1936, Reel 15, General Files of the CIO.

[12] UTWA, Minutes of the Executive Council Meeting, November 12, 1936, box 674, mss 396, TWUA Coll.

[13] UTWU, "Who? and What? are the Amalgamated Textile Workers of America" (New York, n.d.) in box 674, mss 396, TWUA Coll.; Steven Fraser, *Labor Will Rule: Sidney Hillman and the Rise of American Labor* (New York: The Free Press, 1991), pp. 158–160; Report of the General Executive Board to the Twelfth Biennial Convention of the Amalgamated Clothing Workers of America, May 9–17, 1938, pp. 56–57.

14 For examples of this tendency, see the correspondence between Hillman and various UTW officials in folder 9, box 86, Sidney Hillman Papers, Records of the Amalgamated Clothing Workers of America, Labor-Management Documentation Center, School of Industrial and Labor Relations, Cornell University (hereafter cited as Hillman Papers—ACWA Coll.).

15 UTWA, Minutes of the Executive Council Meeting, November 12–13, 1936, box 674, mss 396, TWUA Coll. The help that Lewis ultimately gave to UTW efforts in the synthetic yarn industry contributed to one of the union's rare successes in 1936: the securing of a collective bargaining agreement with the Celanese Corporation in Cumberland, Md. See: Francis J. Gorman to Vice Presidents and Organizers, September 29, 1936; United Mine Workers of America, Press Release, November 20, 1936; and, UTWA, Press Release by Francis J. Gorman, December 3, 1936, see on Reel 15, General Files of the CIO; *Newsweek,* August 1, 1936, p. 13.

16 UTWA, Minutes of the Executive Council Meeting, November 12–13, 1936; Thomas McMahon to John L. Lewis, October 8, 1936, Reel 15, General Files of the CIO.

17 Richard Kelly, *Nine Lives for Labor,* (New York: Frederick Praeger, 1956). p. 67.

18 Data relating to the size and composition of the UTW's membership in early 1937 were gathered by Solomon Barkin, who became research director of the Textile Workers Organizing Committee in March of 1937. See: "TWOC Organizing Data," box 1, series 4A, ms 129A, TWUA Coll.

19 UTWA, Minutes of the Executive Council Meeting, January 29–30, 1937, box 674, mss 396, TWUA Coll.

20 Ibid.

21 L. M. Johnston to John L. Lewis, February 17, 1937, Reel 15, General Files of the CIO. On the CIO's progress see: Robert Zieger, *The CIO: 1935–1955* (Chapel Hill: University of North Carolina Press, 1995) pp. 42–89.

22 *New York Times,* March 5, 1937, p. 3.

23 TWOC, *Building a Union of Textile Workers* (Philadelphia, 1939), p. 10.

24 UTWA, *The AFL Textile Workers* (Washington: Research and Education Department, 1950), p. 26.

25 George Soule, *Sidney Hillman: Labor Statesman* (New York: The Macmillan Company, 1939), p. 190.

26 Interview with Solomon Barkin, November 7 and 9, 1977, Textile Workers Union of America Oral History Project, State Historical Society of Wisconsin (hereafter cited as TWUA-OHP).

27 Soule, *Sidney Hillman,* pp. 189–190; Matthew Josephson, *Sidney Hillman: Statesman of American Labor* (Garden City, New York: Doubleday and Company, 1952), pp. 416–417; Fraser, *Labor Will Rule,* pp. 380–381; Len De Caux, *Labor Radical: From the Wobblies to the CIO* (Boston: Beacon Press, 1970), p. 284; Mary Heaton Vorse, "Bringing Union to Textiles," *New Republic,* October 27, 1932, pp. 331–332; Bernstein, *Turbulent Years,* pp. 616–618; Galenson, *The CIO Challenge to the AFL,* pp. 328; Barkin Interview, TWUA-OHP.

28 Francis J. Gorman to John L. Lewis, August 15, 1938, Reel 15, General Files of the CIO.

29 "Agreement between the Committee for Industrial Organization and the United Textile Workers of America," March 9, 1937, copies in: box 674, mss 396, TWUA Coll.; Reel 2, General Files of the CIO; and, box 86, Hillman Papers—ACWU Coll.

30 UTWA, Minutes of the Executive Council Meeting, March 7, 1937, box 674, mss 396, TWUA Coll.

31 Gorman to Lewis, August 15, 1938, Reel 15, General Files of the CIO.

32 *New York Times,* March 10, 1937, p. 3.

33 The beleagured condition of the textile industry in the mid-1930s is instructively outlined in: H. E. Michl, *The Textile Industries: An Economic Analysis* (Washington: The Textile Foundation, 1938).

34 Hillman's assessment of the difficulties that a southern organizing campaign posed is effectively presented in Fraser, *Labor Will Rule,* chap. 14.

35 *New York Times,* March 7, 1937, p. 27.

[36] *Building a Union of Textile Workers,* p. 8.

[37] *New York Times,* March 11, 1937, p. 11; *The Advance,* March (1937); 3; *Newsweek,* April 10, 1937, pp. 5–8.

[38] *Building a Union of Textile Workers,* pp. 64–66; Bernstein, *Turbulent Years,* pp. 618–619; Fraser, *Labor Will Rule,* p. 387.

[39] Information relating to the TWOC organizing staff can be found in "TWOC Organizing Data," file 4A, box 1, mss 129A, TWUA Coll. Also see: Hodges, *New Deal Labor Policy,* 150–151; *Building a Union of Textile Workers,* pp. 14, 61–63; DeCaux, *Labor Radical,* p. 284; Fraser, *Labor Will Rule,* p. 387. Many of those counted among the TWOC organizing staff were veteran millhands who worked full time in a mill and functioned as organizers only part time. See: Barkin Interview, TWUA-OHP.

Chapter 4

[1] Solomon Barkin, "Report to Textile Workers Organizing Committee on Activities," March 20, 1937, file 4A, box 1, mss 129A, TWUA Coll. Hillman reportedly told textile unionists from the Fall River–New Bedford region that the UTW was to be "practically dissolved" as a result of the TWOC's assumption of jurisdictional authority. See in the file noted above: An untitled report on Hillman's conference with William Batty and others, March 26, 1937.

[2] Mary Heaton Vorse, "Bringing Unions to Textiles," *New Republic,* October 27, 1937, p. 332.

[3] *Newsweek,* April 10, 1937, p. 5.

[4] *Daily News Record,* March 5, 1937, p. 1.

[5] "CIO Textile Plans," *Business Week,* March 20, 1937, pp. 16–17.

[6] Barkin, "Report to the TWOC on Activities," March 20, 1937, p. 3; *Building a Union of Textile Workers,* p. 16; *Daily News Record,* March 13, 1937, pp. 1, 13; *Journal of Commerce,* March 13, 1937, p. 1. The attitude of those employers (nearly all northern ones) who acknowledged the potentially therapeutic effects of collective bargaining in chronically "sick" industries like textiles was well-stated by an executive of the Hickey-Freeman Company, who cordially advised Hillman on March 6:

I think the Textile people will feel they are to be congratulated on your having taken the leadership in this movement, after they have a chance to become acquainted with you. I feel it will be very much to [the] advantage of the textile industry, as well as to manufacturers, as I am sure that you will make a very definite effort to be of help to the Textile industry as you have been to the Clothing industry.

See: E. M. Baum to Sidney Hillman, March 6, 1937, in folder 10, box 86, Hillman Papers—ACWA Coll.

[7] Hillman's attitude is ably explored in: Steven Fraser, *Labor Will Rule,* (New York: The Free Press, 1991), pp. 388–391. See also: Vorse, "Bringing Unions to Textiles," pp. 331–333; Matthew Josephson, *Sidney Hillman,* (New York: Doubleday, 1952), pp. 418–419; James Hodges, *New Deal Labor Policy,* (Knoxville: University of Tennessee Press, 1986), pp. 151–152.

[8] *Building a Union of Textile Workers,* p. 14.

[9] Barkin Interview, TWUA-OHP.

[10] Fraser, *Labor Will Rule,* p. 387.

[11] On Nance's background and stature see: Herman Wolf, "Cotton and the Unions," *Survey Graphic* March, 1938, pp. 146–150, 189; Lucy Randolph Mason, *To Win These Rights* (New York: Harper and Brothers, 1952), pp. 22–25; *Atlanta Georgian,* April 4, 1938, p. 1; Lucy Randolph Mason, "Steve Nance—Labor Statesman and Citizen," April 15, 1938, Reel 15, General Files of the CIO.

[12] Wolf, "Cotton and the Unions," pp. 146–147.

[13] On Peel see: Joseph J. King, "The Durham Central Labor Council," *Southern Economic Journal* 5 (1938), pp. 55–70.

[14] "Nominal Membership of Local Unions Affiliated with the United Textile Workers of America as of March, 1937," in "TWOC Organizing Data," file 4A, box 1, mss 129A, TWUA Coll; *Textile Bulletin* January 27, 1938, p. 1.

[15] Lucy Randolph Mason, *To Win These Rights* (New York: Harpers, 1952), pp. 19–92; Margaret Lee Neustadt, "Miss Lucy of the CIO: Lucy Randolph Mason, 1882–1959" (M.A. thesis, University of North Carolina at Chapel Hill, 1969), pp. 20–23; John A. Salmond, *Miss Lucy of the CIO: The Life and Times of Lucy Randolph Mason* (Athens: University of Georgia Press, 1988), pp. 75–100.

[16] Dodge's background and activities on behalf of the TWOC are described in: D. Witherspoon Dodge, *Southern Rebel in Reverse: The Autobiography of an Idol-Shaker* (New York: The American Press, 1961).

[17] On Horton see: John M. Glen, *Highlander: No Ordinary School, 1932–1962* (Lexington: University of Kentucky Press, 1988); Myles Horton Interview, Southern Oral History Program, Southern Historical Collection, University of North Carolina at Chapel Hill (hereafter cited as SOHP-SHC).

[18] *Daily News Record,* March 5, 1937, p. 1.

[19] *New York Times,* March 19, 1937, p. 3; *Business Week,* March 20, 1937, p. 16.

[20] "Report of Meeting of the TWOC and the CIO," March 19, 1937, File 4A, box 1, mss 129A, TWUA Coll.

[21] *Daily News Record,* March 11, 1937, p. 19.

[22] On the diverse character of the cotton textile industry in the mid-1930s, see: Michl, *The Textile Industries: An Economic Analysis,* pp. 80–194; Herbert J. Lahne, *The Cotton Mill Worker* (New York: Farrar & Rinehart, 1944), pp. 11–25, 240–259.

[23] J. H. Marion, Jr., "Does the South Need John Lewis?" *Christian Century,* May 19, 1937, pp. 465–467.

[24] *New York Times,* March 7, 1937, p. 29.

[25] Ibid., sec. III, p. 9.

[26] Ibid., March 19, 1937, p. 3.

[27] Ibid., March 20, 1937, p. 6.

[28] *Charlotte Observer,* March 18, 1937, p. 1; *New York Times,* March 19, 1937, p. 3.

[29] *New York Times,* March 20, 1937, p. 6.

[30] Quoted in *Newsweek,* April 10, 1937, p. 6. See also: "Textile Wages Raised," *Business Week,* March 27, 1937, p. 22; *New York Times,* March 30, 1937, p. 11.

[31] Marion, "Does the South Need John Lewis?," 645.

[32] *Building a Union of Textile Workers,* pp. 14–15; Lahne, *The Cotton Mill Workers,* p. 265; "Report of Meeting of the TWOC and CIO, March 19, 1937," file 4A, box 1, mss 129A, TWUA Coll.

[33] *New York Times,* March 19, 1937, p. 3.

[34] Barkin, "Report to the TWOC on Activism," March 20, 1937, pp. 1–3.

[35] Fraser, *Labor Will Rule,* pp. 389–391.

[36] Horton Interview, SOHP-SHC; Hodges, *New Deal Labor Policy,* pp. 151–152; Glen, *Highlander,* pp. 72–73; Jonathan Daniels, "Gold Avenue," *The Virginia Quarterly Review,* April 1938, p. 183.

[37] Marion, "Does the South Need John Lewis?," pp. 645–647.

[38] TWOC, *Press Release,* March 29, 1937, file 13A, box 1, mss 129A, TWUA Coll.; *New York Times,* March 30, 1937, p. 11.

[39] *New York Times,* March 30, 1937, p. 18; *Newsweek,* April 10, 1937, pp. 5–8.

[40] *New York Times,* April 20, 1937, p. 14; See also: Sidney Hillman to All Local Unions, March 31, 1937, folder 10, box 86, Hillman Papers-ACWA Coll.; TWOC, Press Releases: March 30, 1937; April 9, 1937; April 10, 1937; April 12, 1937; April 14, 1937; *The Advance* (May 1937), p. 8.

[41] TWOC, "Weekly Letter for Regional Directors," May 1, 1937, Box 86, folder 10, Hillman

Papers—ACWA Coll.; *New York Times*, March 21, 1937, p. 2; March 21, 1937, p. 34; April 20, 1937, p. 14.

42 The TWOC's activities were widely reported in newspapers throughout New York and New England. The *New York Times, Boston Globe*, and *Hartford Courant* provided the most complete coverage. See also: TWOC, Press Release, April 9, 1937; *The Advance*, (April 1937), pp. 4–5; Ibid., (May 1937), p. 8.

43 *New York Times*, March 21, 1937, p. 34; TWOC, "Background Data on Silk Strike," August 10, 1937, file 4A, box 1, mss 129A, TWUA Coll.

44 TWOC, *Press Release* #10, April 14, 1937; *New York Times* April 15, 1937, p. 14; Ibid., April 17, 1937, p. 2. Despite a claim by one union official that organizers enjoyed more freedom of action in Danville, Va., than in any other southern textile center, the huge Dan River and Riverside cotton mills there did not become targets of sustained organizing campaigns by the TWOC. See: Robert Smith, *Mill on the Dan* (Dunham: Duke University Press, 1960), p. 393.

45 *New York Times*, March 21, 1937, p. 34; Ibid., March 30, 1937, p. 11.

46 Marion, "Does the South Need John Lewis?," p. 647. Especially well-informed reports regarding the reactions of Piedmont cotton mill workers to the TWOC's early overtures can be found in box 7, Paul R. Christopher Papers, Southern Labor Archives, Georgia State University. The Myles Horton Interview, SOHP-SHC, is also very instructive on this point.

47 Sol Barkin, "Notes on New Bedford-Rall River Conference," March 26, 1937, in "TWOC Organizing Data" folder, file 4A, box 1, mss 129A, TWUA Coll. See also: Vorse, "Bringing Union to Textiles," p. 332.

48 James Starr to J. B. S. Hardman, June 2, 1937; James Starr to Sidney Hillman, June 2, 1937; Sidney Hillman to James Starr, June 4, 1937, all in box 67, mss 396, TWUA Coll.

49 Solomon Barkin, "Memorandum on Synthetic Yarn Conference," March 29, 1937, in "TWOC Organizing Data" folder, file 4A, box 1, mss 129A, TWUA Coll.

50 *New York Times*, May 24, 1937, pp. 1, 12.

51 Ibid., May 30, 1937, p. 6.

52 TWOC, Press Release No. 35, n.d.

53 *Building a Union of Textile Workers*, pp. 20–21; TWOC, "Background Data on Silk Strike," August 10, 1937, file 4A, box 1, mss 129A, TWUA Coll.; *New York Times*, August 10, 1937, p. 1; Ibid., August 11, 1937, pp. 1, 9; Ibid., August 21, 1937, p. 30; Ibid., August 24, 1937, p. 13.

54 *The Advance* (July 1937), p. 6; *Building a Union of Textile Workers*, pp. 21–22, 38–39. See also: Paul David Richards, "The History of the TWUA, CIO, in the South, 1937 to 1945," (Ph.D. dissertation, University of Wisconsin, 1978), 54–56.

55 "Report on TWOC Progress," October 8, 1937, File 4-A, box 1, mss 129A, TWUA Coll.

56 *The Advance* (October 1937), p. 4. In addition to the reports he received from Hillman regarding the TWOC's progress in Lawrence, John L. Lewis received direct reports from L. H. Bell, a United Mine Workers official assigned to assist with the organizing effort there. See: L. H. Bell to John L. Lewis, May 28, 1937; L. H. Bell to A. D. Lewis, June 7, 1937; L. H. Bell to A. D. Lewis, August 20, 1937; L. H. Bell to A. D. Lewis, August 26, 1937, all in reel 15, General Files of the CIO.

57 TWOC, *Press Release # 44*, September 17, 1937; *The Advance* (October 1937), 4.

58 Vorse, "Bringing Union to Textiles," p. 331.

59 "Report of Sidney Hillman at the CIO Conference, Atlantic City, October 12, 1937, on the work of the Textile Workers Organizing Committee," in "Informal Minutes of CIO Conference, October 11–15, 1937," on Reel 2, General Files of the CIO.

60 A detailed accounting of the organizational progress and financial condition of the TWOC as of October 8, 1937, is provided in union Research Director Solomon Barkin's "Report on TWOC Progress," October 8, 1937, in file 4-A, box 1, mss. 129A, TWUA Coll.

61 The organizing staff employed directly by the TWOC as of July 27, 1937, numbered 488. Of that number, 23 percent, 112 staff members, were assigned to the Lower South. However, the organizing staff that Steve Nance commanded in the region actually totaled 128, since 16 addi-

tional organizers still on the payroll of either the Hosiery Workers or the Amalgamated Clothing Workers were assigned to assist the campaign he directed in the Lower South. See: "A Summary of Textile Campaign," July 27, 1937, and "Organizers Not on TWOC Payroll," n.d., both in "TWOC Organizing Data" folders, file 4-A, box 1, mss. 129A, TWUA Coll.

[62] *New York Times,* May 6, 1937, p. 7.

[63] "Total Number of Pledge Cards Received Through August 7, 1937," file 4-A, box 1, mss 129A, TWUA Coll.

[64] Quoted in: Wolf, "Cotton and the Unions," p. 147.

[65] Lucy Randolph Mason to John L. Lewis, August 31, 1937, Reel 2, CIO Files of John L. Lewis.

[66] Wolf, "Cotton and the Unions," p. 146.

[67] Lucy Randolph Mason to Sidney Hillman, October 2, 1937, Reel 2, CIO Files of John L. Lewis.

[68] "Report of TWOC Progress," October 8, 1937. See also: Hodges, *New Deal Labor Policy,* pp. 164–165; Richards, "History of the Textile Workers Union of America in the South, 1937 to 1945," pp. 56–64. In April of 1938 the TWOC reported that fewer than 3,600 cotton workers were under contract in the four-state region. See: TWOC, *Cotton Notes, No. 1,* April 9, 1938, in file 4-A, box 1, mss 129A, TWUA Coll.

[69] Lucy Randolph Mason to John L. Lewis, September 11, 1937, Reel 2, CIO Files of John L. Lewis.

[70] Mason to Hillman, October 2, 1937.

[71] Lucy Randolph Mason to Southern Editors, October 5, 1937, Reel 2, CIO Files of John L. Lewis; TWOC, *Press Release No. 45,* September 20, 1937.

[72] Mason to Hillman, October 2, 1937.

[73] Ibid.

[74] Lucy R. Mason to Southern Editors, November 5, 1937, Reel 2, CIO Files of John L. Lewis.

[75] Sidney Hillman to John L. Lewis, August 19, 1937; John L. Lewis to Sidney Hillman, September 1, 1937; Sidney Hillman to John L. Lewis, September 8, 1937, al in Reel 2, CIO Files of John L. Lewis.

[76] "Report on TWOC Progress," October 8, 1937, Appendix G.

[77] TWOC, *Press Release No. 43,* September 1, 1937.

[78] Joe Mayo to A.D. Lewis, September 4, 1937, Reel 2, CIO Files of John L. Lewis.

[79] "Report on TWOC Progress," October 8, 1937, Appendix A.

[80] Fraser, *Labor Will Rule,* p. 406; Solomon Barkin to Sol Stetin, September 20, 1989 (in the author's possession); Barkin Interview, TWUA-OHP; Hodges *New Deal Labor Policy,* pp. 150, 169; *The Advance* (December 1937), p. 5. Barkin also insists that when Hillman did finally return to New York in the spring of 1938, he "never did return to the TWOC office," preferring instead to conduct whatever nominal involvement he had in the organization's subsequent affairs from his Amalgamated headquarters. See: Solomon Barkin to the author, October 24, 1987; Donald Stabile, *Activist Unionism: The Institutional Economics of Solomon Barkin* (Armonk, NY: M. E. Sharpe, 1993), p. 18.

[81] Lucy Randolph Mason to Southern Editors, December 18, 1937, Reel 2, CIO Files of John L. Lewis.

[82] *New York Times,* November 7, 1937, Sec. III, p. 9.

Chapter 5

[1] For a detailed picture of the TWOC's status as of late March, 1938, see: "Report on TWOC Progress," March 20, 1938, File 4A, box 1, mss 129A, TWUA Coll.

[2] *Atlanta Georgian,* April 4, 1938, p. 1; *CIO News,* April 9, 1938, p. 2; Ibid., April 16, 1938, p. 2; *The Advance* (May 1938), p. 29.

[3] Lucy Randolph Mason, "Steve Nance: Labor Statesman and Citizen," April 15, 1938, Reel 15, General Files of the CIO.

[4] TWOC, *Press Release #54,* April 16, 1938. On Lawrence's limitations from the point of view of two astute TWUA staffers, see the interviews with Lawrence Rogin and Solomon Barkin in TWUA-OHP. See also: Lucy Randolph Mason to Southern Editors, May 11, 1938, Reel 15, General Files of the CIO.

[5] For an excellent analysis of the TWOC's tireless, but usually unavailing, efforts to redeem the promise of the Wagner Act in the southern textile industry, see: Hodges, *New Deal Labor Policy,* pp. 164–168. On the larger theme of the Wagner Act's ultimately ineffectual force in the protection of workers' rights, see: James A. Gross, *Broken Promise: The Subversion of U.S. Labor Relations Policy, 1947–1994* (Philadelphia: Temple University Press, 1995).

[6] TWOC, *Building a Union of Textile Workers,* p. 26.

[7] *Business Week,* August 27, 1938, pp. 15–16; Lahne, *The Cotton Mill Worker,* p. 243.

[8] *Building a Union of Textile Workers,* pp. 27–28; *CIO News,* April 9, 1938, p. 8. Douglas Woolf, editor of *The Textile World,* urged mill owners in early January to "resist to the last ditch" pressures to cut wages. *New York Times,* January 7, 1938, p. 26.

[9] Building a Union of Textile Workers, pp. 27–28; TWOC, Press Release #56, May 6, 1938; Press Release #57, May 6, 1938; Press Release #58, May 13, 1938; Press Release #60, May 19, 1938; Press Release #62, May 20, 1938; Press Release #65, May 22, 1938; Press Release #62, June 15, 1938; Press Release #68, June 18, 1938. TWOC, Strike Bulletin on the Bigelow-Sanford Carpet Company, No. 1, May 11, 1938, and Sidney Hillman to Sirs and Brothers, July 5, 1938 (plus attachment), both in box 86, folder 11, Hillman Papers—ACWA Coll.

[10] Sol Barkin, "Report for the Conference of the Committee on the experiences during the last year," n.d. [early August, 1938], file 4-A, box 1, mss. 129A, TWUA Coll.

[11] "Report on TWOC Progress," March 28, 1938, pp. 3–4; Barkin, "Report . . . on the experiences during the last year," p. 4.

[12] TWOC, *Press Release #63,* May 21, 1938; *Press Release #66,* June 15, 1938.

[13] TWOC, *Press Release #66,* June 15, 1938; Hodges, *New Deal Labor Policy,* pp. 170–171.

[14] Lucy Randolph Mason to Southern Editors, May 11, 1938, Reel 15, General Files of the CIO.

[15] Hodges, *New Deal Labor Policy,* p. 171.

[16] Fraser, *Labor Will Rule,* p. 408.

[17] Report of the General Executive Board to the Twelfth Biennial Convention of the Amalgamated Clothing Workers of America, May 9–17, 1938, p. 60.

[18] Proceedings of the Twelfth Biennial Convention of the Amalgamated Clothing Workers of America (Atlantic City), May 9–17, 1938.

[19] *New York Times,* July 6, 1938, p. 10.

[20] TWOC, *Press Release #70,* July 7, 1938.

[21] Barkin Interview, TWUA-OHP; Fraser, *Labor Will Rule,* pp. 408–412, 420–421; Hodges, *New Deal Labor Policy,* pp. 170–171. Sol Barkin, who assumed day-to-day responsibility for the operations of the TWOC's New York headquarters after the onset of Hillman's illness in late 1937, is emphatic in his recollection that Rieve was the "acting chairman" of the organization in title only. See: Sol Barkin to the author, October 24, 1987, and Sol Barkin to Sol Stetin, September 20, 1989, copy in the author's possession.

[22] Resentment toward the TWOC and the sometimes officious Amalgamated Clothing Workers personnel who ran it in New England was not long in being expressed by disgruntled UTW members and functionaries in various bastions of textile unionism throughout the region. Local No. 2363 in Fisherville, Mass., a long-functioning local affiliate that UTW Secretary-Treasurer James Starr described as "one of our good ones," abruptly severed its ties to the TWOC before its drive in the region was six months old. In Holyoke, Mass., another area where textile unionism had deep roots, TWOC leaders were busy throughout the spring of 1938 quelling one incipient rebellion after another as local UTW officials and members grew increasingly restive and obstreperous. See: James Starr to Solomon Barkin, August 2, 1937, box 67, mss 396, TWUA Coll. On the situation in Holyoke see the correspondence in James Starr, File 4, box 67, mss 396, TWUA Coll. See also: William F. Hartford, *Where is Our Responsibility?: Unions and Economic*

Change in the New England Textile Industry, 1870–1960 (Amherst: University of Massachusetts Press, 1996), p. 69.

23 Lahne, *The Cotton Mill Worker,* pp. 266–267; *Building a Union of Textile Workers,* p. 27; Lionel Jubinville and Edward Vanasse to John L. Lewis, February 6, 1938, Reel 15, General Files of the CIO.

24 TWOC, *Press Release No 50,* January 22, 1938; Ibid., *Press Release No. 51,* February 10, 1938.

25 Joseph Sylvia to Solomon Barkin, June 27, 1938, box 67, mss 396, TWUA Coll.; TWOC, *Building a Union of Textile Workers,* p. 32.

26 UTWA, Minutes of the Executive Council Meeting, March 7, 1937, box 674, mss. 396, TWUA Coll.

27 Stabile, *Activist Unionism,* p. 14.

28 Ibid., p. 18; Barkin to Daniel, October 24, 1987; Columbia University Oral History Project, "Reminiscences of Solomon Barkin" (1961); Barkin Interview, TWUA-OHP.

29 Transcript of Rogin Interview, TWUA-OHP, p. 21.

30 James Starr to Solomon Barkin, April 12, 1938, and Solomon Barkin to James Starr, April 13, 1938, both in box 67, mss 396, TWUA Coll.

31 Solomon Barkin to James Starr, September 18, 1937, box 67, mss 396, TWUA Coll.

32 James Starr to Solomon Barkin, September 20, 1938, box 67, mss 396, TWUA Coll.

33 Sidney Hillman to Francis J. Gorman, April 13, 1937; Francis J. Gorman to Sidney Hillman, August 24, 1937, both in box 67, mss 396, TWUA Coll.

34 Francis J. Gorman to James Starr, January 24, 1938, box 67, mss 396, TWUA Coll.

35 Francis J. Gorman to Emil Rieve, December 2, 1937, box 67, mss 396, TWUA Coll.

36 Emil Rieve to Francis J. Gorman, December 2, 1937, box 67, mss 396, TWUA Coll.

37 Francis J. Gorman to James Starr, January 24, 1938, box 67, mss 396, TWUA Coll.

38 Bernstein, *Turbulent Years,* pp. 621–622.

39 Ironically, Rieve belatedly sought to mollify Gorman by authorizing payment of some of the expenses that Barkin had earlier disallowed. See: Emil Rieve to Frank Gorman, February 11, 1938, box 67, mss 396, TWUA Coll.

40 Francis J. Gorman to Emil Rieve, February 8, 1938, box 67, mss 396, TWUA Coll.

41 Emil Rieve to Frank Gorman, February 11, 1938, box 67, mss 396, TWUA Coll.

42 TWOC, *Press Release #51,* February 10, 1938.

43 Francis J. Gorman to Emil Rieve, February 15, 1938, box 67, mss 396, TWUA Coll.

44 "Report on TWOC Progress," March 28, 1938.

45 Francis J. Gorman to Sidney Hillman, May 16, 1938, folder 11, box 86, Hillman Papers—ACWA Coll.

46 Francis J. Gorman to John L. Lewis, August 15, 1938, Reel 15, General Files of the CIO.

47 Joseph Silvia to Solomon Barkin, June 27, 1938; Mary Taccone to Solomon Barkin, June 28, 1938; "Resolution Adopted at Conference of the Federation of Woolen and Worsted Workers of America, Affiliated with U.T.W. of A., T.W.O.C., C.I.O., July 17, 1938, Owls Hall, Providence, R.I."; Anthony Valente to [Woolen and Worsted Workers], July 21, 1938, all in box 67, mss 396, TWUA Coll.

48 "Statement of the Providence and Woonasquatucket Woolen and Worsted Council," n.d., file 15, box 86, Hillman Papers—ACWA Coll.

49 Frank [Gorman] to Jim [Starr], July 20, 1938, box 67, mss 396, TWUA Coll.

50 Ibid.

51 Francis J. Gorman to John L. Lewis, August 2, 1938, Reel 15, General Files of the CIO.

52 Francis J. Gorman to John L. Lewis, August 15, 1938, Reel 15, General Files of the CIO.

53 A report by research director Solomon Barkin to the TWOC's leadership on July 27, 1938, indicated that the union was employing only 24 organizers throughout the entire Lower South region. At that same time 38 organizers were on the TWOC's payroll in New England and 20 were employed in the Middle Atlantic region. Nationally, the TWOC employed only 123 organizers.

See: Solomon Barkin, "Report for the Conference of the Committee on the Experiences During the Last Year," n.d. [July 27, 1938], box 67, ms. 396, TWUA Coll.

[54] John Brophy to Sidney Hillman, August 4, 1938, folder 13, box 86, Hillman Papers—ACWA Coll.

[55] TWOC, *Press Release #74,* August 15, 1938.

[56] Ibid.; "Hillman Pushes Textile Drive," *Business Week,* August 20, 1938, p. 33.

[57] James Starr to [Rhode Island Woolen and Worsted Workers], August 10, 1938, box 67, mss 396, TWUA Coll.

[58] Emil Rieve to Sidney Hillman, October 24, 1938; Sidney Hillman to John Peel, October 31, 1938, both in box 576, mss 396, TWUA Coll.

[59] TWOC, Minutes of the Advisory Board Meeting, November 3, 1938, file 4A, box 1, mss 129A, TWUA Coll.

[60] Charles W. Erwin to Sidney Hillman, August 17, 1938, folder 13, box 86, Hillman Papers—ACWA Coll.

[61] Francis J. Gorman to all Textile Locals and Textile Workers of the United States and Canada, December 13, 1938, box 67, mss 396, TWUA Coll.

[62] TWOC, *Press Release #83,* November 30, 1938.

[63] Ibid., *Press Release #86,* December 14, 1938.

[64] *Textile Labor,* (February 1939), p. 1.

[65] *New York Times,* August 28, 1938, pp. 1, 21; Ibid., October 14, 1938, pp. 1–2.

[66] Sidney Hillman to Francis J. Gorman, December 14, 1936, box 67, mss 396, TWUA Coll.

[67] TWOC, *Press Release #87,* December 16, 1938.

[68] Isadore Katz and Alfred Udoff to Emil Rieve, "In Re: UTW, TWOC and Gorman," n.d., box 67, mss 396, TWUA Coll. The eight union locals in Rhode Island that comprised Joseph Sylvia's successionist Providence and Woonasquatucket Woolen and Worsted District Council reaffiliated with the AF of L in November of 1938. See: *New York Times,* November 16, 1938, p. 18.

[69] "Minutes of the Meeting of the Executive Council of the United Textile Workers of America," January 4, 1939, box 67, mss 396, TWUA Coll.

[70] *Business Week,* December 24, 1938, p. 28; *Time,* December 24, 1938, p. 9.

[71] Lee Pressman to John L. Lewis, December 1, 1938, Reel 15, General Files of the CIO.

[72] Solomon Barkin, "Report Presented to the Second Meeting of the TWOC Advisory Council," January 4, 1939, box 67, mss 396, TWUA Coll.

Chapter 6

[1] *New York Times,* May 7, 1939, p. 2.

[2] John Pollard, Unofficial Minutes of the UTW-AFL Washington Convention, May 8–10, 1939, box 67, mss 396, TWUA Coll.; Irving Bernstein, *Turbulent Years,* p. 623; (Boston: Houghton, Mifflin, 1969), Galenson, *The CIO Challenge to the AFL* (Cambridge: Harvard University Press, 1960), Walter p. 342; *New York Times,* May 11, 1939, p. 3; UTWA-AFL, Proceeding of the Special Convention, May 8–10, 1939.

[3] TWOC, Proceedings of the First Constitutional Convention, May 15, 1939; UTWA, Convention Proceedings, May 15, 1939; TWUA, Proceedings of the First Constitutional Convention, (Philadelphia), May 15–19, 1939.

[4] TWUA, Proceedings of the First Constitutional Convention, pp. 147–165, 180–185.

[5] Len DeCaux, *Labor Radical* (Boston: Beacon Press, 1970), p. 285.

[6] TWUA, Proceedings of the First Constitutional Convention, p. 182.

[7] *New York Times,* May 19, 1939, p. 13; "CIO Turns to the South," *Business Week,* May 20, 1939, pp. 27–28; *Textile Labor* (June 1939), pp. 8, 12.

[8] *Business Week,* May 20, 1939, p. 28. Over vehement objections from southern mill owners, the 32½-cent hourly federal minimum wage for cotton textiles was approved by wage-hour

Administrator Elmer Andrews on September 13, 1939. It went into effect on October 24. The TWUA, which had demanded a 40-cent-per-hour minimum, bitterly complained that federal officials had caved in to "the pressure of reactionary and sweatshop employers" in the South. As a result, union officials groused, a law that might have helped a majority of southern millhands was likely to benefit only a few thousand. See: *New York Times,* September 14, 1939, p. 32; *Textile Labor* (June 1939), p. 10; Ibid. (July 1939), p. 10; Ibid. (July 1939), pp. 1, 4.

⁹ TWUA, Minutes of the Meeting of the Executive Council, June 8, 1939, box 1, mss 396, TWUA Coll.

¹⁰ Ibid.

¹¹ J. R. Bell to Emil Rieve, July 12, 1939, Reel 3, General Files of the CIO. The pressure Lewis brought to bear on the TWUA may also have reflected his conviction that CIO affiliates in general were not sufficiently conscientious in meeting their dues obligations. See: Minutes of the Executive Board Meeting of the CIO, October 14, 1939, Reel 1, General Files of the CIO.

¹² Emil Rieve to J. R. Bell, July 20, 1939, Reel 3, General Files of the CIO; TWUA, Minutes of the Meeting of the Executive Council, September 28, 1939, box 1, mss 396, TWUA Coll.

¹³ TWUA, Minutes of the Meeting of the Executive Council, September 28, 1939; Ibid., January 11, 1939; Ibid., May 11–12, 1939, all in box 1, mss 396, TWUA Coll.; CIO, "Receipts Analysis: October 31, 1939–November 30, 1939," Reel 4, General Files of the CIO.

¹⁴ "War Steps Up Textile Tempo," *Business Week,* November 11, 1939.

¹⁵ TWUA, Minutes of the Meeting of the Executive Council, September 28, 1939, box 1, mss 396, TWUA Coll.

¹⁶ Lucy Randolph Mason to John L. Lewis, November 14, 1939, Reel 15, General Files of the CIO.

¹⁷ *Textile Labor* (December 1939), pp. 1, 8.

¹⁸ *New York Times,* September 29, 1939, p. 15; Ibid., October 6, 1939, p. 42; Ibid., October 7, 1939, p. 10; Ibid., December 11, 1939, p. 34; Ibid., December 23, 1939, pp. 7, 22; *Textile Labor* (December, 1939), p. 4; "Textile Wages Rise," *Business Week,* November 18, 1939. See also: Lucy Randolph Mason to Southern Editors, December 5, 1939, Reel 15, General Files of the CIO. A summary of the wage drive's results is in: TWUA, Executive Council Report for 1939–1941 to the Second Biennial Convention, April 21–25, 1941, pp. 5–11.

¹⁹ *Textile Labor* (December 1939), p. 1.

²⁰ *Textile Labor* (February 1940) pp. 1, 3.

²¹ Ibid.; TWUA, Minutes of the Meeting of the Executive Council, September 28, 1939; Ibid., January 11–12, 1940.

²² *Textile Labor* (February 1940), p. 8.

²³ TWUA, Minutes of the Meeting of the Executive Council, May 11–12, 1940, box 1, mss 396, TWUA Coll.

²⁴ TWUA, Executive Council Report for 1939–1941, pp. 12–16; TWUA, Minutes of the Meeting of the Executive Council, April 18, 1941, box 1, mss 396, TWUA Coll.

²⁵ TWUA, Minutes of the Meeting of the Executive Council, March 29–31, 1942, box 1, mss 396, TWUA Coll.

²⁶ "Army Has a Big Job for Textiles," *Business Week,* October 19, 1940, pp. 30–31.

²⁷ Membership figures are compiled from reports to the Executive Council. See: TWUA, Minutes of the Meeting of the Executive Council, October 1, 1940; Ibid., January 24–25, 1941; Ibid., July 24–25, 1941; Ibid., November 13–14, 1941; Ibid., March 29–31, 1942; Ibid., July 16–18, 1942, all in box 1, mss 396, TWUA Coll.

²⁸ TWUA, Executive Council Report for 1939–1941, p. 87. See also: Hodges, *New Deal Labor Policy,* pp. 177–179; Richards, "The History of the Textile Workers Union of America, CIO, in the South, 1939 to 1945," pp. 99–104.

²⁹ *Textile Labor* (April 1941), p. 1.

³⁰ TWUA, Executive Council Report from 1939–1941, pp. 46–47.

³¹ Ibid., pp. 47–48.

[32] Bureau of Labor Statistics, "Hours and Earnings in Manufacture of Cotton Goods, September 1940 and April 1941," *Monthly Labor Review* (December 1941), pp. 1490–1513. Based on a comparison of active cotton spindles, the southern branch of the industry was three times larger than its New England counterpart by 1940 (Table 1, p. 1492).

[33] Hodges, *New Deal Labor Policy*, pp. 178–179; Lahne, *The Cotton Mill Worker*, pp. 270–271; *Textile Labor* (October 1941), p. 2.

[34] *Textile Labor* (October 1941).

[35] Fraser, *Labor Will Rule*, p. 423.

[36] Lahne, *The Cotton Mill Worker*, p. 134.

[37] U.S. Department of Labor, Wage and Hour Division, Press Release No 1443, June 9, 1941, reprinted in *Monthly Labor Review* (July 1941), pp. 170–171. On the TWUA's efforts to boost the federal minimum wage for cotton textile workers see: Hodges, *New Deal Labor Policy*, pp. 180–190; and, Richards, "The History of the Textile Workers Union of America, CIO, in the South, 1937–1945," pp. 123–149.

[38] On the CIO's internal wrangling, see: Zieger, *The CIO*, pp. 102–110; Fraser, *Labor Will Rule*, pp. 441–452; Melvyn Dubofsky and Warren Van Tine, *John L. Lewis: A Biography* (New York: Quadrangle, 1977), pp. 339–370.

[39] Bernstein, *Turbulent Years*, pp. 721–722.

[40] See Rieve's front-page editorial "Support the President" in *Textile Labor* (May 1941).

[41] TWUA, Minutes of the Meeting of the Executive Council, April 18, 1941, box 1, mss 396, TWUA Coll.

[42] *Textile Labor* (April 1941), p. 1.

[43] *Business Week,* March 21, 1942, 74–76.

[44] TWUA, Proceedings of the Second Biennial Convention, April 21–25, 1941, pp. 8–9.

[45] *Textile Labor* (November, 1941), p. 6.

[46] TWUA, Minutes of the Meeting of the Executive Council, November 13–14, 1941, box 1, mss 396, TWUA Coll.

[47] Ibid.

[48] *Textile Labor* (January 1942), p. 1. See also: Nelson Lichtenstein, *Labor's War at Home* (New York, Cambridge University Press, 1982), pp. 70–71; Joel Seidman, *American Labor from Defense to Reconversion* (Chicago: University of Chicago Press, 1953), pp. 80–81.

[49] *Textile Labor* (January 1942), p. 1.

[50] National War Labor Board, *Termination Report,* Vol. 1 Washington, DC: U.S. Government Printing Office, 1947), p. 82.

[51] Ibid., p. 88.

[52] TWUA, Executive Council Report to the Third Biennial Convention: "Textile Workers at War," May 10–14, 1943, p. 45.

[53] TWUA, Minutes of the Meeting of the Executive Council, October 23–25, 1944, box 1, mss 396, TWUA Coll.

[54] TWUA, Executive Council Report to the Fourth Biennial Convention, April 24–27, 1946, p. 5.

[55] Ibid., pp. 46, 49.

[56] *Textile Labor* (June 1942), pp. 1, 10; Ibid., (October 1942): p. 2.

[57] TWUA, "Textile Workers at War," p. 48; TWUA, Executive Council Report to the Fourth Biennial Convention, p. 49.

[58] TWUA, Executive Council Report to the Fourth Biennial Convention, p. 49; Adolph Benet Interview, TWUA-OHP.

[59] Hartford, *Where Is Our Responsibility?*, pp. 72–93; *Textile Labor* (September 1942), p. 8.

[60] TWUA, Minutes of the Meeting of the Executive Council, November 5, 1942, box 1, mss 396, TWUA Coll.

[61] Ibid.; Hartford, *Where Is Our Responsibility?*, pp. 76–78; *Textile Labor* (April 1943), pp. 1–2.

[62] Hartford, *Where Is Our Responsibility?*, p. 78.

[63] *Textile Labor* (April 1943), pp. 1–2.

[64] Ibid.; Hartford, *Where Is Our Responsibility?*, pp. 78–80.

[65] *Textile Labor* (January 1943), p. 2.

[66] Richards, "The History of the Textile Workers Union of America, CIO, in the South 1937–1945," pp. 150–179.

[67] Smith, *Mill On the Dan,* pp. 491–495.

[68] Transcript of Interview with Joe Pedigo, April 2, 1975, Southern Oral History Program, University of North Carolina, Chapel Hill (hereafter cited as Pedigo Interview, SOHP), pp. 35–48.

[69] Smith, *Mill on the Dan,* pp. 491–495; *Textile Labor* (July 1942), pp. 1–2; Ibid. (July 1943) pp. 1–3; *Danville Bee,* July 27, 1942.

[70] *Textile Labor* (July 1942), pp. 1–2.

[71] TWUA, *Textile Workers at War* (New York, 1946), pp. 46–47.

[72] On North Carolina's special prominence in the textile industry, see: Phillip J. Wood, *Southern Capitalism: The Political Economy of North Carolina, 1880–1980* (Durham, N.C.: Duke University Press, 1986).

[73] Pedigo Interview, SOHP, pp. 48–51; Richards, "The History of the TWUA, CIO, in the South, 1937 to 1945," 164–166; *Textile Labor* (September 1942), p. 2; Ibid. (October 1942), p. 7; Ibid. (January 1943), p. 2.

[74] Richards, "History of the TWUA, CIO, in the South, 1937 to 1945," p. 167; *Textile Labor* (December 1943), p. 7.

[75] Richards, "The History of the TWUA, CIO, in the South, 1937–1945," pp. 150–179.

[76] Bureau of Labor Statistics, "Earnings in Cotton-Goods Manufactured During the War Years," *Monthly Labor Review* (October 1944), p. 827.

[77] TWUA, Minutes of the Meeting of the Executive Council, March 29–31, 1942, box 1, mss 396, TWUA Coll.

[78] *Textile Labor* (April 1942), pp. 1, 4.

[79] Ibid. (April 1942), p. 4; Hartford, *Where Is Our Responsibility?*, pp. 84–85; "Textile Wage Row," *Business Week,* March 28, 1942, pp. 64–66.

[80] *Textile Labor* (April 1942), p. 4; Hartford, *Where Is Our Responsibility?*, pp. 84–85; Richards, "History of the TWUA, CIO, in the South, 1937–1945," 184–185; *New York Times,* July 31, 1942, p. 32.

[81] *Textile Labor* (May 1942), pp. 1–2; National War Labor Board, *Termination Report,* vol. 1, pp. 178–179. Barkin's brief is in box 20, mss 129A, TWUA Coll.

[82] *New York Times,* July 31, 1942, p. 32.

[83] *Textile Labor* (June 1942), pp. 1–2.

[84] *New York Times,* August 5, 1942, pp. 1, 10; *Textile Labor* (August 1942), pp. 1–2.

[85] TWUA, Minutes of the Meeting of the Executive Council, November 5, 1942, box 1, mss 396, TWUA Coll.

[86] National War Labor Board, *War Labor Reports,* Vol. 2. In re: Fifty-nine Cotton Textile Cos., August 20, 1942 (Washington, D.C.: Bureau of National Affairs, 1943), pp. 345–399.

[87] TWUA, Minutes of the Meeting of the Executive Council, February 15–16, 1943, box 1, mss 396, TWUA Coll.

[88] *Textile Labor* (July 1941), pp. 1–2.

[89] TWUA, Executive Council Report to the Fourth Biennial Convention, pp. 67–75; TWUA, Minutes of the Meeting of the Executive Council, February 15–16, 1943; "Union Agreement in the Cotton-Textile Industry," *Monthly Labor Review* (March 1946), pp. 413–423; Joel Seidman, *American Labor from Defense to Reconversion* (Chicago: University of Chicago Press, 1953), pp. 122–123.

[90] *Textile Labor* (July 1943), pp. 1, 5, 8; Ibid. (October 1943), pp. 1–2, 7. On labor's battles with the Bureau of Labor Statistics regarding measurements of wartime inflation see: Seidman, *American Labor from Defense to Reconversion,* pp. 122–125; *Textile Labor* (February 1944), p. 6.

[91] TWUA, Minutes of the Meeting of the Executive Council, November 17, 1943, box 1, mss 396, TWUA Coll.; *Textile Labor* December (1943), p. 1.

[92] Seidman, *American Labor from Defense to Reconversion,* pp. 123–130; Lichtenstein, *Labor's War at Home,* pp. 210–212.

[93] *Textile Labor* April (1944), pp. 1, 4, 5.

[94] The Bureau of Labor Statistics noted the decline in employment in the cotton-rayon industry as early as 1942. See: Ruth E. Clem, "Effect of the War on Textile Employment," *Monthly Labor Review* September (1942), pp. 446–458. See also: *Business Week,* May 17, 1943, pp. 76–80.

[95] *Textile Labor* (April 1944), pp. 1, 4; Ibid. May (1944), pp. 1, 9. See also: "Earnings in Cotton Goods Manufacture During the War Years," *Monthly Labor Review* October (1944), pp. 823–835.

[96] *Textile Labor* May (1944), p. 5.

[97] *New York Times,* September 28, 1944, p. 36; *Textile Labor* October (1944), pp. 1–2.

[98] *Textile Labor* January (1945), pp. 1–2.

[99] Ibid. February (1945), pp. 1, 3, 4; TWUA, Minutes of the Meeting of the Executive Council, February 19–21, 1945, box 1, mss 396, TWUA Coll.

[100] For details of the War Labor Board's actions, see: National War Labor Board, *War Labor Reports,* Vol. 21 (Washington, D.C.: Bureau of National Affairs, 1945), pp. 793–846, 876–889.

[101] TWUA, Minutes of the Meeting of the Executive Council, February 19–21, 1945.

[102] Emil Rieve to Hon. Franklin D. Roosevelt, February 20, 1945, reprinted in: TWUA, Minutes of the Meeting of the Executive Council, February 19–21, 1945. The TWUA also requested that other CIO representatives resign from the War Labor Board, but, except for the United Auto Workers, whose leaders agreed that WLB proceedings had become "a time-wasting, meaningless rigmarole," the other affiliates believed that resigning from the board would be counterproductive. See: Seidman, *American Labor from Defense to Reconversion,* p. 126.

[103] *New York Times,* April 20, 1945, p. 14; *Textile Labor* May (1945), pp. 1, 3; Lichtenstein, *Labor's War at Home,* p. 212; *Business Week,* April 28, 1945, p. 84.

[104] *Textile Labor* May (1945), p. 1. Despite the influences that other factors exerted, the TWUA leadership was convinced that its decision to release its members in the cotton-rayon industry from the no-strike pledge forced federal officials to concede the union's demands. See: TWUA, Minutes of the Meeting of the Executive Council, June 11–13, 1945, box 1, mss 396, TWUA Coll.

[105] *Textile Labor* July (1945); pp. 1–2.

[106] TWUA, *Report of the Executive Council to the Fourth Biennial Convention,* p. 56; "Union Agreements in the Cotton-Textile Industry," *Monthly Labor Review* March (1946), pp. 413–417; "Earnings in the Cotton-Goods Manufacture During the War Years," *Monthly Labor Review* October 1944), pp. 823–835; *Textile Labor* October (1945), p. 5.

[107] For a discussion of this issue, see: Timothy J. Minchin, *What Do We Need a Union For? The TWUA in the South, 1945–1955* (Chapel Hill: University of North Carolina Press, 1997), pp. 6–25.

[108] *Textile Labor* September (1945), pp. 1, 7; TWUA, Minutes of the Meeting of the Executive Council, June 11–13, 1945.

[109] "Textiles Enter a New Era," *Business Week,* October 13, 1945, pp. 48–58; Ibid., March 16, 1946.

[110] *Textile Labor* September (1945), p. 1.

Chapter 7

[1] TWUA, Minutes of the Meeting of the Executive Council, June 19–22, 1944, box 1, mss 396, TWUA Coll.

[2] Ibid., June 3–4, 1946, box 1, mss 396, TWUA Coll.

[3] Ibid., December 3–5, 1945, box 1, mss 396, TWUA Coll.

[4] TWUA, Executive Council Report to the Fourth Biennial Convention, pp. 41–49, 55–75. The TWUA's fourth biennial convention should have been held in 1945, but wartime travel restrictions forced the union to postpone it until 1946. Thereafter, the conventions were held in even-numbered year.

[5] TWUA, Minutes of the Meeting of the Executive Council, August 20, 1945; Ibid., February 4, 1946, both in box 1, mss 396, TWUA Coll.

[6] "Wage Structure in Cotton-Textile Mills, April–May, 1946," *Monthly Labor Review* (March 1947), pp. 454–461; Richard A. Lester, "Trends in Southern Wage Differentials Since 1890," *Southern Economic Journal* (April 1945), pp. 317–344; Lloyd Saville, "Earnings of Skilled and Unskilled Workers in New England and the South," *Journal of Political Economy* (October 1954), pp. 390–405; Edwin Mansfield, "Wage Differentials in the Cotton Textile Industry, 1933–1952," *Review of Economics and Statistics* (February 1955), pp. 77–82.

[7] "Union Agreements in the Cotton-Textile Industry," *Monthly Labor Review* (March 1946), pp. 413–423; Seymour E. Harris, "Regional Wage Differentials in an Economy of Large Bargaining Units and Less Than Pure and Perfect Competition in the Marketing of Products: Interregional Competition: With Particular Reference to North-South Competition," *Journal of the American Economic Association* (May 1954), pp. 367–380.

[8] The *CIO News* boasted in March of 1946 that the upsurge in worker militancy after the war had produced $500 million in new wage gains for nearly 1.5 million members of CIO-affiliated unions. See: *CIO News,* March 4, 1946, p. 2.

[9] Hartford, *Where Is Our Responsibility?* pp. 88–89; *Textile Labor* (December 1945), pp. 1, 10; Ibid. (January 1946), p. 1; Ibid., (March 1946), p. 1; TWUA, Minutes of the Meeting of the Executive Council, December 3–5, 1945 and February 4, 1946, box 1, mss 396, TWUA Coll. February 4, 1946, box 1, mss 396, TWUA Coll.; TWUA, Report of the Executive Council to the Fourth Biennial Convention, pp. 50–54.

[10] Minchin, *What Do We Need a Union For?* pp. 67–76.

[11] *Textile Labor* (September 1945), pp. 1, 8.

[12] For a detailed chronology of the Industrial Cotton Mills strike see: TWUA Research Department, "Labor Relations Cases," Report No. 60-A: Industrial Cotton Mills, Rock Hill, S.C., 1942–1953, mss 396, TWUA Coll.; *Textile Labor* May (1946), p. 16.

[13] *Textile Labor* (September 1946), p. 9; Ibid. (January 18, 1947); p. 12; TWUA Research Department, "Labor Relations Cases," Report No. 7: Athens Manufacturing Co., 1944–1948.

[14] *Textile Labor* (July 1946), p. 11; TWUA Research Department, "Labor Relations Cases," Report No. 8: Gaffney Manufacturing Company, 1938–1947. TWUA, Minutes of the Meeting of the Executive Council, June 3–4, 1946, box 1, mss 396, TWUA Coll.

[15] *Textile Labor* (July 19, 1947), pp. 1, 3, 5.

[16] Ibid. (March 1946), pp. 1, 3; Ibid. (February 22, 1947), pp. 1, 3.

[17] *CIO News* (March 4, 1946), p. 7; CIO, Proceedings of the Eighth Constitutional Convention (1946), p. 193.

[18] Allan S. Haywood, "We Propose to Unionize Labor In the South," *Labor and Nation* (April–May 1946), pp. 35–37.

[19] J. B. S. Hardman, "The Southern Union Campaign in the National Interest," *Labor and Nation* (April–May 1946), p. 32.

[20] *CIO News,* March 18, 1946, p. 8.

[21] CIO, Proceedings of the Eighth Constitutional Convention (1946), p. 211.

[22] *CIO News,* April 29, 1946, p. 5.

[23] Ibid., March 4, 1946, p. 7; Ibid., March 18, 1946, p. 8.

[24] Minchin, *What Do We Need a Union For?*, pp. 26–29; Barbara S. Griffith, *The Crisis of American Labor: Operation Dixie and the Defeat of the CIO* (Philadelphia: Temple University Press, 1988), pp. 22–23. See also: Michael Goldfield, "The Failure of Operation Dixie: A Critical Turning Point in American Political Development?," in *Race, Class and Community in Southern Labor History,* Gary M. Fink and Merle E. Reed, eds. (Tuscaloosa: University of Alabama Press, 1994), pp. 166–189; Solomon Barkin, "Operation Dixie': Two Points of View," *Labor History* 31

(summer 1990), pp. 378–385; Marshall, *Labor in the South,* pp. 254–269; Zieger, *The CIO,* pp. 227–241.

25 *CIO News,* March 18, 1946, p. 8.

26 Ibid., April 15, 1946, p. 8.

27 Ibid., July 22, 1946, p. 5; CIO, Proceedings of the Eighth Constitutional Convention, p. 189.

28 *CIO News,* April 15, 1946, p. 8.

29 *CIO News,* May 13, 1946, p. 3.

30 TWUA, Proceedings of the Fourth Biennial Convention (1946), pp. 95–99; *Textile Labor* (May 1946), pp. 1, 13.

31 George Baldanzi, "The South is 32 Million Americans," *Labor and Nation* (April–May 1946), pp. 43–44.

32 Neither Rieve nor Baldanzi is the subject of a serious biography. My characterizations of them are based on assessments provided by several of their contemporaries in the TWUA, including Larry Rogin, Sol Barkin, Sol Stetin, Ken Fiester, Joe Hueter, William Gordon, Norris Tibbetts, and Emanuel Boggs. Taped interviews were conducted by James Cavanaugh of the Wisconsin State Historical Society for the TWUA Oral History Project. Also useful are interviews with Joe Pedigo, Julius Fry, Larry Rogin, Joe Glazer, and David Burgess for the Southern Oral History Program at the University of North Carolina at Chapel Hill.

33 My characterization of Roy Lawrence is also based on impressions of him provided by oral interview subjects (see note 32).

34 See, for example: Solomon Barkin, "The Personality Profile of Southern Textile Workers," *Labor Law Journal* (June 1960), 16 pp, Barkin's first attempt to compile a psychological profile of southern millhands occurred in 1939, when after a brief visit to the South, he volunteered an assessment in a memo to Emil Rieve. See: Solomon Barkin to Emil Rieve, "Re: My Trip, South, Oct. 10–24th, 1939," October 25, 1939, File 1A, box 11, mss 129A, TWUA Coll.

35 George Baldanzi to Emil Rieve, Isadore Katz, Solomon Barkin, and Herbert Payne, "Problems of Organization in the South," April 8, 1942, file 1A, box 1, mss 129A, TWUA Coll.; Richards, "History of the TWUA, CIO, in the South, 1937–1945," pp. 175–179.

36 Transcript of Interview with Julius Fry, August 19, 1974, Southern Oral History Program, University of North Carolina, Chapel Hill (hereafter cited as Fry Interview, SOHP), pp. 43–44.

37 TWUA, Minutes of the Meeting of the Executive Council, September 19–21, 1943, box 1, mss 396, TWUA Coll.

38 *Textile Labor* (May 1946), p. 4.

39 TWUA, Proceedings of the Fourth Biennial Convention, pp. 114–115.

40 Pedigo Interview, SOHP, p. 60. Within three months of the campaign's official kickoff its leaders were claiming that "nearly 300 organizers" were on the job in the South. See: *Textile Labor* (August 1946), pp. 1, 11.

41 On the antiunion onslaught that greeted the CIO's southern organizing campaign, see: Griffith, *The Crisis of American Labor,* pp. 62–160; Minchin, *What Do We Need a Union For?,* pp. 26–47. Both the *CIO News* and *Textile Labor* also chronicled these attacks. See, for example: *CIO News,* June 3, 1946, p. 11 and *Textile Labor* (July 1946), p. 9; *New York Times,* September 3, 1946, p. 1. See also: Helen M. Gould, "Union Resistance, Southern Style," *Labor and Nation* (January–February 1948), pp. 6–9.

42 *CIO News,* June 17, 1946, p. 1.

43 Minchin, *What Do We Need a Union For?* pp. 46–47; Mason, *To Win These Rights,* pp. 178–192; Salmond, *Miss Lucy of the CIO,* pp. 124–145; Griffith, *The Crisis of American Labor,* pp. 106–122; *CIO News,* June 24, 1946, p. 8.

44 Richards, "The History of the Textile Workers Union of America, CIO, in the South: 1937–1945," pp. 154–157; Minchin, *What Do We Need a Union For?,* pp. 37–39.

45 *CIO News,* May 13, 1946, p. 3.

46 Griffith, *The Crisis of American Labor,* pp. 62–87; *Textile Labor* (July 1946), p. 2.

47 CIO, Proceedings of the Eighth Constitutional Convention (1946), p. 191; Griffith. The Cri-

sis of *American Labor,* p. 27; *New York Times,* September 9, 1946, p. 1; Zieger, *The CIO: 1935–1955,* pp. 253–277.

[48] Griffith, *The Crisis of American Labor,* pp. 139–160; Goldfield, "The Failure of Operation Dixie," pp. 166–189; Minchin, *What Do We Need a Union For?* pp. 44–47; DeCaux, *Labor Radical,* pp. 470–485.

[49] *Textile Labor* (July 1946), pp. 1–2, 6.

[50] Ibid., (June 1947), pp. 1, 11.

[51] Ibid., (June 1946), pp. 1, 11; Ibid., (July 1946), pp. 1–2, 6.

[52] Minchin, *What Do We Need a Union For?* 48–68.

[53] *Textile Labor* (September 1946), p. 6.

[54] Ibid.

[55] Ibid., (February 1946); p. 5.

[56] Ibid., (August 1946); pp. 1–2; H. D. Lisk, "Unionize the Organized," *Labor and Nation* (May–June 1948), pp. 46–47.

[57] *CIO News,* July 29, 1946, p. 5.

[58] *Textile Labor* (July 1946), p. 4; *CIO News,* July 3, 1946, p. 6.

[59] Griffith, *The Crisis of American Labor,* pp. 33–35.

[60] TWUA Research Department, "Labor Relations Cases," Report No. 2: Bibb Mfg. Company, 1946–1949; *Textile Labor* (October 1946); pp. 1, 9. See also: Helen M. Gould, "Union Resistance, Southern Style," *Labor and Nation* (January–February 1948), pp. 6–9.

[61] TWUA Research Department, "Labor Relations Cases," Report No. 5: Avondale Mills, 1946–1955; *Textile Labor* (August 1946), p. 4; Ibid., (September 1946), p. 12; Minchin, *What Do We Need a Union For?,* pp. 50–52.

[62] The Cannon Mills debacle is detailed in Griffith, *The Crisis of American Labor,* pp. 46–61.

[63] CIO, Proceedings of the Eighth Constitutional Convention (1946), pp. 57, 117; Griffith, *The Crisis of American Labor,* pp. 42, 57.

[64] CIO, Proceedings of the Eighth Constitutional Convention (1946), pp. 188–194.

[65] Ibid., pp. 211–214.

[66] Ibid., p. 188; Griffith, *The Crisis of American Labor,* pp. 42–45.

[67] CIO, Proceedings of the Ninth Constitutional Convention (1949), pp. 155–156. For a contrary view, one that emphasizes the Taft-Hartley Act's importance as an impediment to the CIO's success in the South after 1947, see: Minchin, *What Do We Need a Union For?,* pp. 31–37.

Chapter 8

[1] Solomon Barkin Interview, TWUA-OHP; Larry Rogin Interview, TWUA-OHP; Ken Fiester Interview, TWUA-OHP; Sol Stetin Interview, TWUA-OHP.

[2] Emanuel Boggs Interview, TWUA-OHP.

[3] Stetin Interview; Joseph Hueter Interview, TWUA-OHP; Fiester Interview; Barkin Interview; William Gordon Interview, TWUA-OHP; Rogin Interview; Paul Swaity Interview, TWUA-OHP.

[4] TWUA, Proceedings of the Fifth Biennial Convention (1948), pp. 75–76.

[5] Transcript of Rogin Interview, TWUA-OHP, pp. 118–119.

[6] Emanuel Boggs Interview, TWUA-OHP.

[7] Herbert Williams Interview, TWUA-OHP.

[8] Gordon Interview; TWUA, Minutes of the Meeting of the Executive Council, April 21–24, 1948; Ibid., June 8–11, 1948, box 1, mss 396, TWUA Coll. On Rieve's motives in regard to the reorganization of the Dyers Federation, see also: Stetin Interview.

[9] TWUA, Minutes of the Meeting of the Executive Council, May 21–25, 1949, box, mss 396, TWUA Coll.; Fiester Interview.

[10] Perhaps because of the poverty that had always plagued textile unionism, Rieve placed great emphasis on building the TWUA's financial reserves during the late 1940s. On the eve of the union's 1950 convention Secretary-Treasurer William Pollock bragged to the press that the TWUA

had amassed nearly $4 million in assets. *New York Times,* April 24, 1950, p. 26. On Rieve's preoccupation with the TWUA's financial solvency see: Stetin Interview, TWUA-OHP.

[11] *Textile Labor,* August 6, 1949, p. 3; Ibid., August 20, 1949, p. 1; TWUA, Proceedings of the Sixth Biennial Convention (Boston, Mass.) May 1–5, 1950, pp. 81–82; *New Republic,* April 2, 1951, p. 7.

[12] Rogin, Fiester, Rogin-Fiester, Barkin, Boggs, Williams, Norris Tibbetts and Wesley Cook interviews, TWUA-OHP. See also: Interview with Joe Glazer, pp. 14–15; Interview with David Burgess, pp. 19–23; Interview with Larry Rogin, pp. 51–55; Interview with Julius Fry, pp. 42–44; all in Southern Oral History Program Collection.

[13] TWUA, Proceedings of the Sixth Biennial Convention (1950), pp. 78–86.

[14] Ibid., p. 65.

[15] Not until a week before the convention began did *Textile Labor* report to the union's membership that "for the first time in the TWUA's 11-year history, there will be a contest for at least one of the three general officers." See: *Textile Labor,* April 22, 1950 p. 1.

[16] TWUA, Proceedings of the Sixth Biennial Convention (1950), pp. 52–66. For a summary of the debate, see: *Textile Labor,* May 13, 1950, pp. 2–4, 13.

[17] Sol Stetin, William Gordon, and Ken Fiester, among others, later insisted that the "democracy issue" was essentially baseless. See: Stetin, Gordon, and Fiester interviews, TWUA-OHP. In contrast, Larry Rogin, who was, like the others, an ardent Rieve supporter, believed that the issue was raised for legitimate reasons. See: Rogin Interview, TWUA-OHP.

[18] TWUA, Proceedings of the Sixth Biennial Convention (1950), pp. 52–66.

[19] Ibid., pp, 66–85.

[20] Ibid., pp. 100–101, 116–117; *Textile Labor,* May 13, 1950, pp. 1, 14; *New York Times,* May 8, 1950, p. 12.

[21] Tibbetts Interview, TWUA-OHP.

[22] *New York Times,* April 8, 1950, p. 19.

[23] *Textile Labor,* May 13, 1950, p. 1; *New York Times,* May 6, 1950, p. 7.

[24] TWUA, Proceedings of the Sixth Biennial Convention (1950), pp. 100–101, 143–145.

[25] Fiester Interview, TWUA-OHP.

[26] Although his practice of using *Textile Labor* "objectively on our side" fooled many outside observers, Fiester later reported, it did not fool Baldanzi, who began addressing him as "Dr. Goebbels" as the fight progressed. Fiester Interview, TWUA-OHP.

[27] Transcript of Rogin Interview, TWUA-OHP, p. 120.

[28] Fiester Interview, TWUA-OHP.

[29] Ibid.

[30] Rieve's letters to the TWUA's membership, as well as Baron's response, are reprinted in *Textile Labor,* March 17, 1951, pp. 9, 11.

[31] TWUA, Minutes of the Meeting of the Executive Council, October 16–19, 1950, box 1, mss 396, TWUA Coll.; Fiester Interview, TWUA-OHP; Hueter Interview, TWUA-OHP.

[32] Even many of Rieve's most loyal supporters and defenders later acknowledged that he had pursued a policy of retaliation and intimidation against union officials and staffers who openly sided with Baldanzi. See: Rogin, Fiester, Stetin, Williams, Gordon Interview, TWUA-OHP.

[33] *New York Times,* March 9, 1951, pp. 5, 14.

[34] Ibid., March 11, 1951, p. 40.

[35] Boggs Interview, TWUA-OHP.

[36] Hueter Interview, TWUA-OHP.

[37] TWUA, Minutes of the Meeting of the Executive Council, June 4–12, 1951, box 1, mss 396, TWUA Coll.; *New York Times,* June 10, 1951, p. 57.

[38] *New York Times,* July 22, 1951, p. 30; Ibid., July 23, 1951, p. 15.

Chapter 9

[1] The refusal of southern mills to match the wage increases granted by northern cotton-rayon mills caused *Textile Labor* to complain, early in 1947, "Obviously the southern mills are trying to bring back the north-south wage differential which TWUA fought for years to wipe out." See: *Textile Labor,* February 8, 1947, p. 5.

[2] For an analysis of the northern textile industry's deepening malaise during the late 1940s, see: Hartford, *Where Is Our Responsibility?* pp. 116–148.

[3] For vivid characterizations of the Pittsylvania County Joint Board from the perspective of two insiders who served it, see: Boggs Interview; Tibbett Interview, both in TWUA-OHP. The TWUA, itself, touted Dan River Mills and its joint board in Danville as partners in an unusually effective labor-management relationship. See: *Textile Labor,* June 18, 1949, p. 6.

[4] Robert S. Smith, *Mill on the Dan* (Durham: Duke University Press, 1960), pp. 509–510; Boggs Interview, TWUA-OHP; Minchin, *What Do We Need a Union For?* pp. 134–141.

[5] Smith, *Mill on the Dan,* pp. 491–511; Boggs Interview, TWUA-OHP; Tibbets Interview, TWUA-OHP.

[6] *Textile Labor,* June 4, 1949, pp. 1, 12.

[7] Ibid., September 3, 1949, pp. 1, 5, 6–7, 11.

[8] Ibid., August 20, 1949, p. 1.

[9] Ibid., June 18, 1949, p. 1; TWUA, Proceedings of the Sixth Biennial Convention (1950), pp. 3–9.

[10] *Textile Labor,* January 21, 1950, p. 4.

[11] Ibid., February 4, 1950, p. 1.

[12] Ibid., July 8, 1950, pp. 1, 5, 6.

[13] Boggs Interview, TWUA-OHP; Tibbetts Interview, TWUA-OHP; Smith, *Mill on the Dan,* p. 508.

[14] Tibbetts Interview, TWUA-OHP. Also useful is "The Danville Story," a special report Tibbetts wrote on the 1950 Dan River Mills negotiations and the subsequent strike there the following year. A copy of the report is in box 672, mss 396, TWUA Coll.

[15] Boggs Interview; Tibbetts Interview; *Textile Labor,* September 2, 1950, pp. 1–2.

[16] *Textile Labor,* August 5, 1950, p. 1; Boggs Interview; Tibbetts Interview.

[17] *Textile Labor,* September 2, 1950, pp. 1–2.

[18] Tibbetts Interview; Boggs Interview.

[19] *Textile Labor,* September 16, 1950, pp. 1, 3, 5.

[20] Tibbetts Interview; Boggs Interview; *Textile Labor,* October 7, 1950, p. 4. Dan River Mills, along with other union mills in the South, voluntarily boosted wages by eight percent in October. See: Smith, *Mill on the Dan,* p. 505; *Textile Labor,* October 21, 1950, p. 6; Ibid., (November 4, 1950) p. 3.

[21] *Textile Labor,* October 21, 1950, p. 2. Roy Lawrence, whom Rieve had stubbornly maintained as the TWUA's southern regional director despite his manifest shortcomings, was reassigned to the union's lobbying office in Washington, D.C., after Bamford's appointment. See: *Textile Labor,* November 4, 1950, p. 1.

[22] Fiester Interview; Transcript of Rogin Interview, TWUA-OHP, pp. 141–147.

[23] *Textile Labor,* November 18, 1950, p. 1.

[24] Hartford, *Where Is Our Responsibility?* pp. 116–148; *Textile Labor,* September 3, 1949, pp. 1, 11; Ibid., December 2, 1950, p. 2.

[25] *Textile Labor,* February 3, 1951, p. 10; Ibid., February 17, 1951, p. 4; Ibid., March 3, 1951, p. 4.

[26] Ibid., March 3, 1951, p. 10.

[27] Boggs Interview; Tibbetts Interview.

[28] Transcript of Rogin Interview, TWUA-OHP, p. 141.

[29] *Textile Labor,* December 2, 1950, p. 2; Ibid., December 16, 1950, p. 5; Ibid., January 6, 1951, pp. 1, 3, 5.

[30] *Textile Labor,* January 20, 1951, pp. 1, 3.

[31] Boggs Interview; Tibbetts Interview; Minchin, *What Do We Need a Union For?*, pp. 124–128; Smith, *Mill on the Dan,* pp. 491–502.

[32] Boggs Interview; Tibbetts Interview. The negotiations are described in illuminating detail in: Minchin, *What Do We Need a Union For?* pp. 124–128.

[33] *Textile Labor,* February 3, 1951, p. 1; Ibid., February 17, 1951, pp. 1, 12; Ibid., March 3, 1951, pp. 1, 4; Boggs Interview.

[34] Tibbetts Interview.

[35] Quoted in: Minchin, *What Do We Need a Union For?* pp. 127–128.

[36] Boggs Interview; Tibbetts Interview; Transcript of Rogin Interview, TWUA-OHP, pp. 141–144; Rogin Interview, SOHP, pp. 54–56; Stetin Interview; Barkin Interview; Gordon Interview; Williams Interview; Fiester Interview; *Textile Labor,* April 7, 1951, p. 5.

[37] *Textile Labor,* April 7, 1951 pp. 1, 3.

[38] Although frequently referred to as a "general" strike, the 1951 southern strike involved only mills whose contracts were expiring or were subject to renegotiation under a reopener clause. The 40,000 union members who did strike comprised slightly less than half of the TWUA's total membership in the South. See: *Textile Labor,* April 7, 1951, pp. 1, 3. The strike also spilled over into Tennessee and Louisiana, but Danville and the leading textile centers of North Carolina were the major battlegrounds.

[39] Minchin, *What Do We Need a Union For?* pp. 99–118; Transcript of Rogin Interview, TWUA-OHP, p. 143; "Textile Tension," *Nation,* May 5, 1951, pp. 31–32.

[40] *Textile Labor,* April 21, 1951, pp. 1, 4; Minchin, *What Do We Need a Union For?*, pp. 128–130; Boggs Interview; Tibbetts Interview; Harry Conn, "Public Relations Goon Squad," *New Republic,* May 7, 1951, pp. 13–14.

[41] Conn, "Public Relations Goon Squad," pp. 13–14.

[42] *Textile Labor,* May 5, 1951, p. 1; Minchin, *What Do We Need a Union For?*, pp. 110–113.

[43] *Textile Labor,* April 21, 1951, pp. 1, 4, 5.

[44] Transcript of Rogin Interview, TWUA-OHP, pp. 141–142; Rogin Interview, SOHP, p. 55; Boggs Interview.

[45] Tibbetts Interview.

[46] *Textile Labor* reported that as the strike neared its end "almost $50,000" had been contributed by local unions and joint boards. See: *Textile Labor,* May 5, 1951, pp. 1, 3.

[47] Tibbetts Interview.

[48] Stetin Interview; Fiester Interview; Barkin Interview; Williams Interview; Boggs Interview; Transcript of Rogin Interview, TWUA-OHP, p. 147. See also: Minchin, *What Do We Need a Union For?*, pp. 141–149.

[49] Boggs Interview; Transcript of Rogin Interview, TWUA-OHP, pp. 70–71; Minchin, *What Do We Need a Union For?*, pp. 119–128, 148–149.

[50] Tibbetts Interview. The company's records indicate that by April 8, 40.3 percent of its first-shift workers, 33.4 percent of its second-shift workers, and 28.6 percent of its third-shift workers were on the job. The discrepancy between union and company figures may be explained by the inclusion of replacement workers in the latter's count. See: Minchin, *What Do We Need a Union For?*, p. 130.

[51] Conn, "Public Relations Goon Squad," p. 14.

[52] The records of the leadership's discussions of the Danville strike situation are in File 1-A, box 20, mss 129A, TWUA Coll. See also: Minchin, *What Do We Need a Union For?* pp. 114–118, 142–149; Boggs Interview; Tibbetts Interview.

[53] *Textile Labor,* May 5, 1951, pp. 1, 3; Ibid., May 19, 1951, pp. 1, 3; "Meeting of the Cotton-Rayon Policy Committee," May 5, 1951, File 1-A, box 20, mss 129A, TWUA Coll.; Minchin, *What Do We Need a Union For?*, pp. 115–116.

[54] *Textile Labor,* May 19, 1951, p. 5.

[55] *Textile Labor,* August 18, 1951, p. 2; Ibid., October 6, 1951, pp. 1, 4; Minchin, *What Do We Need a Union For?* pp. 150–151; Boggs Interview.

[56] Minchin, *What Do We Need a Union For?* pp. 149–153; Boggs Interview; Tibbetts Interview; Williams Interview.

[57] *Textile Labor,* May 5, 1951, Ibid., May 19, 1951, p. 3; Jean Begeman, "Terror in Textiles," *New Republic,* March 19, 1951, pp. 13–14; "Textile Tension," *Business Week,* May 5, 1951, pp. 31–32; John C. Cort, "Unions in the South," *The Commonweal,* February 2, 1951, pp. 434–424; Aleine Austin, "Footnote to Taft-Hartley," *Nation,* July 7, 1951, pp. 10–12; U.S. Congress, Senate, Committee on Labor and Public Welfare, *Report of the Subcommittee on Labor-Management Relations:* "Labor-Management Relations in the Southern Textile Industry," 82d Cong., 2d sess. (Washington, D.C.: U.S. Government Printing Office, 1952).

[58] TWUA, Minutes of the Meeting of the Executive Council, June 26–29, 1951, box 1, mss 396, TWUA Coll.; Boggs Interview; Stetin Interview; Fiester Interview; Gordon Interview; Tibbetts Interview; Paul Swaity Interview, TWUA-OHP; Minchin, *What Do We Need a Union For?,* p. 149.

[59] Stetin Interview; Swaity Interview; Fiester Interview; Hueter Interview; Transcript of Rogin Interview, TWUA-OHP, pp. 135–136; Pedigo Interview, SOHP, p. 57; Watson Interview; Tibbetts Interview; Gordon Interview; TWUA, Minutes of the Meeting of the Executive Council, June 4–12, 1951; Ibid., June 26–29, 1951; Ibid., November 12–16, 1951; Ibid., April 21–24, 1952, all in box 1, mss 396, TWUA Coll.; *New York Times,* July 22, 1951, p. 30; Ibid., July 23, 1951, p. 15.

60 Rieve's complete control of the convention is abundantly evident in the union's formal record. See: TWUA, Proceedings of the Seventh Biennial Convention, April 28–May 2, 1952 (Cleveland).

[61] Ibid., pp. 123–124; *New York Times,* April 29, 1951, p. 17; Ibid., April 30, 1952, p. 20; Ibid., May 1, 1952, p. 23; Ibid., May 2, 1952, p. 17; Ibid., May 3, 1952, p. 14.

[62] TWUA, Minutes of the Meeting of the Executive Council, April 21–24, 1952, box 1, mss 396, TWUA Coll.

[63] John C. Cort, "Baldanzi Leaps Over the Wall," *The Commonweal,* June 13, 1952, pp. 243–245.

[64] *New York Times,* May 3, 1951, p. 14; Watson Interview; TWUA, Proceedings of the Seventh Biennial Convention (1952), pp. 154–155; Cort, "Baldanzi Leaps Over the Wall," pp. 243–245; "Textiles Split," *Business Week,* June 2, 1952, p. 71.

[65] Pedigo Interview, SOHP, p. 57.

[66] *New York Times,* May 16, 1952, p. 15; *Business Week,* June 2, 1952, p. 71. On the debate preceding the UTW's decision to hire Baldanzi see: Francis Schaufenbil Interview, TWUA-OHP.

[67] *New York Times,* May 16, 1952, p. 15; "Revolt in Textiles," *New Republic,* May 26, 1952, p. 6.

[68] Scott Hoyman Interview, SOHP, pp. 13–22.

[69] Pedigo Interview, SOHP, pp. 57–59. Years later Pedigo returned to the TWUA, where he remained until his retirement in 1974. Hoyman Interview, SOHP, p. 15.

[70] Hoyman Interview, SOHP, pp. 15–22; *New York Times,* May 19, 1952, p. 24; Ibid., May 20, 1952, p. 16; "Warfare in Textiles," *Fortune* (July, 1952), p. 58; Minchin, *What Do We Need a Union For?,* pp. 171–172.

[71] Emanuel Boggs to John Harkins, July 17, 1952, quoted in Minchin, *What Do We Need a Union For?,* pp. 171–172.

[72] Williams Interview.

[73] *New York Times,* May 22, 1952, p. 16.

[74] Hueter Interview; *New York Times,* May 18, 1952, p. 33; TWUA, Minutes of the Meeting of the Executive Council, June 16–20, 1952, box 1, mss 396, TWUA Coll.; Hoyman Interview, SOHP, p. 16.

[75] *New York Times,* May 17, 1952, p. 14; Ibid., May 18, 1952, p. 33; Ibid., May 20, 1952, p. 16; "Warfare in Textiles," p. 58; Gordon Interview; Stetin Interview; TWUA Minutes of the Meeting of the Executive Council, June 16–20, 1952, box 1, mss 396, TWUA Coll.

[76] Hueter Interview; Hoyman Interview, SOHP, pp. 17–27; Swaity Interview; Transcript of Rogin Interview, TWUA-OHP, p. 146; Stetin Interview; Rogin Interview; SOHP, pp. 58–59; Minchin, *What Do We Need a Union For?*, pp. 170–173. John L. Lewis, whose personal dislike for Rieve dated from the late 1930s, loaned the UTW $1.5 million to defray the costs of absorbing so many new employees and members, but the union, with no more than 65,000 dues-paying members, was chronically short of money. See: Schaufenbil Interview.

[77] Hoyman Interview, SOHP, p. 23; Williams Interview; Minchin, *What Do We Need a Union For?*, pp. 171–175; "Trouble by the Yard," *Fortune* (December 1952), p. 84.

[78] "Trouble By the Yard," p. 84.

[79] TWUA, Minutes of the Meeting of the Executive Council, June 16–20, 1952, box 1, mss 369, TWUA Coll.; Barkin Interview; Perkel Interview; Transcript of Rogin Interview; TWUA-OHP, pp. 110–115.

[80] *Business Week,* May 10, 1952, pp. 142–143.

[81] "Warfare in Textiles," p. 58.

Chapter 10

[1] On the disillusionment that Baldanzi supporters experienced when confronted by the UTW's internal corruption, see: Emanuel Boggs Interview, TWUA-OHP; Norris Tibbetts Interview, TWUA-OHP.

[2] *Textile Labor,* June 6, 1953, pp. 5–8.

[3] Ibid., September 5, 1953, p. 5.

[4] Ibid., December 20, 1952, p. 5.

[5] Quoted in William Hartford, *Where Is Our Responsibility?* (Amherst, MA: University of Massachusetts Press, 1996) p. 139.

[6] *Textile Labor,* May 24, 1952, pp. 1, 3; Ibid., June 7, 1952, p. 8; Ibid., June 21, 1952, pp. 1, 3; TWUA, Minutes of the Meeting of the Executive Council, June 16–20, 1952, box 1, mss 396, TWUA Coll.; Hartford, *Where Is Our Responsibility?* p. 141.

[7] *Textile Labor,* July 12, 1952, pp. 1, 3; TWUA, Minutes of the Meeting of the Executive Council, June 16–20, 1952, box 1, mss 396, TWUA Coll.

[8] TWUA, Report of the Executive Council to the Eighth Biennial Convention, May 3–7, 1954, pp. 57–58.

[9] *Textile Labor,* July 12, 1952, p. 4.

[10] TWUA, Minutes of the Meeting of the Executive Council, June 16–20, 1952, box 1, mss 396, TWUA Coll.; *Textile Labor,* June 21, 1952, pp. 1, 3.

[11] TWUA, Minutes of the Meeting of the Executive Council, September 8–11, 1952, box 1, mss 396, TWUA Coll.

[12] Kelly, *Nine Lives for Labor,* pp. 40–64; *Textile Labor,* May 10, 1952, pp. 1, 15; Ibid., January 10, 1953, pp. 1, 3.

[13] Transcript of Rogin Interview, TWUA-OHP, p. 121.

[14] In addition to Bishop, who served as its director, the TWUA Organizing Committee included Rieve, Secretary-Treasurer William Pollock, and union vice presidents (and anti-Baldanzi hard liners) William Belanger, James Bamford, Boyd Payton, Sol Stetin, and William Tullar.

[15] TWUA, Minutes of the Meeting of the Executive Council, September 8–11, 1952, box 1, mss 396, TWUA Coll.

[16] Bishop's progress report on the organizing committee's activities was scheduled for submission at the Executive Council's meeting on November 30, 1952. It was withheld, however, owing to the press of other business. The report is printed in: TWUA, Minutes of the Meeting of the Executive Council, March 3–6, 1953, box 1, mss 396, TWUA Coll.

[17] *Textile Labor,* January 10, 1953, pp. 1, 3; Kelly, *Nine Lives for Labor,* pp. 59–64; Fiester Interview; Rogin-Fiester Interview. TWUA research director Sol Barkin, who was rarely generous in his assessments of the ability of others in the union, thought Bishop was generally competent,

but dismissed him in the end as no more than "a good political leg man" for Rieve. See: Barkin Interview.

[18] Transcript of Rogin Interview, TWUA-OHP, p. 166.

[19] Ibid.; Fiester Interview; Rogin-Fiester Interview; Stetin Interview; Barkin Interview; Gordon Interview; Swaity Interview.

[20] Rogin-Fiester Interview. See also: Stetin Interview; Barkin Interview; Gordon Interview; Cook Interview; Hueter Interview.

[21] Rogin-Fiester Interview.

[22] TWUA, Minutes of the Meeting of the Executive Council, January 8, 1953, box 1, mss 396, TWUA Coll.; *Textile Labor,* January 24, 1953, pp. 1, 3.

[23] On the events surrounding Pollock's selection as Bishop's successor, see: Rogin-Fiester Interview; Rogin Interview; Fiester Interview; Stetin Interview; Gordon Interview; Cook Interview; and, Hueter Interview.

[24] Rogin-Fiester Interview.

[25] On the consequences of the TWUA's decline for the northern textile industry, see: Hartford, *Where Is Our Responsibility?*, pp. 149–171. See also: Barkin Interview; Perkel Interview.

[26] Rogin-Fiester Interview; Fiester Interview; Barkin Interview.

[27] Fiester Interview.

[28] *Textile Labor,* November 21, 1953, pp. 1, 3; TWUA, Minutes of the Meeting of the Executive Council, September 22–23, 1953, and November 9–12, 1953, box 1, mss 396, TWUA Coll.; Schaufenbil Interview; Stetin Interview. Even after the formal merger of the AFL and CIO at the end of 1955, the TWUA and UTW, though interested enough in the idea of reconciliation to discuss it frequently, could never agree on how it might be accomplished. See: TWUA, Minutes of the Meeting of the Executive Council, May 7–11, 1956, box 1, mss 396, TWUA Coll.

[29] On the TWUA's grim perceptions of the textile industry's economic plight at the beginning of 1954, see: TWUA, Minutes of the Meeting of the Executive Council, February 23–26, 1954, box 1, mss 396, TWUA Coll.

[30] Ibid.

[31] TWUA, Proceedings of the Eighth Biennial Convention, May 3–7, 1954, pp. 9–19, 100–106.

[32] Fiester Interview; Rogin-Fiester Interview; TWUA, Minutes of the Meeting of the Executive Council, April 26–28, 1955, box 1, mss 396, TWUA Coll; TWUA, Proceedings of the Ninth Biennial Convention (1956), pp. 14–15.

[33] TWUA, Proceedings of the Ninth Biennial Convention (1956), pp. 14–15.

[34] Fiester Interview; Rogin-Fiester Interview; Stetin Interview; Hueter Interview; Cook Interview; Gordon Interview; Watson Interview; Williams Interview.

[35] "The End of Textile Unionism?" *Fortune,* December 1957, pp. 230–232.

[36] Barkin Interview; Perkel Interview; Stetin Interview; Gordon Interview; Swaity Interview.

[37] TWUA, Minutes of the Meeting of the Executive Council, November 27 to December 1, 1955, box 1, mss 396, TWUA Coll. For a detailed assessment of the union's "bargaining from weakness" strategy, see: TWUA, Minutes of the Meeting of the Executive Council, March 7–11, 1963, box 1, mss 396, TWUA Coll.

[38] Transcript of Rogin Interview, TWUA-OHP, pp. 155–163; The Reminiscences of William Pollock, pp. 32–33; TWUA, Minutes of the Meeting of the Executive Council, February 27 to March 2, 1956; Ibid., July 19–23, 1956; Ibid., November 12–15, 1956; Ibid., March 11–15, 1957; Ibid., June 17–21, 1957; Ibid., September 16–20, 1957, all in box 1, mss 396, TWUA Coll. See also: "The End of Textile Unionism?," pp. 230–232.

[39] TWUA, Minutes of the Meeting of the Executive Council, November 17–21, 1958, box 1, mss 396, TWUA Coll.; "Textile Strategems," *Fortune,* April 1959, pp. 200–202.

[40] TWUA, Proceedings of the Tenth Biennial Convention, May 12–16, 1958, pp. 105–106.

[41] Ibid., pp. 114–115.

[42] TWUA, Minutes of the Meeting of the Executive Council, August 4–8, 1958, box 1, mss 396, TWUA Coll. The union's increasing preoccupation with legislative solutions to its problems

is reflected in the quarterly deliberations of the Executive Council. See, for example: TWUA, Minutes of the Meeting of the Executive Council, February 2–6, 1959, box 1, mss 396, TWUA Coll.

[43] Stetin Interview; Swaity Interview. The union's dilemma in the South is also analyzed at length in the two interviews of Scott Hyman conducted by researchers from the Southern Oral History Program at the University of North Carolina, Chapel Hill. See also: "The End of Textile Unionism?," pp. 230–232; and, U.S. Congress, Senate, Committee on Labor and Public Welfare, Report of the Subcommittee on Labor and Labor-Management Relations, *Labor-Management Relations in the Southern Textile Industry,* 82d Cong., 2d Sess. (Washington: U.S. Government Printing Office, 1952).

[44] For detailed accounts of the Harriet-Henderson strike, see: Daniel J. Clark, *Like Night and Day: Unionization in a Southern Mill Town* (Chapel Hill: University of North Carolina Press, 1997); and by Linda Jean Frankel, "Women, Paternalism, and Protest in a Southern Textile Community: Henderson, N.C. 1900–1960," (Ph.D. dissertation, Harvard University, 1986), and "Jesus Leads Us, Cooper Needs Us, the Union Feeds Us," in Leiter, et al., eds., *Hanging by a Thread: Social Change in Southern Textiles* (Ithaca, NY: ILR Press, 1991), pp. 101–120. See also: John C. Cort, "Turning Back the Clock," *The Commonweal,* October 23, 1959, pp. 99–101; "A Town's Bitter Taste," *Newsweek,* April 27, 1959, pp. 85, 88; "Struggle in Dixie," *Time,* November 30, 1959, p. 19.

[45] TWUA, Minutes of the Meeting of the Executive Council, February 2–5, 1959; Ibid., April 27–May 1, 1959; Ibid., September 14–17, 1959; Ibid., November 30–December 3, 1959, all in box 1, mss 396, TWUA Coll.

[46] Ibid., July 25–29, 1960, box 1, mss. 396, TWUA Coll.; Clark, *Like Night and Day,* pp. 196–198.

[47] TWUA, Minutes of the Meeting of the Executive Council, February 14–22, 1961; Ibid., May 22–26, 1961; Ibid., August 21–24, 1961, box 1, mss. 396, TWUA Coll.; Clark, *Like Night and Day,* pp. 199–207; *New York Times,* June 25, 1961, p. 58.

Chapter 11

[1] "The End of Textile Unionism?," *Fortune,* December 1957, p. 232.

[2] *New Republic,* July 6, 1959, p. 10.

[3] Richard Gorrell, "Roger Milliken and the Textile Union," *The Reporter,* January 3, 1963, p. 32.

[4] On the Darlington case see: James A. Gross, *Broken Promise: The Subversion of U.S. Labor Relation Policy, 1947–1994* (Philadelphia: Temple University Press, 1995), pp. 174–176. See also: *Labor Unity* (January 1981), p. 3.

[5] On the postwar degradation of labor's rights, in general, and on the politicization of the NLRB, in particular, see: Gross, *Broken Promise.*

[6] TWUA, Minutes of the Meeting of the Executive Council, July 25–29, 1960, box 1, mss 396, TWUA Coll.

[7] In an article entitled "The End of Textile Unionism?," *Fortune* contemplated the TWUA's demise as early as 1957.

[8] Stetin Interview; Cook Interview; Schaufenbil Interview; Benet Interview; TWUA, Minutes of the Meeting of the Executive Council, February 2–6, 1959, box 1, mss 396, TWUA Coll.; *U.S. News and World Report,* October 4, 1957, pp. 128–129; Ibid., March 28, 1958, pp. 99–100.

[9] *Business Week,* March 22, 1958, p. 94; TWUA, Minutes of the Meeting of the Executive Council, May 5–8, 1958, box 1, mss 396, TWUA Coll.

[10] Cook Interview; Stetin Interview; Gordon Interview; Heuter Interview; Fiester Interview; Perkel Interview; Watson Interview; Williams Interview.

[11] Members of the majority faction on the Executive Council went so far as to bring a lawsuit against Pollock and Chupka to force them to implement various decisions that had been adopted on a series of 12 to 10 votes. See: TWUA, Minutes of the Meeting of the Executive Council,

November 11–13, 1963, box 1, mss 396, TWUA Coll.; *New York Times,* November 17, 1963, p. 86.

[12] Julien Cloutier to John Chupka, November 21, 1963, reprinted in TWUA, Minutes of the Meeting of the Executive Council, March 31–April 4, 1964, box 1, mss 396, TWUA Coll.

[13] "Statement of General President Pollock," in TWUA, Minutes of the Meeting of the Executive Council, April 22–26, 1963, box 1, mss 396, TWUA Coll.

[14] Cook Interview.

[15] *New York Times,* June 3, 1954, p. 28.

[16] TWUA, Proceedings of the Thirteenth Biennial Convention (1964), pp. 125–131. *New York Times,* June 4, 1964, p. 34.

[17] TWUA, Proceedings of the Thirteenth Biennial Convention, pp. 208–211.

[18] Ibid., p. 212.

[19] Watson Interview; Cook Interview; Stetin Interview; Swaity Interview.

[20] Stetin Interview.

[21] Gross, *Broken Promise,* pp. 180–181.

[22] On the company's history see: Lloyd Ferguson, *J. P. Stevens and Company, Inc.: From Family Firm to Corporate Giant* (Boston: Federal Reserve Bank, 1964); and, Richard Whalen, "The Durable Threads of J. P. Stevens," *Fortune,* April 1963, pp. 3–12.

[23] James A. Hodges, "J. P. Stevens and the Union: Struggle for the South," in *Race, Class, and Community in Southern Labor History,* Gary M. Fink and Merl E. Reed, eds. (Tuscaloosa: University of Alabama Press, 1994), pp. 53–56.

[24] Walter Guzzardi, Jr., "How the Union Got the Upper Hand on J. P. Stevens," *Fortune,* June 19, 1978, pp. 86–88; Stetin Interview.

[25] Hodges, "J. P. Stevens and the Union," pp. 57–58.

[26] Quoted in Hodges, "J. P. Stevens and the Union," p. 58.

[27] TWUA, Minutes of the Meeting of the Executive Council, August 26–September 1, 1965, box 1, mss 396, TWUA Coll.

[28] Hodges, "J. P. Stevens and the Union," pp. 53–59; Gross, *Broken Promise,* pp. 176–181; Kenneth G. Slocum, "A Campaign to Organize Southern Plants Meets Formidable Opposition," *Wall Street Journal,* May 11, 1966, p. 1; *New York Times,* May 16, 1965, p. 73; Ibid., May 23, 1966, p. 33; Ibid., August 19, 1967, p. 13.

[29] James R. Wooten, "When Unions Try to Gain Ground in Southern Textile Mills," *U.S. News and World Report,* December 22, 1975, p. 60; Guzzardi, "How the Union Got the Upper Hand on J. P. Stevens," pp. 87–89; Gross, *Broken Promise,* pp. 177–179; William Pollock to Hon. Adam Clayton Powell, January 27, 1966, reprinted in: TWUA, Minutes of the Meeting of the Executive Council, February 14–17, 1966, box 1, mss 396, TWUA Coll.

[30] U.S., Congress, House, Committee on Education and Labor, Hearings on Investigation of the Administration of the National Labor Relations Act, as Amended, by the National Labor Relations Board, 89th Cong., 1st sess. (1965); Ibid., Hearing before the Select Subcommittee on Labor, To Amend the NLRA to Increase Effectiveness of Remedies, 90th Cong., 1st sess. (1967); Ibid., Special Subcommittee on Labor, NLRA Remedies: The Unfilled Promise, 90th Cong., end sess. (1968); TWUA, The Hollow Promise (New York, 1968); New York Times, August 31, 1965, p. 24; Ibid., August 11, 1967, p. 38.

[31] TWUA, Minutes of the Meeting of the Executive Council, July 22–25, 1968, box 1, mss 396, TWUA Coll.

[32] Ibid., May 22–26, 1967, box 1, mss 396, TWUA Coll.

[33] Stetin Interview; Swaity Interview. On the rising employment of African Americans in the southern textile industry see: Timothy J. Minchin, *Hiring the Black Worker: The Racial Integration of the Southern Textile Industry, 1960–1980* (Chapel Hill: University of North Carolina Press, 1999). See also: Mary Frederickson, "Four Decades of Change: Black Workers in Southern Textiles, 1941–1981," in *Workers' Struggles, Past and Present,* James Green, ed. (Philadelphia: Temple University Press, 1983), pp. 62–82.

[34] Stetin Interview; Williams Interview; Cook Interview; TWUA, Proceedings of the Ninth Biennial Convention (1956), pp. 161–173, 213; *New York Times,* May 19, 1956, pp. 1, 40.

[35] Stetin Interview; Williams Interview; Swaity Interview; Cook Interview.

[36] TWUA, Minutes of the Meeting of the Executive Council, January 22–25, 1963; Ibid., April 22–26, 1963; Ibid., August 26–30, 1963; Ibid., November 11–13, 1963, all in box 1, mss 396, TWUA Coll.; Stetin Interview.

[37] Hodges, "J. P. Stevens and the Union," p. 56; Stetin Interview.

[38] Transcript of Hoyman Interview, SOHP, pp. 37–38.

[39] Stetin Interview; Cook Interview.

[40] TWUA, Minutes of the Meeting of the Executive Council, May 22–26, 1967, box 1, mss 396, TWUA Coll. Transcript of Hoyman Interview, SOHP, p. 38.

[41] Quoted in Hodges, "J. P. Stevens and the Union," p. 60.

[42] Stetin Interview; Transcript of an interview with Sol Stetin conducted on April 19, 1976, by Steven Kramer for an oral history project undertaken by students of my graduate labor history course at the School of Industrial and Labor Relations, Cornell University (hereafter cited as ILR-OHP), pp. 1–24; Videotaped interview with Sol Stetin conducted on October 21, 1987, by students in my undergraduate labor history seminar at the School of Industrial and Labor Relations, Cornell University (hereafter cited as Stetin Video Interview).

[43] Cook Interview; Gordon Interview.

[44] Rogin-Fiester Interview; Stetin Interview; Hueter Interview; Watson Interview; Swaity Interview.

[45] Although the TWUA guarded data on its dues-paying membership as if it were a state secret, even as early as 1963 the union was paying a per capita tax to the AFL-CIO on behalf of only 130,000 members. See: George Meany to John Chupka, January 16, 1934, in TWUA, Minutes of the Executive Meeting, March 31–April 4, 1964, box 1, mss 396, TWUA Coll.

[46] Stetin Video Interview.

[47] Transcript of Hoyman Interview, SOHP, p. 48.

[48] Stetin Interview; Schaufenbil Interview. William Pollock's reports on merger discussions with the UTW can be found in the minutes of TWUA Executive Board meetings throughout the 1960s.

[49] Stetin Interview; Watson Interview.

[50] Stetin Video Interview.

[51] Ibid., Stetin Interview; Swaity Interview; Perkel Interview; Stetin ILR Interview, pp. 37–38; James R. Wooten, "When Unions Try to Gain Ground in Southern Textile Mills," *U.S. News and World Report,* December 22, 1975, p. 60.

[52] *AFL-CIO News* June 10, 1972, p. 1; *New York Times,* June 4, 1976, p. 11.

[53] Stetin Interview; Stetin Video Interview.

[54] My analysis and characterizations of the merger negotiations are, unless otherwise noted, based on the interviews with Sol Stetin cited earlier.

[55] For Stetin's detailed explanation of the merger agreement's central provisions, see: TWUA, Proceedings of the 19th Biennial Convention (1976), May 31–June 2, 1976, pp. 69–77.

[56] Watson Interview.

[57] Stetin Video Interview.

[58] Ibid.; *New York Times,* August 15, 1976, Sec. III, p. 11.

[59] Stetin Interview; Stetin Video Interview.

[60] TWUA, Proceedings of the Nineteenth Biennial Convention (1976), pp. 5–17; *New York Times,* June 2, 1976, p. 40.

[61] ACTWU, Proceedings of the Merger Convention, June 3–4, 1976, (Washington, D.C.); *New York Times,* June 4, 1976, p. 11.

[62] A. H. Raskin, "J. P. Stevens: Labor's Big Domino," *New York Times,* August 15, 1976, Sec. 3, p. 1. See also: "The All-Out Campaign Against J. P. Stevens," *Business Week,* June 14, 1976, p. 28; *New York Times,* October 6, 1985, Sec. 3, p. 6.

[63] Victoria Byerly, *Hard Times Cotton Mill Girls* (Ithaca: ILR Press, 1986), pp. 201–218; Hodges, "J. P. Stevens and the Union," p. 61; *New York Times,* October 24, 1980, p. 22.

[64] See, for example: Terry W. Mullins and Paul Luebke, "Symbolic Victory and Political Reality in the Southern Textile Industry: The Meaning of the J. P. Stevens Settlement for Southern Labor Relations," *Journal of Labor Research* (Winter 1982)., pp. 81–88.

[65] *Washington Post,* October 20, 1980, p. 22. See also: "A Gathering Momentum Against J. P. Stevens," *Business Week,* March 20, 1978, p. 147; Ibid., "Is the J. P. Stevens War Over?," June 9, 1980, p. 85; Ibid., "The Ripples Spreading from the Stevens Pact," November 3, 1980, p. 107.

[66] *New York Times,* October 21, 1983, p. 16.

[67] *Los Angeles Times,* August 25, 1985, Sec. 5, p. 1; *Washington Post,* October 10, 1985, p. 3; *New York Times,* October 20, 1985, Sec. 3, p. 1; *Charlotte Observer,* March 23, 1999, p. 1.

[68] For details of the campaign and election, see: *Charlotte Observer,* March 23, 1999, p. 1; Ibid., June 25, 1999, p. 1.

Index

Abt, John, 121–122
ACTWU. *See* Amalgamated Clothing and Textile Workers Union (ACTWU)
ACW. *See* Amalgamated Clothing Workers (ACW)
AFL. *See* American Federation of Labor (AFL)
AFL-CIO
  ACW-TWUA merger and, 272–278
  Industrial Union Department of, 267–268
  nonraiding agreement and, 241
  Stevens campaign and, 265, 267–268
African Americans. *See* Racial issues
AFTO. *See* American Federation of Textile Operatives (AFTO)
Alabama, strikes in, 44–45
Amalgamated Association of Iron, Steel and Tin Workers, 8, 67
Amalgamated Clothing and Textile Workers Union (ACTWU)
  creation of, 272–278
  inaugural convention of, 277–278
  merger with ILGWU, 279–280
Amalgamated Clothing Workers (ACW), 3, 5, 11, 40, 57, 61, 68
  funding of TWOC, 83, 94, 101–102, 122
  influence in TWOC, 73, 83
  merger with TWUA, 272–278
  1938 convention, 101–102
  revitalization of, 273
  support for TWUA, 128, 129
Amalgamated Textile Workers of America, 61
Amazon Mill, 143
American Communist Party, 8
  dual unionism and, 27, 30
  New Bedford strike and, 26
  NTWU and, 27–28, 30, 38
  Operation Dixie and, 172, 174, 179
  Passaic strike and, 26
  Third Period strategy, 27, 30
American Cotton Manufacturers Association, 77
American Federation of (Full-Fashioned) Hosiery Workers, 24–25, 29, 80, 89, 107, 139–140, 255
American Federation of Labor (AFL). *See also* AFL-CIO
  American Federation of Full-Fashioned Hosiery Workers and, 24–25, 29
  CIO and, 10
  craft union domination of, 5–6, 10, 40, 57

disciplines Gorman, 125
IWW and, 3
Lewis's conflict with, 5–7
National Union of Textile Workers and, 16
1929 convention, 35
1934 convention, 5–6
1935 convention, 6–7
Piedmont strikes and, 32, 35–37
procapitalist stance of, 23–24, 28
southern strategy of, 37
support for UTW, 58
UTW and, 18–19, 33, 57–58, 125–126
American Federation of Textile Operatives (AFTO), 26, 140
  feud with NUTW, 18–19
American Thread Company strike, 25
American Viscose Company, 78, 81, 83, 103, 142
American Woolen Company, 77, 78, 86, 133, 139
Asheville Normal and Teachers College, 69
Athens Manufacturing Company strike, 159, 160
Atomic Workers Organizing Committee, 180
Automobile industry, unionization of, 8–10, 64
Avondale Mills, 175, 179

Baldanzi, George, 60, 170, 258
  ambition of, 165–166, 188–189
  as anticommunist, 173
  Baron and, 200–203
  community-based unionism and, 169
  Dan River strike and, 208–212, 218
  Danville campaign and, 142–143
  defeated in 1952 election, 222–228
  in Dyers and Finishers Federation, 186, 189
  elected TWUA vice president, 127
  Hillman and, 186
  Lawrence and, 168, 186–189
  New Bedford campaign and, 140
  at 1946 CIO convention, 181–182
  at 1946 TWUA convention, 165
  Operation Dixie and, 163, 164–170, 186
  popularity of, 166, 190–191, 197–198
  presidential campaign of, 204
  proteges of, 168–169, 190–191
  racial issues and, 173
  reelection of, 197–198
  replaced by Bamford, 210